Advance F

Songlines of the Soul

"Veronica Goodchild has written an important counter to the oppressive scientism that tends to silence our connection to those aspects of reality that are not readily amenable to empirical study. She shows us that there is more to reality than we have been led to believe, and she introduces us to these mysteries in a provocative and scholarly manner. Read this book, and the universe suddenly becomes deeper and more intriguing than we could have imagined."

—Lionel Corbett, author of *The Religious Function of the Psyche, Psyche and the Sacred,* and *The Sacred Cauldron: Psychotherapy as a Spiritual Practice.*

"This rich and multifaceted book merits long and careful contemplation. Veronica Goodchild has given us an allusive and authoritative chart to help negotiate these tumultuous times."

—Michael Glickman, writer, crop circle commentator

"An alchemical mystical treatise, *Songlines of the Soul* takes us on an extraordinary journey into realms of the imaginal that expand our consciousness and our map of reality. Goodchild's keen intelligence and visionary capacity hunt and track down patterns of fundamental mysteries about the nature of the psyche and psychoid that take us into phenomena on the edge of consciousness that knock at the doors of the known world: Mystical Cities, UFOs, crop circles to name a few. Anyone interested in depth psychology and the mysteries of our times will get a vast drink of the living waters of the psyche with *Songlines of the Soul,* where Veronica's work has driven a tap root down into this soul nourishing realm."

—Monika Wikman Ph.D. Jungian analyst and author of *Pregnant Darkness: Alchemy and the Rebirth of Consciousness*

"Veronica Goodchild's book *Songlines of the Soul* speaks of the deeply emotionally touching and transmuting aspect of UFO phenomena. As she writes, every UFO encounter and 'abduction' is a call for initiation into the reality of the subtle body phenomenon neither explainable by natural science nor superficial psychology. We need a completely new worldview based on the reality of the *unus mundus* (C.G. Jung) or psychophysical reality (Wolfgang Pauli) to understand such phenomena. Today, in more and more people, this new worldview is constellated. To me, this is a great hope for our world in danger of being extinguished by our completely destructive behaviour. "

—Remo F. Roth, author of *Return of the World Soul*

"*Songlines of the Soul* is a book whose time has come. The irruption of the imaginal realm into our conscious reality is a sign that great changes are afoot in human consciousness. In a world that so often feels like it is is full of choking darkness, this book sings out that it is also full of wonder, enchantment and the mysterious—and it is these very things that have the power to illuminate and transform the darkness. That such strange subjects as UFOs, crop circles and other paranormal experiences are finally restored to their rightful place in the pantheon of human experience as arbiters of a new consciousness is of enormous importance. I can't recommend this book highly enough!"

—Karen Alexander, co-author with Steve Alexander of
Crop Circles: Signs, Wonders and Mysteries, and *The Crop Circle Yearbooks*

"Veronica is [what I call] a reliable Witness. I learned about this term from a Catholic prelate at a conference in San Marino in April 1999, who reported that the Vatican takes UFO phenomena seriously because there are so many reliable Witnesses. The Church relies on this notion when evaluating miracles. The Witness is in a sacred tradition. The Zen master too speaks of the Witness as having a clarity of mind, and a purity of expression. They bring something of extraordinary importance to the culture, because they are receiving information from whatever source this phenomena emanates from that says: Human beings have to change; we have to open our consciousness, and stop the destructive path we are on. Veronica is such a Witness."

—Dr. John Mack, Harvard psychiatrist, researcher of extraordinary
experiences, and author of *Passport to the Cosmos*

Songlines
OF THE
SOUL

Pathways to A New Vision for a New Century

VERONICA GOODCHILD, Ph.D
foreword by Thomas Moore

NICOLAS-HAYS, INC.
Lake Worth, Florida

Published in 2012 by
Nicolas-Hays, Inc.
P. O. Box 540206 • Lake Worth, FL 33454-0206
www.nicolashays.com
Distributed to the trade by Red Wheel/Weiser, LLC
65 Parker St., Unit 7 • Newburyport, MA 01950-4600
www.redwheelweiser.com

Cover photography © Steve Alexander. This crop circle appeared at
Wansdyke Path, Stanton, St Bernard, Wiltshire, England on July, 2, 2009
Photographs on pages 175, 183, 184, 189, 190, 192, 193, 199,
200, 203, 204, 206, 207 and 208 © Steve Alexander,
reproduced by kind permission of Temporary Temple Press, www.temporarytemples.co.uk

Library of Congress Cataloging-in-Publication data available on request.

ISBN: 978-0-89254-168-3 (pbk)
ISBN: 978-0-89254-578-0 (ebook)

Cover and text design by Kathryn Sky-Peck
VG
Printed in the United States of America

To Suhrawardi, invisible guide and Friend of my heart

To The Lady Melissa, guide from the City of Ladies

*To my Grandfather Goodchild, whose unspoken story
about his sojourn with the Aboriginal elders in the early part
of the twentieth century finds some voice here*

*And to the Native American warrior in the dreamtime, who taught me
about the Ghost Dance and how to be invisible*

I give you my deepest gratitude

This book is for you

"[W]hen the universe as we each know of it emerged, it was whole and complete, harmonious and sounding a resonant note. Each and everything, every being and species uttered a sound that harmonized with each other. They formed a song that was more beautiful than we can imagine. But gradually, notes of disharmony crept into the song. There were those within every species, our own included, who became unable to recognize the note they produced. This led to greater and greater unbalance and disharmony. Within the shape of the universe many things came into being then that added to this disharmony. It could be said that one of the tasks of all species is to find their true note and sound it once again."

THE SIDHE

Contents

PART ONE

An Introduction to the Subtle Body and Subtle Worlds

PART FOUR
Mystical Cities and Healing Sanctuaries

Acknowledgments

F irst, my husband's love, interest in and support of my project, in addition to our many conversations, was a continuous gift, especially during the times when I would lose faith in what I was doing. Robert's confidence in my work has been an inspiration, providing much needed encouragement along the lonely path of writing. He is also a great editor! He read a final draft of my book and made many fine editorial suggestions.

Along this path of reflection, research, and writing, my allies have been my dreams, visions, active imaginations, feelings, and my intuitive mind. I have been inspired and supported also by the dreams, visions, and thoughts of others. I have read, and often re-read slowly, the background material that seemed to belong to my areas of interest. Here I hardly need mention the work of Jung, especially his later work on alchemy and his revision of the nature of the archetype to include its psychoid dimension, and the work of Henri Corbin who has chartered the subtle worlds of imagination both from an intellectual point of view and also, like Jung, from the direct experience of such worlds. I have found with both these writers that the "gems" of their knowledge are given up only slowly, for they are writing of realities that, although very ancient, are nevertheless not included in our current worldview. Jung, Corbin, and Marie-Louise von Franz have been powerful spiritual mentors for me throughout my life and have chartered a course into the realm of the soul that made it possible for me to have a creative personal and professional life. I feel deep gratitude for their courage and vision.

I also had many enlightening discussions with friends, both professional and personal. In particular I must mention my soul friend Anne Baring, a

Jungian analyst in England, whose acquaintance I made by way of her beautiful website just before 9/11, and whom I subsequently met in person, sharing many times together in England as well as here in the States, and in Italy at the time of the Venus transit of the sun in June 2004, which we observed together (through special glasses) from Assisi. Anne's trust in the visionary imagination and her commitment to speaking and writing about what we know of the soul in a world gone mad has helped me to develop my own trust in and responsibility toward speaking up even when I hesitated to do so. Gratitude goes to the late Dr. John Mack whose pioneering and fearless work on behalf of UFO/ET experiencers is unparalleled and who provided much encouragement to my own research. I also wish to acknowledge Dr. Remo Roth with whom I had many rewarding conversations on the topics discussed in this book, interests that, quite independently of one another, we discovered we shared. Remo helped me clarify some of my own insights and thoughts at early stages of the writing and for that, I am grateful.

Many thanks also to my courageous and trail-blazing friend, Tayria Ward. Much love and gratitude to my soul friends Monika Wikman, Virginia Apperson, Marea Classon, and Lisa Sloan, who, though inspired by Jung, also belong to the ancient shamanic and oracular traditions, and who embody the divine Feminine with such care, fierceness, and grace. Many thanks to Lanara Rosen who led me to the Celtic Sidhe, to Deanne Jameson for the *Kingdom,* and to Kathy Atwood for her journeys to the City of Light.

Thanks also to the many students and patients who contributed their material and from whom I continue to learn so much. I would like to mention in particular Candy Kleven, Judith Orodenker, Robin Palmer, Kas Sarah Robinson, Samina Salahuddin, and Laura Smith, whose work appears here, and to acknowledge those whose work appears in the book but remains anonymous. And there are many others whose work though not in print here will remain an inspiration for years to come.

Gratitude goes also to my colleagues at Pacifica Graduate Institute. I particularly wish to thank Dr. Steve Aizenstat, Chancellor of Pacifica, for providing an educational venue in which one's deepest pedagogical and research interests are encouraged to deepen and flourish.

Love goes to my two children, Sarah and Timothy, whose humor, creativity, intelligence, and compassion bring a light into this world, and who have contributed material for this book. Sarah first alerted me to Christine de Pizan's *The Book of the City of Ladies*, so special thanks for that.

Deep gratitude goes to my editor, Joy Parker, an author, teacher and healer, who embodies a rare combination of gifts. She not only has a fine editorial hand and a keen sensitivity to the material presented in this book but also a deep devotion to the imaginal realm and to the feminine mysteries. In its final form, this book also owes much to the way in which Kathryn Sky-Peck, editor at Nicolas-Hays/Ibis, communicated with me about my project with such care, focus, clarity, and grace.

On a final note, I would like to honor my earliest dream that recurred regularly throughout my childhood and adolescence. I dreamt of golden circles arising out of a dark night and approaching me, becoming wider and wider. Sometimes this dream was quite frightening to me; at other times it seemed to be holding me and beckoning to me until l was ready to bring forward that portion of fate granted to me by the Invisible world. Now, much later in life, I know a little about the gold that alchemy speaks of as arising out of a black, blacker than black. I hope in some small way, in this book and in my life, to at last be able to bring forth into reality some of that gold. Many thanks are also due here to Rose-Emily Rothenberg, for helping me to see this important link during an early stage of writing, and to Brigitte Jacobs for unconditionally supporting me and, from my dream world, for awakening me to The Lion Path and the Egyptian Mysteries.

Foreword

BY THOMAS MOORE

A week after a visit to my ninety-seven year-old father, I called to see how he was doing. "Did I tell you what happened the day you left?" he asked.

"No," I said, worried that he had fallen. He is in wonderful shape but walks on shaky legs with a cane. He has been a devout Catholic all his life and went to church every Sunday. Now that he doesn't drive—he stopped only a year ago—he likes to watch Mass on television. Recently my brother installed a new television for him and this set has a different list of channels, and my father, who lives alone, couldn't find the Mass on it. After I left, he laid down on the couch and fell asleep. In his sleep he heard the most beautiful woman's voice he could imagine, speaking to him. "3-2-9," she said softly. When he woke up he tried channel 329 on the television, and there was the Mass.

This is a small, mundane excursion from rational life, but the story stunned and charmed everyone in my circle who heard it. There is something liberating and uplifting in it, a release from the heavy mechanical laws by which we live our everyday lives. I particularly like the simplicity of it, the revelation of a television listing.

Magnify this story by a factor of a hundred or more, and you get the spirit of this book by Veronica Goodchild. It, too, is liberating, enchanting, and full of hope. This is not only a good book; it is an important one. It could lead us out of the twentieth-century embrace of scientific laws and the moralism of those who insist on a materialistic, quantified, and rigid natural philosophy. Many laud the last century for all its achievements. I, for one, am happy to be done with it, to let go finally of its cruelty and the closed cosmos that it expected of its children and those of us who tried to make a life within its narrow borders.

It may take the reader a while to find a place in discussions of UFOs, synchronicity, dreams, crop circles, ET encounters, visitations of Mary, and near-death experiences. Keep the title in mind: Songlines of the Soul. Veronica discusses a number of unusual phenomena as hints about how to find ourselves in the cosmos and in the psyche, remembering that the two are profoundly connected. The anomalies she explores in loving detail are not curiosities or mere marvels to be treated as spiritual entertainments. They are indications of how we might be healed, learn to love, and live in a living world, a world that could fulfill our longings and free our souls.

It's as though we are in a small prison cell with only a chink of a window giving us hints of what is outside our confinement. The songlines Veronica gathers together in this visionary book show how full of wonder the world is and how much serious delight is to be found in it for us. I use the word with William Blake in mind, who said, "Energy is eternal delight." I mean a joyous and fulfilling experience of the world that addresses the emptiness we often feel and the sickness of body and soul that appears when delight disappears. Veronica uses the word "eros," which can sometimes be defined as delight.

Veronica writes like a traveler who has seen the wonders of the world and is ready to see more. She has neither the cold, skeptical preoccupations of the modernist critic nor the bug-eyed over-enthusiasm of a gullible devotee. She brings a new kind of intelligence to the study of a world now revealed to have infinitely more dimension than previously accorded it. Yes, the scientists have explored outer space, but they have seen only what their instruments, designed and used with limited purpose and scope, can perceive. Veronica is instructed by traditional peoples and visionaries. Her mind takes in more than the average person can entertain comfortably.

She is a pioneer going out boldly to visit Terra Incognita, the heretofore unknown earth.

Part of the modernist temperament stops research at the point where it feels mentally satisfying. Expectations have either been verified or refuted. We have a new fact or the satisfaction of knowing that a presumed fact is spurious. Veronica, in contrast, is in search of knowledge that heals and that makes possible an increase in loving connection with the world and with each other. This increase in loving is a crucial, profoundly innovative aspect of method. In the twenty-first century our devoted work has an ethical purpose: to discover the principle of love. In this, Veronica is simply enacting what the religious traditions have been teaching for millennia.

As you read this book, you may find one of those twentieth-century voices speaking up—either the skeptic or the devotee. Each has something to offer. You should always ask, can this be real? Where is the evidence? Am I being led along a too-rosy path? You can also relax and enjoy the thrill of considering a world of magic and outrageous well-being and beings from Other worlds in space. The idea is to bring all your rich intelligence to bear on the subjects that Veronica introduces with her own graceful blend of doubt and allowance. I picture her spending the winters teaching with innovation and rigor and the summers visiting crop circles and miracle sites. A psychological secret that is rarely discussed is the human capacity to do many things at once. You can be critical and indulgent at the same time. One attitude, fully enjoyed, corrects the other.

If you are like me, this book will feel like an invitation to live in a much larger, more interesting world. It will serve as a key to open the handcuffs that have kept your spirit in check for too long. It will give you ideas, facts, and a language for living more from your pulsing heart than your frowning head. It will help you make sense of things you were taught earlier in your life, understood then only naively. It may inspire you to hope for a strong dream, an overwhelming coincidence, or a UFO encounter. It will certainly free you from the particular depression that comes from a habit of modern skepticism.

Our planet is still full of cruel behavior on the part of individuals and groups. Children die of starvation and wartime bullets. It is difficult to travel the world safely and gather the experiences and sights that educate our hearts in the fullness life has to offer. But it doesn't have to be this way forever. We could recover a sense of common destiny and the need for common caretaking. But first we would have to break out of the mythic mold that shapes our understanding and emotions. We need to hear the music of a larger and different cosmos—the songlines that feed the soul and enliven the spirit.

Preface

*The psyche is the greatest of all cosmic wonders and the
sine qua non of the world as an object.*

C. G. JUNG

My interests have led me on a strange and unexpected journey
with innumerable twists and turns, and so the writing of this
book has taken much longer than I initially anticipated. This
in itself has educated me about approaching a subject with an open mind,
and particularly with an open heart. I have discovered that the soul reveals
its depths only in increments determined by our attitude and even perhaps
our patience. In any event, I could not have expected what has unfolded in
these pages and, in a way, find it difficult to judge the merits of my long
searches. All I can confirm is that I have followed a thread with as much
care as I could.

I have always been interested in the more esoteric side of C. G. Jung,
and Jung's work will resonate throughout these pages as one of the "songlines" I have pursued in my own journey toward exploring a new vision
of reality, a new worldview. I have been fascinated by that point where
the threads running from his doctoral dissertation on occult phenomena,
through his paranormal experiences and accounts of direct experiences
of the psyche in hauntings, visions, certain types of dreams, active imaginations, synchronicities, and his near-death-experience (NDE) come full

circle in his publications on synchronicity, the psychoid archetype, and "flying saucers." Here Jung can perhaps be seen—often more implicitly than explicitly—to be pointing toward a new kind of consciousness, one that dissolves the usual boundaries of inside/outside, subject/object, to produce a richly tapestried subtle body world ruled not by causality but rather by acausality, uncertainty, and unpredictability; not by past, present, and future, but by the boundless yet immediate realm of the here-and-now, of Presence. In my view, this new consciousness is ruled not so much by logos (rationality), but more by the feeling ambiguities and the depth of eros (interconnectedness and love).

I suppose that my version of Jung derives from my own interest in these irrational forces in our lives. I am intrigued by the power of mystical experiences, dreams, synchronicities, and extraordinary events of one kind or another to change our lives, to transform our consciousness toward a deeper gnosis, toward the sacred in nature and in the body. Also, I long to challenge thinking that equates the mystical experience with a spiritualizing tendency which denies or dishonors our divine-given physical form. On the contrary, mystical experience, synchronicities, and UFO encounters—in the way that I will be presenting them—are phenomena that counteract the historical Christianizing tendency to artificially split spirit from matter. The goal of this book is to reconnect the two parts of our nature, to let us once again appreciate how the transcendent is actually immanent, that is, fully present and grounded in this world and not "out there" somewhere. In reality, this union of psyche and matter is the rich field wherein soul and body are one, and wherein the third domain, that of the subtle body, comes into being.

An Invitation to the Reader

But the moment when physics touches on the "untrodden, untreadable regions," and when psychology has at the same time to admit that there are other forms of psychic life besides the acquisitions of personal consciousness...then the intermediate realm of subtle bodies comes to life again, and the physical and the psychic are once more blended in an indissoluble unity....We have come very near to this turning point today.[1]

W e live in a time of tremendous suffering and strife—and also a time of great possibility and change. Seemingly everything is in collapse—systems of governance, the environment, the economy, relationships, educational approaches that continue to stress objectivity, rational thinking, and scores on tests at the expense of vision, creativity, intuition, and quantum leaps into new possibilities. It is time for transformation and change. A global transformation of human consciousness is absolutely necessary NOW. Every heart can make this choice. A new consciousness is arising in us and around us. We long for it and we need to help each other strengthen its reality in our everyday lives.

This book proposes a new paradigm of reality, a new worldview. The signatures of this new reality are arising both in our own experiences and are to be seen all around us if we care to stretch wide open the often too narrow lens of conventional approaches that stubbornly persist in spite of enormous changes in our understanding of the world during the last century.

---

1   C. G. Jung, *Psychology and Alchemy*, from *The Collected Works of C. G. Jung*, tr. R. F. C. Hull (Princeton, NJ: Princeton University Press, 1970), Vol. 12, par. 394. (From now on, I will refer to Jung's *Collected Works* as *CW*.)

In the sciences, life is now seen as an interconnected and dynamic whole in which each part is coherently related to and involves the entire web of being. Rather than the parts determining the whole as in the old view, now the whole is seen as determining the activity of the parts.

Consciousness itself is part of this dynamic whole and is now thought to exist everywhere in the universe, not just associated with our brains. An underlying field, a silent invisible intelligence permeates everything from the DNA in your body to the swirling galaxies in the cosmos. We live in an interconnected, conscious, and holographic universe, a cosmos where we are both creation and also co-creators. We can connect with this extraordinary intelligence in a variety of ways: by reconnecting with the wisdom of the ancient mystical traditions to paying attention to non-ordinary states of consciousness. In addition, I will show in this book how dreams, synchronicities, UFO/ET encounters, Crop Circle mysteries, and NDEs all point to the new unfolding vision of reality that give us a taste of the new worldview and inspire us to become participants in its unfolding. Non-ordinary events are awakening us to the next phase in human evolution.

Just before his untimely death, former Harvard professor John Mack wrote that we live in a time in which we simply cannot just go on as usual.[2] The politics of fear, the increasing oppression of civil liberties, and the move toward fundamentalism worldwide that have taken hold require reflection and a response from each of us. Our response cannot arise out of the limitations of the ego, in other words, out of what we already know. As Einstein acknowledges, "A problem cannot be solved at the level at which it was created." At the end of an age when the answers offered by systems of governance or traditional religion are no longer sufficient for increasing numbers of individuals, a vision of renewal must—as it always has in the past—arise, first through visions, dreams, and journeys to other dimensions of consciousness.

After two thousand years of Christianity, of folding ourselves into one religion or another, we have almost forgotten the invisible realms and Invisible Ones who reside in the subtle domains. Later I will describe what I mean by these terms but for the moment I simply want to say that this is a good time to be quiet and to be listening, to go into an underground place, even in

---

2 John Mack, "The Current Crisis: Looking More Deeply" (unpublished lecture, dated June 10, 2004).

the imagination. Perhaps the outpouring of chaos in our world could be the birth pangs of a new era. But in these disturbing times, we need to go still and deepen our connection to those immortal guides who bestow wisdom, truth, and justice from realms beyond our limited perceptions, and who wish to help us. We can then try to bring this deeper knowledge back to the here and now and apply it to our daily lives in the world.

We are at a turning point in our history. In the words of, psychologist Carl Jung, our time is ripe for a "metamorphosis of the gods," what the Greeks call the *kairos*—the right moment—for a change in our perception regarding the fundamental principles and symbols that orchestrate reality.

This metamorphosis is already reflected cross-culturally in Hopi, Aztec, Mayan, Hindu, Tibetan, Maori, Zulu, Dogon, and Egyptian cultures, and their prophecies concerning the ending of an age and the constellation of a new myth, often associated with the year 2012. Interestingly, there are strong similarities among the different cultures about both the endings of the current time and the potentials of the new aeon, "Fifth World," or "Time of the Sixth Sun." Briefly, the endings point to a cataclysmic crisis in climate, cultures, and consciousness, owing to our separation from the sacred, and the beginnings of a new possibility based on the awareness of unity between diverse cultures, between science and ancient healing methods, between spirit and matter, and between the individual and the cosmos. In these insights, we see the attempt to bridge the (necessary) developments in ego consciousness with the wisdom of ancient and indigenous knowledge—in other words to restore our self-reflective capacity to a vision of the whole, to a *conscious* perception and experience of the interrelatedness of all being.

The book is titled *Songlines of the Soul* because it explores a reality that reaches far beyond the limitations of rational thinking. Readers will journey toward an attunement to intuition and a visionary and mytho-poetic sensibility, often responding to insights and stories that have come to me from the land of dreams, encounters, "miracles," conversations with soul friends, deep subtle experiences of my students and patients, and the dark unknown. The ancient word "songline," (*oime* in Greek) is relevant for its meaning refers to a pathway to another world and to the nuances of these non-ordinary and subtle realities. According to indigenous Aboriginal cosmology, the dreamtime and its songlines rule the universe. The ancestors were thought to have scattered words and musical notes along their trails as they walked over the land. These "dreaming-tracks" provided ways of communication between widely dispersed tribes, and a song was both map and direction-finder to those who shared one's Dreaming. The body also had its songlines; in fact, for Aboriginal Australians, "the vibratory song of an object must be known and sung before it can come alive."[3]

Today, the ancient idea of the music of the spheres is returning to us with the recent revelation that the entire solar system can be seen as a "tuned quantum resonant structure."[4] In my own life, music was the soothing vehicle through which my emotional and secret unspoken life was held like a treasure during my childhood and adolescence. For many people, music is the carrier of deep soulful experience giving expression to feelings often difficult to articulate with words.

Songlines have an ancient and resonant history. They are those soul-tracks that form grids or patterns that allow subtle communication, sometimes over very long distances. These musical notes comprise not only the foundations of reality, but also the imaginal geography of our journeys, the maps of our destinies and the secret pathways of the soul. If we follow their call, they are the passport to our vocation and the direction-finder to our beloved. Indeed, in ancient Greek epic poetry the word for "road" and the word for "song" are almost identical. This ancient identity has even older roots, for the aboriginal culture goes back thousands and thousands of years, to a time when the poet was a shaman and his song opened a journey to another world. When we acknowledge these profound and subtle ways of knowing that are returning to us today, we realize we are interdependent with all creation. This knowledge brings us to the place where we desire to live ethically and with compassion for our fellow human beings, the earth and the cosmos.

It is not known yet how we will navigate this earthquake of change. Indeed, we do not know whether we will even survive it at all. When we think of the dire state of things in Darfur or Iraq (the list could go on) and the kind of driven martial consciousness that initiates such atrocities, when we remember the devastation brought about by the tsunami wave the day after Christmas, 2004, the devastation of Hurricane Katrina, the cata-

---

3   Arnold Mindell, *The Quantum Mind and Healing* (Charlottesville, VA: Hampton Roads, 2004), p. 93.
4   Jude Currivan, *The 8th Chakra* (Carlsbad, CA: Hay House, 2007), Chs. 1 and 2

strophic earthquakes in Haiti, Japan . . . we may well find ourselves sinking into despair. But there is also a voice in us that insists that we not give in to despair and not lose heart, in spite of how things appear, in spite of all of humanity's collective suffering.

This text has been written in a voice that aims to keep hope alive, that envisions chaos and death as the harbingers of new life. However, this book also looks at why the *symbolic* and experiential realities of death and renewal are key to preventing the literal growth of these forces on our planet. Developing this kind of consciousness demands much from us, one individual at a time.

Songlines of the Soul tries to show us that visionary experiences of the psyche, synchronicities, UFO encounters, events that involve moments of "missing time," and journeys to the mystical and luminous cities of the soul, are all contemporary expressions of ancient ways. They belong to the mystery and esoteric traditions and earlier shamanic cultures, and can be fruitfully situated in these ancient ways as contemporary explosions of our need to resituate our historical lives back into the sacred streams of history. These streams have been known since the beginning of time, and can be restored to us once again by the ancestors and the invisible guides of the soul who are visiting us once again today.[5]

This book, then, seeks to articulate the possibility of a new worldview, first suggested by Carl Jung, and then further developed in the fifty years since his death by people who have increasingly experienced all sorts of anomalous events relating to altered states of consciousness. Our cultural fascination with near-death experiences, contemporary forms of mysticism, the spectacular "miracles" of the crop circles, the many visions of Mary, Tara, and the Black Madonna, and the reflections about them represent the desire of so many individuals to connect to a reality beyond the secular and profane worldview of our time. These are just some of the many ways this new healing "shamanic" energy, what we might imagine as the holistic, connected, and indigenous level of the psyche, is entering into our precarious world. In this book I hope to show what some of the features and qualities of this new worldview might be like.

---

5 Nicholas Goodrick-Clarke, *The Western Esoteric Traditions: A Historical Introduction* (Oxford: Oxford University Press, 2008).

Carl Jung felt that each of us was responsible for a worldview. In fact, he exhorted each of us, like initiates or shamans returning back to the everyday world following exposure to events and lessons experienced during altered states of consciousness, to be responsible for moving beyond our own suffering and giving expression to what we have learned in a larger context that includes our relationship with others. In this way, through the hard-won resolution of our own issues, we can bear our part of the collective suffering in the world in a way that is both practical and manageable in our individual lives. Each person's suffering leads to an archetypal core which is essential to an understanding that, if we are indeed able to penetrate deeply enough into these altered states and *make them conscious*, we will help to raise the level of collective consciousness. In this way, we can help to alleviate unnecessary suffering in the world.

It is difficult to account for all the ingredients that go into writing a text. Some are known, others are more invisible and deeply mysterious, as if some unknown force or character in the background—an angel or *daimon* perhaps—keeps nudging us along until we complete the task that has been handed to us, and in which on some level we have agreed to participate. As I persevered in the task of writing and researching this book, what emerged over time was the sense that the "reality" of our world is far vaster than we could ever know; it holds more mysteries than we can account for. We hunger for these mysteries and are starving for lack of them. On the one hand, the absence of this kind of deep knowledge is contributing to the violence that seems to pervade our world locally and globally and that may eventually destroy us. On the other hand, the irruption of all kinds of anomalous and paranormal events in our time seems to signal another possibility. I have come to view these events as signs and symptoms of the re-emergence of the ancient idea of the subtle body, and of its access to subtle worlds.

The pre-Socratic philosopher Parmenides, for example, wrote an epic poem about his underworld journey to the goddess in an altered state of consciousness and what she taught him about the nature of reality and illusion, justice and truth. It is a journey into the heart of our deepest longing where we are taught divine and eternal truths in a subtle world where opposites meet and are transcended. Because we have become so far removed from our longing and depths today, increasing numbers of people are finding themselves in the world of neither dreaming nor waking, and in that Other world are seeing through illusion into the depths of a divine reality that feeds our souls.[6]

Because such knowledge is paradoxical and hard to articulate, often the ineffable nature of such experiences was translated into a poem or a song, a vehicle that could allude to the mystery, and embody its tone or vibration indirectly, though effectively, for the listener. Hence the title of this book, *Songlines of the Soul*, derives from this recognition of how difficult it is to translate the invisible into the visible. But I am neither poet nor singer. So my medium is prose, and I do my best to use it as a tool for reflection and storytelling, including many direct examples from the world of the soul. Dreams, visions, synchronicities, imaginal encounters, active imaginations, accounts of unidentified flying object (UFO) sightings or extraterrestrial (ET) meetings—all these must be my poems and my songs, which I hope will just as effectively evoke the rich heritage of that subtle world from which they arise: an alternative world that seems to be encroaching on our everyday world once again as we move beyond the limitations of our failed materialistic and rationalistic prejudices.

In addition to recognizing the subtle world, I have tried to write specifically about the key elements and characteristics which comprise it. I touch on how this new worldview is supported by scientific explanations such as modern physics and the new cosmology. Much of my evidence takes the form of reporting our direct experience of its domain. Hence, I speak of how a subtle embodiment erodes the divisions of mind and matter, psyche and world, and points to a non-dual and psychophysical unity in the background of our world. I have further suggested that the unpredictable nature of anomalous events and the experience of them psychologically lead us in the direction of a deep and subtle eros awareness that we are called to nurture. Advancements in the new physics as well as psi research (such as telepathy and remote viewing) also suggest that the paranormal should be included in a fuller description of reality. Anomalous experiences—particularly synchronicities, UFO-ET encounters, Crops Circles, NDEs, and journeys to the Mystical Cities of the Imaginal World—are the signatures

---

6   Elizabeth Mayer, *Extraordinary Knowing* (New York: Bantam Dell, 2008).

of a new mythic landscape in our time. As we live physically within the interconnected web of all life, and psychically in Earth's visionary geography, these signatures and their subtle body field mark the possibility for our own transformation.

Songlines of the Soul places its energy into hoping for a miracle, so that we can move beyond killing and destroying each other toward a greater wisdom to be made manifest on our beautiful planet. The goal of this book is to help all of us remember who we truly are, to become the midwives for this evolution in eros consciousness, and become like notes in a cosmic symphony resounding throughout creation in devotion to a unified vision of reality, to the ancient notion of the world or cosmic soul.

I have divided this book into four parts. Part One: Introduction to the Subtle Body and Subtle Worlds, re-acquaints the reader with our ancient mystery traditions and introduces the notion of an intermediate and inter-mediating reality between spirit and matter that usually exists outside our conscious awareness. Part Two: Synchronicity: Doorways to the Deep Mysteries of the Psyche, presents a subtle sensibility as the mechanism that puts us on the path to the recovery of deepening human consciousness toward eros awareness. Part Three: A New Emerging Myth: UFOs and Crop Circles, sets the stage for a new reality by outlining the emergence of a new myth and the signatures of this emerging myth as we transition from one age to another. Finally, Part Four: Mystical Cities and Healing Sanctuaries, explores the features of the new consciousness and ways we can incarnate and embody the new emerging myth. Throughout this volume, theoretical material is balanced by the inclusion of many examples from students, patients and colleagues.

My book seeks to support the creative imagination and its access to this subtle wisdom field on behalf of a much-needed "course correction" for our planet, from a race toward disaster to the re-embracing of the cosmic soul. Drawing on Jung's revolutionary understanding of the psyche and how psyche and cosmos are at bottom really one, my book will give many examples of the intuitive accessing of a wisdom of the heart, an evolution in consciousness gaining ground in our time and one that is needed for the maturing of our own Earth home.

Part One

AN INTRODUCTION
TO THE SUBTLE BODY AND
SUBTLE WORLDS

Chapter One

THE RETURN OF THE MYSTERIES

The dream is over.
God is a Concept, John Lennon

The Age of Aquarius will involve the true discovery of the Divine Guest within us,
and with it the need to recognize this in all people and in nature, as well: it will be the
dialectic of the individual and the cosmos. . . . a deep understanding of the interdependence of
all life. . . . the unus mundus of the mystics and the alchemists. . . . the reemergence of
Hagia Sophia, the feminine wisdom hidden in nature and in us.[1]

There is a knowledge that secretly and imperceptibly tries to make its
way into our world from time to time over the course of history.
This knowledge is subtle, residing in a space that is neither precisely inside nor precisely outside—it is found in the intervals between waking, sleeping, and dreaming. From the earliest philosophers and shamans,
to the alchemical mystic philosophers, to the Sufi Gnostics and Western
mystics, through to Jung's psychology of the transpersonal unconscious and
beyond to his observations about the "transpsychic"[2] landscape of reality,
we can glimpse the streams of underground initiates, who through direct
experience of this reality, sought to keep this vital knowledge—sometimes
called the *aurea catena* or golden chain—alive.

Today, however, this knowledge is no longer the province of the mystical few. All of us, in our own unique way, are being asked to participate in
a new spiritual flowering on our planet Earth, a blossoming that gives as
much room to eros (interconnectedness and love) as is has heretofore given

---

1 Alice. O. Howell, *Jungian Synchronicity in Astrological Signs and Ages* (Wheaton, IL: Quest Books, 1995),
pp. 207–209.
2 C. G. Jung, *CW* 14, pars. 410–411.

to logos (rational thinking and the scientific method). It is often extraordinary experiences of a non-ordinary or rare and wondrous kind that give us glimpses of this golden chain, expand our sense of who we are and set us on a path of personal transformation.

In focusing on these kinds of experiences and the changes in consciousness that arise from them, I am suggesting in this book that we can detect a new vision of life emerging, a new worldview for a new millennium. A new and expanding human being is gradually emerging from the death of outmoded containers of thought and from the ashes of our civilization that is disintegrating all around us. The notion of the unconscious in Freud and Jung's work—the idea of a secret and "unknown" world that informs our feelings and actions—has been incorporated into the life of the *mind*—both in psychology and in almost every discipline beyond psychology. Now it is time for the imagination, for the *soul*, for eros and love to help balance and re-orchestrate the energy that is falling out of all the old forms that no longer serve our survival either physically or spiritually.

The new physics and transpersonal psychology are discovering this silent intelligence as a fundamental reality as each discipline explores its separate territory. Though mechanistic Newtonian ideas in science are useful for the world of everyday reality and for technology, they are useless for explorations into the subatomic world in the deeper realms of matter and, in the same way, rational modes of discourse are inadequate for deeply spiritual experiences in non-ordinary states of awareness. Nevertheless, both the quantum physicist and the depth psychologist or mystic rely on empirical observation; the one from his experiments, the other from her experiences of the different levels of consciousness. Both now are compelled to include their own consciousness as part of a reciprocal unfolding of reality: in physics this is called the observer effect; in psychology it is called the predisposition or "personal equation" of the individual. Moreover, both are on the frontiers of exploring a reality way beyond the ordinary senses and both are dealing with multi-dimensional realities that are extremely difficult to describe in ordinary language. Furthermore, it is increasingly acknowledged by both scientists and depth psychologists that intuition, feeling, and the creative imagination are indispensable ingredients for a fuller description of reality. The new human is both scientist and mystic, both rational and visionary! We are experiencing the return of the mysteries.

My Dream of Suhrawardi

To give you an example of how this wisdom tradition is making its reality accessible to a modern 21st century woman, and what it has meant for my life personally, let me share a pivotal dream I had about Suhrawardi, a twelfth-century Sufi mystic, who has become a guide within my inner landscape. At the time of the dream—September 20, 2000—I had begun a very early draft of this book, which, at that time had been initiated by a desire to deepen my understanding of extraordinary events and unusual encounters that seemed to take place in a space that was neither dreaming nor waking.

In the dream, which takes place within the context of some sort of public event, an enlightened holy man who is old but nevertheless seems quite young, is dying, passing over into the beyond. Before he passes, he is trying to tell me something. He has a gentle demeanor, and a smile on his face that contains depths of feeling, pathos, and compassion. He tells me that he is so happy that he has been able to save or liberate a young boy. Although I do not yet know the boy, I understand that the holy man means to place the young boy in my care, and in the dream this has a deeply spiritual significance for me. Then the holy man—he seems to be a Tibetan monk—slowly and calmly dies. The next day I had a strong emotional response to this dream as I wrote it out. In ways that were quite incomprehensible on a rational level, it was very moving to me. In addition, quite unconsciously, I put on a red silk jacket with gray Tibetan tantric symbols woven into it—the double dorge (or visavajra)—signifying the sacred union of the hard, penetrating masculine and the multifaceted, reflecting feminine energies. (At the time, I was completely ignorant of the meaning of these symbols, but some colleagues later pointed them out to me.) While wearing the jacket, I had this curious sense of the enlightened being from my dream being present and surrounding me.

Since I was not familiar with this holy man who had made his appearance in my dream, I decided to engage in an active imagination exercise to find out more about him. I withdrew into a quiet, meditative state. Suddenly, a bird started to sing. The sound was so clear, so ethereal, so otherworldly, that it penetrated into the core of my soul. It felt like a song from another land. Then, all at once, the holy man in the dream and the bird became one.

I thought, "So! He's appeared in the form of this bird." Then I asked, "Who are you? What is your name?" Immediately, the name of the twelfth-century Sufi mystic Suhrawardi came to my mind. The dialogue that unfolded led me to do some research on this Persian Gnostic. The only book I had in my own library at that time that mentioned his name was Dan Merkur's *Gnosis*.[3] I opened to the appropriate section and read that one of Suhrawardi's mystical treatises was entitled, "The Treatise of the Birds." It is a story concerning the journey of the soul into the visionary landscape of the *mundus imaginalis*, revealed in his book as a beautiful city atop a mountain.

Suhrawardi (1153–1191) was a Persian Sufi visionary martyred at age thirty-eight for his defense of the ontological reality, the "really realness," of visionary states. Though he was also a logician, he developed a theory of visionary knowledge and illuminative wisdom, emphasizing the integrity of altered states of awareness, and valuing the union of gnosis—direct experience of these states—with rational reflection. Suhrawardi felt that the imaginal world was a reality upon which we could utterly rely. The initiates of his mystery school were called the "people of love,"[4] and their journey took them in the direction of "opening the heart." Upon reading this, I was overcome by a strong sense of belonging , the belonging of my soul to this mystical, visionary tradition, and a feeling, even deeper, of already knowing this man, this Friend of my heart. The only discrepancy was that the enlightened holy man in the dream was a Tibetan Buddhist, and Suhrawardi was a Persian Gnostic. What, I wondered, might be the link between these two traditions?

Tibet is the preserver and custodian of enlightenment teachings. The Tibetan Buddhist tradition accesses its insights by meditative practices involving the third eye, an organ of visions rather than of sight, that opens to the subtle world of imagination. In this imaginal domain, guides of the soul, spiritual mentors, enlightened historical teachers, masters and mentors from all the great spiritual traditions of the world, such as Suhrawardi, reside. Sufi Gnosticism, which follows a similar process, therefore has direct links with the practices and beliefs of Tibetan Buddhism.

---

3   Dan Merkur, *Gnosis: An Esoteric Tradition of Mystical Visions and Unions* (Albany, NY: SUNY Press, 1993), pp. 222–225.
4   Merkur, *ibid.*, p. 224.

It is both my belief and experience that this channel to the *mundus imagi-nalis* is being opened up again in our world today—and we need this knowledge desperately if we are to save ourselves. Once a culture has become too overwhelmed by materialism or destructive practices such as war, and the individual has been buried in a morass of conventional attitudes, often driven by fears that do not resonate with our truest essence, the soul begins to sense its terrible separation from the deeper waters of wisdom and compassion. Slowly, however, many individuals within our culture have begun to awaken, to recall our desire for freedom, our longing for an individually meaningful connection with the depths of existence, the joy of enlightenment, and a sense of unity beyond the self to all creation. The image of the holy man in my dream and his message within the context of a larger collective event—witness the figure of the young boy transferred to my care—strongly suggests that this significant awakening is upon us. So important has this figure become in my life that I strongly suspect that he is the guide, aiding me in my work of writing this book.

Non-local Communication

But the appearance of Suhrawardi in my dream has a further implication. As recent research into phenomena such as telepathy and remote viewing reveal, the human mind also acts non-locally. In such instances we can see and know things beyond the range of our physical senses. Communication can transcend space-time and therefore does not rely on a signal within our local, cause-effect universe. What this means is that at non-local levels we can access other dimensions of consciousness and reality, other times and places in history including the future coming toward us, other beings in other star systems who can reach us. In short, non-locally we can access the "always-everywhere" Akashic field and are being invited to tune in to the deeper nature of the cosmos.

Similarly, the sacred teachings of the Tibetan tradition were thought to have originally come from another place, sometimes called the Pure or Noble lands. These mystical lands, acknowledged by other spiritual traditions as well, have many names such as Shambhala, Avalon, and Hurqalya. The wisdom, the sacred knowledge, of these subtle imaginal worlds becomes accessible to us only under certain spiritual and emotional conditions. Following the "golden chain" tradition of which Suhrawardi was an initiate, the chapters in this book will share many accounts of direct experiences of the subtle world—historical as well as modern—and reflect upon what these sorts of experiences might mean for our further development not only as individuals, but as citizens of a living, consciously aware and interconnected cosmos. Achieving wholeness and awareness of who we truly are depends upon the inclusion of both experience and reflection.

My dream and its exploration led me to see that unusual events and encounters, such as the crop circle phenomena, near-death experiences, visions of Mary, and ET visitations—reflections upon which were preoccupying me at the time of the dream—are part of this tradition of love. It is once again seeking a way to enter our lives so that the esoteric truths of the past can become relevant once again today, converging toward a fuller description of reality and a more comprehensive worldview. One key to this ancient tradition that is trying to visit us once again is the power of vision and the imagination—true imagination, *imaginatio vera*, as it was called by the alchemists, as opposed to flights of fancy. In this way we can access the spiritual truths of the subtle imaginal interworld where the sacred knowledge is held, and assist in the evolution of consciousness.

Subtle Worlds and Imagination: The Work of Henri Corbin

Ultimately, the aim of this book is to recover the imaginal world of the soul, enabling readers to experience it as another dimension of being and awareness—not as an esoteric upper world or lower world but, as Suhrawardi claimed, an ever-present *Other* world that defies logical explanation because, as he writes, it is both within the body spatially and outside it as a separate location in the cosmos. The term *imaginal* originates with the recovery—from the ancient texts and practices of twelfth century Sufi mysticism—of what philosopher and theologian Henri Corbin calls the *mundus imaginalis*.[5] This *mundus imaginalis* is a truly real though subtle landscape located in a

5 Henry Corbin, "*Mundus Imaginalis*, or The Imaginary and the Imaginal." In *Swedenborg and Esoteric Islam* (West Chester, PA, Swedenborg Foundation, 1995), pp. 1 – 33.

"third domain" that is neither precisely spirit nor matter, but lies somewhere in-between the purely intellectual world of angelic intelligences and the sensible world of material things and participates in both.

The imaginal world is a "really real" place where an interiority becomes the threshold to a new "outside," a spiritual landscape where beings have extension and dimension of a subtle or "immaterial" kind. This is a world where space, being the outer aspect of an inner state, is created at will.

This third domain, the *mundus imaginalis*, is to be distinguished from purely imaginary or idealized ideas such as the notion of a utopia. In fact, Corbin considers utopian ideologies to be a displacement of the imaginal world. The key to experiencing this subtle realm with its own inhabitants, topographies, and mystical cities is through the faculty of imagination, or *imaginatio vera* as it was called in alchemy, to distinguish it from the fictive or self-aggrandizing fantasies of the ego. This "true imagination" is a spiritually creative force, connected with the feminine figure of Sophia, or Fatima in Persian mysticism, and it is also the subtle organ that enables visions and new creations.

The imaginative faculty is a spiritual power independent of the physical body and therefore surviving it. Many people who have endured near- or after-death experiences also attest to this fact as they record floating above their bodies in another form invisible to other people, yet watching (quite accurately) doctors and nurses trying to resuscitate their physical forms.[6] The imagination is the formative power of the subtle or imaginal body, which, according to Corbin, is forever inseparable from the soul, or the spiritual individual.

Corbin contends that this imaginal realm got lost with the rise of man's "agnostic reflex," when thinking and being became divorced in the West. He dates it back a thousand years to the destruction of the Avicennian cosmology with its angelic hierarchy, and indicates that with it the imaginative power of symbol-making got lost. Once this universe and its souls disappeared, the imaginative function itself was devalued. Corbin suggests that it will not be recovered until we have access to a cosmology structured with a plurality of universes arranged in ascending order, as once before. All the wondrous discoveries of modern science relating to our physical universe alone do not

---

6   See, for example, Raymond Moody, *Life After Life* (San Francisco: HarperSanFrancisco, 1975/2001), p. 24ff.

begin to touch the reality of the imaginal realm, because this latter realm exists beyond the purely physical, yet it is present here and now. Until that time, Corbin claims, our will to power will be a never-ending source of horrors.

Corbin allows for the possibility that this loss of the *mundus imaginalis* was necessary to allow for the horrible, the monstrous, the miserable, and the absurd to surface. Perhaps while science attempts to give us the quantum world, dark matter, worm holes, black holes, and string theory, in a movement toward a renewed multidimensional universe lost in the rise of our secular and all-too-human interests, all the ghastly images, for example, of aliens and abductions are the dark chaotic shadow side that also comes into being as part of our initiation into the new age.

Corbin describes the manifold function of the *mundus imaginalis*. Lying between matter and spirit, it is that world that materializes spirit and spiritualizes, or "imaginalizes," matter, creating symbols that, like a painting, a symphony, a sacred dance, or an esoteric piece of literature, have the peculiar quality of linking something known with something that remains an unknown mystery. The *mundus imaginalis* is the world where mystical visions and visionary events at death "take place" and "have their place." It is also the place of mystical epics such as the Grail legends, symbolic acts that become initiation rituals, liturgies and their symbols, and the "composition of the ground" in various methods of prayer (for example, the ancient circular labyrinth that provided a walking meditation through the seven chakras and the four elements on the floor in Chartres Cathedral). Corbin summarizes other events that are dependent on the *mundus imaginalis:*

> the validity of dreams … the reality of *places* constituted by intense meditation, the reality of inspired imaginative visions, of cosmogonic relations and of theogonies, the authenticity of the spiritual *meaning* decipherable under the imaginative data of prophetic revelations …briefly, everything that surpasses the order of common empirical perception and is individualized in a personal vision, undemonstrable by simple recourse to the criteria of sensory knowledge or rational understanding.[7]

---

7 Henry Corbin, *Spiritual Body & Celestial Earth* (Princeton, NJ: Princeton University Press, 1977), p. 87.

Without the true spiritual imagination, then, none of this has a place, or can take place, any more.

Corbin elucidates the necessity for musical terminology when opening to the imaginal world, for penetration into the *mundus imaginalis* cannot be achieved by force, nor will logic, proof, or rational reasoning get you to those subtle worlds. Rather, it is an attunement to a different octave of experience, one that also includes our feelings and intuitions. A musical chord displays a harmony that includes the repetition of the lowest note at the top. In other words, the same note is played again, but in a higher octave. It is the image of "same but different," a qualitative difference, repeating and amplifying with feeling and experience the same note or theme but at another vibratory level. This is the language, the songline, required for the journey, not of the intellect or physical senses per se, but of the true imagination, which is the soul's way of knowing. This journey is a penetration to those deeply subjective yet completely reliable visionary or mystical events, to those regions so utterly different from "my" psychic space, a journey that opens us once again to the perception of a multi-dimensional universe.

Access to the *mundus imaginalis*, a psycho-cosmic landscape also known as the "Eighth Climate," or "Na-koja-Abad," the "land of No(n)where" (reminding us of the invisible quantum field or hyperspaces of physics), always involves a breach, a break with geographical coordinates and chronological time. It involves a discontinuity, therefore, a rupture with the laws of the physical world, like that provided for example by a near-death encounter, an out-of-body journey, or intense meditative practice. The traveler, however, is not conscious of the precise moment of this break. She only realizes it later. Hence, she cannot show the way to others. She can only describe it afterwards. Speaking of that subtle moment of non-ordinary awareness, Corbin writes in his book *Spiritual Body and Celestial Earth*, "Everything is strange ... when one sets foot on that Earth where the Impossible is in fact accomplished."[8]

Entry to the *mundus imaginalis* cannot be demonstrated rationally, or to those who deny or reject such ideas. It is a gnosis granted by virtue of having suffered the dark night of the soul, the death of the ego, the death before

---

8 Corbin, *ibid.*, p. xxix.

you die. A descent into these depths leads to a knowledge that links the initiate with ancient Hermeticism, spiritual alchemy, the mystical traditions, and the death and rebirth mysteries. It is not a rational knowledge, it is the soul's knowledge that through a spiritual birth, opens to the perception of hidden things, and often involves the appearance of a spiritual guide (like Philemon for Jung, or Suhrawardi for me), or the connection with one's immortal *daimon*, angel, or being of light often described in the near-death literature.

The initiate, the true philosopher and lover, begins to discover a central authority and ethic as her soul awakens to consciousness of a transpersonal or celestial kinship that supports the marriage of intuition and imagination. She becomes the spokesperson for the invisible world and Invisible Ones, often developing a passionate desire to see world conditions improve. This can clearly be seen in the story of a patient of mine named Robin, a former executive who gave up a lucrative career in order to follow her desire to become a novelist. Robin responded to a calling to rewrite fairy tales for today's young adult readers. The catalyst for this vocational change was a mourning process constellated by her reliving of the trauma of her own mother's suicide when she was six years old. Robin courageously entered a 12-Step program for her alcoholism and overcame a deep sense of her own unworthiness to tap into deep reservoirs of the personal and collective unconscious. Squarely facing and exploring the tragedies and inadequacies of her own upbringing, she vowed to create books for today's adolescent youth that shared a different vision and offered greater possibilities than she herself had inherited. Through deep work on herself by undergoing her own grieving and rebirth process, Robin eventually achieved a multi-book deal with a major publisher. Following her dreams, she re-imagined the theme of the abandoned and orphaned child—a theme common in fairytales—in her own writing.

So we see how this Other world has been experienced and kept alive not only by practitioners of Sufism and Tibetan Buddhism, and by shamans, mystics, poets, alchemists, and certain philosophers across the globe for thousands of years, but also by ordinary individuals willing to endure self exploration and personal transformation. Access to this world demands an introverted, reflective, and open attitude structured by eros (the heart) more than by logos (the intellect), an awareness that is at home in paradox, ambiguity, and the unfamiliar—even the impossible. Entering these domains requires a willingness to slow down and embody each experience in the present moment through images and with attention to the power and subtleties of feeling that they contain. As my own example illustrates, entering these domains requires also an openness to dreams as a legitimate mode of knowledge.

We are ill-equipped for this orientation to reality because the overwhelming mindset of our time is an extraverted, heroic ideal, which expresses itself mainly in empirical and rational terms. A mindset often goal-oriented and hurried, it creates an artificial compartmentalization between what is "inner" and "outer," perpetuating the familiar split between body and mind. This book, however, proposes that the subtle world of the imaginal is a third realm of being, as described by Corbin, pressing up from the depths of the psyche in certain kinds of dreams and waking visions, disclosing itself in synchronicities, arriving from "outer space" as UFOs, revealing itself in so-called ET encounters, emerging from the earth as crop circles, and appearing in all kinds of anomalous and paranormal events, such as the now well-researched near-death experiences (NDEs). We need to attune ourselves to the possibility that these events are signaling a shift in our collective unconscious that will lead toward a vastly expanded sense of who we are.

In the new worldview, the imaginal world is becoming our reality. These subtle events, which take place in the world "between" seem to enter our awareness when we are sufficiently open and permeable to them. The following example from my journal tells how my husband and I experienced this type of awareness throughout the course of a day.

JOURNAL ENTRY: SUBTLE SYNCHRONICITY

My husband Robert and I are out on our deck, sipping our morning coffee in the blue-green light of a southern California Spring morning. He is telling me a dream that he had the previous night about my father, who had actually died sixteen months ago, but who in the dream is not quite dead and who keeps making bizarre, physical gestures that suggest he might still be somewhat alive. Robert says that the dream feels disturbing, but he cannot really see why he had it or what it connects with in his life. We wonder if it might have to do with a visit that he is soon to make to his eldest son, and if the dream contains some disturbing features of his own fathering attitude. But that is a stretch and it doesn't seem to really fit emotionally. Robert wonders in a reflective and intuitive way if somehow my father feels that he hasn't been mourned adequately.

We let it go and move into our day.

Early after lunch I receive a phone call. Surprisingly, it is from my brother who lives in Bristol, England. I have always felt close to my brother, but although we had sporadically exchanged correspondence over the past year, we had not spoken to each other on the phone since my father's death. William is calling to let me know that my one remaining uncle on my mother's side of the family died yesterday, and that he thought I would like to be told. We pause. I thank him.

In the course of our rather lengthy trans-Atlantic conversation, I mention Robert's dream and his intuition about it. Will replies that, amazingly, he awoke at 4 am that morning overwhelmed with feelings of sadness and loss about our uncle's death. He goes on to say that he was surprised that he was having such intense feelings for an uncle that he was not even particularly close to. However, he was concerned that, apart from a strong feeling of loss at the moment of our father's death over a year ago, he hadn't really felt much conscious grief about his death after that. He told his wife Rachel that he wondered if perhaps he hadn't mourned our father's death adequately.

At that moment, the atmosphere of our conversation shifts, and there is the sense of another presence entering into our world.

This story tells of a synchronicity, an affectively pregnant moment having to do with acausally related events taking place in both the dream world and the waking world, happening in two different countries at roughly the same time, linked and made conscious by a phone call, and held together within the archetypal field of death. In such a moment, death becomes both a human and a trans-human event, a powerful moment of sorrow, and, paradoxically, a moment of grace in which awe enters the world. In that moment the human and eternal realms momentarily meet and infuse each other with their discrete ways of being.

Such events break open the usual kinds of distinctions we hold about reality. In such moments, we discover that each of us is not only a separate individual with a beginning and an end, but also that each one of us constitutes a luminous presence with neither a beginning nor an end. In such moments, psyche and matter seem to be but two different expressions of one eternally present ground of being, a "soul field" that embraces both modes of being, disclosing other realms of perception in addition to our normal sense of reality. For example, what, we may ask, is being disclosed to us in synchronicities and paranormal phenomena, UFO/ET encounters? What does humanity have to learn from the dim memory, or experience, of mystical kingdoms such as Shambhala or Belovodia in Tibetan Buddhism, Olmo Lungring in Bon Buddhism, the strange lands of Avalon in the Grail Legends, and Hurqalya in Sufi mysticism? These are all imaginal "third world" domains, realms of heightened emotional intensity and experience in which soul and body, are one.

What has been excluded by linear, rational, and logical ways of knowing as exceptional, irrational, mystical, along with the deep psychophysical feeling states that accompany these experiences, are seeking an honored place in our lives once more. For it is only through exposure to realms beyond the boundaries of ordinary time and space that we can truly heal and reclaim our birthright as liberated and enlightened beings devoted to wisdom and love within the domain of our ordinary, everyday world. The following provides another story by a graduate student of a journey to the *mundus imaginalis*.

Songlines and the Call of the Soul: The Green Lady

Kas Robinson, a psychotherapist and doctoral student at Pacifica Graduate Institute, was an orphaned newborn whose first memory was of a colorful heavenly mother spirit holding her in her arms. In her grief and terror at having been abandoned, she called out for help and this luminous spirit held her close against her warm breasts, giving her a sense of belonging and home. Kas writes: "This early experience with my spirit mother provided me with a connection to the unseen world, the world behind the veil. It enabled me to survive my grief and gave me a worldview in which everything was alive and filled with enchantment. As a child, the birds and trees talked to me, I had imaginary friends who were with me always, and my ring had magic powers of protection. My bedroom was filled with animated objects, and I spoke to God daily and God spoke to me." Growing up in a culture dominated by rationalism she eventually lost her connection to this Other world, but she also fell into a depression on account of this loss, a sadness that eventually led to her recovering the enchanted world of her childhood and integrating it into her everyday life and practice as an adult. Kas is now writing her dissertation on "The World Behind the Veil," focusing on the healing value to be found within anomalous experiences of the Other world.

One day while Kas was on the beach reflecting on her dissertation topic, she sat down next to a piece of driftwood that provided a sort of shelter and listened to the waves, opening herself to guidance about her work. She writes about what happened next:

My eyes were closed, and I suddenly saw a vision of myself in a rickshaw on a road in India traveling up a mountainside to the temple of a female goddess. The rickshaw passed a marketplace that was colorful, noisy, smelly, and filled with many people. It was dusk and the light was beautiful. It was quiet on the mountain. I arrived at the temple, which was like a cave and made from the rock of the mountain. I saw a woman sitting on part of the rock outside the temple, and she was dangling her green legs over the side. I recognized her as the Green Lady, a figure who visited me once before in a time of great need. She was green all over—her clothes, her skin, her eyes, and even the blood pumping through her body. She was dressed in what looked like a green tunic, and her head and face were veiled. I began to cry at the sight of her. I asked her what she wanted from me, and she simply continued to swing her legs back and forth. The feeling atmosphere was pungent with the force of life; everything was animated. It was an experience that permeated my being and got into my bones. I felt her love penetrating me, and she opened me to a sense of mystery—her green legs swinging back and forth all the while.

Then the Green Lady grabbed my hand and we dove into the ocean. We dove down deep to the bottom of the sea, where we saw a treasure: a bright orange object glistening within the water. Then, suddenly, we were back at the temple, and I sensed a message that the Green Lady was communicating to me without having to speak. The message just arrived in my awareness. She told me that nature is my ally and friend; that I am a nature spirit, and that nature can speak to me and advise me.

Kas writes that after this experience she was once again plagued by doubts about the reality of the Other world, and an inner voice associated with her critical father put her down for being so stupid about thinking that she could survive in the "real world" when her head was in "make-believe" all the time. After acknowledging this resistance, however, she was able to suspend her disbelief long enough to reflect on the experience of being in the presence and color of the Green Lady, which reminded her of the New Zealand bush from her childhood. "As a child, I spent all of my free time in nature—the birds, the trees, the animals, and nature sprites all spoke to me and I spoke to them. Magic and mystery were everywhere." At this point, her resistance returned, and she was reluctant to stay with the image of the Green Lady, preferring instead to remember and explore the rickshaw and the wild and colorful market in India.

Kas felt that the Indian market was a more comfortable place for her and she associated it with the part of her that values quickness, extraversion, and change. However, the image of India was also associated with magic and spirituality and so, like the Green Lady, also related to anomalous experiences, visions, and the reality of the Other world. Nevertheless, India has a place in this world and a rhythm that seems more acceptable, while the Green Lady was a part of a non-ordinary experience that still felt less "real." Struggling with these resistances and conflicts, Kas felt the deep longing in herself for the magical world of her childhood, for the relationship with nature, and for shamanic otherworldliness. Suddenly she had an epiphany that perhaps the mother spirit of her infancy united both the experiences of the Green Lady and the colorful market in India. She knew that she needed to honor both her deeply altered states of awareness together with her unpredictable colorful states, and that these marginalized experiences carried the deepest, most meaningful threads in her life.

Staying with this feeling, and suspending the disbelief that kept haunting her, Kas moved on to do some research into the symbolism of her experiences. She began with the color green that tends to represent new growth and change. Indeed, the color green is the "color of the plant kingdom, particularly of awakening springtime." At the time, Kas was feeling that her dissertation topic had gone stagnant and that there was little life or new growth, so she was surprised and delighted with the hint of an emerging vitality. Moreover, she discovered that green is not only a predominant color of nature, but that it is often linked with "otherworldliness—the mystic color of fairies and little people from other space." This definition linked more specifically with the Green Lady, who was both otherworldly and deeply connected with the earth. Furthermore, she discovered the African indigenous teacher Malidoma Somé's moving account of his vision of a cosmic green woman during an initiation who told him secrets and filled him with unconditional love. Kas's experience of this deeply feminine presence had also been of a penetrating, unearthly, intuitive kind of love.

The emphasis on the feminine aspect of this profound experience—and in Africa, green is also connected with the feminine—was supported for Kas by Jungian analyst and writer E. C. Whitmont's description of this neglected pole of human experience within the patriarchal worldview. "The feminine," he writes, in *The Return of the Goddess*, "implies an approach to life that focuses not on planned striving, but rather on playfulness and imagination, seeing the world of fantasy and reality as but opposite sides of the same coin. This emphasis upon sensuality and bodily experiencing over abstract thinking and rationalism permits greater openness to the intangible, as well as a greater susceptibility to the realms of the magical, mystical, mediumistic and psychic."[9]

We are so thoroughly indoctrinated to feel that reason, logic, and external action are the only legitimate modes of experiencing reality that Kas became even more convinced that, in order to value imaginal and anomalous experiences, and the changed quality of time and place associated with them, as well as the deep feelings and intuitions that arise with them and penetrate into our bones, we have to "step outside patriarchal consciousness and be open to other energies in the field."

Returning to her vision of traveling to the temple of a female goddess, Kas discovered that temples are symbolic of "the cosmic center linking underworld, earth and heaven, or the ascending path toward spiritual enlightenment."[10] She felt that this image of the temple could represent the linking of the worlds and could assist her in holding the tension of the rational and irrational worlds, the everyday and the imaginal worlds, and the psychological and anomalous worlds. To highlight this need for integration, the Green Lady guides her from the temple and dives with her into the sea, the primeval source of life (and often a symbol of the unconscious in

9   E. C. Whitmont, *Return of the Goddess* (New York: Crossroad, 1992), p. 129.
10 J. Tressider, *Dictionary of Symbols: An Illustrated Guide to Traditional Images, Icons, and Emblems* (San Francisco: Chronicle Books, 1997), p. 201.

psychology), for transformation and renewal. Here, just as Dante, Orpheus, and Inanna descend into the underworld and return transformed, so too did Kas feel transformed by her dive into the depths of the great maternal sea where she is shown a treasure, a bright orange object, suggesting "fertility, splendor, love and fire." Though the treasure remains a mystery, pointing to things yet to be revealed, Kas muses that perhaps the love and fire aspects of the orange object are the passion that fuels her vocation to write this dissertation on the world behind the veil. Upon her return to the temple, the Green Lady communicates to her that nature, including her own psychic nature, is her guide. Kas summarizes this extraordinary experience:

It seems that throughout my life, there have been otherworldly presences holding, guiding, and healing me. The mother-like spirit who came to me as a baby and held me, the Green Lady who is veiled, and the orange object that remains partially mysterious are all figures from another dimension who bring important information that our materialist patriarchal world has chronically overlooked. With this overview of the symbolism in my vision, I feel certain that my vocation to my dissertation topic came from these figures from behind the veil. The veil between the visible and non-visible worlds can open during altered states of consciousness such as ecstatic states, shamanic trances, deep stillness, spontaneous waking visions, and certain night dreams. Indeed, my worlds opened when I allowed myself to go into this state of reverie, and the Green Lady took me down into the depths of the ocean where there is little light from our conscious, rational world, and where we discover the treasure of the irrational and anomalous, which I have been asked to bring into the light of day.

Commenting on the significance of these sorts of experiences in her work as a healer, Kas writes: "Having worked in the managed care system as a psychotherapist for many years, the abandonment of anomalous experiences and the mediumistic/intuitive is very apparent. Psychotherapy in these environments focuses on motivational interviewing, outcomes, time efficiency, and behavioral changes. It grievously abandons the depth, healing and transformative possibilities of the soul. Going deeply into feeling worlds, connecting with the earth, and having anomalous experiences can bring depth and richness to the practice of therapy. It can also bring forth knowledge that seems irrational but holds the very essence of soul work. By allowing the anomalous experiences into the therapeutic process, it may help to animate the world of the client, the therapist, and indirectly the larger community. My dissertation is the song of my soul calling me to address the separation between the "worlds," to look behind the veil and notice marginalized anomalous experiences in an attempt to discover and affirm their potential usefulness as a central therapeutic force."

∽◦∽

Kas's personal story, like the others told here, are part of a larger pattern that is a breaking through as a new myth in our time. These stories are crucial to this work for two reasons. First, each personal story is a singular vibration that resonates with this larger pattern breaking through into our world. Second, by situating these personal experiences into the larger pattern, my hope is that those who have these experiences will not feel so isolated and will feel more encouraged to bring them forth. In the next few sections, therefore, I describe some of these larger patterns.

Epiphanies of the Imaginal World in the Work of Jung

Freud and Jung showed us that symptoms, complexes, conflicts and dreams revealed the subtle world of the soul. They showed us that psychological suffering, such as depression and anxiety, pointed often to unacknowledged emotional realities of a wounded heart buried deeply beneath the surface of limited social mores. To help relieve the suffering caused by these symptoms that seemed to lie in neither a purely physical nor mental source but somewhere in-between, Freud came up with his famous "talking cure." Just as it did in Freud's day, the intermediate world often emerges through suffering, arriving first through what deeply disturbs us, as I can see in my own work with clients.

Like Freud, Jung considered this world of the soul or psyche to be neither strictly the realm of mind nor matter. Yet psychic reality for Jung seems to have an ontological reality or ground of being that goes beyond Freud's understanding, seeming instead to resemble the interworld or imaginal reality described in sacred traditions. This is an aspect of his work that has not always been sufficiently understood, and about which Jung himself is not always clear. However, the recent publication of *The Red Book, Liber Novus*, an account of Jung's early dreams and meditative writing which is, as he himself claims, the source of all his later work, emphasizes in visionary and visceral ways Jung's direct connection to the imaginal world of the soul.

One of the major differences between the theories of Freud and Jung is this: for Freud the unconscious is a secondary phenomenon composed largely of forgotten or repressed memories (though he did appreciate its mythic dimension); for Jung the psyche, which he called in later writings the objective psyche, is an *a priori* phenomenon of general human character, and much more extensive than simply our individual egos and personally repressed material. This collective or transpersonal unconscious, whose capacity for producing symbols accompanies us here at birth and whose contents contain universal or archetypal images, patterns of behavior, energy and emotional feelings—often storied in myth—is initially experienced by us via our personal complexes, or in fantasies, paranormal experiences, and dreams.

Amazingly, we can even respond to images and symbols that transcend the limited cultural and historical contexts in which we grow up. Jung demonstrates this in his researches as well as in his autobiography, where he explores how the mythic images of Egyptian, Greek, Indian, and other cross-cultural symbolic systems picture for us our emotional conflicts and maturational challenges. When viewed symbolically, these ancient patterns can assist us with our search for a meaningful life and help us feel vitally alive. Jung viewed the unconscious, then, as a source and well-spring of the not-yet known that could help a person lead a creative and individual idiosyncratic life, and that functioned to heal the wounds of the past as well as to link us with deeply felt emotional, intuitive, and spiritual realities in the soul.

Thus the "reminiscences" of Freud's hysterics became for Jung the necessary wounds that we needed in order to remember, beyond our personal biographies, our ancestral and soul origins in the stars; in other words, our complexes could help form a link with the unknown transpersonal spheres. In this regard, our soul life takes place at the intersection of the horizontal and the vertical, of the historical moment and the *kairos* of divine intervention. This sensibility restores the capacity for healing, for "making whole," through recovering a sense of the mystery of life, balancing our more rational sides with an experience that includes the dark intimations of secrets not yet fully disclosed or revealed. These are the moments on which the soul thrives, and which often deepen our capacity for love.

The Psychoid Archetype

However, Jung was required by his own unusual experiences to develop further his ideas. The in-between world of the soul revealed in synchronicities and other paranormal events made it necessary for Jung to re-evaluate his concept of the archetype in a radically new way. Though this concept has multiple meanings and eludes simple definition, it was initially conceived primarily as an inherited *inner* structure of the human mind that organized patterns of behavior, gave expression to images and instincts, and in its numinous power made deeply spiritual experiences available to individuals. However, synchronicities occurred in the space between the psyche and an event in the world, so the archetype as an expression of the psyche or soul could no longer be conceived as only residing with*in* the human personality. The soul is not only in us; we are *in it* as a drop of water is held within the ocean. Removing the soul from inside to outside, as it were, restored the ancient alchemical idea of the *anima mundi*, the world soul, thought to be an active natural force equated with the Holy Spirit and responsible for all the phenomena of life and the psyche. The *anima mundi* was imagined as the animating principle of the *unus mundus* or One world of the mystic philosophers and we could experience its eros quality directly in moments of synchronicity.

Furthermore, the underlying unity of psyche and matter suggested by synchronicities gave an inkling that the archetype could no longer only be psychic; it also extended into the world of physical matter. Jung now described this essentially unknown factor as "quasi-psychic" or "quasi-physical," meaning resembling but being neither psychic nor physical, and he renamed this deeper region that transcends the distinction between soul and matter, the psychoid archetype.[11] This paradoxical and subtle reality, however, made sense of subtle experiences such as the many paranormal events that Jung himself had experienced and been keenly interested in since his childhood . The archetype then was expanded to include not only the union of instinct and spirit, but also the union of psyche and world. In the new myth, psyche and nature are one and we participate in this interconnected web of being in increasingly attuned and coherent ways depending on the nature of our awareness. This evolution in consciousness led Jung to describe what he calls a "mystic" consciousness, a subtle awareness evoking

---

11 C. G. Jung, *CW 8*, pars. 367–368.

both our feelings and deepest reflections, symbolized by the color violet, a dark purple blue that links instinct (red) and spirit (blue), yet remains a color in its own right.[12] This paradoxical union in human nature was given expression by the alchemists in the ancient symbol of the Uroborus, the serpent eating its own tail, whose meaning included both cosmos and eternity, nature and psyche. As we deepen our psychological awareness we begin to see not only how our inner reality is reflected in our outer circumstances (and vice versa), but also how we are each the expression of the cosmic mind coming to know itself.

Jung felt that the psychoid archetype as an unknowable ground of being was incapable of becoming conscious and probably belonged, as it were, to the extreme ends of a spectrum where both spirit (at one end) and matter (at the other)—neither of which we truly understand—"disappear" into a transcendent world. Drawing on an analogy with quantum physics, Jung notes that objective reality now requires a mathematical model based on invisible factors, because the smallest particles, though impossible to represent, nonetheless produce experimental effects from which a model can be created. Similarly, postulated "invisible-in-themselves" archetypes produce effects in images, feelings, and synchronicities. Perhaps then if both physics and psychology have come up with elements that finally always elude our representations of them, it is no longer a question of two background realities—the material and the spiritual—but only one. For Jung, it seemed that both physics and psychology had reached the same frontier and uncovered what appeared to be a potential psychophysical background unitary world, the *unus mundus* of the alchemists. Jung writes:

> Since psyche and matter are contained in one and the same world and moreover are in continuous contact with one another and ultimately rest on irrepresentable, transcendental factors, it is not only possible but fairly probable, even, that psyche and matter are two different aspects of one and the same thing. The synchronicity phenomena point, it seems to me, in this direction, for they show that the nonpsychic can behave like the psychic, and vice versa, without there being any causal connection between them. Our present

---

12 *Ibid.*, par. 414.

knowledge does not allow us to do much more than compare the relation of the psychic to the material world with two cones, whose apices, meeting in a point without extension—a real zero-point — touch and do not touch.[13]

Zero-point energy (comparable to the Akashic quantum information field noted by philosopher and consciousness researcher Ervin Laszlo) refers to the idea that space itself, far from being empty and lifeless, is filled with its own powerful, fluctuating energy. The psychoid archetype turns out to be a radical notion that suggests that we not only experience the unconscious indirectly through its effects as Jung believes, but also more directly through an expansion of the range of our awareness into the more subtle and psychoid levels of reality, which is the central theme of this book. Jung's colleague, the analyst and writer Marie-Louise von Franz, hints at this when she records the dream of a patient who painted an image of the Holy Spirit not as a dove, but as a spiral. Von Franz comments that this image suggested a further development of religious understanding because the axis of the spiral neither moved upward toward greater spiritual height nor downward into the realm of matter, but into the background of the picture, "to another dimension."[14] Interestingly, as we shall see later in the book, many crop circles use circular designs that suggest to observers this spiraling to another dimension.

Yet this "further development of religious [or spiritual] understanding" into the psychoid levels of reality, and of consciousness itself evolving into the capacity for appreciating the subtle imaginal worlds of the soul, have remained largely ignored in Jungian and other psychological circles. In my view, the new vision of reality for a new century requires us to go in this exciting direction. Jung helped us understand the polarities of human consciousness and how holding the "tension of opposites" could yield to a new level of awareness that honored, yet transcended, each separate state. Still, in Jungian psychology, we tend to privilege symbolic, "as if," *interpretations* over appreciating the wisdom of *direct experiences* of an Other world. In spite of

---

13 *Ibid.*, par. 418.
14 Marie-Louise von Franz, "The Process of Individuation," in C. G. Jung, *Man and His Symbols*, Part 3 (Garden City, NY: Doubleday & Co., 1964), p. 226.

years of therapy many people either do not, or rarely, achieve a truly new creative life, a quantum leap into a new paradigm from insight to new vision and a lived vocational passion.

In spite of Jung's own many experiences of this Other world (that we will explore in chapter 3) together with his acknowledgement of the arising of the subtle body world, the active engagement of the psychoid subtle imaginal world and finding ways to stabilize non-ordinary or anomalous experiences in our everyday world through deep reflection and the conscious practice of non-local communication—with its access to guides, wisdom, and unconditional love—is a task for the future. What I am proposing is a new therapy, a second stage beyond insight and interpretation that aims to realize a more complete apprehension of consciousness, of our natures, and of the nature of the world and the cosmos. This might be called psycho-cosmotherapy. We will explore this new paradigm as it co-emerges with the new interconnected worldview, in Part Four of this book.

The possibility of richly textured experience whereby we are continuously alert to the deep organizing river and its song beneath the bubbling chatter of our ordinary lives is recovered for us by exposure to the potential One World, and reflected in these words of the poet Wordsworth:

> *There was a time when meadow, grove, and stream,*
> *The earth, and every common sight,*
> *To me did seem*
> *Appareled in celestial light,*
> *The glory and the freshness of a dream.*[15]

This poem beautifully describes the open-heartedness of the mystical sensibility toward which we are all moving in the new worldview. Everything is holy, and everything matters; everything resonates with the invisible reminder of its Source, its angelic presence. Rilke, too, suggests that consciousness is a mystical force of co-creation when he says, "Earth, isn't this what you want? A re-arising in us?" This mystic realization suggests a vast expansion of consciousness, a deepening of vision toward cosmic

15 Wordsworth, "Ode: Intimations of Immortality." *Wordsworth: Poems* (Oxford: Everyman's Library Pocket Poets, 2005), p. 63.

consciousness. Such a consciousness is not fixed; it involves our openness and curiosity. It must always include and be aware of the unknown. In the new vision of reality, we can be content that we both create and discover meanings, and that our knowledge always, of necessity, remains both provisional and full of creative potential in every moment. As quantum physics also recognizes, uncertainty is now part of reality.

Other Epiphanies of the Imaginal World in Our Time

At exactly the same time that Freud and Jung were investigating the soul of humankind, the whole Newtonian view of the world was beginning to be challenged by research into the micro-levels of the universe. This field later became known as quantum physics. Interestingly, this new physics arrived at the same conclusions about the nature of consciousness as Freud and Jung—an awareness of a similar kind of in-between realm where it was impossible to make any kind of observation of sub-atomic matter without taking into account the consciousness of the observer. In other words, they discovered that *how* you look at something effects *what* you will see. So-called reality, then, really arose at the interface between the individual and the world. Thus the worldview that there was a simplistic inner/outer dichotomy was once again seriously challenged.

In the field of philosophy this in-between interface between individual and world became the domain of phenomenology, which is based on the premise, initially articulated by Edmund Husserl, that consciousness is an intentional act which co-creates the world. In other words, phenomenology undercuts the dualism of subject and object at the same time as depth psychology and quantum physics do. Each makes consciousness a part of the equation of reality. Later, Merleau-Ponty deepened Husserl's notion of consciousness as an intentional act and described it as embodied, thereby opening the perceptual space of interaction as an erotic play between incarnate flesh and the body of the world.

At this same time, artists such as Pablo Picasso were experimenting with the breakdown of conventional structures and forms in paintings such as "Les Demoiselles d'Avignon," while Impressionists such as Claude Monet and Mary Cassatt were exploring novel ways of depicting light and its vicissitudes. Furthermore, Camille Claudel's sculpture is an example of the portrayal of emotional intensity in art, a feature, as we shall see, that is often central to paranormal experience. Closer to our own time, Jackson Pollock's work continues the tradition that began in the first decades of the twentieth century, the play of the unconscious in the creative process. Moreover, in literature we have only to think of James Joyce's work, particularly *Finnegan's Wake*, and the single, emblematic novel of Alain Fournier, aptly titled *The Lost Domain.*[16] These books reflect the apparent intent of the authors to evoke and recover the mystical in-between world of consciousness as an imaginative power for which we seem to have such a deep nostalgia.

Over the last several decades, the field of cosmology has further revised our view of reality, from one in which we are separated from an essentially "dead," mechanical and predictable Newtonian world to one in which the new physics tells us that we are indivisibly connected to a sacred, living ecological-cosmological reality humming with the tremendous chaotic forces of creation, destruction, and ever-emerging possibilities. This dynamic interconnectivity is going on all the time in the tiniest of invisible places as well as in the vast spiraling galaxies. Another relevant fact here is that String Theory, astonishingly enough, speaks of a vibratory universe in multidimensional hyperspace, recovering for contemporary times the ancient laws of harmony, octaves, and chords—found, for example, in Pythagoras' teachings. The universe can now be seen as a vast cosmic musical score in which we are each a note. Metaphorically, therefore, the songlines of the soul have been recovered in cosmology. Seeing matter structured as atoms is now "out" of vogue, and seeing matter as invisible, unknown, dark—even missing!—and mysterious is now "in"! This "reality" is conceived as a higher octave capable of transporting us to parallel worlds, a subtle harmonic which echoes with the sounds of the A-U-M of ancient Hindu thought or the notion of the origins of the universe as Word, Sound, Vibration.[17]

---

16 Alain-Fournier, *Le Grand Meaulnes* (Harmondsworth, Middlesex, England: Penguin Modern Classics, 1979/1913). This is the title given to the English edition.

17 See, for example, Fritjof Capra, *The Tao of Physics* (Boston: Shambhala, 2000), Paul Davies, *God and the New Physics* (New York: Touchstone/Simon & Schuster, 1983), Brian Swimme and Thomas Berry, *The Universe Story* (San Francisco: HarperSanFrancisco, 1992); Duane Elgin, "We Live in a Living Universe," in *Sufi Magazine* (London: Khaniqahi Nimatullahi Publications, 2005), pp. 34–44; Charles Goyette, "Tying It All Together," in *America West Magazine* (July 2005), pp. 93–97; and theoretical physicist, Dr. Michio Kaku's website: mkaku.org.

All these developments in thought from the end of the nineteenth century into the twenty-first, demonstrate that between the two sources of conventional knowledge—sense perception and the categories of the intellect—there has begun to emerge an interworld, a third domain, first documented in the field of psychology by observations about the symptom and the dream. These early "sightings" are now blossoming full force in our time as accounts of this in-between world have increased, manifested in all kinds of anomalous experiences, along with the *felt* transformed view of oneself and the world that often accompany such experiences.

Despite the witnessing and documentation done by Freud, Jung and their followers, as well as artists, sculptors, writers, and scientists, many have tried to squeeze these newly emerging realities into the old Newtonian paradigm, a model based on an all-pervading law of causality. This old model preserves our conventional sense of history and time as a linear and chronological movement from point A to point B, and our conventional sense of space as something to be marked on a map with the coordinates of longitude and latitude. But most anomalous events defy these familiar time and place-markers, taking us instead to realms unfamiliar to our conventional sensibilities, though by no means "new." An emerging potentiality for change is being threatened, even lost, here.

The intention of this book is neither to disavow the level of three-dimensional space and a fourth time (space-time), nor to discount the importance of psychological work related to our personal life and personal unconscious, especially work on our shadows (which is an ongoing endeavor throughout life), but only to point out that our notion of reality cannot become stuck here. It cannot become stuck here because all the emerging paradigms of reality suggest that there are other dimensions of being intersecting with our own and that these are increasingly making themselves felt. These other domains, these lost worlds, are challenging us to change our attitude—especially in view of the technological power we have amassed—from one of drivenness and control over creation, to one of wisdom, co-operation and love on behalf of creation. These domains are urging us to re-examine our values and recover a sacred sensibility. They seem to reveal, often in quite stark ways and to quite ordinary people, the necessity of not simply going on as usual, but *waking up* to ourselves in a way that will truly reveal our role as custodians of planet Earth. For example, Al Gore has alerted us in his documentary film that we live in a world of "inconvenient truths," and to these we must turn and be educated if we are to survive. In the same way, the soul itself is a threatened species and needs our support to vision new possibilities for our world.

The Grail Myth

In the West, the mythic structure of this new creative potential can perhaps most clearly be seen in the legends of the Grail, which emerged centuries ago and can be seen most recently in the popularity of Dan Brown's book *The Da Vinci Code* and Sue Monk Kidd's beautiful novel *The Secret Life of Bees*, both of which focus on the beauty and eroticism of the figure of Mary Magdalene and her connection with the mystery of the Grail. The Grail stories began to emerge in the twelfth century (paralleling the Sufi mystics), picking up on themes less developed in orthodox Christianity. They later went underground and have reappeared only in the last one hundred years or so. Sadly, we have not yet been willing or able as a culture to consciously embrace the new values of the heart and feminine eros that accompany this myth, and so we have been dominated by their destructive aspect, witnessed in two major world wars, and now in the threat of a third.

The group of stories that make up the Grail myth, with their familiar cast of Parzival, Gawain, Blanchefleur, the Loathly Damsel, King Arthur, and Merlin, are subtle and complex. We will look at some aspects of these stories in more detail later, but suffice it to say here that they emphasize the themes of questing and journeying, liberation from impersonal values arbitrarily imposed from without, an appreciation for the body and of the chalice of feminine values of wisdom, intuition, oracular knowing and personal feeling, and the inhibition and transformation of violence and aggression into ethical and creative forms. Of particular importance in the Grail myth is the discovery of and experimentation with new ways of loving beyond the conventional dichotomies of mother/father and wife/husband that allow for greater mutual respect, the following of one's own true vocation, and an honoring of the dark as well as the light elements in our natures, and perhaps even the overcoming of the terrible prejudices that divide nations.

My own interest in these stories lies in how they connect with the secret gnosis of the esoteric traditions of Sufi mysticism and Arabic poetry. Indeed, according to one story of its origin, the Grail is rumored to have arisen out of these Gnostic streams. For example, Parzival eventually discovers that he has a Muslim half-brother, Feirfiz, whom he engages in a fight-to-the-death until he realizes that he is fighting his own kin.[18] Here is an example of how the mysteries of this Other world are breaking through to correct its initial destructive appearance as a war of cultures. The Grail is also significantly linked to the traditions of "spiritual alchemy" with their emphasis on the development of the subtle body and the creative imagination, and the sacred sexuality of the Tantric traditions that appreciate the vitality of divine eros in the transformation of consciousness and in the refinement and evolution of modes of loving.

These traditions are compatible with an understanding of the Grail myth as an initiatory tale. These esoteric streams in our cultural history that include both the shadow of our aggression as well as our neglect of the divine feminine and wisdom traditions, not to mention their lively beauty and celebration of Life, have yet to be harvested, especially on the collective level.

We also see in Jung's psychology the continuation—in contemporary times—of the Grail themes, especially the value of individuation as an initiatory ordeal toward authentic self-expression. Jung's psychology, unlike Freud's, tried to recover the ancient tradition of the esoteric and mystical schools with their emphasis on the journey of the soul and the transformations of consciousness through initiations that accompanied such *pèlerinages de l'âme*. These "soul journeys" that epitomize the theme of the "quest" emphasize experience over theory and method, and honor knowledge gleaned from the dream world and active imagination as much as that gained from rational thinking. Perhaps they have more in common with shamanic initiations than with conventional psychological analyses, which run the risk of sorting all experience into predetermined categories, including Jungian ones.

Here is an example of such over-categorizing. One of my students told a class how the expression of her longing for the divine was *automatically* reduced by her Kleinian therapist to a parental issue involving the recent

---

18 Lindsay Clarke, *Parzival and the Stone from Heaven* (London: HarperCollins, 2001).

death of her father. Apparently, there was no space in this paradigm for the integrity of the soul's yearning as an *a priori* religious longing or as an instinct irreducible to something else. In this regard, the Jungian approach that incorporates the archetype of Spirit behind the personal father offers a fuller articulation of the richness and totality of our experience that needs to be honored, *in addition to* a fuller exploration of the student's grief over her father. In the Kleinian interpretation, it almost seemed as if the meaning of her experience had already been determined as soon as she said something. By contrast, in the unfolding process of individuation, the emphasis is on developing a personally meaningful myth from direct experiences of the psyche that unites the individual with a transpersonal center. Moreover, as we have noted, there are domains of experience that seem to go beyond even the transpersonal and the mythic, toward another transpsychic level of reality, the *mundus imaginalis*. Jung himself evokes this imaginal realm in his description of his guide, Philemon, or in some of his mystical dream experiences, visions, or accounts of his active imaginings. Here is an example of how the creative power of the imaginal world, experienced in a spontaneous numinous vision, inspired transformation and long lasting change in a woman who suffered from a very difficult relationship with her mother.

DREAM: MOON VISION

The woman, Laura (not her real name), a therapist in her early 50s, tended to get caught by her mother's emotional and physical problems, which she (the mother) used to try to manipulate her daughter to gain attention. Laura was about to go on a trip that she had been looking forward to when the mother intervened, trying to make her feel guilty for leaving as she possibly had (it had not yet been confirmed medically) a cancerous lesion on her skin. Also, the daughter's going abroad meant that she would not be present for her mother's birthday. During one of our therapy sessions, Laura told me that she was starting to feel both angry with her mother and also sad that her mother was unable to communicate more directly with her. She went on to express that she felt an even deeper sadness that she had simply never really felt an attachment to her own mother. This filled her with grief, yet at the same time she said that she was finally beginning to accept that her relationship with her mother was never going to change. That night she had a dream vision. She recounts it in the following words:

In the early morning, I don't know when exactly, a very strange thing happened. I don't know if I was awake or asleep, or in that zone between waking and sleeping, but, though my eyes were closed, yet I "saw," as if I were completely awake, a huge magnificent full moon on the horizon. I "knew" it was the moon, although it could easily have been the sun because of its bright yellow color. The moon was just above the horizon, but the purple pink light surrounding it was such that I didn't know if it were dawn or dusk; it could have been either. My whole body was filled with awe and complete peace as I took in the sight. At the same time, I heard coyotes shrieking in a loud chorus, so loud that it felt as if they had to be close by. (This was interesting because sometimes you can hear the coyotes up in the hills near our house, but never as loudly as this. Yet this was the part of the dream that made me wonder if I might actually be awake. Also, in reality it was, in fact, the time of the full moon.) At the same time, I "knew" that though I was seeing as if I were awake, I was also "seeing" through my third eye. I knew that I was having a complete third eye opening. I could see everything completely clearly in a way that brought a whole range of complex and contradictory feelings together— grief, love, and total peace. I felt the moon as the feminine eye of the divine, that wise Presence that is behind me, my mother, and that complex field of image and emotion, longing and loss that surrounds all mothers and daughters, including my own daughter and my love and devotion to her. I wanted to hold onto this direct experience of the full moon forever because it was enabling me to penetrate deeply into a feeling of compassion for the wounds of women, a feeling that proved to be both liberating and healing. I felt momentarily freed from a deep ancient wound, but paradoxically, it was not that the wound had gone; rather in some way my relationship with it had transformed. The grail tells of a story of a wound that doesn't heal. This wound for me is connected with my mother and her wounds, with the desire to redeem the feminine soul, and to find support for living an authentic life as a woman. With this gift of the full moon I could feel how She longs for us to live within Her fullness.

For my patient Laura, this dream vision involved a spontaneous opening of her third eye and exposed her to the world of imagination where she was given guidance from the Other world, the mystical lands. There, through the unifying symbol of the moon—a bright yellow moon that also reminded her of her mother's spoiling tendencies —her wounds paradoxically became gold and her personal loss became situated within a universal context that gave meaning to her vocation as a healer and helped restore her lost values. Such experiences initiate us into spiritual transformations whose aim seems to be to bring more compassion and wisdom into life. Throughout the book, I will elaborate more on these epiphanies from the subtle world and consider their implications for an emerging worldview.

There is, however, strong resistance to this emerging consciousness. This can be seen only too clearly in the continuing disregard for the psyche and the environment, the potential outbreak of biological or chemical warfare, and the horrific acts of terrorism such as those witnessed at the World Trade Center and the Pentagon on September 11, 2001, and subsequently in other parts of the world, including our own country's violent response to this tragedy. Such destruction and violence can point to our own refusal to change or our own destructive capacity. Through making conscious our own potential for "acting out" in harmful ways, behavior often fuelled by fear, we can face the necessity to change our lives and to choose our actions consciously and ethically. Through the awareness and integration of our own mistrust of life, and its accompanying grief and sorrow that often lies just beneath the surface, we can hopefully find the courage to adopt paths of creativity and the wisdom of love. We need to embrace life, we need to support the psyche, and we need to build our capacity for kindness and compassion.

Conclusion

In this chapter, I have tried to draw attention to an emergent reality that is neither the inner world of the mind, nor the outer world of nature, but an Otherworld. This is an intermediate and intermediary world lying between the sensory world of empirical study, and our mental thoughts about it. It has been my experience that the irruption of this interworld into ours brings with it a whole new sense of reality, one that beautifully and vastly expands our familiar horizons. It is my belief that this Otherworld wishes to help us to restore certain values that have been lost to us over the last few centuries, and to raise our awareness of what these values mean.

The values of this lost world that resides on the border of time and eternity are renewing our sense of Mystery about life, reconnecting us with the sacred ground of Being and of Creation, teaching us a heightened sensibility in the realm of loving and being loved, and challenging us to live our lives with deepened integrity and with greater creative expression in our work and in how we live day-to-day. This Other world brings with it access to the terrors of beauty and opens the door to ecstasy, *ananda*, joy.[19] It invites us to move beyond our addiction to suffering, not by denying or ignoring it, but by moving through our shadows toward an increasingly refined and energetic celebration of life. It encourages us to build our subtle bodies, vehicles of truth that survive physical death—as the alchemists, Tibetan Buddhists, and the ancient Gnostics affirmed—so that in bringing another reality into this one we may assist others toward a deepening truth and a reconnection to the stars from which we came. This emergent subtle world encourages us not only to expand our views of extraterrestrial intelligence and planet Earth's place in the larger cosmos, but also to expand our multidimensional range of consciousness and awareness, recovering the angelic forms and multiple universes among us. In short, we are being invited to recover an embodied mystical consciousness and awareness, centered in the heart, that has practical implications for everyday living.

DREAM: ANGELS AND THE SUBTLE REALM

To help the reader understand this process, I will share the following dream, which was told to me by a close friend whose journey through a very painful divorce slowly opened her to a deep level of the psyche where she began to feel in touch with deep sources of guidance that she was able to bring into her work as a healer and teacher Tayria writes:

I am at an Art Institute and have just passed an intensive course on "angelology," becoming something of an expert. The dream has an interesting aspect of past, present and future all being the same thing, because I simultaneously have the sense of having completed the course and become something of an expert, while at the same time being enrolled in the course and

---

19 Verena Kast, *Joy, Inspiration and Hope* (College Station, TX: Texas A & M University Press, 1991).

continuing to presently work on it, and also having the sense that I am just signing up to take it. But it starts out with this sense of completion, and then moves into these other two phases.

I am asked to summarize the course, and as I do I have the sudden realization that the reason I have been hurting so much at the cellular level during my recent dark night of the soul experience is because our (human's) matter is changing so that we are not so dense, so that we can be more permeable, open and in flowing communication with other realms and kingdoms, like the angel kingdom.

Then I am walking down a street with a wise older woman past holes cut in the street where work is being done underground. I ask the woman if she thinks that humans will ever have evolved to a state in which we will have a more conscious, visual, verbal communication with these other realms. She replies, "Yes, absolutely." It is happening, we are evolving in this direction.[20]

Tayria shared with me that while she was experiencing the excruciating process of mourning the loss of her marriage within her dream, this experience also was becoming an initiation for her, an undoing of fixed positions she held, not only at the level of consciousness but at the cellular level as well. She was also experiencing a new connection to a deep source of wisdom and guidance from another dimension of consciousness where the past, present and future could all be experienced at once, as well as in distinctive stages. Furthermore, this dream conveyed a feeling of hope to her about the survival of our species, something that deeply concerned her, as well as reassurance about the evolution of human consciousness toward connection with other streams of knowledge that could assist us at a time when the world seems to have gone mad. The dream, like a guiding spirit, conveyed these assurances directly, without interpretation, and helped her continue with her vocation to teach and write about these subtle realities that she now finds both in the dreamtime and from working with attunement to the subtle body and voices of the natural world—mountains, trees, animals.

Throughout this chapter I have given some examples of the irruption of the Other world into our quotidian world in order to indicate that such experiences are not the province of the special few. In a sense we are all ordinary

20 Tayria Ward, PhD, runs dreams groups and mountain retreats in western North Carolina. See her website: www.tayriaward.com.

mystics. In this context I want to end this chapter with another example from my own life.

This experience occurred with my children several years ago. It describes how a walk on the beach transformed into the wider arc of creation:

I am walking on the beach with my children after school. We are a little tired and weary at the end of a busy day. The early evening has a soft glow. We walk and talk in a lazy way. The smell of the salty air is fresh on our faces. Then, suddenly, out of the blue, one, no two, no, a whole school of dolphins start leaping and playing in pairs, groups, splashing, skimming the water with amazing speed, feeding, circling. We find ourselves laughing, delighted, pleasure beyond measure to see such sport. People, complete strangers, find themselves stopping and smiling at each other, sharing their common delight with those creatures of the deep. We watch and watch, dreaming, imagining, making up stories about dolphins and asking, "Do they sleep at night?" The whole ambience of the evening is miraculously changed. What might have been just the obligation of dreary homework suddenly becomes an aliveness charged with vitality and hope. The dolphins move on. We go home bathed in mystery, happy and laughing together. A subtle shift has taken place. We can't see it, but we feel it. It's in the atmosphere. It's as if everybody knows it. Animal and human are partners; an ancient memory stirs.

In moments like this we are relieved of the limitations of rational understanding and showered with luminous fibers of a larger cosmic consciousness, one that nourishes our souls, invites us to play, activates the imagination, and bestows knowledge about the mystery and interconnectedness of all life.

Chapter Two

ANOMALOUS EXPERIENCES AND THE SUBTLE WORLD

*[The Sufi mystic,] Suhrawardi's otherworld was not an invisible aspect of the
world we know .... Was also not a spatial extension of this world .... It was not an
upper world, high in the sky, as in heaven .... Suhrawardi's Other world was a different
dimension or order of existence, whose mystery defied logical description and explanation. It
was spatially both within a person's earthbound body and a distinct region of the cosmos.
It was not simply upper, or invisible. It was distinctly other.*[1]

T he emergence of the imaginal world as an Other world in our time
is giving rise to anomalous events—unusual experiences that are
not only irregular and unexpected, but that also break our habitual
molds of what is acceptable and what is considered real. These anomalous
events are often known only through direct experiences of a subtle and elusive
nature. We have seen already in the previous chapter how these often non-
ordinary events help individuals go beyond their normal and conventional
understandings of reality and encourage them to realize more of their potential. These extraordinary events are the songlines of our souls, the pathways
into an Other world, taking us to a new vision of reality for a new millennium.
They are the signatures of our participation in a new living myth, a new story
whose mystery we do not yet fully understand. Historically, there were traditions and spiritual practices that dealt with these sorts of experiences, helping
the individual to understand them. The traditions of alchemy, for example,
were directed toward an attempt to understand the union of the mysteries
of matter and psyche and the emergence of a subtle body world. While the

---

1   Dan Merkur, *Gnosis* (Albany, NY: SUNY Press, 1993), p. 224.

adept was involved with experiments in the alchemical laboratory, he would be aware of his visions in both worlds, and would record the changes in both as he proceeded with his great work. However, since the rise of modern science in the seventeenth century and the demise of spiritual alchemy, science has advanced by focusing on the experimental aspects of alchemy and exploring the mysteries of matter and the physical world in an increasingly objective way. The importance of the spiritual dimension in scientific research and of the processes of psychological transformation that can result got left behind until Jung's alchemical dreams led him to pick up on this aspect and demonstrate, through his research, how alchemical symbolism was actually an expression of the collective unconscious containing universal images of initiation that lie deep in the soul of all people.

Now, however, the confluence of modern quantum physics and Jungian psychology has led to further developments in understanding the spiritual implications of science. An exploration not only of the spiritual aspects of alchemy, initiated by Jung but, once again, the mysteries of the union of both psyche and matter are being explored. The quantum physicist Wolfgang Pauli, whose dreams Jung and von Franz analyzed, writes, "It is my personal opinion that in the science of the future reality will neither be "psychic" nor "physical" but somehow both and somehow neither."[2] It seems to be the case that anomalous events are often the expression of a neither/nor subtle body nature that unifies, yet transcends, both psychological and physiological aspects of our nature. It is significant that in his alchemy studies Jung does mention this development of the union of psyche and matter in a subtle body, although this aspect of his work is not usually emphasized.

Individuation as Initiation toward the Creation of a Subtle Body

Jung's individuation process—the long and difficult task of differentiating ourselves from identification with outer collective cultural values and inner archetypal figures so that we can live our own authentic individual life—has been effectively compared to an initiatory ordeal. Both Jung himself and those who came after him, especially first generation Jungians and others

---

2   Pais, A. "Wolfgang Ernst Pauli," *The Genius of Science* (London: Oxford University Press, 2000).

who continue to follow this early classical approach to the psyche, have seen and discussed this connection.[3] Nevertheless, the aim or goal of this initiatory work, which is to create and establish the subtle body, is less frequently acknowledged as an aspect of this transformation process. In my view, this is an unfortunate omission that preserves our cultural paradigm of a body/ psyche split that the creation of the subtle body aims in part to overcome.

The notion of a subtle body[4] is perhaps more familiar to us from Eastern religions, but there are mystical and metaphysical traditions in the West as well, in addition to alchemy, that preserve this reality for us, such as the Platonic and Pythagorean schools, which reach back to Orphism, as well as in Neo-platonic thinkers such as Proclus and Plotinus, Renaissance philosophers such as Ficino, Hermetic physicians such as Paracelsus and Dorn, and forward into the theosophical schools of thought.

Jung discusses this notion of linking individuation with the development of the subtle body when he writes about receiving a translation of a Taoist alchemical text called *The Secret of the Golden Flower* from the well-known sinologist Richard Wilhelm. Jung relates how between 1918–1919 at the end of WWI, he had been reflecting on *mandala* symbolism and its relationship with the transformative path to the center or Self. At this time he had just painted a picture with a golden castle in the center, which struck him as having a Chinese quality. Soon afterwards, he received the manuscript from Wilhelm. This was a momentous synchronicity that confirmed many of Jung's own ideas. In honor of this event, he recorded his experience on his painting, noting how the image of the yellow castle represents ""the germ of the immortal body.""[5] In the Taoist text he received there is mention of the *Book of the Yellow Castle* and the "golden flower," which is the elixir of life.

Furthermore, in his volume *Psychology and Alchemy*, Jung speaks of the need to understand the sacred art of alchemy not just in contemporary scientific psychological terms as the projection of the collective unconscious onto or into matter, but also as a representation of a real experience tak-

---

3 For example, Joseph Henderson, *Thresholds of Initiation* (Middletown, CT: Wesleyan University Press, 1967).
4 C. G. Jung, *CW 9i*, par. 202, *CW 11*, pars. 160 & 848, *CW 13*, par. 262.
5 C. G. Jung, *Memories, Dreams, Reflections* (New York: Vintage Books, 1989), p. 197.

ing place within the in-between realm of subtle bodies.[6] In fact, alchemy is full of images that refer to the subtle body, and we need only mention the philosopher's stone, the *lapis aethereum*,[7] to glimpse a paradoxical reality that is made up of both psyche and matter, yet curiously transcends each of these. For example, the philosopher's stone refers to the creation of an enduring spiritual reality in our human body. Other terms, such as the *resurrection body*, the *elixir* ("healing remedy"), or the *aqua vitae* ("water of life") or *aqua permanens*—all sometimes associated with the philosopher's stone and imaged as a pearl, treasure, or star hidden within us at birth—as psychophysical images of the goal of the work that can bring health and healing to the adept, are also mentioned by Jung in his texts of alchemy and his work on the psychology of the transference.[8] Furthermore, alchemical terms such as the *lumen naturae* ("light of nature"), a spiritual force found in the natural world, and the *unus mundus*, the background psychophysical basis to the world—terms that Jung wished to bring back into contemporary usage—guide us in this direction of a subtle reality and its association with eternal wisdom.

In the Nietzsche Seminars he delivered between 1934 and 1939,[9] Jung writes specifically on the nature of the subtle body as a kind of invisible somatic unconscious. According to the alchemists, this body is formed when we suffer intense feelings and emotions related to carrying our burden of suffering that, with consciousness, can open us to transformation. This "incorruptible" body as St. Paul describes it (as opposed to *sarx* or our biological flesh) is difficult for the mind to grasp, as it is a transcendent concept outside time and space. Yet our psychological knowledge, both conscious and unconscious, is embedded in our bodies so that we cannot know precisely where matter becomes psyche and psyche becomes matter, nor can we assume the total immateriality of the psyche.[10]

Jung explores this idea later when he writes about the nature of synchronicity and the tantalizing appearance of UFOs, which seem both con-

---

6 C. G. Jung, *CW 12*, par. 394.
7 C. G. Jung, *CW 13*, par. 137.
8 See, for example, Jung, *CW 16*, par. 486, and *CW 8*, par. 390.
9 C. G. Jung, *Nietzsche's "Zarathustra": Notes of the Seminar Given in 1934–1939 by C. G. Jung* (Princeton, NJ: Princeton University Press, 1988) 2: 967–8, 1067–8, 441–5.
10 C. G. Jung, *CW 9i*, par. 392.

cretely real and symbolic of a psychological state. These ideas led to his reformulation of the archetype as psychoid, that is, essentially unknown yet extending into nature. Marie-Louise von Franz writes that in addition to the psychoid system referring to the "really absolutely unconscious," Jung uses the expression in a specific sense as "the part of the psychic realm where the psychic element appears to mix with inorganic matter."[11] The new physics was also faced with the difficulty of the relationship of consciousness and matter, yet the observer effect (referring to changes that the act of observing will make on the phenomenon being observed) and the concepts of uncertainty (describing the impossibility of measuring both the position and momentum of a particle at the same time) and of non-locality or "action at a distance"—that also point beyond time and space—have now been included in our cultural vocabulary.

The creation of this subtle body through what Jung referred to as individuation, or authentic personal development, has its parallels in the alchemical *opus* of establishing the "resurrection body," "immortal body," *corpus glorificationis*, or "diamond body." It enables us to create a "body" believed to survive physical death. This body—a kind of psychic body that nevertheless had "substance" and contained one's essence (*quinta essentia*)— was also imagined as the *rotundum*, suggesting roundness and the fulfillment of a completed life. In other words, you would take it with you when you sloughed off your earthly form. The implication of a deified human body was of course a heretical notion in orthodox Christianity.

Other Sightings of the Subtle Body

In 1919, with words that echo Jung's, the author, esotericist, and influential member of the Theosophical Society, G.R.S. Mead, wrote about the history of the subtle body in western civilization. His writing includes a discussion of the different terms used for the notion of the subtle soul-vehicle or body. He distinguishes between the "spirit-body" (that pervades and surrounds the physical body), the "radiant body" (an everlasting celestial or star-like body that links the individual with the cosmos)—both particularly famil-

---

11 M-L. von Franz, *Psyche and Matter* (Boston & London: Shambhala Publications, 1992), p. 4.

iar in alchemy and the mystical traditions—and the "resurrection-body" (the Christian term for the various ideas from the "gross materialism … to the high spiritualism" of a "restored physical body").[12] Mead stresses, however, that the notion of our physical forms as the expression of an invisible subtle essence is an extremely ancient belief. (Both the Upanishads and the Zohar, for example, posit the existence of subtle bodies). This belief is occluded only by the materialist and rationalist prejudices of our times which, even back in the early 20th century, were beginning to erode as science and psychology began to penetrate more deeply into the invisible mysteries of matter and mind. The ancient intuition of the journey of the soul through incarnation from a place of constraint in the "gloom-wrapped" region toward freedom and enlightenment in the "light-wrapped" region, is returning to us.

In the last century, esoteric schools associated with Madame Blavatsky (founder of the Theosophical Society and Order of the Golden Dawn) and Rudolph Steiner (founder of Anthroposophy, Waldorf Education, and Eurythmy—the art of movement that gives expression to the archetypal gestures associated with speech, emotion and music), also developed theories of the subtle body.[13] Today, an understanding of the subtle body is increasingly being used in healing, and in the training of healers and psychotherapists. For example, the Reverend Rosalyn Bruyere, director of The Healing Light Center Church, and author of *Wheels of Light*, and Barbara Brennan, MA, PhD (a former research scientist for NASA), founder of the Barbara Brennan School of Healing and author of *Hands of Light*, use the human aura and energy field in their "hands on" healing work. They describe seven levels of this subtle body auric field related to the seven chakras of the body. The first three levels/chakras relate to our physical, emotional, and mental functioning, while the fourth, fifth, sixth, and seventh levels/chakras, relate to love, responsible self-expression, vision and care for all things, and our spiritual identity, respectively. Knowledge of these levels/chakras, that are expressed in a rainbow range of colors from red at the physical end to violet at the crown, and that connect to specific organs and glands in the body,

12 G. R. S. Mead, *The Doctrine of the Subtle Body in Western Tradition: An Outline of What the Philosopher's Thought and Christians Taught on the Subject* (Wheaton, IL, Theosophical Publishing House, 1919).
13 See, for example, Robert McDermott, *The Essential Steiner* (New York: Harper Press, 1984).

can, as Brennan writes, "be a bridge between traditional medicine and our psychological concerns."[14]

Scientist and healer, Jude Currivan, Ph.D, elucidates and further differentiates the nature of five more chakras when we are grounded in the first seven. The eighth chakra of the universal heart (positioned between the fourth and fifth chakras) is the pivot point between our ego-based personality and our higher transpersonal awareness. The vibration of this chakra is unconditional love and increasing global compassion. The ninth, or earth-star, chakra, six inches beneath our feet extends beyond our physical rootedness to increasing alignment with the devic and elemental beings of the living Earth. The tenth chakra about six inches above our heads connects us with the entire solar system, and aids us in remembering our identity at terrestrial, intra-terrestrial and extra-terrestrial levels. The eleventh chakra at eighteen inches above our crown reaches into galactic levels of awareness, helping us to access the "wisdom and guidance of the multi-dimensional realms of the cosmos and our own highest awareness and intuitive guidance." The twelfth chakra (at about thirty-six inches above our heads) connects us with the unity consciousness of the entire cosmos, the One which transcends and gives rise to all other levels of awareness and gives us a glimpse of who we truly are. These five transpersonal chakras are the ones that are awakening in our new age.[15]

Quantum physicist and Hindu scholar, Amit Goswami, also delineates the nature of the subtle bodies in his discussion of alternative medicine and quantum healing. He makes the case for the quantum or non-local nature of vital energy (*prana* in Indian Ayurveda and *chi* in Chinese medicine) required for a feeling of well-being, and describes integrative healing strategies that involve acupuncture, chakra medicine, and meditation for correcting vital energy imbalances as well as homeopathy, appreciation for different body types, yoga, and the contribution of mind and meaning in healing. Furthermore, Goswami suggests updating *The Tibetan Book of the Dead* by making the post-mortem subtle body Bardo states it

---

14 Rosalyn Bruyere, *Wheels of Light: Chakras, Auras, and the Healing Energy of the Body* (New York: Fireside, 1994); Barbara Brennan, *Hands of Light: A Guide to Healing through the Human Energy Field* (New York: Pleiades Books, 1987), p. 43.
15 Jude Currivan, *The 8ᵗʰ Chakra* (London: Hay House, 2006), pp. 108–109.

describes, a practice while we are still living. In this way, we can see that dying, often feared in the Euro-American West as a ruthless ending from the point of view of the ego, is also—potentially—about creative living, a teaching confirmed by many NDEers. In uniting physics and spirituality, Goswami's teaching aims to connect us with non local levels of reality transcending space-time, for here we can move beyond the limitations of our conditioning to the creative, compassionate, and telepathic aspects of the subtle quantum mind.[16]

Jungian analyst and process-oriented psychologist, Dr. Arnold Mindell, offers a view of the subtle or quantum level of reality, calling it "the force of silence," and linking this deep form of intelligence to both the songlines of the Australian Aboriginal peoples, and also to the hyperspace concept in physics. In his latest book, *The Quantum Mind and Healing*, he suggests that along with the power of sound there are many practical ways to increase our awareness of this background subtle world, which expresses itself in the sub-atomic levels of the body, in working with symptoms. Mindell proposes that we are located both locally in time and space and also, in the land of dreams, spread throughout the universe. A too narrow view of ourselves can create emotional and physical symptoms. In addition to his belief in the usefulness of experimentally verifiable classical medicine, he proposes that focusing on nonconsensual subtle subjective experiences helps us get to the dreamtime, to the immeasurable source, tendency, and intention of the symptom. In this multileveled, "rainbow" approach, we can be helped with creative and transformative answers to the many issues and questions troubling us.[17]

In one example, Mindell describes sitting with a relative and inviting him to sit quietly, breathe, do a body scan, and then just focus on anything that caught his attention. After a pause, the relative described a "dryness" in his throat. Mindell asked him to dwell on the dryness, even amplify the sensation until he could easily imagine it. Soon, he imagined a vast desert and a Native American sitting on the ground speaking to his ancestors. The

16 Amit Goswami, *The Quantum Doctor* (Charlottesville, VA: Hampton Roads, 2004).
17 Arnold Mindell, *The Quantum Mind and Healing* (Charlottesville, VA: Hampton Roads, 2004). I only came across Mindell's book after I had completed my own, but his many practical exercises for accessing the subtle body world I have found to be extremely useful. See pp. 29–30 for the following example.

SONGLINES OF THE SOUL

ancestors told him to let go of his relationship troubles and to stop feeling so responsible for others. The relative, laughing and somewhat embarrassed, admitted that he felt that the ancestors were speaking to him, for he did indeed feel overly responsible for those around him. Mindell inquired about what was wrong in feeling responsible. His relative answered that there must be something wrong because it led to fits of coughing. But how was this connected to the dryness, Mindell asked, believing that (the relative) already knew the answer himself? The relative immediately responded by saying that he himself should not *feel* responsible for others but *be* more responsible to the ancestors, a very important distinction.

Mindell comments that this story illustrates how tiny sensations can initiate creativity, fantasy, stories, and dreams that give us important information about ourselves. He points out how these tiny symptoms contain their own healing medicine (being *with* the ancestors instead of being a caretaker). Mindell feels that the importance and usefulness of focusing on tiny nano-like subtle events has been underestimated in psychology and physics, and that attending to them can vastly expand our consciousness to a kind of lucid dreaming awareness, helping us get to a source of wisdom embedded in the body.

Subtle Body and Subtle Worlds

In addition to building the subtle body associated with the individual, we can also, as we have already noted, achieve access to Other worlds of a subtle nature under certain conditions. Marie-Louise von Franz confirms in *Psyche and Matter* the presence of an intermediary, subtle body realm of autonomous, symbolic images.[18] This is the *mundus archetypus*, an imaginal psychoid realm lying between the Platonic forms and the visible, material world, and accessible to a visionary, alchemical sensibility. The subtle earth of "invisible cities" such as Hurqalya or Shambhala contain the imaginal forms of the *mundus archetypus*, forms and events that will later become manifest in our visible three-dimensional world. Von Franz particularly emphasizes (following ideas presented by the alchemist Avicenna, 980–1037) how the soul in its passions and ecstasies is not limited or bound within an individual,

18 Marie-Louise von Franz, *Psyche and Matter* (Boston: Shambhala, 1992), p. 190.

but deeply rooted in a cosmic intelligence. It is precisely because the soul's essence derives from a cosmic intelligence that it is able to both influence matter and nature and to reach subtle worlds beyond the local self.

Another recent exploration of this in-between subtle world that is neither precisely waking nor dreaming can be seen in Oxford scholar Peter Kingsley's original translations of ancient Greek texts in which he recovers for us the spiritual tradition that lies at the origins of western civilization. He writes of the pre-Socratic philosophers' dream incubation techniques that, much like the practices of shamans from all cultures stretching back thousands of years, refer undeniably to spirit journeys to another reality, and the bringing back of knowledge from this real but subtle world. The dream and meditative practices of these philosophers—"lovers of wisdom" as opposed to the rational thinkers of the last few hundred years—were believed to contribute to building the immortal body that could be created only by being true to one's deepest reality. This journey is described by Kingsley as "dying before you die."[19] Regrettably, we have mostly lost this sensibility, but there are indications (as in the healing modalities described above) that this Otherworld may be returning to us. An example of this return of the subtle "invisible cities" is given here by my husband, professor and writer, Robert Romanyshyn.

ACTIVE IMAGINATION: THE CITY IN THE CLOUDS

It was after my second brain surgery to remove a benign pituitary tumor that I began to feel exhausted and slightly depressed. Every breath seemed to take more energy than I could muster and there were times when I felt indifferent about living and dying. It was while I was in one of these moods that my wife suggested to me that I do some active imagination in order to get more deeply in touch with my feelings. I had practiced this method of soul work before and I was familiar with the "guide" who visited me on these occasions. I won't reveal his name here, but suffice it to say that it was he who showed up in response to my invitation. For the sake of this description I will refer to him as A.

A said to me that he felt my indifference and in response to it he wanted to show me the place where souls go who have exited this life before their time. What appeared was a gray somewhat cloudy plane, which seemed rather flat and two-dimensional, as if it was the surface of a wall. Within this space I saw people, or rather the outlines of people. They were without

---

19 Peter Kingsley, *In the Dark Places of Wisdom* (Inverness, CA: The Golden Sufi Center, 1999), p. 61.

substance, more like the shadows of people, thin shapes without depth. They were at the same eye level as myself and from my vantage point they were moving back and forth from right to left. I thought I detected some slight moaning, but it was clear that they were not in pain. If anything, the soft moaning sounded like the cry of lost souls, and I thought of Limbo, which in Catholic doctrine is the in-between world where sinless but un-baptized souls go.

A then said to me that he wanted to show me another place. In an instant what appeared before me was a beautiful city in the clouds. It was made up of many buildings, which gave the city the appearance of immense depth. The buildings in the forefront had towers, which made them look like castles. The city was very far away, certainly much farther from me than the previous scene, as if it was at the top of a very high mountain. But there was no earth on which it rested, so it seemed to be hovering in the air amidst the clouds. I was awed by its beauty, especially by its shining appearance. It was made of white diamonds and green emeralds, which at first glance seemed to sparkle, like jewels in the sun. But then I realized that the city was vibrating and I knew that its jewel-like structure was actually composed of musical sounds. The city was changing shape, expanding and contracting, like a breathing organism. I could "hear" the music but not with my ears. It felt like I was hearing it with my heart. I had an overwhelming sense of beauty. I felt calm, peaceful, and bathed in an atmosphere of love. Time seemed to disappear and it only reappeared when A said the following words: "Your task is to gather the sparks of beauty from your world with which to build this city." I knew that A was speaking not just to me but also to us. This was our task as human beings living in this world. I knew then that my indifference about living and dying had been dissolved.

In this example, we observe how a symptom, a feeling of depression relating to the after effects of major surgery, and the willingness to attend to its subtle underlying field, opens the seeker to the possibilities of two different worlds. In one, there is a landscape composed of those who have not fulfilled their potential but who nevertheless continue to exist as shadowy lost souls; and in the other, an alternative world is offered whereby one's own creative efforts are perceived as meaningful, indeed as helping to establish a bejeweled and musical city that is alive with breath. The sighting of this city bestows a feeling of beauty, peace and love, a direct experience of an opening of the heart that transforms the paralyzing feeling of gray indifference into a renewal of life. Attending to the symptom that could be so easily dismissed or overlooked (or in our society mindlessly medicated with anti-depressant drugs) constellates the invisible guide of the soul, and opens the individual to wonderment, an altered outlook, a sense of vocation, and a feeling of well-being. We also see how our suffering, if related to with interest and care, can lead to an "aha" moment that changes us. When we change, our behavior toward others also transforms. The magic that I mentioned in chapter I seeps invisibly into the atmosphere around us. Moreover, this example allows us to appreciate how the spiritual or "true" imagination and what the alchemists called the *meditatio*—conversations that took place with an invisible guide, or "good angel" (often reduced in our day to making things up and hallucinating respectively)—are key ingredients to the establishment of the subtle body and subtle world.

The capacity for uncertainty and curiosity about our experiences can carry an emotional power and spiritual depth. Our time-bound life is recognized, as in the esoteric traditions, as being linked inseparably with a rich cultural-historical heritage, as well as with the transpersonal domains and their landscapes and inhabitants. In this way our local selves are expanded to include many parallel worlds and domains of experiencing, a richly textured subtle body field, the "force of silence."

The Need for Initiation

We can see that the long enduring mystical traditions of both East and West have retained the importance of the transformation of consciousness through initiation and incubation, through the death and rebirth mysteries. Jung had the special gift and insight to realize that we fall into illnesses because we have lost our connection to these Other worlds of consciousness in which healing is to be found and in which a subtle vision of the whole can be restored to us in the modern world. Much to our detriment, even perhaps to our eventual destruction, we have lost the ancient initiatory path and contact with those realms where sacred knowledge is preserved. Today we even pride ourselves on defining ourselves as historical beings in a predominantly desacralized cosmos. In fact, we could even define our lives by the noticeable absence of any meaningful rites of initiation. Certainly there are vestiges of such rites in Christian baptism or confirmation and their equivalents in the Jewish bar mitzvah and bat mitzvah, and in other coming-of-age ceremonies, but these practices are usually little more than social occasions instead of rituals evoking the challenging ordeals of death and renewal. As Jung observes in his autobiographical account of his own confirmation ceremony, and as I experienced in my own confirmation, we are often left cold by these pale imitations, and do not feel an actual experience of the divine, or of a meaningful "death/rebirth" process, in them at all. The absence of puberty rites for our youth, for example, may contribute to their sense of alienation, suffering, and feeling so lost. This may perhaps contribute to acting-out behaviors, drug problems, and gang violence. In fact, youth gangs are most likely a misguided attempt to create an initiation into man- or womanhood.

When we see ourselves only as historical beings we become dis-eased. One of the themes of this book is the need to recover the ancient way of initiation and the deep shamanic-indigenous layers of the psyche that are the birthright of every human being and are being sought by many today. In some cases, this process is even being imposed upon us by dreams, visions, and UFO experiences. Through conscious suffering, through turning inward and observing our dreams and reflecting on our relationships, we temporarily suspend a full engagement in life, while surrendering to the processes of descent and psychological dismemberment. If we can sustain this ancient practice, the effort may be rewarded by the eventual renewal of life and reconnection with the immortal guides through dream and active imagination, experiences that can help give us a greater vision of life, one from which meaningful work can arise. So one's temporary withdrawal from the world to seek initiation is not therefore for one's sake alone, but for a larger purpose. As with the early philosophers and shamans of all times, that purpose is to become a citizen of and spokesperson for the cosmos and the mysterious knowledge it holds that can benefit all of humanity.

As the religious historian Mircea Eliade points out, it is the aim of initiation to learn the particular mystical relations between the tribe or group and the Supernatural Beings or Invisible Ones and Guides.[20] These relations were established at the "beginning of Time," that is, a kind of vertical or deep time, a time before or out of time, the dreamtime, the Source point in another dimension of consciousness as opposed to the origin point at

---

20 Mircea Eliade, *Rites and Symbols of Initiation: The Mysteries of Birth and Rebirth* (New York & London: Harper Colophon Books, 1975).

the moment of our biological birth. Initiation provides the means of learning the myth or "sacred history" in which we are situated, for this Source informs all life and custom which, in truth, belongs properly to and derives meaning only within the context of this sacred history. Instruction, ceremonies, and ordeals gradually expose the initiate to this sacred history and to direct encounters with the divine and with the Invisible Ones or Divine Beings who link us with the Heart of Creation.

Martin Prechtel in his book *Long Life: Honey in the Heart* (as well as Malidoma Somé in *Of Water and the Spirit*) has told many stories of the initiation process. For example, Prechtel talks about how for the Tzutujil Mayans the "violating and mining mentality of war" characteristic of the Euro-U.S. West is an indication of "uninitiated behavior" and of a "hungry ghost" soul condition that creates generations of addicts and sociopaths, and leads "whole tribes to ruin or war ... to feed its bottomless dependent existence." Without the "ancient intelligence," maturation, and rigors of initiation, young people would be "suspended in eternal childhood." Adolescents needed to be saved from the narrow-mindedness and survival opinions of their families and prepared for their lovers, life in the bigger family—the village—and eventually the spirit, by their elders. Prechtel writes of the significance in one ordeal of, treacherously, hanging the young men in trees throughout the night, "swaying [them] into manhood, lurch by lurch," under the watchful eye of Grandmother Moon. Suspended there, between drowsiness and dreaminess, they are reminded that they are the fruit on the tree of life, and that their soul obligation, rather than taking life for granted, is to re-member the Goddess by acknowledging that everything they could see, taste, feel, carry, grieve and love, was really the face and fruit of the Earth that gave of herself to help humans. Listening to the sacred stories of their people while hovering between earth and sky, the young initiates were directly prepared for facing the dangers and challenges of their lives. Every human being's eventual goal was "the pursuit and maintenance of the sacred" through ritual and ceremony that honored the web of all Being, and through different levels of initiation throughout adult life, undertaken by desire or the promptings of the divine within themselves.[21]

---

21 Martin Prechtel, *Long Life, Honey in the Heart* (Berkeley, CA: North Atlantic Books, 2004), pp. 39–40, 44–45, 52, 56, 87–89, 106–117. See also Somé, *Of Water and the Spirit* (New York: Penguin, 1994).

Symbolic Death

The rituals of initiation continue to regenerate the world, always making it new, always connecting history with Source, time with the timeless, because participants are reminded of the creative power of the gods and goddesses, and are constantly being resituated within the sacred forms of creation. The ritual repetition of linking with beginnings regresses into Chaos, into "pre-creation," annihilating the "old world" through such symbolic practices as extinguishing fires, for example, and restoring the cosmogony by lighting them again. "Death" leading to Chaos portrays the necessary end of a mode of being, the end of ignorance and irresponsibility. This is the indispensable condition for the emergence of new life for humankind. The new life is imagined as a second birth, a rebirth that is a spiritual birth, representing life or existence that is truly human because it is opened to the values of spirit, values conveyed by the Supernatural Ones and Invisible Guides since the beginning. Hence true existence can only be achieved by openness to the sacred experiences released during initiation.

This linking to Source can itself only be achieved through "death," through the annihilation of the present status quo, through death of our identification with social and collective values that throw a miasma of illusion over us. This symbolic death has other names in different traditions, for example, *nigredo* ("blackening") in alchemy (often, for example, signaled by a depression), or *the dark night of the soul* in the mystical traditions, and is associated with images of being in the belly of the monster or whale, or in the dark, such as a cave or womb, and so on. Nevertheless, initiatory death is the *sine qua non* of rebirth to a higher plane of being, and even already includes the germination of new life within itself, imaged by seeds or the new moon, or by the meeting with spirits and ancestors. Prechtel writes of literally "risking life, limbs, and sanity to descend into the Underworld to face the Gods of Death, to help retrieve the Goddess of Water and Growth back to her rightful throne here on this earth in our village." The initiation processes help to create young adults who are able, courageous, and useful to the larger community and who are necessary to renew and remake all of life each year.

Moreover, the earth, stars and moon, and all things, according to Tzutujil sacred knowledge, are powered by a sacred music, by the sounds of each thing being itself. Humans, just by being ourselves and forgetting our true nature, disrupt the symphonic song of all creation, by our noisy disturbances, "our strange wailings and wars." So the drum and flute music that accompany dance rituals and ceremonies that are part of the initiations are considered offerings for the restoration of harmony and reconnection with the ancestor spirits.

Civilization in Transition

We pride ourselves on going our own way and doing our own thing, but in fact we do not create ourselves. We are also created, by the wisdom of spiritual masters, by the ancestors, by the already initiated elders, and by those others who help guide us toward Source. This is a process that must be experienced, lived through, and embodied; it cannot be learned solely by reading about it in books. Books, however, like guides, can awaken us to knowledge beyond actual words because when we read we also fantasize and dream. For example, when I first read Jung's autobiography *Memories, Dreams, Reflections* at the age of 21, I felt I had "come home," and it inspired in me a "knowing" that became the foundation for my personal and professional life. We are creatures of time and history, but we are at home only when that time and history are linked with the timeless dimensions of the soul and the immortal lands of sacred cosmogony and myth. It is the recovery of this profound insight and reality that I believe is emerging into our culture again today, for we have so completely and grievously lost our connection to Source and to other dimensions of being that we need this "visitation" from the Otherworld.

In fact, I would venture to suggest that in the absence of meaningful rituals, all the killing, violence, and wars that characterize our times and give us an inchoate feeling of "everything being terribly wrong," are an unconscious, symptomatic attempt to "annihilate" our world in order to recreate it. At the same time and in the same way, our age is also characterized by an exponential rise in the interest in healing, alternative methods in medicine and psychotherapy, spiritual practices from East and West, the return of shamanism in both analytic practice and among ordinary people, hunger for transpersonal experience in yoga or breathwork practices, as well as care for a beleaguered environment—interests that could be seen as symptomatic attempts at renewal and rebirth. Since Jung's late but significant interest in the "flying saucer" phenomenon (and also since his death in 1961), there has been a huge increase in reports of extraterrestrial (UFO and ET) encounters, near- and after-death experiences, out-of-body travel, and all kinds of other spontaneous anomalous experiences that, in my view, can lead us to a renewed interest in the reality of the subtle body and subtle worlds, and to the importance of consciousness research, endeavors supported by the emergence of quantum physics and holographic theory in the sciences.

If we put these two divergent and seemingly opposite trends—an insistence on death on the one hand, and a commitment to a spiritual life, on the other—into one picture, perhaps they are significant as pointers to coordinates of a new worldview that is trying to emerge as we move from one cosmic era toward another. This new worldview is characterized by the evolution of consciousness toward self-awareness, integration of the shadow, a recovery of the feminine Sophianic wisdom left behind in the Old Testament and before, and a direct connection of the individual with other dimensions of consciousness and the cosmos—all powerful dynamic realities arising from the transpsychic or psychoid unconscious.

We all have an obligation to assist in this transformation of human consciousness. However, as we mostly no longer have the rituals in place to help us with this profound transformation, we often have to find our own way, either alone through sustained practice and study, and/or by meeting others on the path of self discovery, or by participation in small groups or communities. This book, rooted in this felt sense of obligation, is an attempt to gather us in these lonely struggles toward a new myth for our time. I will close this chapter with some remarks on this emerging myth.

Anomalous Experiences and A Modern Myth

Jung's synchronicity studies furthered his alchemical researches by pointing to this intimate connection that we have with nature and the cosmos. Moreover, these "meaningful coincidences" open us in a feeling way to our connection with the Earth, the interrelated web of all life, and the *unus mundus* background world, and offer a new creative possibility to the individual, one disclosed by the ego's connection to a deeper transpersonal reality. Furthermore, UFOs as examples of the union of psyche and matter were synchronicities appearing on a collective level. Here, a more intense psychophysical experience suggests that the *imaginatio vera* or subtle organ of visions is activated and opens the witnesser to a transpsychic or psychoid world peopled by figures and landscapes with color and extension. A subtle world is revealed compatible with the *mundus imaginalis* of the alchemists and Sufi mystics, and the temporary altered state of consciousness makes available to the individual deep sources of knowledge not usually accessible under ordinary conditions.

With both synchronicities and UFO encounters, therefore, we experience the strange paradox, noted by Suhrawardi in the quote at the beginning of this chapter, that the Other world is a different dimension of existence experienced both in the body and as a separate region of the cosmos. Such experiences can give us exposure to the same processes released during initiation. Jung's heart attack combined with his NDE (described in the next chapter), Mindell's relative's dry cough that led him simultaneously to the Native ancestors in the desert, and Prechtel's accounts of young men feeling themselves to be fruits on the Tree of Life, are good contemporary examples of this union.

Jung felt that these paranormal or non-ordinary imaginal events, *as a new third arising between psyche and matter, and as examples of spontaneous acts of creation out of the world soul*, gave evidence for the constellation of a new and living myth in our midst. I call such subtle events signatures of the new myth; they unite symbolic and non-symbolic reality together. Jung observes that in view of the individual and cultural need to reconcile opposites and, particularly, to make the psychological and ethical move to own the personal shadow (that is, instead of killing each other, to use the aggression to kill off our illusions, "the death before you die,") that the current wave of UFO sightings was possibly both an activation of compensating archetypal contents (the disc shape evoking the symbol of wholeness) *and* physically real events. The new myth involves the union of psyche and matter, both individually and collectively. Out of this union a subtle energy guidance system that is non-local and hyper-dimensional—which is not bound by time and space yet enters our world forming a bridge between psyche and matter—is arising all the time. Through the co-creative possibilities of our conscious awareness and imaginative capacities, we can access this subtle field and its guiding intelligence—just like the alchemists did while they were pursuing their experiments and the Tzutujil Mayans do in their rituals and ceremonies—through our symptoms and relationship difficulties, our dreams, imaginings, and encounters. In this way we can dream reality forward with wisdom and vision.

Insensitivity to this relationship of psyche and nature—its shadow aspect, if you will—is perhaps best summed-up in Jung's phrase, "what we do not realize in our own psyches, we meet up with as fate." In other words, if we disregard important psychic factors, these will impose themselves as if from the outside. Illness is often a way that the psyche brings to our attention that which we are overlooking, and the field of psychosomatic medicine now acknowledges this important synchronistic connection between body and psyche. Let me give an example.

After a life transforming journey to a small temple sanctuary on the island of Crete, to a dream incubation and aqua wellness program in the mineral springs of Bad Sulza, and attending lectures and visiting crop circles in the U.K. during the spring and summer of 2008, I found it very difficult to resume my regular teaching schedule and professional duties on returning to the U.S. I returned home feeling vital, renewed and inspired, but what I also felt was that I couldn't get my whole self back to this country; my physical body was here, but my soul felt elsewhere. I couldn't get *back*. Almost immediately upon my return I injured my lower back. Attempting to continue my normal routine, I eventually suffered so much pain that I could no longer stand or sit. I spent a couple of months lying almost exclusively on my back (the diagnosis of a herniated disc having been confirmed), forced into a contemplative mode in which I had to confront the deep changes that were occurring within me on account of writing this book and trying to live its insights and practices. Refusing the medical advice of surgery, I opted to try to let my body heal itself, listening in to its messages and dreams with the help of cranio-sacral and healing touch therapy that views the body not as an assembly of parts but as a seething mass of energy and intelligence reaching into the heart and the deeply informing intuition that comes out of stillness and silence.

Once again, I had to face my inability to fit myself in with a system I no longer felt supported by or that I had outgrown perhaps and to be open to the reality of the guidance I was receiving from the Other world. Dreams I had at that time pointed to preserving knowledge "based on the old Dionysian model." Dionysus is regarded as a god of inexhaustible life. He is the dark god of change, of chaos, death and renewal, of nature and longing. Dionysus is also known as the "god of women" and deep emotional interiority. He is the god of music, ritual and ecstasy, who supports aggression transformed into authentic self-fulfillment and genuine relatedness. Dreams suggested further that I "put aside the play written by someone else" in order to "sing my own song with joy out of the healing waters of life." A context for being in the world was ending for me, even as another was opening up. I was overwhelmed with a feeling of sadness and needed to grieve the losses, suffer the anxieties of change, while trying to trust the new creative energies emerging. In another dream, I was making a pilgrimage with others to the middle of a dark green forest where there was an ancient sanctuary of the Black Madonna. She told me, "I am the lady of the wild beasts; I am ancient and come to remind you what your heart longs for; I am the lady of the rose; my thorns are here to wake you up." My encounter with the Black Madonna helps give me the strength to obey the new dispensation in service to the heart.

On the collective level, the events of 9/11, the tsunami, hurricanes, earthquakes and fires since that time, and the volatile economic crisis of 2008, can also be regarded as fateful events alerting us to what we have refused to pay attention to. Similarly, accounts of traumatic abduction in UFO encounters, or indeed, the splitting of the atom to create bombs that threaten nations and the earth itself, may indicate that we have not yet found the right attitude in relation to the new challenges of the evolution of consciousness toward re-learning how to develop and connect to the subtle body and its wisdom.

A change from one mode of being to another, however, whether individual or collective, is always a crisis—both a danger and an opportunity. As the ancient way of initiation has always recognized, it involves a "death," or an outpouring of chaos, as well as a rebirth to another level. We are in the midst of such times, but we cannot really see the change precisely because we are so deeply in its midst. Through symptoms, synchronicities, UFO encounters, and other anomalous experiences such as the mystery of crop circles we are being called to remember a mode of being we have forgotten, a reconnection to the Other world, to its guides and to our Source in a sacred ground that will help us retrieve our true humanity, which exists as a multi-dimensional reality.

In the new myth, we move primarily from a psychology of images to be interpreted, to a psychology of encounters to be experienced. In the new myth, we move from knowing the unconscious primarily from its effects in images and dreams, to developing an attunement to different times (past lives, future incarnations), different spaces (three-dimensional to non locality and multi-hyperspaces), and different realities (from the ordinary every-day to the subtlest, most subjective, synchronistic, and anomalous). In the new worldview, we learn to navigate the subtle imaginal Other world, the songlines of our dreaming non-local soul. We do this by paying attention to our experiences of anomalous events—these will expand the range of our consciousness into the complex and multiple levels of reality, so that our personal visionary discoveries can be linked with our work on behalf of the broader planetary matrix of which we are a part. In the next chapter, we explore Jung's relationship with the subtle imaginal Other world.

Chapter 3

THE MYSTICAL TRADITIONS AND JUNG'S SUBTLE IMAGINAL WORLD

*In the end the only events in my life worth telling are those when the imperishable world
irrupted into this transitory one. That is why I speak chiefly of inner experiences,
amongst which I include my dreams and visions. These form the* prima materia
*of my scientific work. They were the fiery magma out of which the stone that
had to be worked was crystallized.*[1]

In this chapter we will explore more thoroughly Jung's own experiences
of the Other world and situate them within the tradition of mystics,
visionaries, and shamans. Today, those who are experiencing anomalous,
subtle and non-ordinary experiences are also part of these ancient traditions and are helping to initiate us into the new worldview, the new myth of
continuing creation. I will weave some contemporary accounts with Jung's
own stories.

Jung is sometimes "accused" of being a mystic, and this critical if not
derogatory attitude implies that his scientific work is suspect and not to
be taken too seriously. The notion that one could be both a mystic *and* an
empirical scientist simultaneously seems foreign to the contemporary worldview. This perspective in itself is somewhat strange as many scientists are
reputed to have had their theories revealed to them in dreams or visionary
states, only later working out the demonstrable details. For example, French
mathematician, Henri Poincare, "discovered" the formula for the so-called
automorphic functions in a half-awake, half-asleep vision. The prominent

---

1   C. G. Jung, *Memories, Dreams, Reflections* (New York: Vintage Books, 1989), p. 4.

nineteenth century German organic chemist, August Kekule, claimed that he discovered the ring shape of the benzene molecule after having a waking vision of a snake biting its own tale (the ouroborus). And in 1953, Cambridge University's Francis Crick glimpsed the double helix nature of the structure of DNA and its four base pairs of molecules purportedly during an LSD trip. Together with his colleague James D. Watson, they unlocked the secret of the building blocks of life itself from a powerful altered state of consciousness, which later they went on to confirm scientifically. Of course, in these instances the experiences were preceded by arduous and rigorous scientific investigations. Nevertheless, they also clearly indicate that reason is also related to the dream.

Usually, however, we hear less about the mystical or visionary origins of scientific theories than we do about their reproducible data. This is no less true of Jung's work. While many are now familiar with concepts such as shadow, animus, anima, and Self, far fewer tend to remember the experiences Jung had that gave rise to such theories. In fact, most of Jung's research was first initiated by dreams or visions from the subtle imaginal world.

For example, the historical basis of Jung's work within the traditions of alchemy as the link between ancient Gnosticism and his own psychology of the unconscious was presaged in a dream in which he found himself stuck in the seventeenth century.[2] It took Jung decades of research to elucidate this connection between the undifferentiated wealth of his own unconscious mind—the *prima materia* noted in the quote above—and the confusing wealth, *massa confusa*, of alchemical symbolism initiated by the dream. Too, it was the imaginal presence of his winged guide Philemon, who appeared to Jung in both dream and waking life, who taught Jung about the reality of the psyche as a world that existed apart from his own thoughts, desires, and intentions. For Jung, dreams, visions, and imaginal encounters (which were not unusual for him) were considered to be events that needed to be taken seriously by both the scientific mind *and* as emotional experiences of a psychic nature. They were disclosures of the Other world—that background, dreaming, hyperspace world—that gave rise to feelings and sensations in the body, and challenged his own thinking in a creative way.

---

2 Jung, *ibid.,* pp. 202–203.

In order to "check" his own subjectivity—a consideration in all experiences of a psychic nature, which are vulnerable to doubt—Jung carried out both empirical and hermeneutic research on these visionary and spontaneous dream *facts*, to ground, amplify, and culturally situate his theory of the unconscious in the scientific spirit of the times. For example, in *Symbols of Transformation*, Jung's volume that marks his separation from Freud and Freud's more reductive approach, Jung amplifies with cross cultural mythic material the written fantasy reflections of a young woman, Ms. Miller, whom he never met. In doing so he demonstrated the creative and regressive flow of psychic energy that is active in all human beings and, furthermore, the depth of unconscious material that is present in the background in all creative acts including his own written works.[3]

Sadly, however, the scientific spirit has too often rationalized and codified Jung's rich experience of the landscapes of the soul into interpretive concepts that turn the vitality and transformational depth of direct experience of the psyche into a dried-up, second hand dogma, far removed from the subtleties and suffering of a mythopoetic sensibility and feeling imagination. This same scientific attitude continues to silence the mystic and brand him as a heretic; therefore, the mystic continues to reside as a shadow character within individuals and their culture.

This is no accident. The prevailing collective consciousness of our times is overburdened by rationalism, unrelated sexuality and aggression, extraverted exploration, and power defined as domination over others. We might call this logos, rational or patriarchal consciousness. The mystical and esoteric traditions, however, have always had access to another dimension of reality, a world behind this one, characterized by waking visions and revealed knowledge. The central characteristic of these traditions is the attainment of *cardiognosis*, heart knowledge, and an opening to the transpersonal that often leads to creative work. For example, the mystic and visionary Hildegard of Bingen (1098–1179) was a theologian, musician, painter, poet, healer, and counselor whose work remains inspirational to many today. She was in touch with her wondrous, creative, multidimensional nature. We, too, long to be in tune not only with our local but also with our non-local selves.

---

3   C. G. Jung, *CW 5*. See also his *Analytical Psychology: Notes of the Seminar Given in 1925* (William McGuire, Ed., Princeton, NJ: Princeton University Press, 1989), especially Lecture 4, pp. 26–34.

Jung's psychology, through its work of recovering the autonomous nature of the world behind this one—the imaginal world of the soul—by valuing dreams, visions, and synchronicities, is more than a clinical, developmental psychology. It is simultaneously an attempt to help shift human consciousness from an overemphasis on logos toward an eros awareness centered in the heart. The fact that in our time the mystical side of Jung quickly got lost and is generally no longer valued suggests that the conservative forces of the psyche resist the transformation of our consciousness in the direction of eros and inter-relatedness. We are still unwilling to learn the difficult lessons posed by love.

Our dark shadows, it seems, rule the world, as can be seen in the increasing violence in all corners of the world as well as the advance of global warming. In recovering Jung's imaginal world—what he calls the reality of the psyche—my hope is to draw attention to the kind of potential transformation that such chaotic times offer to us. This wake-up call is accomplished by direct exposure to the expressions of the collective unconscious or objective psyche via certain types of dream or waking vision, an exposure that awakens us to eros consciousness and creativity.

Contrary then to the idea that a rational person should dismiss Jung as a mystic, I want to emphasize that the mystical is central in Jung's work and that mystical or visionary consciousness—precisely *because* of its impact on the body—is a consciousness that aims at embodiment. Archetypal vision and bodily instinct are not split realms—the one "out there" in some kind of imaginary airy-fairy realm, the other here, firmly rooted in reality. They are always connected together in a "psychophysical parallelism."[4] For example, in his essay "The Psychology of the Transference,"[5] Jung writes explicitly of the constellation of eros in the field between analyst and analysand, as always made up of a combination of fantasies and meaning as well as visceral and instinctual responses occurring simultaneously. Jung gives a good example of this when he describes how a young woman patient of his,

---

4 C. G. Jung's interest in the connection between psyche and body is evident as early as his essay, "The Psychology of Dementia Praecox," *CW 3* (Princeton, NJ: Princeton University Press, 1907), pars. 1–316, even suggesting that the term "psychophysical parallelism" be used for his approach: "All psychic processes are correlates of cell-processes, according to both the materialistic view and that of psychophysical parallelism" (par. 7). He elaborated his "psychophysical parallelism" view in later descriptions of the archetype, and used it in reference to UFO phenomena in his essay, "Flying Saucers: A Modern Myth of Things Seen in the Skies," *CW 10*, pars. 589–824, as I will be showing later on.
5   C. G. Jung, *CW 16*, pars. 353–539.

a philosophy student, remained caught between a persistent emotional tie to her father (who had died) and a relationship with a man that she could not reach emotionally. Jung reports how in the ensuing conflict, the patient's unconscious transferred onto him the image of the father and simultaneously made him the substitute for the would-be lover. In this temporary solution to the conflict, the doctor becomes overvalued, as if he were a savior or a god-like figure. In fact, in the patient's dreams Jung appeared as a combination of the patient's father and the image of a giant nature god, holding and rocking the patient in his arms like a tiny child. The energy of this transference was so strong, Jung writes, that it seemed to portray a vital instinct, even a passionate religious longing that must, therefore, have a purpose. As his patient journeyed through the process of holding together both her conscious feelings and her unconscious dream images, Jung observed the subtle development of a third position, a guiding transcendent function that gathered to itself what was formerly placed on the overvaluation of the analyst. At the same time, the patient's relationship with her lover imperceptibly deepened, loosening her personal tie and projection onto the doctor. Out of the collective unconscious, an ancient archetypal motif of the divine emerged for this patient, not a Christian image that she might have inherited from childhood, but an archaic image of god as a nature-daemon, as the wind, *pneuma, ruah,* or spirit. It was as if her infantile love transformed and deepened into a mature eros relationship experienced both as a mystical spirituality and also erotic love for another human being.[6]

Jung makes it clear in this clinical vignette and in his essay on the transference that a person's ability to tolerate such deep affect and its accompanying images has a specific purpose. It helps us to build a transformed "quintessential" subtle body that endures, and moves us in the direction of a paradoxical consciousness, one in which our rationality is joined with a transpersonal value, and thus becomes the experience of a mystery. Increasingly we live in a synchronistic world held together within the timeless, unified field of divine Love. The *elixir vitae,* which is the goal of the alchemical process of individuation, gives us a hint of our immortality, here and now in this life. This is an intuitive feeling experience of everlasting value that

---

6   C. G. Jung, *CW* 7, pars. 206–217.

cannot be taken away. Such a religious attitude provides a sense of vocation for our earthly life and gives meaning and depth to what otherwise might remain empty and banal.

The Mystical Traditions

The mystical and visionary traditions—echoed above in the example of Jung's patient—have been a venerable source of wisdom and knowledge for millennia. Since time immemorial we have wondered about our place in the universe, our link with the stars, our emergence from millions of years of history that predate us. Early philosophical traditions, which were devoted to a love of wisdom beyond rational and discursive thought, continued their links with the mysteries, with spiritual alchemy. Such knowledge was once linked with the realization of gnosis, with direct experience of the invisible realms and the invisible Ones.

Every religious system began with the power of a revelation or disclosure from a transpersonal source of consciousness. Ceremonies were put in place to honor the "unknown" mystery. In the West, Gnostics, alchemists, and mystics relied heavily on the disclosures of voices, visions, angels, and *daimones* to help discern the presence of evil or negative forces. In the East, meditative practices to learn how to discriminate between reality and illusion, and to focus on the development of the many bodies from the physical level to the subtle levels of transpersonal vision, have been part of the road to enlightenment. Self-knowledge leading to knowledge of the divine was often embodied in attitudes of compassion and wisdom and expressed in inspired, creative acts. The visionary, the mystic, the seer, the shaman, through authentic transpersonal vision, helped create the myths and stories that people felt sustained them, that advanced human consciousness and produced classic works of art, music, literature, and sacred architecture.

For example, in a cave at Lascaux in France some 14,000 years ago someone painted an animal-shaman figure dancing on the wall. Shamans were thought to receive divine messages via animal spirits while they were in trance states and their souls traveled to the beyond, to the invisible world on which this world rested. Wisdom, sacred songs, and ceremonial dances were conveyed to the chosen one while he or she waited in solitude for a vision of what to teach or how to proceed. Christ, the Buddha, and Mohammed all received visionary experiences that gave birth to myths—powerful stories that, as Joseph Campbell has suggested, engage the soul at a deep level and influence and structure whole cultures.

Jung claimed that the Judaeo-Christian myth was in decline and that our culture needed a new vision in order to survive. His suggestion was to find new perspectives on life through our own dreams, a place where revelation may be trying to reach us if only we could become attuned to it. In *Modern Man in Search of a Soul*, Jung comments:

> The living spirit grows and even outgrows its earlier forms of expression. It freely chooses the men [and women] in whom it lives and who proclaim it. This living spirit is eternally renewed and pursues its goal in manifold and inconceivable ways throughout the history of [hu]mankind.[7]

Jung adds that this spirit, often imaged by the archetype of the wise man or woman, is awakened from its dormant home deep within the unconscious when times are out of joint and characterized by a false or one-sided attitude. Then, instinctively, these images begin appearing in individual dreams, and in the visions of artists, poets, and seers, in an attempt to restore balance and equilibrium.

DREAM PILGRIMAGE TO VÉZELAY

A patient named Victoria (not her real name) dreamed recently that she and her husband were on a pilgrimage to a sacred site in France that was devoted to Mary Magdalene. There they met two others, one of whom was Rick Tarnas, whom she had recently heard giving a lecture on his new book, *Psyche and Cosmos*.[8] The patient commented that she had been struck by Tarnas' valuing of the union of the accomplishments of patriarchal consciousness and rational thinking, "solar" consciousness, together with the wisdom of the visionary imagination and the deep feeling, evidenced in "lunar" consciousness. Indeed, he had brought many opposites together in his talk as

7   C. G. Jung, *Modern Man in Search of a Soul* (London: Routledge and Kegan Paul, 1933), p. 197.
8   Rick Tarnas, *Psyche and Cosmos* (New York: Viking Press, 2006).

an unfolding possibility for a new myth in our times. The sacred site in the dream was on the grounds of the beautiful Romanesque cathedral at Vézelay, a church like many others in France, devoted to Mary Magdalene. In the dream, the landscape was not exactly like Vézelay, as there was now a healing sanctuary built there with a clinic for patients (the fourth person, an unknown woman, was working there), a meditation room, a vast library, a beautiful dining-room, stone steps circling down to a labyrinthine basement, and sacred springs filling bathtubs for incubation and immersion mysteries in service to the divine feminine. The patient particularly loved the image of Mary Magdalene, who for her represented the union of spirit and instinct, holy longing and dark eros, an image that belonged to the lineage of Sophia, Aphrodite, and Isis, all symbols of the sacred feminine and with whose holy bridegrooms symbolize the sacred union that unite above and below, male and female, and who encourage us to *be* who we *truly are*.

Furthermore, the sacred site in the dream was situated in a place of great natural beauty that suggested both a particular village in the Swiss Alps where St. Nicklaus had his visions (a place that reminded her of Jung) as well as the rolling hills of Burgundy, places that the patient had explored during a time in her life when she was reading the stories of the grail as a way of helping her heal her unfulfilled spiritual past. The patient felt that her dream, which came after a period of great suffering, was pointing to the restoration of the equilibrium that Jung spoke of above, and was also drawing her further into her current researches into the divine feminine and its relationship to healing, not only for herself, but for others also.

The title of Tarnas' book, *Psyche and Cosmos*, also reminded the patient of a passage she had recently read by religious studies professor, Christopher Bache, who described a vision he experienced while experimenting with Stan Grof's holotropic breath work. Bache recounts a journey to the unified field underlying physical existence, and how this field dissolved all boundaries and divisions between species, incarnations, spirit and matter, revealing all life to be a "diversified manifestation of a single entity." He continues:

> [T]he most poignant aspect of today's session was not the discovered dimensions of the universe themselves but what my seeing and understanding them meant to the Consciousness I was with. It

seemed so pleased to have someone to show Its work to. I felt that it had been waiting for billions of years for embodied consciousness to evolve to the point where we could at long last begin to see, understand and appreciate what had been accomplished. I felt the loneliness of this Intelligence…and I wept for its isolation and in awe of the profound love which had accepted this isolation as part of a larger plan. Behind creation lies a Love of extraordinary proportions, and all of existence is an expression of this love. The intelligence of the universe's design is equally matched by the depth of love that inspired it.[9]

In traditional and indigenous cultures, this seamless web of soul, nature, culture, and cosmos held together by love continues to be upheld. Since the rise of western science in the seventeenth century, we have, however, increasingly lost touch with those traditions that honor the interconnectedness of all beings. Instead ego consciousness has developed as an organ of knowledge that has become separated from its ground in the transpersonal matrix which once held our culture. While the development of consciousness separated from nature can be appreciated and applauded for many reasons, particularly the advances of medical science and in the creation of technologies that have allowed global communications and explorations of cosmic space, its current *disiunctio* (a rupture from a sacred or participatory context) has created dangerous disturbances in the collective psyche and brought us to a terrifying imbalance. Power motives and the ascendancy of violence and aggression, together with the increasing inability of the Judaeo-Christian myth to engage the soul at the deepest level—including Christianity's disregard of the body, of the shadow, and of the wisdom of the heart—have put the human race into extreme danger. Some of the cultural symptoms of this dangerous imbalance include eating-disorders, the outbreak of violence in schools, and the lack of differentiation of the feeling function, not to mention the omnipotent fantasy and hubris of ego consciousness concealed within the Star Wars Project and other military experiments.

Revelation, which may now be trying to reach us through the lens of a new scientific paradigm—for example, membrane or M theory (the "M"

---

9   Christopher Bache, *Dark Night Early Dawn* (Albany, NY: SUNY, 2000), p. 70.

standing for Mother, Magic, Majestic, or Madness, all images of the divine feminine!), a theory linking strings and dimensions, parallel worlds and the idea of what Ervin Laszlo calls a multiverse—is itself rendered suspect by a collective consciousness that excludes anything "non-rational," and by a materialist prejudice that reduces the visionary imagination and consciousness itself to a by-product of the physical brain. In this dogmatic and arrogant view, the divine is unnecessary and the soul is irrelevant. Even when I studied theology at the University of London as a young undergraduate, my fellow students laughed when I suggested that we ought to be reading the literature of the mystics, which was nowhere to be found on the syllabus, an echo of that historical bias that dismissed interest in such topics as evidence of insanity, demonic possession, or hysteria.

Contemporary Forms of Mysticism

At the same time, however, there is a flowering of interest in spirituality and the sacred as the soul searches once again for the transpersonal and numinous experiences that nourish it. It searches also for meaning and creativity beyond the isolating preoccupations of the ego and the collective pressures to conform that threaten individual expression. Individuals, many of whom no longer feel held by conventional religious institutions (or even conventional forms of psychotherapy), are experimenting with shamanism, altered states of consciousness, channeling, prayer, card readings from a variety of traditions, spiritual alchemy, Jungian dream work, and contemporary forms of mysticism, meditation, and yoga practice.

There have also been increasing reports of anomalous experiences. Such experiences are often characterized by a quality of intense or heightened reality that is neither interior nor exterior in an ordinary sense. Jung's acknowledgement that in so far as the psyche has a non-spatial aspect, there may be a psychic region "outside-the-body" suggests that he was familiar with these alien dimensions.[10] From after-death experiences (ADEs) and NDEs to UFO sightings, crop circle enigmas, and so-called extraterrestrial and other kinds of encounter phenomena (including the Orbs of light that are gaining attention), the irrational, the mystical, and the visionary are

---

10 C. G. Jung, *CW 14*, par. 10.

returning with a vengeance. Often these irregular sorts of events are still mostly hidden, kept secret by individual witnesses who fear ridicule, not being taken seriously, or being treated with suspicion. Their experiences are reduced by psychology to some type of complex, or their stories are attacked as inflated, exaggerated, or surely a sign of either mental illness or a lurking psychosis. When I first spoke of my own UFO experience to two different Jungian analysts, one overacted with extreme alarm, and the other, though he tried to understand the event symbolically, was completely unable to agree with me that what I described could have happened. It was because of these responses, or rather lack of them, that I silenced myself for almost ten years. Yet in my view, we should perhaps at least be curious and wonder why this disclosure of other dimensions of consciousness is occurring. What crisis of the soul is attempting to find a voice or be exposed here?

Jung himself kept many of his own mystical experiences hidden for, like many people today, he was afraid of being labeled insane. In response to an inquiry in a letter dated January 30, 1934 (Jung was 58 years old at the time), about whether he "possessed any "secret knowledge" surpassing his written formulations," Jung confessed that he did have "secret" experiences of an "ineffable" and incomprehensible nature. He feared to tell of such numinous disclosures, he wrote, because "99 percent of humanity would declare I was mad if they heard such things from me." He goes on to say, however, that the exploration of the unconscious recovers the ancient way of initiation, and further that "it is not merely my "credo" but the greatest and most incisive experience of my life that this door [to initiation] leads to the secret of transformation and renewal." Jung adds: "Now you will understand why I prefer to say "scio" [I know] and not "credo" [I believe]."[11]

The kind of knowledge that Jung refers to here as distinct from belief is known as *gnosis*, that is, knowledge gained not only from the reading of books or from discursive, rational thought, but from a living relationship to the reality of the psyche. This is the knowledge obtained from dreams and waking visions or experiences of a revelatory nature, knowledge from the reality of an Other world that makes its presence felt in this one. In calling this an Other world, I am and have been drawing a more or less

---

11 C. G. Jung, *Letters 1: 1906–1950,* selected and edited by Gerhard Adler in collaboration with Aniela Jaffe, trans. R. F. C. Hull (Princeton, NJ: Princeton University Press, 1973) pp. 140–142

clear distinction between the general use of the term unconscious (which covers all kinds of dreams, fantasies, slips of the tongue, and so on) and a more specific reference to an inter-world. This intermediate and intermediating world is another dimension of experience, a parallel world if you like, with its own inhabitants and landscapes. In many esoteric, mystical, and folkloric traditions, these inter-world "places" have names, for example, the fairy lands of the Celts, Avalon (in the Grail myths), Shambhala (in Tibetan Buddhism), and Hurqalya (in Sufi Gnosticism). For me, the designation of these names suggests that these landscapes have an external reality, albeit non-ordinary, and are not just symbolic of various states of consciousness.

Knowledge as *gnosis* links Jung's work to the vitality and perils of the death and rebirth mysteries of ancient initiatory traditions. It links the work of individuation with the goals of spiritual alchemy, shamanic rituals from indigenous cultures, and the mystic paths of East and West. These all represent the achievement of an illumined consciousness centered in the heart, achieved by a descent (or series of descents) through the dark night of the soul. In fact, in the film *Matter of Heart*,[12] Jung explicitly speaks of his psychotherapy as a pedagogical procedure more like "antique philosophy," an initiatory process of death and renewal through the "death-before-you-die" journey.[13] The wide popular appeal of such films as *Harry Potter, The Lord of the Rings, K-Pax, The Sixth Sense, A Beautiful Mind,* and *Big Fish* indicate an increased attunement and hunger on the part of all of us to be connected to these realms of rich imaginal soul activity.

Interestingly, many of the extra-ordinary and anomalous experiences noted above follow this initiatory patterning. In NDEs or extraterrestrial encounters, individuals can suffer a precarious shattering of self and their worldviews, and undergo deeply disturbing and disorienting experiences comparable to the "death before you die" experience. Yet, if they are able to restructure their lives after such an encounter, they are often profoundly altered in their vocational occupations, being called upon now to write or to paint, to create music, to become healers and therapists, and often to work on behalf of ecological or social justice issues. Such individuals also can become bridge builders between

---

12 Suzanne Wagner, *Matter of Heart: The Extraordinary Journey of C. G. Jung into the Soul of Man.* Mark Whitney, Director. (Kino International Corporation, 1980).
13 Peter Kingsley, *In the Dark Places of Wisdom* (Inverness, CA: The Golden Sufi Center, 1999), p. 65.

different levels of consciousness or dimensions of reality. Like the shamans and mystics of old, who are often called into this "double vision" by breakdown, serious illness, catastrophic loss of a loved one, or of one's own soul through depression, an out-of-body journey, or a powerful visionary dream, they press beyond the boundaries of the known helping to rebuild a new myth for our times. For example, Anne Baring writes of the British artist Cecil Collins who "trusted his visionary imagination in the face of contempt and neglect by the art establishment, [and] wrote these words:

> "My works are a visual music of the kingdoms of the imagination. There is in all human beings a secret, personal life, untouched, protected—won from communal life; and of which all public life is the enemy. It is this sensitive life which my art is created to feed and sustain, this real life deep in each person.""[14]

Psychotherapy can often be inadequate to the task of dealing with these altered states of awareness, these other-than-consensual-reality states of consciousness, for these events do not fit neatly into clinical categories, such as I described above in regard to my UFO experience. Stan and Christina Grof created the Spiritual Emergency Network to help individuals cope appropriately with spiritual experiences that were often not being understood properly by conventional psychotherapy techniques. Sometimes individuals experience anomalous experiences spontaneously and repeatedly. At other times they seek them out deliberately because of the hunger in their souls for a guiding transpersonal vision no longer provided by our society, and not provided by traditional therapy.[15] Grof's Breathwork has helped thousands of individuals with an expansion of consciousness to include parallel worlds. Perhaps, too, clinical practice is so bound to the mother archetype in its impersonal emphasis on creating a safe environment, and in its reductive interpretations, that it may actually be preventing the possibility of more radical transformation and change, thereby inadvertently pushing individuals to seek other containers for their experience.

---

14 Anne Baring, www.annebaring.com, Lecture 1, "The Relevance of Visionary Experience to Culture," p. 8, and for this whole section.
15 See, for example, Christopher Bache, *Dark Night, Early Dawn* (Albany, NY: SUNY Press, 2000).

Naturally, psychotherapists share a legitimate concern that the egos of their patients will become overwhelmed by archetypal imagery and numinous energies. There is also the difficulty of relating to and embodying the deep changes in body-consciousness, and making the images and feelings conscious, not to mention relationship and lifestyle upheavals that can come in the wake of overwhelming experiences of the transpersonal realms. For example, Hildegard of Bingen kept many of her "secret mysteries and wondrous visions" that she experienced—not in dream, nor in frenzy but while "awake and alert with a clear mind"—to herself throughout her childhood and early life. She writes, however, that she was continually ill until she began, through instruction from the Light that warmed and opened her heart, to paint and write down her visions, and to share them with close supporters.[16] We forget perhaps that rituals like baptism were once life-threatening and that initiatory journeys undertaken to discover one's life vision or purpose held no certainty of survival.

Moreover, as Jung mentions about his own confrontation with the unconscious, he entered dangerously disorienting and psychotic states at times. Many of us who have personally experienced these breakdowns of our constructed worlds know that they can lead to deep levels of depression. We forget perhaps that the word "psychosis" originally meant "I give life," and that our underworld journeys and chaotic disturbances yield to renewed life and new depths of love that often fuel our creativity. Nevertheless, the dangers and shadows of transformation inevitably lead us into the chaotic waters of the alchemical *nigredo*, the dark, sometimes very black, night of the soul. The soul requires impossible situations in order to mature and deepen, and to create a body that can withstand the numinous.[17]

Even though we do care about the very real clinical issues and problems that can result from such soul journeys, I am concerned that we might be too one-sided with our care, which then results with psychotherapy becoming a hindrance to the irruption of this Other world. After all, the transpersonal levels of the psyche *do* visit us and not always at the *right* or convenient time (at least from the ego's point of view). That is the blessing and the curse of being open to these dimensions of experience. Most importantly,

---

16 Baring, *ibid.*, p. 4.
17 *Ibid.*, please note the end of the article because she reviews the dangers of visionary experience.

however, Jung suggested (and perhaps we know first hand from our own experiences) that what the Sufi mystics confirm as "The Great Tremor"[18] is the real locus of transformation and healing, precisely because of its experiential intensity. The intensity relates to the energetic shifts felt deeply in the body, the numinous and dynamic aspect of the archetype, and points again to the relationship between spirit and matter. Eastern traditions recognize these transformational potentials in their descriptions of *kundalini* activation in the body—*kundalini* energy imagined as a coiled serpent that resides at the base of the spine at the lowest chakra, and that when awakened, moves up the spine, opening the different energy centers until Samadhi, detachment from ego consciousness and enlightenment, is achieved.

The transpersonal domains need us, and seek a relationship with us. Many traditions attest to the fact that the Divine wants us to be the vehicle through which It comes to know itself. This reciprocal movement between the divine and human realms was Jung's radical "Answer to Job,"[19] that is, the disturbing claim that not only does the divine seek incarnation, but that humans, through conscious awareness, are thus raised to the status of divinity. While God may be a *complexio oppositorum*, a union of opposites, Jung suggested that the cosmological dimension of human consciousness consisted of holding these opposites *in awareness*. Holding this multiplicity of existence as One, makes human consciousness (as opposed to God's unconsciousness) "a second world creator."[20] We bring the world into being by our conscious awareness of it. *How* we relate to the unconscious then *really matters*. We have not yet developed this realization, this anamnesis, this "un-forgetting" of what we once knew and need to remember. Perhaps we might view the events of September 11, 2001, as a devastating reminder of the urgency of this fact. Jung's insight was that if we could not balance the tension of opposites between our rational consciousness and its dark shadow, the world around us would live out this conflict. Yet, tolerating our paradoxical nature *consciously* also leads to the possibility of a further development in consciousness, one that gives us a direct experience of the mystical heart of creation.

---

18 Henry Corbin, *The Voyage and The Messenger* (Berkeley, CA: North Atlantic Books, 1998), p. 158.
19 C. G. Jung, "Answer to Job," *CW 11*, pars. 553–758.
20 C. G. Jung, *Letters 11, 1951–1961*, selected and edited by Gerhard Adler in collaboration with Aniela Jaffe, trans. R. F. C. Hull (Princeton, NJ: Princeton University Press, 1975), p. 487.

This movement toward us on the part of the Divine or the Other world also occurs through certain types of dreams or visionary events that have an autonomy and "really real" quality to them. In other words, experiences that are not made-up fantasies in our heads, or dreams that we might misinterpret only on a subjective level. The events I am talking about here are externally real, however, not "physically real" in the ordinary sense. As an example of these sorts of experiences, Jung writes about his Ravenna vision, which I explore later in this chapter, that "something interior can appear to be exterior, and ... something exterior can appear to be interior." Through them, we move into a subtle body world, a central quality of which is not only the relativity of time and space but also the subtle feeling ambience of the event.

These types of experiences are well documented in the visionary literature—Dante's *Divine Comedy* comes to mind or Suhrawardi's mystical treatises and visionary recitals—and are key features of the mystical, Gnostic, and alchemical traditions of West and East. Although Jung claims he was reluctant to speak of some of his own experiences, he does recount some of his dreams, encounters, and visions in his autobiography *Memories, Dreams, Reflections.* Now we also have *The Red Book,* for a more detailed account together with Jung's visionary art. If we pay close attention to some of his accounts, we can see similarities to the flowering of all kinds of anomalous experiences in our own time—experiences that many people, too, are reluctant to share. I suggest that these experiences demonstrate the irruption of the imaginal domain into our world and the return of the visionary world. These events occur for the purpose of individual and cultural transformation of consciousness toward greater depth, wisdom, integrity, and love.

Jung's "Reality of the Psyche"

In his autobiography Jung often describes the reality of the dream as a force of nature that comes from elsewhere. So, for example, after relating the dream in which he protects a tiny light cupped in his hands from the force of a giant black figure behind him, he asks himself,

> Whence comes such a dream? . . . Something must . . . have been
> at work behind the scenes, some intelligence, at any rate something

more intelligent than myself. For the extraordinary idea that in the light of consciousness the inner realm of light appears as a gigantic shadow was not something I would have hit on of my own accord.[21]

Describing his initial phallic dream, "a dream which was to preoccupy me all my life," Jung writes, "Who spoke to me then? Who talked of problems far beyond my knowledge? Who brought Above and Below together, and laid the foundation for everything that was to fill the second half of my life with stormiest passion?"[22] At the end of his school years, when he was in conflict about the direction of his vocational life, he was able to use two dreams—one of digging in a burial mound and discovering the bones of prehistoric animals, and the second of discovering a beautiful giant jellyfish in a pool in the middle of a dark wood—to reach a decision about his future. He accomplished this not by analyzing the dreams, but by opening himself to their unequivocal guidance and intensity.[23] The dreams themselves inspired in Jung an eager desire for knowledge about the natural world, and so he elected to study science. One could suggest that greater wisdom or intelligence knew that to get to spirit Jung would need to know matter.

We all have such dreams. However, there are times when Jung suggests a slightly different nuance in the dream. For example, six weeks after his father's death, Jung dreamt about him twice. Later, he says, "I kept asking myself: "What does it mean that my father returns in dreams and that he seems so real?"" He adds: "It was an unforgettable experience, and it forced me for the first time to think about life after death."[24] Here Jung confronts us with an impression that the dream is so "real"—the presence of his actual father—that it goes beyond his trying to understand what the dream might be saying merely about himself subjectively, that is, the image of the father as an aspect of Jung's psychology. No, in fact it made him think not only about life after death but also our relationship with after-death reality and the dead's relationship with us, as well as the possibility of reincarnation and what form it might take. Moreover, if death is not an end but the doorway to a new life, then death can also teach us how important the quality

---

21 C. G. Jung, *Memories, Dreams, Reflections*, pp. 87–89.
22 *Ibid.*, p. 11, p. 15.
23 *Ibid.*, p. 85.
24 *Ibid.*, pp. 96–97.

of our own life is now. How we mature and love here on earth may inform what happens next.

There are many other examples of the reality beyond the psyche, such as the "experience" (he does not use the word "dream") he had after his wife Emma's death: "[I] suddenly awoke one night and knew that I had been with her in the south of France, in Provence, and had spent an entire day with her."[25] Provence is, of course, the landscape of the Grail, the Troubadours, and the Cathars, the domain of Emma's lifelong work and interest. Jung's story suggests that he *knows* that Emma is continuing her work in Provence in another dimension of consciousness or parallel world and that he was privileged to go beyond the veil into the imaginal world to be with her there for a day. I myself have found that in the south of France, in Provence, and in the Luberon and Languedoc regions—the land of Mary Magdalene as well as the grail—it is not difficult to sense the reality of this Other world as being present and very close.

Jung's glorious descriptions of his own mystical experiences during an NDE after his heart attack when he was 68 years old, in the chapter titled "Visions" in his autobiograpy,[26] have the quality of being "utterly real." Jung writes that the ecstatic beauty and intensity of emotion of these visions were "not a product of imagination [here meaning unreal fantasy] .... there was nothing subjective about them; they all had the quality of absolute objectivity."[27] An account of this extraordinary event and the subtle body self as a quintessence related to the stone of alchemy follows.

Jung's Near-Death Vision

In early 1944 Jung had a heart attack and, hovering close to death, suffered many tremendous visions. From a height of about a thousand miles he saw the Earth bathed in a blue and green silvery light. Eventually turning away from the globe he saw a dark block of stone, a meteorite, about the size of his house floating in space as he himself was. At the entrance to the stone, a black Hindu in a white robe sat in a lotus position, awaiting Jung, and

25 *Ibid.*, p. 309.
26 *Ibid.*, p. 289ff.
27 *Ibid.*, p. 295.

guarding the gate to a temple. Innumerable tiny niches containing lighted candles surrounded the gate in a wreath of bright flames that reminded Jung of a similar sight he had once seen at a Temple in Ceylon.

As he approached the rock, Jung felt everything that constituted his earthly existence slough off—an extremely painful process—yet his essence and the sum of his experiences remained with him, an experience both humbling and fulfilling. He felt that in entering the temple he would enter an illuminated space and would meet there all the people to whom he belonged, and finally understand where he came from and where he was going. Suddenly, an image of his doctor arose before him in the form of a king of Kos, the Greek island that was home to a temple of the god of healing, Asklepios. This island was also the birthplace of Hippocrates. Dr. H. told Jung that it was not yet time for him to leave earth. At that point his (Jung's) vision ceased, but he had tremendous resistances to returning to earthly life, which now seemed like an illusion, a prison that boxed him in. At the same time, he feared for the life of his doctor who had appeared to him in his archetypal form, a fear that was soon justified as the doctor was taken ill and died in early April.

During the weeks that Jung was recovering from his illness, he felt depressed by day, but late into the night, after he had slept for awhile, he would fall into a kind of blissful ecstasy, "floating ... in the womb of the universe—in a tremendous void, but filled with the highest possible feelings of happiness." He thought he was in the Pardes Rimmonim, the garden of pomegranates (the title of a sixteenth century kabbalistic text), witnessing the wedding of Tifereth and Malchuth, the male and female aspects of the divine. Yet at the same time he experienced himself as a representation of this mystic marriage. Then followed the joyful Marriage of the Lamb in a festive Jerusalem with angels and light present. Finally, he arrived at a classical Greek amphitheatre in a beautiful green valley where, on a flower-decked couch on the stage, the *hierosgamos*, or mystic marriage, was being celebrated by Zeus and Hera, as described in the *Iliad*. During this time, his room was filled with an inexpressible sanctity, which he feared might even be harmful to his nurse or other people.

Jung comments that it was "impossible to convey the beauty and intensity of emotion during those visions. They were the most tremendous things I have ever experienced." By contrast the day world was limited, too material, clumsy and crude, yet it had a kind of hypnotic power. He writes that although his belief in this world eventually returned, he could never free himself from the impression that this life is a segment of existence which is "enacted in a three-dimensional boxlike universe especially set up for it." The Other world of visions gave him a glimpse of eternity, an ecstatic feeling state wherein past, present, and future are one—a state almost impossible to imagine or fabricate. Jung experienced this state once again in his life, in a breathtaking vision of his wife after her death in her most beautiful dress, a vision that somehow contained the whole history of their life together, and conveyed an image of completion.

After these glimpses of eternity, Jung writes that he surrendered to the flow of his thoughts, and a period of great creativity followed. He also was able to give an unconditional "yes" to things as they are, and affirm his own destiny, mistakes and all! Furthermore, in a way that I found particularly liberating, he also realized that "one must accept the thoughts that go on within oneself of their own accord as part of one's own reality ... part of our wholeness." These thoughts are more important than our evaluations of whether they are true or false which, for Jung, was merely of secondary importance. Yet, our judgments toward them must not be suppressed either, for these too are our thoughts!

Jung also describes the overpowering and recurring vision he had in 1913 of a frightful catastrophe that threatened civilization itself. He writes that during the second vision, which was particularly bloody, an inner voice said, "Look at it well; it is wholly real and it will be so. You cannot doubt it."[28] At the time, he says, the possibility of war had not occurred to him. Later on that same year, he describes the moment when he decided he had to explore his fantasies, "drop down" into them. "suddenly it was as though the ground *literally* [emphasis mine] gave way beneath my feet, and I plunged down into dark depths."[29] The quality of the active imagination (or vision as he calls it) of the wounded blond youth, the black scarab, the rising sun, and the blood—all beneath the glowing red crystal—have a vital aliveness and reality to them:

---

28 *Ibid.*, p. 175.
29 *Ibid.*, p. 179.

I squeezed past [the mummified dwarf] through the narrow entrance [to a dark cave] and waded knee deep through icy water to the other end of the cave where, on a projecting rock, I saw a glowing red crystal …. I discovered a hollow underneath [the stone] …. [T]hen I saw that there was running water. In it a corpse floated by, a youth with blond hair and a wound in the head. He was followed by a gigantic black scarab and then by a red, newborn sun, rising up out of the depths of the water …. Then a fluid welled out. It was blood …. I felt nauseated.

Later in the book, Jung shares two other particularly striking examples of this other kind of reality. One is an account of Jung's second visit to Ravenna in 1933,[30] and the second is his alchemical vision of Christ a few years later.[31]

Jung's Ravenna Vision

In Ravenna Jung fell into a strange mood at the tomb of Galla Placidia. Even during his first visit in 1913, the place had held a compelling aura for him. On this second trip, Jung and his traveling companion, Toni Wolff, walked into the tomb's Baptistery, which Jung describes as filled with a strange blue light whose source is not visible.[32] There they come across four extraordinarily beautiful mosaic frescoes that Jung could not recall seeing during his first visit. These frescoes depicted various water scenes from the Bible, the most notable one being Christ holding out his hand to Peter who was sinking beneath the waves. This inspired a fairly lengthy discussion about the original meaning of baptism as a treacherous death and rebirth ritual.

Although Jung remembered the details of the mosaics with great clarity, he was unable to find photographs of them afterwards. Later in Zurich he asked an acquaintance who was going to Ravenna to pick up some photos for him, but the colleague was unable to oblige as the mosaics *did not exist*. By this time, Jung had already lectured on baptism and the Ravenna frescoes, and Toni Wolff also remained equally convinced of their reality.

30 *Ibid.*, pp. 284–287.
31 *Ibid.*, p. 210.
32 Blue light often seems to be associated with profound spiritual experiences. See Corbin, *Spiritiual Body Celestial Earth*, p. 74, and my account of "missing time" in chapter 11.

Jung comments that this story was among the most curious in his life. Acknowledging the cultural level of archetypal experience, he suggests that a strong identification with the highly cultivated Galla Placidia (d. 450) as an anima figure (the personification of the feminine in a man's unconscious) may have been responsible for this event, mentioning that the anima (like the animus) has a strongly historical character. Galla herself had survived a stormy boat crossing from Byzantium to Ravenna and had vowed to build the Baptistery and mosaics if she survived her dangerous journey. The mosaics were destroyed in a fire in the Middle Ages, but a sketch of Galla in a boat remains in the Ambrosiana in Milan. (Moreover, there is a striking resemblance between a mosaic picture of Galla from Ravenna and photographic footage of Toni Wolff.)

Jung writes that he, too, had suffered a near drowning in the waters of the unconscious, but his ability to integrate and realize their contents adequately saved him from this fate. His baptism in the waters of the psyche was an example of an initiatory process, a submersion in a perilous underworld journey that linked him with all initiates of the death and rebirth mysteries. The one fresco that had particularly drawn Jung's attention—sinking Peter with outstretched hand to the Christ—could be seen as a quintessential image of his psychology of the unconscious. So, it was the constellation of the archetype of Initiation that lent a numinous quality to his visit. All very good "Jungian" observations!

But these interpretations, correct as they may seem, do not account for the peculiar nature of the *experience itself*. He writes:

> Since my experience in the baptistery in Ravenna, I know with certainty that something interior can appear to be exterior, and that something exterior can appear to be interior. The actual walls of the baptistery, though they must have been seen by my physical eyes, were covered over by a vision of some altogether different sight which was *as completely real as* the unchanged baptismal font.[33]

Here Jung impresses upon us the "objective" reality of the visionary realm as another world that is as equally real as the empirical world of the

---

33 C. G. Jung, *Memories, Dreams, Reflections*, p. 287. Emphasis mine.

senses. He also describes the event as "deeply stirring." He describes the "incredible beauty" of the four mosaic frescoes that had replaced the windows he remembered from his first visit, though he could not believe that his memory had been so unreliable. And then there was the lovely quality of the light—the blue light that had no apparent source, a fact that he did not question at all.

Jung comments on the vision as a "new creation by the unconscious,"[34] occasioned by unknown factors pertaining perhaps to previous integrations of unconscious material, but in the end relating to deeply felt sensibilities about himself, and to the mystery of his nature. He goes on to say that such an event is completely unexplainable in rational terms, and adds, sadly, that it "finds no place in the official view of the world."[35] In spite of its extraordinary significance, the mystical event and its repercussions have no home in our culture any more.

The quality of the landscapes of mystical and visionary—or perhaps we might say "psychospiritual"—experiences is particularly well articulated by the French philosopher and theologian and close colleague of Jung's, Henri Corbin. First, there is a break or discontinuity with ordinary space and time. Second, even though the beholder of this realm *knows* they have been elsewhere, it is impossible to describe the way to anyone else. It is also often impossible to describe the journey itself. People often do not speak of such experiences because they fear being misunderstood. In addition, descriptions of the *mundus imaginalis*, or disclosures of the mystical cities, often include intense feelings of beauty that stir the imagination toward a deep pathos and an opening of the heart.

This sense of penetration through a veil to another reality—or alternatively, the irruption of another world into ours—is illustrated by an image reproduced in Jung's essay "Flying Saucers: A Modern Myth," in a woodcut captioned, "The Spiritual Pilgrim Discovering Another World" that Jung thought came from the seventeenth century.[36] In this picture, the pilgrim, circumscribed by the arc of a circle representing this world, leaves ordinary space-time behind with its trees, towns, sun, moon and stars, and with her

---

34 *Ibid.* p. 286.
35 *Ibid.* p. 287.
36 C. G. Jung, "Flying Saucers," *CW 10*, 1959, pars. 589–824, Figure VII.

head through the *fenestra aeternitatis* ("window onto eternity") gazes into the timeless eternal world. In the Other world, which seems strange and filled with a subtle light, the double wheels of Ezekiel's vision are present, suggesting that visionary events are an experience of the synchronistic union of the eternal and the temporal, the timeless with the time-bound. They are the meeting point at the mystical center where psyche and matter are one. Temporarily, the *unus mundus* breaks through, and the pilgrim feels close to a miracle, while her heart opens in awe to the full intensity of divine Presence. Afterwards, the "window" closes, and the flow of events resume their ordinary patterning.

There are more recent examples of such journeys to the *mundus imaginalis*. Some of the shamanic initiations of the Russian psychiatrist Olga Kharitidi, M. D. in the Altai mountains of Siberia, and of the West African teacher and scholar Malidoma Somé, reported in their respective autobiographies,[37] also pertain to these strangely altered landscapes that Jung describes as taking place "outside," not in an ordinary outside, but in a region "utterly different from "my" psychic space."

Jung's Alchemical Vision of Christ

The other visionary experience of Jung's that I wish to recall occurred in 1939 while he was working on the studies for *Psychology and Alchemy*.[38] Alchemy for Jung was important as a heretical mystical philosophy that lay hidden in the underbelly of the more dogmatic and institutionalized Christianity, and was significant for him as the historical parallel to his own psychology of the unconscious. In attempting to bring Christianity up to date with the spiritual needs of the times, Jung realized that his penetration into the seemingly incomprehensible imagery and texts of the alchemists (research itself initiated by dreams) in fact portrayed a useful sequence of events relating to the transformation of consciousness also observed in the individuation process. A key feature of this process is the transmutation of spirit into matter and matter into spirit, which is also a function of the *mundus imaginalis*.

---

37 Olga Kharitidi, *Entering the Circle* (San Francisco: HarperSanFrancisco, 1996), and Malidoma Somé, *Of Water and The Spirit* (New York and London: Penguin/Arkana, 1994).
38 C. G. Jung, *Psychology and Alchemy*, CW 12, 1944.

While Jung was working on his alchemy studies for his book, he was also working in other areas of study. He was giving a seminar on the *Spiritual Exercises of Ignatius Loyola* and was preoccupied with the *Anima Christi*, one of the meditations of the *Spiritual Exercises*. He writes: "One night I awoke and saw, bathed in bright light at the foot of my bed, the figure of Christ on the Cross …. and I saw that his body was made of greenish gold." He adds that though experiencing visions was not unusual for him, this one was "marvelously beautiful" and he was "profoundly shaken by it."[39] Jung had already made links between the psychological figure of Christ and the central symbol of the alchemists, the *lapis*, or stone, so he was able to realize that this was not a literal Christian vision. Here, the "green gold" referred to the analogy of Christ with the *aurum non vulgi* ("not the common gold") and the *viriditas*, the greenness of manifested life, of the alchemists. Hildegard of Bingen also uses the term *viriditas* to express the manifestation of cosmic energies in the created world and in the individual human soul. Jung understood this image, then, as referring to the divine spirit poured out in all of nature and the cosmos, as well as in us. His vision pointed to the necessity for the recovery of the *anima mundi*, the animating principle of the *unus mundus*, the subtle world behind this world, radiating as a life force throughout the whole of creation.

In his vision of the green-gold Christ, Jung in effect recovered an alchemical gnosis for our times, in the image of Christ as a *mystical union of spiritually alive and physically dead matter.* The history of Christianity, Jung writes, recalled a story of the gradual separation of the spiritual from its home within the body, and the extrapolation of impersonal ideals at the expense of valuing the instinctual life, the wisdom of the creative feminine, and living in close harmony with one's feelings and the natural world. Matter and spirit were increasingly split off from each other. Indeed, the developing power of ego consciousness as an autonomous force of will separated from its instinctual roots in a psychic non-ego left matter with no life at all, and consciousness at the mercy of its own driven power motives. The violence of our times mirrors back to us the destructive effects of rationalism divorced from spiritual values centered in the heart, and of a view of nature and the cosmos without soul.

---

39 C. G. Jung, *Memories, Dreams, Reflections*, p. 210.

Jung's alchemical vision restored matter as sacred and nature, the physical world, and our bodies as elements infused with the divine. In this way he corrected the misconception of Christianity that dissociates matter from the divine, inviting the evolution of a different kind of consciousness, one informed with eros awareness that aims to reunite thinking and feeling, passion and vision, spirit and matter, humankind and cosmos. In his vision, Jung glimpsed the psychophysical background to the world, an experience that eventually led him to conceive the archetype as psychoid, that is, at bottom an unknown mystery, yet extending from a transcendent background into and including matter.

The value of alchemy was that it envisioned the transmutation of consciousness as a process that simultaneously was affected by and had an effect on nature, for example, the astrological influence of the stars or the effects of the alchemist's imagination on the experiments. The practice of alchemy also was affected by and had an effect on the physical body, specifically. Through a continuing series of *coniunctios* and *nigredos* (unions and deaths) that simultaneously psychized/sublimated matter and embodied spirit, the opus (outcome of the work) was aimed at the development and refinement of a third space, the subtle body, accompanied by its rebirth imagery. This "resurrection body" (the conscious self now reconnected with its celestial partner or "I") was thought to survive physical death.

Jung's alchemical vision gives us a hint of how in the union of psyche and matter our exposure to the reality of the subtle world of the *mundus imaginalis* is aiding us in this transformation of consciousness demanded in our times. I should like to draw attention once again to the emotional and numinous nuances of this vision for Jung. Not only is Jung describing another event belonging to that psychic landscape "outside the body," but he is also remarking on both the beauty of the Presence in his room and the emotional impact of this experience upon him. We are left with the deep impression that in being "profoundly shaken," his heart was penetrated and that this transpersonal vision not only gave rise to developing his thoughts further about the relation of the Christ figure to his alchemical psychology, but that his body was infiltrated by the feeling values of an eros consciousness arising directly out of the collective unconscious, or objective psyche. What burns through this mystical visionary perception is the conscious recovery of the *a priori* unified world, the subtle world behind and infusing this one, held together by the numinous energies of love.

This exposure to a transpsychic sphere is deeply transformative to body and psyche through the intense power of beauty, feeling, and an opening to the divine. At the same time, access to this realm far beyond the limitations of ego consciousness, encourages a creative furthering of one's own work. Logos and eros are brought into a new synthesis. This is simultaneously felt as a healing balm for the embodied soul and has an all-round deepening effect on our nature that penetrates to the core of our being. The feeling, too, of being initiated into a cosmic secret or divine disclosure endows our life with a sense of worth and meaning beyond the finite limitations of everyday reality. At such a moment we might also feel a sense of gratitude at having been granted such an insight, and experience a union of both humility and joyous devotion to a spiritual value beyond ourselves. For a moment we no longer feel so alone, but united with the forces of creation as one note in a cosmic symphony.

Yet in spite of the overwhelming significance of these kinds of events for the development of consciousness toward heart knowledge, visionary or mystical perception is mostly undervalued, if not outright ignored—sometimes even envied and "spoiled"—in much contemporary psychology and psychotherapy. Consequently, individuals who have had such experiences are left to wander alone with them, without support or without any means to integrate them into life. *The Songlines of the Soul* is an attempt to open a space for such experiences and thereby with a spirit of hospitality invite readers to remember and give voice to them. Epiphanies of the Other world as "new creations" belonging to a new vision of reality are also to be found in experiences of synchronicity. To these we will turn in the next chapter.

Part Two

∞

SYNCHRONICITY:
DOORWAYS TO THE
DEEP MYSTERIES OF THE PSYCHE

Chapter 4

SYNCHRONICITY
AND THE SOUNDS OF SILENCE

*The living mystery of life is always hidden between Two, and it is the true mystery which
cannot be betrayed by words and depleted by arguments.*[1]

"What nature leaves imperfect, the art perfects."[2]

So far in this book I have tried to show how individuals are transformed
by experiences that put them in touch with the Other world. These
experiences, as I have shown, initiate a journey into one's true nature.
Through the power of the creative and true imagination, these experiences
continue the creation of the individual. In this chapter my focus shifts toward
synchronicity as the bridge between individual transformation from the alchemy
of our dreams and imaginings, and the collective signs of transformation in
which we are enfolded and to which we are called to awaken.

Synchronicities move us beyond interpretation and beyond dichotomies
to a direct relationship with the songlines of our souls. Synchronicities are
a kind of dreaming while awake. They draw, therefore, our attention to the
nature of consciousness itself and to the wide range of its possibilities. Are
we rigid and fixed, or are we open to a broad spectrum of modes of appre-
hending the world?

Although Jung spoke of the psyche as a symbolical realm, an "as if"
reality that we think of as being "inside," he also spoke of it in another way.
He alludes to a world "outside," albeit in a subtle form, that we can, never-

---

1   C. G. Jung, *Letters 11: 1951–1961*, selected and edited by Gerhard Adler in collaboration with
Aniela Jaffe, trans. R. F. C. Hull (Princeton, NJ: Princeton University Press, 1975), p. 581.
2   C. G. Jung, *Psychology and Alchemy*, CW 12.

theless, experience directly. As we have seen, we can know this subtle world through paying attention to our symptoms, in certain kinds of dreams, in waking visions, and in some active imagination processes. The organ of perception and cognition of these subtle states is the *imaginatio vera* (true or spiritual imagination) of alchemy that Corbin, as we have seen, also elaborates. This organ is a subtle one, and rather than being connected with the sharp focus of the intellect, it resides in the chambers of the subtle heart and opens us to a world that under ordinary reality remains unseen or eclipsed. True imagination also participates in new creations, and Jung suggests that, rather than remaining fixed in a Christian "imitation" where everything is already settled and remains fairly predictable, consciousness has the transformative power of participating in a continuing creation, *creatio continua*, in which each moment has a never-before-imagined creative potential.

In this chapter, we turn to the phenomenon of synchronicity that also opens us to the subtle body of the world, points us toward evidence of continuing creation based on an acausal foundation, and relies on the co-creative contribution of consciousness through the act of giving "meaning" to this on-going creation. Jung's observations, then, on the phenomena of synchronicity and the psychophysical unity of the world suggested by such unusual events were an effort to bring the mediaeval alchemical ideas on the non-local and confusing relationship between psyche and matter, up to date.

There are four main reasons to connect synchronicity with alchemy. Once again, in synchronicity, as in alchemy, there is a connection of inner and outer events not linked by the laws of cause and effect. Second, the individual can experience this connection as meaningful beyond a purely personal level through the participation of consciousness that can be compared to the alchemical *imaginatio vera*. Third, synchronicities tend to cause a profound shift in attitude, resulting from an emotional encounter that opens us to the subtle worlds of the numinous, such as the direct experience of imaginal figures in the visions of the alchemists at various stages of the work. Finally, these experiences, like the continuous alchemical operations that serve as metaphors for the deep pools of feeling that belong to the individuation process, reveal life and our involvement with it as an ongoing creative process and not something that is fixed, linear, or determined from the beginning.

According to Jung, the key feature of visionary alchemy, the spiritual *imaginatio*, indispensable for the creative transformations of the work, is the observing consciousness of the individual (or individuals). Indeed, the deep participation and emotional involvement of the individual are required, in synchronicities, to make these "miracles" affectively meaningful. Consciousness creates a new meaning, a predominantly spiritual creation arising out of the ego's reconnection with a wiser source that is, nevertheless, simultaneously registered in the body as intense feeling. Synchronicities depend on our interest in them, and this interest is rewarded by our being granted an experience that is often treasured as a carefully guarded secret, only reluctantly told. Synchronicities are "aha" moments that deepen the atmosphere around us and reshuffle the events of our lives. We have an enlivening sense of our participation in the continuing creation of the world and, by momentarily healing our doubting self, we experience a reconnection to the Source that inspires our creative work, re-vitalizes our life, and makes us feel less alone.

Jung's work on synchronicity represents his first attempt to explicitly challenge the Cartesian heritage that has traditionally split mind and matter. In his essay *Synchronicity: An Acausal Connecting Principle*, and in the companion essay, *On the Nature of the Psyche*, Jung links synchronicity with developments in the new physics to put forward a hypothesis for a new emerging reality that opens up and recovers the subtle world for contemporary times. In this way, he is able to point out the striking affinities between psychic, biological, and even microphysical processes. This connection begins to move rational consciousness toward a new paradigm: the grounding in science not only of a unified psychophysical and subtle reality, but also of the paranormal in general, for example, telepathy, clairvoyance, and other extraordinary and anomalous experiences. Synchronicities more accurately, then, provide an up-to-date link between the alchemists' visionary world and Jung's imaginal world.

Jung wrote his essays on synchronicity late in his life, although he had thought about the phenomenon and its implications for many years because of his own experiences and those of his colleagues, friends, and patients. There may be reasons for his hesitancy to speak out sooner. Synchronicities are problematic because in the same way that quantum physics requires a re-visioning of reality toward probability, indeterminacy and the "uncertainty principle," synchronicities feature unpredictable events and attributes of consciousness relegated to the margins of our rational, scientific minds that tend to be disregarded. Perhaps we can understand this reluctance to look too closely at what is happening, for synchronicities herald not only the breakdown of everything we think of as normal, they actually provide beginning hints of a new worldview coming into consciousness, one to which we are being invited to pay close attention to enable us to balance and expand the more familiar coordinates of reality.

Jung mentions how synchronicities tend to appear at moments of intense psychic urgency. For example, he writes of awakening from a terrifying dream in which a bullet passed through his head, to learn the next day that one of his patients had committed suicide by shooting himself in the head during the night.

This psychic urgency may be happening on a cultural level as well. British Jungian analyst, Julian David, comments that the difference between causality and synchronicity can be understood as two styles of being. He writes that causality is related more to the ego and represented, mythologically, by the god Apollo, while synchronicity is connected to the mysteries of the luminosities of the unconscious and personified by the god Dionysus. The weakness in Western culture is that it cannot recognize the dark depths of Dionysus and so the ensuing hubris and inflation of a culture out of balance has led to a path of increasing warfare, corruption, and self-destruction.[3] Maybe this collective ruin is a signal to us that it is time for transformation and change. The powerful emotional energy generated by the 2008 election of President Obama in the U.S. and rippling out across the world signals this urgency for something new in the political sphere, but perhaps beyond as well.

One of the central themes of Jung's theory is his emphasis on synchronicities as the irruption into our world of a new unified reality that, in Julian David's terms, would remember Dionysus. Here Jung moves beyond psychology toward articulating a new worldview based on the conscious union of instinct and spirit, psyche and matter. In fact, his "fervent interest" in a new cosmology is reflected in a response to a letter from British Jungian analyst, Michael Fordham, in which Jung addresses Fordham's *psychological*

---

3   Julian David, in *Psychological Perspectives*, "The Mystery of Synchronicity," #45, 2003, pp.62–85.

interest in the archetypal implications of synchronicity. Significantly, however, Jung adds, "but I must say that I am equally interested, at times even more so, in the *metaphysical* aspect of the phenomena, and in the question: how does it come that even inanimate objects are capable of behaving as if they were acquainted with my thoughts?"[4]

In my own life, this curious familiarity, even intimacy, between psyche and world, has from time to time made a deep impression. Here are some simple examples from my own therapeutic experiences.

SYNCHRONICITY: "MIRACLES" IN THE THERAPY ROOM

When I think back to my first analysis some twenty-five years ago, I do not remember much that was said, but the relationship itself lingers as the container for a process—actually more like a rollercoaster ride—that changed my life, and in which I discovered my vocation. Some images remain, however, as if asking not to be forgotten. One such memory is the initial dream I had following my telephone call to the analyst to make my first appointment. In addition to setting out the issues of the work we would do together, this dream described almost perfectly the layout of my analyst's office, something I realized as I was recounting the dream during our first meeting. This made a deep impression on me. What kind of consciousness knew about this before I knew? How could an event that later unfolded in time already exist somewhere?

Later on, when I shared a dream in which a Voice spoke of my need to talk about intimacy—(I had had great difficulty talking about my feelings toward my analyst)—two doves, birds of Aphrodite, flew into the garden outside the consulting room, and perched on the open windowsill by my chair. Their gentle presence gave me courage to speak about things that at that time were fraught with terror, embarrassment, and numinosity for me.

Another time, when I was weeping, overcome with sadness and grief, the petals on a flower in full bloom in a vase on the table next to me fell to the ground. My therapist knelt down, picked them up, and handed them to me. This was such a beautiful and spontaneous gesture (on the part of the flower as well as my analyst)—one that did not attempt to take my grief away or respond to it with already rehearsed words—that over two decades later I remember it as a simple and silent moment of lasting change.

I remember, too, the day when almost an hour passed by without a word spoken between us. Toward the end of the session, I lifted my head and looked at my analyst. His face began to transform in front of me, becoming eternally old. The edges of it dissolved into what looked

---

4   C. G. Jung, *Letters 1 1*, p. 344. My emphasis.

like white mist or clouds. "The Ancient of Days," I whispered without voice. That was perhaps one of my most memorable sessions, a song without words. I had always felt so embarrassed and full of shame about my shyness and inability to speak or communicate my thoughts, especially in social groups. Here, in this moment, the silence in the field between and surrounding us deeply accepted my heretofore "unacceptable" characteristics. It simultaneously transformed them in such a way that I both felt and envisioned a divine presence.

I experienced a more humorous moment of synchronicity many years later when I was seeing another analyst. In the two years following my divorce, I had felt mostly a lifeless depression. Then gradually I began to sense the forces of eros, love, returning to me. However, I had only a dawning awareness of this feeling. One day as I arrived at my analyst's office (which was connected to his farm), all the donkeys in the field were breaking through the bounds of their fence and running wild and free. I spent the first fifteen minutes of my session helping to herd them back into the paddock. The feeling of unmitigated life and the power of natural instinct breaking through the prison of my depression—just like the misbehaving donkeys!—made me aware of how the forces of life were indeed returning from the underworld into my ordinary daylight world once again.

But, there can be painful synchronicities too. For example, the very day I was journaling about the motorcycle accident of a friend's brother, I discovered that my daughter was involved in a serious bicycle accident. I had just finished writing in the early afternoon and was about to go out, when the phone rang and I received the news. I myself found no solace in nature or people that day. I was flung into a high state of anxiety and concern as I immediately made my way to the airport to fly to Portland, Oregon, to be with her in the hospital where she was. Fortunately, she recovered fairly quickly, and though it is hard to say I have discovered a meaning in the event for myself, nevertheless I have reminded myself that there is always a shadow to what we do, and that I must not forget that shadow in my own creative thinking and writing. On my daughter's part, she feels that since her accident, she has allowed herself to become more vulnerable, and has come to reflect more seriously on the nature of her vocational life and to take steps to live it.

Jung's Experiences of Synchronicity

Jung observed in his own life the powerful resonances of synchronistic events and the critical junctures at which they often occur. For example, Jung's war visions coincided with the outbreak of the First World War and his own disturbing descent into the unconscious (following his break from Freud) that proved so critical for his later work. Jung's painting of a "Chinese" mandala depicting the circumambulation of the Self as the goal of psychic development was followed by a letter from Richard Wilhelm enclosing *The Secret of the Golden Flower.* This letter made Jung feel at last that he had an affinity with something and someone beyond himself in relation to the *experience* of the alchemical goal of individuation as the establishment of the "immortal body." Later, the visions of his numinous near-death experience in relation to a heart attack, set against the backdrop of eternity, allowed him to surrender more fully to the flow of his thoughts, which gave him the courage to write his final and centrally important texts. These include *Aion*, which elaborates astrological synchronicity, exploring how Christianity coincides with the age of Pisces through the symbol of the fish, *Mysterium Coniunctionis* and its central theme of the *Coniunctio* or Sacred Marriage uniting psyche and matter, and the essay *Flying Saucers: A Modern Myth of Things Seen in the Skies*, which Jung suggests is synchronicity on a collective level.

These examples point to deepening aspects of experience that provide a different kind of attunement to the world and reality than our rational and conventional ways of being and thinking. But the point is, as Jung states, they are to be regarded as just as important, just as real, and to be taken just as seriously as the rational. Only in this way are we enabled to complete our ordinary experience and ways of knowing with non-ordinary and mystical ones. Jung considered the unpredictable and unrepeatable nature of synchronicities—and the spontaneous arising of a new meaning beyond the ego—to be new creations on the part of nature and the psyche. He therefore calls them "acts of creation in time," and states that for that reason they are signs of the continuing creation. For example, we see in the examples just noted how much synchronicity confirmed and deeply inspired Jung's creative writing and the evolution and content of his own ideas.

Further, these types of acausal connections between psyche and nature or the world demonstrate the ancient idea of the interconnectedness of all being, and recovers it for contemporary times. For example, Fritjof Capra, in *The Tao of Physics*, explores how various concepts in the Eastern religions of Hinduism, Taoism, and Buddhism reflect "the quantum understanding of interrelated and inseparable phenomena, of the centrality of consciousness to the world, and the unity of all appearances in a domain that transcends space-time."

Of course, this sense of a unified whole has always been true for some individuals, indigenous cultures, shamans, and mystics, and was true for some philosophers in the West prior to the rise of science in the seventeenth century. The founder of neo-Platonic philosophy, Plotinus (204–270 C.E.), for example, notes how the world soul and individual soul are related by sympathy or antipathy, *regardless of distance*. The oneness of all being is familiar in Chinese thought with the interweaving patterning of physical and psychological events in the form of the Tao. Jung notes particularly how insight into the background of synchronicity is provided by mantic methods like astrology and the *I Ching* that take the position that individual details are part of the whole interplay of the cosmic dynamics of Yin and Yang. But the perspective of perceiving life as an inter-related whole, with synchronicities providing unique expressions of this unity, has been excluded as a legitimate form of experience in western culture until recently. Contemporary trends in scientific thought, however, are beginning to give credence to the idea of the interrelationship of all being. For example, the rise of quantum physics has provided a powerful foundation for this idea, particularly in its observations of non-locality (action at a distance), and the so-called "observer effect." Life is a richly interwoven tapestry in which we are mutually involved. What may seem separate from certain points of view are parts of an integral unity of being in which we participate. We have an impact on other life forms and human beings and are affected by them in kind.

In presenting Jung's work on synchronicity, this chapter focuses on both the psychological aspects of synchronistic experiences, and the appearance of these "miracles" as signs of a new emerging worldview.

Synchronicity: The Golden Scarab

One of Jung's favorite examples of the power of synchronicity to transform and change consciousness was the patient who was stuck in her therapy because her brilliant intellectual abilities and her attachment to rational consciousness prevented her from surrendering to the flow of the intuitive and irrational and, therefore, to the transformational aspect of the individuation process. However, she had a dream in which she was given a golden scarab. While she was telling Jung her dream, which had already by-passed her intellect and touched her feelings and the deep wisdom inside her, a gold-green beetle, a common rose-chafer, began tapping at the window behind Jung's chair. He got up and opened the window, saying, "Here is your scarab" as the insect flew into the room. The combination of the dream, the patient's valuing it and sharing it, and the simultaneous visit of the flying insect (the closest available analogy to the golden scarab), at such a key moment—*together with Jung's openness and attunement to the significance of such events*—all conspired—*in a way that could not have been anticipated*—to provide his patient with the necessary *irrational* force to break through her defenses. This enabled her to open to her feelings, and shift her attitude from being purely rational toward becoming more dependent on her own instinctual, archetypal, true nature.

Such a renewal of consciousness is often accompanied by symbols of rebirth like the golden scarab from Egyptian mythology. This woman's therapy process was released into the flow of life, the Tao, and, therefore, could proceed on an authentic foundation. As Einstein notes, "The significant problems we face cannot be solved at the same level of thinking we were in when we created them." They require intervention from a wiser source beyond the ego's limited knowledge, the spontaneous intervention of the non-local, irrational, archetypal-instinctual psyche.[5]

Synchronicity: "Dark Light"

Here is another example that demonstrates the transformational power of the irruption of a wiser source into reality. It was recounted by a graduate student named Samina Salahuddin at Pacifica Graduate Institute in one of my classes. She wrote the following:

---

5   C. G. Jung, "Synchronicity: An Acausal Connecting Principle," *CW 8*, pars 843–845, 982.

"Once during a therapy session with an adolescent boy, seventeen years old and addicted to drugs, a strange thing happened. I did not know how to move on with his case as he had been in and out of rehab only to relapse again. He had been through a lot of abuse and neglect while growing up in an extremely dysfunctional family and was later moved to a foster home. He was finding it really hard to cope with life. He said that he saw no light at the end of the tunnel. I always used to try and run the therapy sessions, giving him a lot of advice on how to live his life, while he in turn, gave me a lot of excuses. One function of the dream in therapy is to move therapist and patient out of these fixed ego positions. In this particular session, my patient came with the following dream:

> It is night and it's very dark. I find myself outside a farmhouse. There are dogs, horses, and other animals sleeping together with some children and their parents outside the house on the ground. I try to go into the house, which has a gate made of strong iron bars followed by a regular front door. Both the gate and door are open so I walk in. It is dark inside and the house seemed haunted. I feel scared to stay in so I come out. It starts to rain heavily and at the same time the lights come on in the house making it look very bright. The family and animals sleeping outside wake up and they all start to come inside the house. I now feel the house to be very welcoming and full of life.

"At that very moment, when he had completed describing his dream, there came a huge reflection of light on his face. The light had come from the sun's rays being reflected from the window on the hand-painted mirror hanging in the room. The light was so intense that he had to shut his eyes and cover them with his hands. He then sat quietly, as if dumbfounded, and then started to weep. That was a big breakthrough in therapy after which he started to heal. He had realized that there were higher powers and connections much greater than the world in which he lived, which gave him hope and confidence to live his life in a more meaningful way. My patient had indeed received the "divine light" that day during therapy. Looking back I realize how synchronicity had worked during my therapy session without my even trying to do anything. It seemed like the whole world was in unity while the incident was happening."

Samina concluded after this event that, even though the dream itself prefigured the healing, it was the impetus for transformation within her as well. From that point on, Samina felt her attitude as a therapist begin to change. She stopped trying to force a meaning out of every situation or dream that was brought into the therapy session and instead focused on "being present," that is, allowing meaning to be created on its own, arising out of the field with the patient. By adopting this attitude she followed Jung, who said repeatedly that when sitting with patients, he tried not to "know" in advance, but to let the unconscious take precedence in creating meaning.[6] If we can develop this kind of trust, these kind of ordinary miracles happen, and we play our small but not insignificant part in the unfolding of creation.

Synchronicity: Four Essential Features

Jung's notion of synchronicity can be summarized in the four following ways, though these features overlap each other in the wave-like moment of a synchronistic experience.

#1: Acausal Connection, Meaning, and the Elasticity of Time and Space

In a true synchronicity, Jung writes, an inner psychic event (the golden scarab dream) is linked with an event in the outside world (the beetle at the window) with no intervening cause. This acausal parallelism can occur either simultaneously (during the telling of the golden scarab dream) or at a distance in time (Richard Wilhelm sending Jung *The Secret of the Golden Flower*). However, the connection between the two events is a third factor created by the participant through the act of giving these events a greater *meaning*, the "indispensable criterion of synchronicity." Jung is clear here that by "meaning" he is not merely referring to an intellectual interpretation of the experience. On the contrary, he believes the rationalism of the West is a prejudice in need of correction. The rationalism of modern science is a way of thinking that appeared in the last few centuries. Alongside its strengths it tends to constrict Nature's revelations through its own limited theoretical biases. With Jung's patient, for example, the meaning arose from the ego's connection to a transpersonal reality, not

---

6   C. G. Jung, *CW 9i*, par. 528.

via an interpretation but via the direct impact of the numinous dream scarab and its appearance (as a beetle) in her world. As an alternative to rationalism, Jung mentions many alternate ways of "thinking" cross-culturally, from the Chinese Tao, to astrology, alchemy, and intuitive and prophetic procedures, modes of thinking that include nature and "chance." These approaches were for centuries a part of the Western worldview. Jung especially likes using the term Tao to refer to the spiritual meaning arising out of synchronicities. Taoist thinking unites psyche and nature, visible and invisible, rational and irrational, time and timelessness, into a paradoxical complexity that cannot be grasped by the intellect alone, and must include intuition and feeling in order to attune to the rippling, *qualitative* aspect of a moment that pervades the atmosphere in subtle ways.

The Tao beautifully expands our ordinary understanding by allowing us to open to the Mystery. The Tao includes the potentiality of "nothingness." One way to envision this is to think of a door, a vessel, or a window which only has meaning through the paradoxical mystery of including empty space. In reality, this "empty space" is a fullness that surrounds us. In order to correct the imbalances in the modern world, Jung felt that there was a necessity for us to expand our consciousness into the invisible realms of the visionary imagination, realms that could heal our fractured sense of ourselves, creating an experience of our wholeness, both visible and unseen. Normally, in ordinary everyday reality, we marginalize this dreaming songline world but, if attended to, it comes out of the force of silence with unforeseen creative possibilities and makes life sing.

Acausality (and the comparable non-locality in physics) has implications; it goes hand in hand with alterations in the space-time continuum. Jung valued the American psychologist, J. B. Rhine of Duke University, whose experiments with subjects guessing the faces of playing cards before they were drawn from a deck, offered powerful evidence that neither space nor time are prohibitive factors in these psychic events.[7] Elsewhere, Jung writes of this time-space relativity. In fact, in a letter to Rhine in November 1945, Jung comments on the relationship between the new physics and his psychology—even hinting at the affinity between matter and psyche—by writing: "In the microphysical world the relativity of space and time is an established fact. The psyche, inasmuch as

---

7   C. G. Jung, *CW* 8, pars. 833–836.

it produces phenomena of a non-spatial or a non-temporal character, seems to belong to the microphysical world."[8] This functioning of the psyche outside normal time and space—not only in synchronicities, but also in precognition, ESP, and other parapsychological phenomena such as remote viewing—again points to the relativity of time and space in the unconscious. Jung links this with the nature of the archetype as "always-everywhere," in a letter dated 21 October, 1957, to Stephen Abrams:

> We conclude therefore that we have to expect a factor in the psyche that is not subject to the laws of time and space, as it is on the contrary capable of suppressing them to a certain extent. In other words: this factor is expected to manifest the qualities of time- and spacelessness, i.e., "eternity" and "ubiquity."[9]

Through the relationship of inner and outer events characteristic of synchronicity, the archetype shows itself to be not localized in one person, but active in the whole environment. In another letter, in response to his college friend Albert Oeri, Jung already in 1929 proposes a radical idea:

> The nature of the collective unconscious [is] … like an omnipresent continuum, an unextended Everywhere …. [W]hen something happens here at point A which touches upon or affects the [collective unconscious], it has happened everywhere.[10]

Since synchronistic events are unrelated to causality (and occur therefore outside space and time), they give us an experience of an altered state of ordinary consciousness. Recall the example of the golden scarab dream and rose-chafer beetle described in relation to Jung's patient. When the beetle is flying around, it is in ordinary space-time. When the patient is speaking to Jung she is in ordinary space-time. But when the beetle hits the window in Jung's office *at the same moment* that the patient is telling the dream, the link between patient and beetle is not caused. *In that moment*, we are no longer in ordinary space-time. This produces an altered state of consciousness, and this altered state leads us to the second feature of synchronicity.

---

8   C. G. Jung, *Letters 1: 1906–1950*, selected and edited by Gerhard Adler in collaboration with Aniela Jaffe, trans. R. F. C. Hull (Princeton, NJ: Princeton University Press, 1973), p. 394.
9   C. G. Jung, *Letters 11*, p. 398.
10 C. G. Jung, *Letters 1*, p. 58.

#2: *Direct Experience Through Feeling of Another World While in This One*

A key feature of synchronicity is our *experience* of it, which involves our feelings. Synchronistic events belong to those kinds of subjectively significant experiences that, as Jung remarked about his Ravenna vision, are so often critical in our life. They seem to deepen the mystery of our nature, express our unique creativity, and expand our understanding beyond rational arguments to embrace those "carefully guarded secrets" that speak of our vocation. These secrets reveal the powerful background of a subtle world that irrupts from time to time into this one with its own images, figures, and landscapes. Jung suggests that his patient who dreamt of the golden scarab was changed irrevocably because she had an emotional experience that was powerful enough to dislodge her fixed Cartesian rationality. When the archetypal content of the initial dream event—a golden scarab—was presented to her, this image infused her body and imagination with its transpersonal numinous energy. Then the significance of this archetypal event was confirmed by an actual event in the world that, like a miracle, echoed the dreamtime, as if event and dream were working together.

Jung observed that the numinosity of synchronicities relates to the constellation of archetypal patterns and energies. According to Jung's theory, archetypes are the invisible background structure of instinctual patterns of behavior that also have a "specific charge" that enables them to express themselves as emotional intensities. These emotions produce what Jung calls an *abaissement du niveau mental*, a lowering of conscious rational thought processes that simultaneously raises a particular content to heightened intensity. The resultant constriction of ego consciousness produced by the affect creates a favorable opportunity for the unconscious to fill the space, as it were, and thus inhibited or unexpected contents can break through. Jung further observes that synchronicities are often found in association with intensely emotional and universal events such as death, birth, or other processes of initiation such as the psychological death and rebirth associated with life transitions or rites of passage.

In synchronicities our affects and feelings become the doorway to the numinous, an irrational force that seems to seek the transformation of our consciousness. Synchronicities are small unanticipated miracles that open us to the ground of all being, the subtle state of what Jung refers to as the *unus mundus.* They reinforce the "astounding importance" of the subjective element in making new creations and linking us with personal mystery, creativity, and fate. Synchronicities open us to the divine and therefore give us a direct experience of the opening of our heart. We are granted access to deep feeling, and to those levels of consciousness that complete in the irrational mysteries of the transpersonal world an experience taking place in ordinary time and space. With such experience our ordinary life changes as well.

#3: Openness to Thoughts We Did Not Know We Had

With synchronicity we are momentarily situated in an emotional field peopled by images and constructed by invisible yet dynamic archetypal forms. Synchronicities, therefore, reconnect the time-bound participant with the timeless dimension of the transpersonal, archetypal realm, the *unus mundus*, and such moments open us to knowledge or hints of things to which we ordinarily have no access. Jung calls this the opening to "absolute knowledge," or "foreknowledge," and he conceives of it as knowledge stored in the *mundus archetypus*, or imaginal world. Jung gives other examples of this kind of psychic knowing. One is a woman whose husband died quite unexpectedly from the medical point of view, but whose wife seemed to have a foreknowledge of his death. She felt anxious because at the time of his return from his consultation with his doctor, a flock of birds had assembled on the roof of their house, something that had also occurred at the impending deaths of both her mother and grandmother.[11] Jung also reports the case of a patient who fell into a coma after giving birth and losing a lot of blood, yet whose consciousness continued to perceive "from the ceiling" the frightened faces of her husband and mother, and the somewhat frantic attempts of the medical staff to revive her, all of which seemed unnecessary to her as she knew she was most certainly not going to die. One of the interesting aspects of this account is the patient's report of the knowledge of a beautiful green meadow with resplendent and intensely colored flowers behind her that she knew was the entrance to another world. If she were to turn around, she would be tempted to enter.[12]

---

11 C. G. Jung, *CW 8*, par. 844.
12 C. G. Jung, *ibid.*, pars. 950–955.

In dreams and visions, this kind of direct knowing from the Source is often imaged by the symbol of the "Book of Knowledge." In dreams, this knowledge of the meaning of one's life, or of the gift of all knowledge, for example, is often forgotten upon waking, and often one spends the rest of one's life searching for this lost wisdom. In fact, the meaning behind such a dream might be this continuing search for deepening self-knowledge and the capacity for love.

Synchronicity seems to be one of the doorways to this hidden knowledge, as if under certain circumstances we have access to the "images of all creation,"[13] a kind of unconscious perceiving that our rational consciousness has eclipsed or perhaps when exposed to it, immediately dismisses because of our collective prejudice against such a source of knowledge or oracular way of knowing. Synchronicity, however, leads us to honor our deep intuitions and deep knowing. It invites us to take seriously those irrational thoughts that seem so alien to ego consciousness, yet nevertheless come to us as illuminations and insights from another source, often requiring considerable reflection and research on our part.

#4: Transformation and New Creations

Synchronicities expose us directly to a richly textured event, which *in itself* is transformative for us. The intensity of its emotional impact enlivens the whole body and sets the cells dancing energetically. The power of the epiphany is also perceived as meaningful, not as a rational imposition from the ego, but as a spiritual creation that arises out of a union of personal and transpersonal knowledge. The spiritual meaning is a new creation, a "just-so" event, without beginning or end. It is knowledge from a well of wisdom, not knowledge as information or knowledge for personal gain. The moment of change opens us to new creative possibilities, and this led Jung to suggest that, like the discontinuities of physics, synchronicities are like individual dips into the quantum world essential for creativity and renewal. Hence he called synchronicities "acts of creation in time." As such, they demonstrate that creation is not fixed, but continually renewing itself, through the intervention of the "always everywhere"

---

13 C. G. Jung, *ibid.*, par. 931.

SONGLINES OF THE SOUL

vertical dimension of the unconscious or imaginal realm that reaches from outside space-time (and therefore outside history) into the realm of the time-bound embodied soul.

Synchronicities bring us to the present, and resituate us in the Tao. The impact of this link between the finite and the eternal, the time-bound with the timeless, in a state in which ego and non-ego are in momentary harmony, is often a powerful confirmation of one's life path, like a cosmic kiss from the divine. Often this moment encourages us to follow a new creative path, to pick up that project we had put aside. Suddenly the world becomes a magical place again and we feel encouraged to proceed in places where we had doubted and lost our confidence. Surely, one of the major effects of synchronicities is the urge to realize something, a new creation that is primarily a spiritual creation, like the initiatory event brought about by Jung's patient's scarab dream and real life rose-chafer, and birthed by the irruption of the background *unus mundus* world into our individual domain.

Jung's definition of the spontaneous occurrences of synchronicities as evidence of the "transgressivity" of archetypes into nature contributing to "acts of creation in time," can now be regarded as part of a new worldview. These "transgressions" of events into time are comparable to the singularities described by physics, special and irregular instances of a complementary order of reality—acausal orderedness—that exists right alongside classical determinism. This new worldview is one in which inner and outer worlds are no longer separate but united in the background world of the *unus mundus*. As Jung's alchemical vision of Christ suggested, nature too has a soul, and now psyche and world can be viewed as irreducibly and perhaps continuously linked together within this field of soul. This new perspective—in which Jung was proposing a new principle of nature as well as valuing rare and unusual events—required Jung to revision his hypothesis of the archetype from an intrapsychic factor to one that now extended into all of nature. He calls this psychophysical unity in which soul and matter are in seamless contact with each other and of which synchronicities are an expression, evidence of the psychoid archetype.

The Deep Mysteries of the Psyche

It could be that Jung's story of the golden scarab remained so emblematic for him because it reflects the difficulty we all have in surrendering to the radical implications of synchronicity and what it asks of us: namely, to move beyond our cherished ideals and rational consciousness toward deeper wisdom. Jung tells of a dream in which he had to sacrifice his heroic ego, an action symbolized by the slaying of Siegfried, a German figure who represented the imposition of will, "having one's own way."[14] He describes hearing Siegfried's horn sounding over the mountains at dawn and seeing him driving furiously down the rocky slope in a chariot made of bones of the dead. When he turned the corner, Jung and his "brown-skinned savage" companion shot and killed him. Jung was overcome with remorse and compassion: the loss of something so great and so beautiful; the grief that accompanies the sacrifice of conscious attitudes now outgrown. The dream took place in late 1913 and Jung realized that it marked a situation that was also being lived out in the world. The will to power still dominates collective consciousness, so the profound implications of synchronicity to live in harmony with values that transcend the ego's will in devotion to the interconnectedness of all life, still remains a task for the future.

Jung describes this dream as part of his initiation into the deep mysteries of the psyche, where he had to recognize the importance of the transformative value of the imagination that resided in an *other* realm. He had to bow to a higher knowledge, to appreciate not just the causes but also the aims of his psyche, which suggests a "knowledge" prior to all consciousness, and one that desires the rebirth of the personality and the integration of lost values. This initiation breaks our illusion of separation and isolation from creation, and restores the link to a transpersonal and mystical gnosis, informed by eros. In such a moment, reality is experienced in a multidimensional complexity, personal and archetypal, inner and outer, rational and irrational, time-bound and timeless, present and future oriented.

It is perhaps not inconsequential that right after Jung's dream of Siegfried he relates another imaginal journey to the Other world. In his descent, which was also like a "voyage to the moon," he meets a wise old Elijah and

---

14 C. G. Jung, *Memories, Dreams, Reflections* (New York: Vintage Books, 1989), p. 180.

a beautiful young and blind Salome. They have a black serpent living with them. Jung comments that he is distrustful of Salome and, though the serpent shows interest in Jung, he remarks only on its connection to the hero myth. Here we are presented with Jung's (and our culture's) own distrust of and undeveloped relationship with eros and the feminine—feelings, intuition, and wisdom—also brought forward in synchronicities. For the snake is ancient, earthy and wise like the Great Mother, yet her energy can travel from the chthonic to the divine enlivening all the subtle chakras of the body. She represents the creative power and dynamism of the Goddess in pre-patriarchal times, in Hindu cosmology, and is a powerful image of love, healing and transformation in contemporary Native American cultures. The snake has been worshipped cross-culturally as a symbol of death and rebirth, fertility and regeneration. With the rise of patriarchy both the Goddess, her serpentine symbols, and the values of instinct and intuition that came with them were demonized and feared. Jung's dream and the many other ways in which this serpent power is returning in people's dreams today as well as in the phenomenon of synchronicity, are inviting a renewed appreciation for feminine consciousness and our unity with nature and the cosmos.

Synchronicities restore us to the sense of the deep mysteries of the psyche and of a rippling background source of subtle Being; they evoke reverence, and help still the mind; they situate the ego humbly in service to a larger vision; they restore the impossible and irrational as *psychologically* necessary. Such gifts of grace can even help make suffering tolerable. Perhaps, too, the gold-green color of the rose-chafer beetle discussed in relation to Jung's patient's dream reminded Jung of his gold-green alchemical Christ figure, and this dramatic incident became another reminder that all of nature is holy and imbued with a divine spirit. Surely we too are being invited to embrace this mystery once again.

We might consider also that this knowledge—if we are linked in some invisible way in an unseen dimension with all creation—must surely have an impact on our relationships and ethical commitments. We cannot mindlessly project the shadow onto the enemy or continue to rape the environment, for example, if we are linked to one another, to the buzzing bee and the shining star. For all nations and ecosystems are held in a web of life that nourishes the whole, all the beings—animals, insects, trees, oceans, weather, deserts, as well as people—on the planet. We must also consider how we are negatively impacting the wider expanse of the universe and its inhabitants by the destructive choices we make on our own planet.

Having offered numerous examples of synchronicity and having discussed its meanings and implications for a new emerging myth for our time, it seems fitting to close this chapter with a personal example of synchronicity in order to underscore the point that I have been drawn into this work through experiences of it.

SYNCHRONICITY: THE CRANE

Early on in our relationship, when we were more or less settled into our new life together, Robert and I decided to have a ceremony to mark our commitment to one another in a more formal way, although at this time we were not actually legally married. We wanted to do this spiritual marriage at our home surrounded by our children and parents. Soon after my parents' arrival from England, however, my father was taken very ill and was diagnosed with colon and liver cancer. We still managed to perform the ceremony, but almost immediately afterward my father was hospitalized for over two weeks following surgery for the cancer. This tragic event threw a pall over the whole affair, and we were sadly reminded of the intimate connection between love and death.

On one of the days following my father's surgery, my mother and I went by car to the hospital to spend some time with him. As we were approaching the onramp to go north on the highway, we were startled by the appearance of a large white crane that came flying toward us in a fluttering descent, swooping magnificently downward toward the road and alighting on the shoulder just at the point where the ramp and highway joined. To see such a huge bird in such an inhospitable place was actually quite shocking to the senses, and we immediately and simultaneously experienced it—within the powerful circumstances surrounding both my marriage and my father's illness—as an angelic visitation from the spirit world, and possibly as an omen of death. All of this happened very quickly, in a matter of seconds, during which we turned toward each other with our mouths dropping open, aghast. Only afterwards, as we made our way along the road, could we begin to articulate our feelings and fears to each other.

My father actually lived another three years, eventually succumbing in part to the cancer and its ravaging post-op treatments, and in part simply to old age, a death that his medical treatment had wonderfully postponed for the duration of that time. He died in a rather simple way, in the family house in Devon, surrounded and held by those he loved—my mother, sisters, brother, and I—in an aura of love and sweetness. A piercing shaft of sunlight breaking through dark brooding clouds lifted him up at the moment of transition.

Three months after my father's death, and for a number of practical reasons having to do with our children, the provisions of our wills, insurance and the like—and because the timing felt right—my husband and I decided to go ahead and perform the legal aspect of our union. We decided this spontaneously while the children were at school. It was a cool, breezy, sunny, spring day, and I decided to wear the beautiful silvery green dress that I had worn for our ceremony three years previously.

We drove down the hill from our house toward the highway on our way to the court house. At the bottom, as we were turning right onto the main road heading toward the ramp, we saw—opposite us—a large white crane standing still on a piece of uncultivated grassland, as if waiting for us. The sight of this bird in such an unlikely place, so near to the roar of the highway, immediately brought back the memory of my father, so recently passed on to the other side, and of the visitation of this bird to my mother and me in inauspicious, yet strangely sacred circumstances.

We turned the car around and retraced our path, parking right next to where the crane was standing so still. As we sat there quietly looking at the crane, it was as if the landscape of our marriage now suddenly opened up to a numinous realm in which this bird appeared as an emissary from another realm, as the presence of my father bestowing a blessing on our union. This time the feeling was one of a favorable augury, and we knew at once, with great certainty, that we were no longer on a purely practical mission, and that there is no such thing as "only" a legal ceremony.

It was a moving moment, one of extreme subtlety that transcends the immediate, a moment in which our somewhat casual attitude about this civil rite seemed full of a kind of human hubris. We were opened to a larger world, one that humbled our ego intentions and resituated them within the sacred. This world seemed to reshuffle all of the pieces of our lives that we had so far lived together and inexplicably transform them, making them all new. We felt part of a patterning of events and connections that seemed to belong to a harmonious patterning of the world, even extending beyond time to the transpersonal realm of the dead. To put it in another way, we felt we had dipped into a stream of life beyond time and space, to the eternal realms. It was a feeling of being in the Tao: the inner world and the outer cosmos were in a corresponding harmony. We were in the flow of nature. We proceeded on toward the Court House, aware now of this wider field of creation. Interestingly, the judge never showed up and a priest who had just married another couple performed our ceremony. My father was an Anglican clergyman. A mere accident, then, that the judge did not show up, particularly as we were told he was very reliable?

A week later, I was strolling through the local museum with my daughter. We began our visit in the oriental section. In one of the cases was a beautiful silk ceremonial wedding robe, several centuries old. It was covered with images of cranes. The notice read: "Cranes are a symbol of lasting happiness and good fortune in marriage." I was again deeply moved by this epiphany, as if an ancient memory stirred in me.

But the story does not end here.

Just over two and a half years later, right after Thanksgiving, I received a phone call from my family that my youngest sister had died during her sleep, apparently of an epileptic seizure, a disorder she had suffered since her early teens. This news was quite a shock, for although we were not particularly close, and her life was filled with difficulties, she was only in her mid forties, and her death seemed premature. She had recently begun a new relationship and had found happiness for the first time in several years.

Two days following, I was driving my husband to the local airport. We had stopped briefly at a shopping center on the way. There on top of a tree, right on the edge of the shopping center, was a large white crane. We sat in the car and marveled at its strange appearance, as if at an apparition. Naturally, we recalled the two other times that the crane had made such a visit, and as we did so, the bird flew out of the tree, swooped over our car, and landed on top of another tree on the other side of the parking lot. While my husband ran his errand, I sat there and looked at the bird for twenty minutes and wondered at its presence.

I fell into a reverie in which I remembered my sister and some of the events of her life and our times together, some of which were bittersweet, some more painful. She was one of those individuals who, it always seemed to me, never quite made it all the way into this incarnation. She could be overly demanding and needy, yet at her best she had a certain kind of sweetness and a wonderful sense of humor. She also had a musical talent which, since her adolescence, had remained largely undeveloped. Above all, she was extremely intuitive, although this faculty never found a home in our all too rational world. So, like any undeveloped organ, it could possess her in a destructive and impulsive fashion, without regard for the sensitivities of relationship. In another time, she would have been helped to develop her psychic abilities, perhaps becoming a medial sort of woman with a deep relationship to the mysteries. But the overriding impression I had was that she was finally free of what for her, sadly, had been the burden of her body, and that she was now once again with my father in that world beyond this one.

She died shortly after 9/11. It was unusual times, those first uncanny months after the horrors of September 11th, and I could not escape the strange impression that in freeing herself my sister was helping to free others also.

⚮

The Great Awakening

Synchronicities are moments of epiphany that slow us down and bring us to the present moment. This slowing occurs not by *thinking* about the moment, but by directly experiencing another world in the ordinary one. In the moment of awakening to another order of reality, we recover the old idea of *kairos*, divine timing, the sense of union between the timeless and time-bound in the here and now. Future and past dissolve and our normally changing world is stilled by the penetration into our awareness of a still small voice and a feeling of time stretching out radially like a star. Feeling our own reality linked with a larger background Reality or Source eclipses history, helps restore the mysteries, and opens us to the sacred, to the complex subtleties of the wholeness of being. We recover mystical consciousness, not by some flight away from the body into a rarified spiritual sphere, but by deep immersion into the stuff of our lives embedded in nature, and by a deepening of the atmosphere all around us.

Attunement to the present moment and awareness that moments have qualities as well as moving along chronologically, also suggest that we need to be attuned to what specific quality is called for in the moment. Sometimes it might be a gentle response and sometimes it might be fierceness. It might be appropriate for me to be angry just now, or to confront you, or perhaps to be filled with grief. At other times, I should stop writing or talking, and go for a walk in the woods. Who knows who or what might be calling? In the new worldview that includes attention to synchronicity, we learn to tune in to the songline of moments and to become highly discriminatory about their "tunes," or at least to be open to this possibility. Then, instead of merely focusing on details, we expand our repertoire to include the Taoist "thinking in terms of the whole,"[15] which as Jung points out is a key to synchronistic consciousness.

Although synchronicities return us, almost immediately, back into the flow of ordinary time and space, we have been "in the twinkling of an eye" elsewhere, and this journey to the Other place invites a new way of expressing ourselves. This new voice is an experience of eros, a shamanic

---

15 C. G. Jung, *CW 8*, par. 924.

sensibility, a poetic awareness, and a metaphoric consciousness that recovers an Orphic presence. This Orphic presence recalls the mythic figure of Orpheus who as shaman-poet-lover was the only poet whom Plato allowed back into the city. Orpheus' songlines reawakened the sleeping soul to its cosmic destiny, which is why Plato excluded Orpheus from his banishment of the poets. When synchronicities awaken us to the songlines of our own souls, Orpheus is near.

With this new voice, there is no one truth, but a vision, an unveiling, a glimpse of something beyond our ordinary sphere. The sojourner is now invited to capture this elusive visitation, to reflect on it, find its possible meaning, and to express the almost impossible task of translating the invisible and dark intuition to visible form. There is a story to be told. The telling belongs to a language that involves feeling as well as thought, wisdom as well as common sense, ambiguity as well as clarity, image as well as sound, the irrational as well as the rational, speech as well as silence.

A New Archetypal Constellation: The Coniunctio, Union of Opposites, and the Figure of Eros/Sophia

I mentioned above, in Jung's account of Elijah, Salome and the serpent, about Jung's—and our own culture's—distrust and suppression of eros and the feminine. This has been brought to the forefront of our attention by the recent films about Sabina Spielrein, an early patient of Jung's, with whom he had an erotic, creative, and painful relationship, but whose story was lost and forgotten. Sabina was healed by the "talking cure." She trained to become a doctor, and became a creative force in the early psychoanalytic movement, providing inspiration for the theories of both Jung and Freud, but whose significant contributions were not acknowledged at that time. The energies of eros that erupted at the origins of depth psychology need to be acknowledged. This is the task of the twenty-first century. Synchronicites also signal the presence of eros. Synchronicities stop us in our tracks and our usual distinctions, power motives, endless thinking, and repetitive conflicts, are stilled by the intensity of feeling which allows the forces of Eros to flood consciousness. The transformation of our egos toward eros awareness to which these experiences lead us are also often accompanied with the powerful forces of longing—what the Greeks call *thumos*[16]—filling us with desire, eros, raw energies and appetites that fuel the soul's journey "as far as longing can reach"[17] and take us where we need to go. This longing is related to the power of our imaginations and the fulfillment of our creative possibilities.

With synchronicities, the primacy of reflective thought gives way to an emotional intensity structured by exposure to the irruption of Eros, that broad field of love that can foster a full range of experience from deep sorrow, rage, and loss, to the fullness of divine pleasure, joy, and bliss.

Yet Eros is seriously wounded in our modern-day culture. The Grail myth that erupted in the twelfth century, and is re-emerging again today speaks of this wound. The wound of the fisher king is a wound located in his thigh that does not heal, perpetuating the wasteland. The compassionate question, "What ails thee?"—a question that would release him from his suffering—is not yet being asked. At the point in the Grail story where Parzival is about to be knighted by King Arthur for his fighting accomplishments, he is met by a powerful woman, Cundrie, who comes riding into court on a mule. The aristocratic, royally dressed, highly educated ("spoke all languages...was on easy terms with...dialectic and geometry"), yet ugly (hair like boar's bristles, nose like a dog's and tusks jutting from her jaws) and "loathsome female" Cundrie—so ambivalently described in Wolfram's thirteenth century tale perhaps because she is inadequately honored in patriarchal cultures—is sorceress, healer, and Wise Old Woman, who humiliates Parzival.[18]

Cundrie draws attention to how the continued insistence on knightly conquests and the willful pursuit of warring aggression, to the exclusion of attention to suffering, love, relationship, bonding, and soul values—values associated with the discovery of the Grail, the alchemical lapis—marks a failure of dire proportions that will keep us trapped in the wasteland. There we will stay until our grief at our failures and our acknowledgement of how lost we truly are can humble us enough to begin the search for a more whole attitude to life, one that begins with the recognition of our own shadows, what we have neglected either by omission or deliberate commission.

---

16 Peter Kingsley, *Reality* (Inverness, CA: The Golden Sufi Center, 2003), p. 27.

17 *Ibid.*, p. 26.

18 Wolfram von Eschenbach, *Parzival* (London & New York: Penguin Classics, 1980), pp. 163–164.

We have been traitors to the heart, to a way of knowing and being that cannot be achieved by acts of will, or heroic pursuits. The failure to ask the right "question" is a failure of feeling. It is the presence of Sophia, who is present in the Cundrie figure, in images of the Black Madonna and, especially in our times, in the figure of Mary Magdalene with her associations to the Grail, who help shift our priorities toward the development of compassion and toward an imagination fuelled by our passion and vision. Cundrie and the Magdalene symbolize for us the divine feminine as High Priestess and Initiator into the divine mysteries where spirit is no longer divided from matter, but embodied as divine Eros in a sacred marriage of opposites.

The loss of the Grail is caused by a wounding to love, and its recovery is the most difficult task of all. It will be possible only through devotion to self-knowledge by asking the right question. We must claim the freedom to quest, each in our own way, into the wilderness and through our heartbreak, to find the highest and deepest value of all for our souls. The Grail story mirrors a story in heaven, one that describes a wounded god. The wounds from our conflicts will visit our children and grandchildren until a genuine evolutionary advance in consciousness and path to renewal is found. Synchronicities open us to a direct experience of this path to Eros/Sophia. They briefly expose us to the mystical and the numinous, through our connection not with some transcendent beyond, but with a transcendent now immanent in the world of nature. This Other world is here now, and such an experience has a deep impact on our bodies and our consciousness. It encourages us to take up the task of living an embodied life in the present moment, embraced as a vocation and expressed creatively.

By uniting soul with the natural world, relating the ego to a transcendent factor, and uniting the timeless and the time-bound, the synchronistic moment moves us boldly toward new formulations, allowing us full reign of our intuition, irrationality, our feelings. We can say those things we might not ordinarily dare to speak, and become a person at once both strange and yet so curiously familiar. We can recall how Jung's "scarab" patient was dislodged from the superficiality of her intellect to the depths of a new birth through a dream and a visitation, falling finally into the waters of initiation and transformation that belong to the geography of the soul. Likewise in my vision of the crane, the visit of this creature in such unlikely circumstances brought me to a reformulation of my marriage, the realization that my father was bestowing a blessing from the realm of the dead, and the intuition that my sister was perhaps assisting those others who, like her, had died so prematurely and unexpectedly in those Twin Towers.

In describing the union of individual consciousness with a transpersonal source, allowing possibilities of new unions based on difference as well as joining, Jung has suggested that we are held in a mystery "between Two." Within the mystery of the subtle psychophysical background world, the *unus mundus* field that holds the apparent opposites together in the field of Eros we embrace a new constellation, the archetype of the *coniunctio*, the Sacred Marriage of Opposites. Here, the image is no longer that of conflict, suggested by the two fishes swimming in opposite directions that characterizes the Christian aeon of Pisces. Rather, it is the figures of Eros/Sophia, whose complexity allows a stretch from the highest reaches of heaven to the darkest depths of hell, without splitting. Eros/Sophia holds the tension of union and separation, what we hold sacred and what we feel ashamed of.

Moving out of rational consciousness located in an historical frame based on linear time, with its focus on goals, achievements, ambitions, and aims, and with its emphasis on aggression over love, and ego desires over wisdom, synchronicities take us to a realm in which opposites reside together. Now we are momentarily, quite literally, in an Other world that brings dichotomies together and weaves them into a rich emotionally laden tapestry. Here we are outside ordinary time and space, fleetingly dipping into the *unus mundus* world where psyche and matter, body and soul are One in a differentiated harmony. Here the usual divisions of reality are both deeply felt and simultaneously transformed—nothing is left out, nothing is forgotten, but everything shifts. Something else has happened.

A new world is seeking to be born, quietly, invisibly, making its presence felt to those with eyes to see, ears to hear, a new worldview with a different kind of consciousness. Synchronicities draw our attention to one-off events, but these isolated and rare occurrences are also held within a larger context. The synchronistic field points toward a less certain and less predictable world, a world that is continually creating and being created, a world in which our affects, interests, intuitions, and irrationalities find a home. In fact, the irrational and impossible become the transformative moment. The irrational and impossible are, therefore, *psychologically* crucial. Such miraculous occurrences are required for our wholeness. The soul longs for such moments.

Synchronicities recover the songlines of the soul and often serve as those wake-up calls that aim to help us remember what we once knew but have forgotten. It could be that this psycho-cosmic reality is also expressing itself in the UFO phenomenon as well as in the annual appearance of crop circles, both of which seem to provide spontaneous and "impossible" examples of the Great Awakening. The fact that synchronicities point to a compromise in the normal experience of the time-space continuum indicates that under certain conditions there should be an "acceptable" view of the paranormal in general. Thousands of sightings of UFOs and reports of extraterrestrial contact as well as the amazing and mysterious Crop Circles—photographed and seen by untold numbers of people each year as well as the thousands that visit them—are good evidence for the fact that our ideas of reality are changing and that our Earth may be more "cosmopolitan" than we thought. We will turn to these anomalies in the following chapter.

Part Three

A New Emerging Myth:
Ufos and Crop Circles

Chapter Five

UFOs, Collective Synchronicities, and Transformation

If [flying saucers are] a rumour, then the apparition of discs must be a symbol
produced by the unconscious . . . . If [they are] a hard and concrete fact,
we are surely confronted with something thoroughly out of the way . . . .
The phenomenon of the saucers might even be both, rumour as well as fact.
In this case it would be what I call a synchronicity.[1]

A s we have seen, synchronicity plays a key role in Jung's later work. In the previous chapter I looked at the major characteristics and implications of synchronicity. On an individual level, synchronicities express that union of psyche and matter which is at the heart of Jung's studies in alchemy. The psychoid nature of the archetype is the foundation for this union and the opening to the imaginal world of the soul. With UFOs and their "incomprehensible nature" (as well as with Crop Circles), we move from individual experiences of synchronicity to synchronicities on a collective scale. In the move from individual to collective expressions of synchronicity, there are both similarities and differences in their characteristics which we will explore. A central feature, however, is that with UFO encounters there is an *intensification* of experience that engages both psyche and body in such a way that not only is consciousness changed but also matter. This transmutation of consciousness and matter leads to the experience of a psychophysical subtle body.

I   C. G. Jung, *Letters II, 1951–1961*, selected and edited by Gerhard Adler in collaboration with Aniela Jaffe, trans. R. F. C. Hull (Princeton, NJ: Princeton University Press, 1975), p. 3.

As Jung suggests in the subtitle to his essay on *"Flying Saucers,"* in *CW* 10, *Civilization in Transition*, UFOs as collective expressions of synchronicity are the signature of "a modern myth," a new story for the twenty-first century. This new story opens the imaginal world of the soul as a *mundus imaginalis*, an Other world. Synchronicities, UFOs and Crop Circles, which I explore in the next chapter, invite us to see the Earth and ourselves in a new way.

In my book *Eros and Chaos*, I began my initial and somewhat tentative reflections on my own UFO encounter, struggling to understand what might have happened to me on that strange night in May of 1989.[2] Since writing that material, I have continued to explore and dwell on what has been called (unfortunately, because of its negative connotations) the "abduction" phenomenon, seeking to deepen my insights, and to allow an ongoing creative engagement with these kinds of anomalies to inspire and educate me.

This chapter marks a further development of my own reflections and research, which have moved strongly in the direction of trying to articulate the coordinates of a new worldview that the multi-faceted and complex aspects of the encounter experience significantly and boldly draws to our attention. As Jung indicates, the appearance of UFOs coincides with the end of an era, and their disconcerting presence indicates how surely incomplete our knowledge is. We can see around us the dire consequences of flawed and inaccurate data about the state of our society and our world, perpetuated through disinformation, inadequate reporting, or not being willing to face "inconvenient truths." Unless we suffer from the arrogance of thinking that we already know everything there is to know, surely it should not be surprising (or at the very least we could entertain the notion), that the nature of reality, and consciousness itself, is evolving. In my view, a contemplation of the "flying saucers" phenomenon aids us in this adventure.

I have been fortunate during this time to have had many conversations with, and to have co-presented aspects of this material at conferences with the late Dr. John Mack. While a professor at Harvard, Mack conducted pioneering research with hundreds of what he preferred to call "experiencers," doing the careful work of taking them seriously and listening compassion-

---

2   Veronica Goodchild, *Eros and Chaos: The Sacred Mysteries and Dark Shadows of Love* (Lake Worth, FL: Nicolas-Hays, Inc., 2001), chapter 6.

ately to the actual accounts of those many individuals or couples who have had encounters with beings and crafts from what seems to be Other worlds, or perhaps even other dimensions of consciousness. His book, *Passport to the Cosmos*, was the first publication on this topic that finally made me feel less alone with what I had experienced. Significantly, when I first read it, I was delighted to see that Dr. Mack was already making the same connections between the encounter experience and, for example, shamanism and mysticism that I myself was beginning to make. In addition, I felt that I was also contributing other perspectives into this compelling material, drawn from my own insights and explorations, with help too from the work of Jung, Corbin and others.

There was one particular moment, however, following a presentation I gave at an international conference in Siena, Italy, that gave me the courage to proceed with this writing. It came about through a synchronicity that helped me to realize that I myself must approach this material not only from the perspective of a reflective mind, but also in union with the subtle field of complex emotions and feeling sensitivities that reach deeply into the core of my own being. I have found that only this kind of attitude honors the range and depth of direct experience to which most "experiencers" are exposed with such encounters. As with any profound religious or mystical experience, words are, in the end, inadequate to the task of translating the invisible, the impossible, and the unknowable into a form that can be communicated coherently to others. This should not prevent us, however, from making the attempt, as Jung suggests, to prepare ourselves—carefully and ethically—for the incomprehensible nature of the realities before us. We live in a time when unseen realms that challenge our rational and mechanistic principles—in both science and depth psychology—are leading us toward a new worldview.

Perhaps at the very least we might remain open to the mysteries of experience, to the question of how we know things, to the places in ourselves where we remain fixed in our opinions. We might also stay open to those areas where we find ourselves wanting to go beyond conventional positions, over the edge, over the borders of the known. The poet John Keats called this capacity "negative capability" and described it as the ability to remain "in uncertainties, mysteries, doubts, without any irritable reaching after fact and reason."[3] Rather than needing to solve problems rationally or explain things definitively —a peculiarly modern prejudice—we can allow ourselves to be initiated into uncertainties, into the irrational and intuitive depths of the unknown and unknowable mysteries, depths that nourish the soul's reality. We can learn to sit with experiences that push the envelope of the "possible," letting our understanding of them come to us with time. In Zen philosophy, this attempt to put aside our preconceptions and arrive at fresh insight is called a return to Beginner's Mind.

SYNCHRONICITY: AN EXAMPLE

Here is an account of my experience with synchronicity and the resulting shift in perspective it gave me. I was participating in an international seminar organized by F. David Peat at The Pari Centre near Siena, Italy, entitled "New Paradigms of Reality" and had been asked to tell the group about my UFO experience. Interestingly, at the end of my story, the electricity failed in the building we were in, and in the ensuing confusion to regain light and heat, the thread of my story was lost, so we moved on to other things. Reflecting later on this strange coincidence, I realized that I was telling my tale in a context that was not appropriate to its contents. A group of people whom I did not know, with whom I had no previous history, had asked me to share an account which had had a significant impact on my life, challenging everything I knew about my prevailing worldview and sense of reality. Since this event had initiated a radical change in my own life, it had been exceedingly difficult at the time to speak about it with others who—at best—had not known how to respond. After speaking so frankly at the conference, I was left with an uneasy feeling that did not sit well with me. Once again, I felt terribly exposed in a setting with others I did not know and whose response I could not gauge. Did they think I was mad or making something up? Was I giving voice to events of which they themselves had knowledge? It was certainly not their fault that I felt so uncomfortable; I should not have been so naïve, and I should have been more protective of myself.

Worldviews hold the integrity of the psyche together. Events that undermine or destroy our worldview—be they a profound loss or grief, or

---

3   Letter to George and Thomas Keats, 21 December 1817.

an incomprehensible or awesome *something*—can undo us and lead us into dissolution, chaos, and psychic death. Alchemy speaks of the *nigredo*, mysticism of the dark night of the soul, and Zen of the "the great death." The disillusionment and *mortificatio*, "psychological death," that accompany the dissolution of images of self, other, world, and culture cannot be underestimated nor treated lightly. These processes challenge our character and reach deeply into our psychic and physical resources in ways that led Jung to believe that neither necessity nor convenience by themselves were adequate for the task of transformation. For the work of transformation conscience and "vocation" were also needed. For Jung, true transformation occurs only when we really have no choice in the matter because we have been addressed by the voice of a god, or by a power or *daimon* that makes a claim on us.

When I addressed the participants in the Siena, Italy, conference, I did not know, beyond their curiosity, where the group stood on these delicate matters, nor into what deep waters their life circumstances had led them. Telling certain stories requires a circle of psychic protection and the possibility for deeply receptive listening, not merely the conditions of ordinary conversation.

The day following my presentation at the conference, I was sitting on a veranda looking out on the lovely spring country landscape of Tuscany, feeling surrounded by presences, as if I could "see into" the life force of the virgin green hills and olive groves spread out before me, could sense the lively spirits of the place, of the earth and of the clouds, and could dance to their unheard tunes as they welcomed the slow renewal of life after the long and protracted winter cold of that year. The beauty of the morning was almost too much to bear. My husband, who was quietly sitting with me, asked again about my UFO encounter. This time a great sadness overtook me as I deeply felt, once again, how difficult it had been to have this uncanny experience and to keep it secret for so many years simply because it was impossible to communicate with most people about something that had no acceptance in consensual reality, in our collective view of the world. It gradually dawned on me as I sat quietly, that although I had kept silent for so long, then finally made an attempt to come to grips with my UFO encounter in my writing and teaching, there was a dimension to the experience that I had not yet allowed to come fully into my awareness.

With that dawning thought, an epiphany emerged out of the unseen background world, infusing every cell in my body, and I realized that the UFO encounter had been an initiation, a moment of change. This initiation had filled me with a profound feeling of being addressed by a reality that was creating an irrevocable shift in my life. Somehow I knew that when the shock waves of this change had fully penetrated, nothing would ever really be the same again. This moment on the veranda in Tuscany became the moment when those shock waves found a true home in my body. Finally, I could embrace more fully what had happened to me because of my husband's quiet and caring inquiry. The atmosphere between us suddenly softened and invisible walls of protection dissolved. I felt all at once as if my beloved's ability to "truly see" me in this moment healed all the pain of the separation and terrible isolation that my UFO encounter had created. Now I had to commit to further exploration of the knowledge that had been given to me. This ability to commit arose out of the field of love that had, in that unexpected moment, reshuffled everything again, bringing a kind of renewal into my body. A new level of support for the adventure infiltrated my system, and I began to sense the courage to proceed even with all the unknowns that were still present, the parts of the experience that I could not yet remember.

One of my most significant realizations was that, from now on, I could only tell my story in ritual space, because only ritual space provides the appropriate domain for tales of the sacred, tales of the numinous, tales of the gods and goddesses. In this domain we are protected because we have declared our intent to the unseen presences and invisible guides of the soul to tell the truth, our truth. For this reason, they seem to provide the necessary support and containing Presence we need to "safely" share our story. Too, in ritual space there is caring regard for the reality of the deep psyche and its emotional effects. This involves sensitivity toward the feeling tone of a story and its archetypal and symbolic resonances that work directly on the core of our being, and should not be interrupted by premature leaps of rational thinking, doubt, interpretation, or analysis.

The soul appreciates mysteries far beyond the reasoning mind, and we need space for the necessary silence in which these mysteries can work their numinous effects on us. Not to embrace this sensitivity can result in a kind of backlash in which feelings are wounded, and an archetypal significance or healing potential can be missed. Our interpretations and understandings might perhaps be shared with caution, with an attunement to the proper timing and with the knowledge that such commentaries can remove or separate us from direct experience. This separation can feel destructive of our experience. We need to take time to understand "incomprehensible" events, or to seek help in interpreting them. Only when we can slow down, experiencing the sensitivity of feeling that comes with a calm atmosphere, can we consciously attune ourselves to these sensitivities.

Moreover, in his essay "Flying Saucers: A Modern Myth of Things Seen in the Skies," Jung cautions that psychological explanations of what people are seeing when they report a UFO sighting do not exhaust the value and significance of these living symbols whose mythological character may not be immediately recognized and, therefore, easily overlooked. The psyche often provides anticipatory and preparatory dreams whose symbolic language we may not understand without, for example, historical amplifications, or indeed until much later in life. So, too, with UFO encounters. Furthermore, the deeply spiritual quality of archetypal events, such as the persistent "rumors" surrounding UFO sightings, work on us and stimulate deeper reflection about them until we discover what future developments are being prepared in the unconscious psyche of modern humanity and what these events may mean. Jung writes:

> It depends on us whether we help coming events to birth by understanding them, and reinforce their healing effect, or whether we repress them with our prejudices, narrow-mindedness and ignorance, thus turning their effect into its opposite, into poison and destruction.[4]

It is with this type of feeling sensibility and attempt to understand that I write about the UFO encounter and its potential relationship to the creation of the subtle body and the exploration of subtle worlds. I also do this with the hope of furthering the evolution of reality and consciousness toward greater wisdom. Although this chapter deals with the UFO phenomenon, it is important to recall that the Crop Circle mysteries, the

---

4   C. G. Jung, *CW* 10, par. 731.

Marian apparitions, Out-of-Body and Near-Death Experience Research, Holotropic Breath Work opening to multiple levels of consciousness, spontaneous shamanic or mystical experiences, waking visions or certain types of vivid dreams—indeed, any paranormal event that hints at the permeable "barrier" between the unseen world and our material world—belong to the same category of events. Since Jung's death, paranormal events have been increasingly studied by others. These anomalies are drawing our attention to a strange and inexplicable reality, to the subtle depths of the world that are brimming with psychic life. Although we do not fully understand their significance, we need to take them seriously and prepare ourselves for them.

Since the end of the Second World War in 1945 and the dropping of the atomic bomb, which may in itself be significant, reports of UFO sightings and extraterrestrial or close encounters have increased at a considerable pace. Many publications view these strange phenomena through the lens of the empirical scientific paradigm, focusing on whether they are physically real or not, hoping to move conclusively toward confirming or debunking the reports. Though governments have tended to deny, ridicule, or explain away empirical-based accounts (particularly in the U.S. though not so much in other countries, for example, Russia, Mexico and some countries in South America), most serious researchers suggest that "alien" intelligent life forms have been here on Earth or visiting Earth since long before humanity arrived. Indeed, some writers suggest "their being here actually made our being here possible."[5] In other words, the purpose of human life to experience the highest spiritual states while in a physical body was achieved with the involvement of many extra-terrestrial families. Moreover, it is not at all uncommon for individuals to feel—especially in deeply relaxed states such as meditation—that they did not originate here on this planet but that they came from elsewhere.

My approach to these phenomena is to view them from the point of view of those numerous credible witnesses who have actually experienced

5   See Richard Leviton, *Signs on the Earth: Deciphering the Message of Virgin Mary Apparitions, UFO Encounters, and Crop Circles* (Charlottesville, VA: Hampton Roads Publishing, 2005), chapter 5, pp. 127ff. This is an excellent book rich in material on the subtle geography of our Earth and its galactic connection, which I only came to late in my own writing. Uncannily the themes are very similar to my own although Leviton writes as a clairvoyant and geomancer, which I am not, so he adds many details from these perspectives.

these complex anomalous encounters, as well as from the point of view of Jung's "quantum" psychology. Military, Pentagon, and defense personnel as well as astronauts, astronomers, and politicians have increasingly come forward to speak about their UFO sightings or encounter experiences. For example, Jimmy Carter saw a craft and when he was President sought to learn more about the phenomenon. There is evidence that other Presidents (including Truman and Eisenhower in the 1950s and Reagan when he was still an actor) have seen crafts and/or met with star-being races. Rep. Dennis Kucinich of Ohio had a close encounter and was very moved by it. He describes how the smell of roses drew him out on a balcony at the then home of Shirley MacLaine in Washington State where, when he looked up he saw a gigantic triangular craft, quiet and watching him. It hovered and then sped away at an unimaginable speed. Kucinich said he felt a connection in his heart and heard directions in his mind.[6]

---

6   Shirley MacClaine, *Sage-ing While Age-ing* (New York: Atria Books, 2008), pp. 115–181, is full of interesting details about the UFO/ET phenomenon and the names of individuals in prominent government and military, etc. positions who have been involved with this reality. Please also see www.spiritofmaat.com, which has posted online the book *The Report on Unidentified Flying Objects* by Edward J. Ruppelt, former head of the Air Force investigation code-named "Project Blue Book," that studied UFOs beginning in 1947. This is the original evidence that proves conclusively that the United States Government has engaged in an ET and UFO coverup since June 24, 1947 until the present.

    During the writing of this chapter on UFOs, there have been some well-publicized UFO sightings. For example, on Wednesday, May 12, 2004, on CNN television in Europe, at the height of atrocities in Iraq—prison inmate abuse by U.S. forces was already in the headlines, and Nicholas Berg's execution had just been announced—the sighting of 11 UFOs by the Mexican air force was reported. I am not sure if all these 11 were visible to the naked eye. Apparently the sighting had happened two months previously in March, and was only now being publicly disclosed. According to the news account, air force planes detected only 3 of the 11 unidentified flying objects on radar. The video photos on TV showed just six lights "flying" in what appeared to be a coherently patterned formation. Apparently, these six lights were observed when the pilots turned on the infra-red cameras on their planes. The report said that when the air force pilots had chased the "objects," the lights had surrounded their planes and the pilots were quite alarmed. When the pilots called off their pursuit, the lights disappeared. The reporting of this UFO event on public television as part of the regular news and not part of some sensational program on UFOs (it was actually part of a weather report!) seems significant to me. I was on sabbatical leave in Italy at the time, involved in writing a first draft of this chapter, when I happened to see the news at the moment when the story was being told. This in itself was a little odd, as I did not have television in the village I was staying in, but on this day I was on a week's drive through Umbria and was spending the night in a hotel with one English speaking channel on the room TV! It was therefore personally significant to me as well, something of a synchronicity itself. I do not know if this major sighting was also reported on U.S. television.

    More recently there have been two major sightings. On January 1, 2007, NPR reported a UFO sighting by credible witnesses, United Airlines employees, at O'Hare Airport in Chicago. The story was reported in the Chicago *Tribune*. It had happened in early November 2006. Melissa Block interviewed the reporter.

Public opinion via Gallup polls also seems to be in favor of the idea of life on other planets and belief in UFOs visiting earth. France and Great Britain have made their UFO files available to the public. On a cultural level, ETs are popular in movies, TV shows and commercials. Moreover, certain geographical areas such as the Hudson River Valley in New York State or Topanga Canyon near Los Angeles are considered to be hot-spot UFO venues. And we have already seen how evidence for the energy or auric field of human beings as well as evidence for the subtle body world and its landscapes and denizens is by no means a recent idea. Visionaries and geomancers who study Earth's visionary and subtle geography have long spoken of ourselves and our planet as possessing a multi-dimensional reality.

So I am less interested in "proving" that UFOs exist—though in fact the evidence seems overwhelmingly to support their presence—and more interested in trying to understand how their presence relates to a new vision of reality unfolding in our times. In this context, I shall limit myself to a consideration of those tales in which some type of spiritual insight or transformation was felt to occur, either at the time of the encounter and/or later, since merely "seeing lights in the sky," as interesting as that might be, does not necessarily transform anything in the human heart, just as going to church or attending synagogue does not automatically make one grow spiritually. I relate my own UFO encounter in chapter 11, "Missing Time and Mystical Cities," in Part Four of this book, *Mystical Cities and Healing Sanctuaries* as the focus of my own story is the four or five hours of "missing time" associated with it.

A year later, on January 16, 2008, there were multiple witness sightings of a UFO near Stephenville, Texas. A "Larry King Live" program on this UFO event was scheduled soon afterwards. Moreover, I just received an email from a friend alerting me to the following, posted on Ufodigest.com on February 13, 2008. "Source Reveals Secret UFO Meeting at U.N.," by Michael E. Salla, Ph.D. He writes: "I received the following email from two trusted colleagues (Clay and Shawn Pickering) regarding a reliable source informing them that a secret meeting occurred yesterday morning (Feb 12) at the New York office of the United Nations concerning the recent spate of UFO sightings. It appears that a number of nation states are concerned about the impact of increased UFO sightings and wish to be briefed about what is happening. Their source, who currently works in the diplomatic corps, had to travel for an early morning off the record meeting at the UN. Their source revealed that a secret UFO working group exists that is authorizing the release of such information to the public, in an effort to acclimate others to what is about to unfold. A date of 2013 was given as the time for official disclosure and/or when extraterrestrials show up in an unambiguous way. In the interim there will be acclimation related releases of information. Importantly, the source revealed that the events leading up to official disclosure will involve more ethically oriented extraterrestrials, and they will not pose a military threat to the world.'" It seems as if there is a gradual acceptance of UFOs emerging in the collective.

Richard Leviton's Visionary Experience

Clairvoyant and visionary geomancer, Richard Leviton, describes observing a group of Pleiadians at Fajada Butte (the Navajos call it "Holy Rock") in Chaco Canyon, New Mexico, who were phasing in and out of human-like forms alternately becoming pillars of light. Leviton writes that they were not really inside the rock but more accurately were in the *same place* but at one or two dimensions removed from the stone. He says they were inserting what he calls "time caves or wombs" in a complex light matrix situated inside a blue crystalline basin. They were working holographically involving many dimensions and time tracks that included both the Earth's geomantic web and other solar systems throughout the galaxy. A time cave, according to Leviton, is like a hollowed-out space filled with time, a galactic uterus in which life can evolve. When the Anasazi (Navajo for "Old Ones"), an enigmatic and sophisticated religious culture, inhabited Chaco Canyon (around 1020–1220 A.D.) they had access to this time portal at certain points. Time was viewed not as a straight line but as both vertical and horizontal so that you could witness the multiple ripples that any event creates. What was the meaning of this, Leviton asks? "Interaction with the time portal [there are 45 on Earth] enables you to consolidate all your time bodies—the residues of previous lives lived in Earth time—into a wisdom body." The Pleiadians are our mentors in this focusing and consolidation of our wisdom essence spread out over the vast terrain of our past lives.[7]

Dr. Steven Greer's Close Encounter

Though much attention has been given to forced and traumatizing abduction accounts by the widely recognized large-headed, dark almond-eyed alien Grays popularized, for example, in Whitley Streiber's *Communion: A True Story* (1987), these are by no means the only ET family here. Many

---

7   Leviton, *ibid.*, pp. 157–158. Also, a personal communication from my editor, Joy Parker: the Mayan Indians believed in the special "quality" of specific elements of time and planned their activities, such as war, building temples, traveling, etc., according to this belief. That was one of the reasons why they had so many interlocking cyclical calendars—so that they could compare the quality of a moment in history of a past beneficial event with the present day. In the modern traditional Mayan villages, the role of looking at the quality of time and choosing when to act is handled by diviner/advisors known as "day keepers."

"abductions" are now considered epiphanic spiritual initiations. In 1990, Dr. Steven Greer, a medical doctor and a respected researcher and authority on Extraterrestrial Contact, decided to revisit some encounter experiences he had had twenty years earlier as a college student and practitioner of transcendental meditation. As he recounts, one day he decided to perform the protocol for close encounter contact that he had developed telepathically with ETs on board a space ship some two decades earlier. While meditating, he showed them precisely where he was located in Asheville, North Carolina, then he fell asleep. He writes:

> I woke up with a beautiful craft semi-materialized out in the front yard of the house, in the wee hours of the morning, and found myself consciously floated on board. We were all in a quasi-materialized astral state, and as we floated out and went out into space I could look back and see the beautiful earth receding away, floating in infinity.[8]

Greer continues that, as they moved away from earth, he saw enormous space ships hovering silently over what appeared to be the moon, discharging large amounts of magenta colored plasma toward its surface. He was told by the ETs that these craft were making preparations for the coming decade. As they continued further out into the solar system, the ship became translucent, invisible yet somehow still surrounding him. He notes that at this point his consciousness transcended into unity consciousness: "I was infinitely awake and the entire cosmos was awake and perfectly synchronized as one." As he looked around at the dark empty space between the planets and stars, he could see fields of energy and light. He sensed that this was the infinite Mind of God from which the material cosmos emerges.

This experience of unity consciousness recalls astronaut Edgar Mitchell's account of returning from his moon landing. He had a mystical and ecstatic experience of "samadhi" (enlightenment) in outer space. This visionary experience created an opening of his inner heart in which he realized his inter-connective unity with the sun, the moon, and the stars, perceiving himself and them as merely different expressions of a seething coherence

---

8   Steven Greer, *Hidden Truth Forbidden Knowledge* (Crozet, VA: Crossing Point, 2006), p. 74.

of energy. Following this experience, which changed his life forever, Mitchell committed himself to uncovering the connections between his scientific training (which now seemed to present an incomplete picture of the world) and his mystical experience. First he began to explore the religious traditions of the world, and then he created the Institute of Noetic Sciences, an organization whose mission is to "advance the science of consciousness and human experience to serve individual and collective transformation," which continues to pursue this type of research on the confluence of science and spirituality. Edgar Mitchell also believes that there is strong evidence that ETs are here and that we are being visited.

As Greer gazed at each planet, he could directly perceive that each one had a "specific tone and personality," a song that he would have been able to recreate, had he been more musically inclined. He observed that Earth was "definitely female," with a very beautiful musical note emanating from her. Moreover, the Earth communicated to him an "infinite and crushing... love," which was so powerful that, for years, he could not tell this story without weeping. However, he also felt a melancholic sadness for "the damage being done to her and the suffering of humanity upon her." Greer states that this was one of the most emotional and moving experiences of his life. His heart chakra opened fully and "an enormous love and celestial perception dawned...all things [were] suffused in love.... I heard all the distant worlds, every star and planet and the entire creation, singing as one—like a trillion tones blended into the one pure tone of the creation."[9]

By blending the songline of his soul with the songline of the cosmos, Greer realized that the music of the spheres is a reality, and that within the tone of the divine, we can transcend to the infinity of cosmic Being. He remarks that he stayed in this state for what seemed like an eternity. Finally, profoundly transformed and with this unity consciousness vibrating through him, he found himself back in his bedroom where he could see the glow of the craft still outside the window.

Shortly thereafter Dr. Greer formed CSETI, The Center for the Study of Extraterrestrial Intelligence, and the Close Encounters of the Fifth Kind (CE-5) Initiative, which is designed to create an "interplanetary ambassador

---

9   *Ibid.*, p. 75.

program" whereby "humans deliberately welcome and make contact with extraterrestrial people by using a set of protocols to vector them into an area to interact with them."[10] He has also been active in pursuing the need for disclosure of documented human/ET contacts throughout the world and has reported numerous interviews with top government and military officials who know firsthand of this ET contact. These can be seen in his film, *The Disclosure Project*.[11]

There is, however, relatively little material on UFOs from the point of view of Jung's psychology. Even less evident, as far as I know, are references to Jung's thoughts on these "incomprehensibles" in relation to his hints about the necessity to reflect on identifying the mythic, archetypal, and psychological implications of the change from the Age of Pisces to the Age of Aquarius.[12] In the introductory paragraph to his "Flying Saucers" essay, Jung suggests that UFOs signal, or even possibly are,

> Manifestations of psychic changes which always appear at the end of one Platonic month [a two thousand-year astrological shift] and at the beginning of another. Apparently they are changes in the constellation of psychic dominants, of the archetypes, or "gods" as they used to be called, which bring about, or accompany, long-lasting transformations of the collective psyche.[13]

Jung alerts us here to the *psychic consequences* of an astrological change from Pisces to Aquarius, a change that also gives rise to a transformation of the god-image or archetypal dominants. When he says it is not "presumption" but his "conscience" as a doctor that drives him to take the risk of writing about such things, he is implying that depth psychologists like myself have an ethical obligation to attend to and prepare humanity for this evolution in consciousness taking place in the collective psyche. UFOs belong to those incomprehensible "coming events" that seem to be ushering in that evolution in

---

10 *Ibid.*, p. 78.

11 See Steven Greer's website: www.cseti.org; and an article by him at www.earthportals.com.

12 Aniela Jaffe in *Jung's Last Years and Other Essays* (Dallas, TX: Spring, 1984) p. 45, implies that synchronicity requires a new worldview but does not elaborate beyond summarizing Jung's writings. Robert Hopke, in *A Guided Tour of the Collected Works of C. G. Jung* (Boston & London: Shambhala, 1999), p. 152, also remarks how Jungian authors have not further developed Jung's ideas on UFOs.

13 C. G. Jung, *CW* 10, par. 589.

consciousness. They point to an intensely felt subtle body reality that the true imagination experiences, and the body registers as both psychical and physical.

Here we can remind ourselves of Jung's observation that both the psyche and the subatomic world of quantum mechanics produce phenomena that point to a compromise within the space-time continuum. We might conjecture from this that not only might the psyche and the quantum world be two aspects of the same thing, but also that UFO events belong to the subatomic world and, hence, to those subtle domains where spirit and matter are transmuting back and forth, giving us felt expressions of the psychoid archetype, and a new feeling for the alchemical belief that "as above so below."

As with synchronicity, this union of psyche and matter, which can take us to deeply altered states of reality, as evidenced by Richard Leviton's and Steven Greer's accounts above, again indicates the constellation of the archetype of the *coniunctio* (Sacred Marriage) on a collective level. I have already noted that the symbol of the Ouroborus, the snake that holds its own tail in its mouth, is an alchemical image of this union of eternity and cosmos. And again, the figure of Eros/Sophia is at the center of this new subtle union— indeed, Leviton explicitly mentions the Pleiadian assistance in the creation of our wisdom body—bringing love and its shadows and a deep imaginal consciousness into a viable whole. In his encounter, Greer emphasizes his experience of profound feelings of cosmic love as the pulse of creation, as well as the sorrows of what we are doing to each other and to Earth.

Furthermore, I suggest that "other beings" often encountered in UFO events are heralds of a new living myth who are seeking to help us renew our vision of the world, expand our awareness of other dimensions, and help us remember that we are part of a much wider galactic community. Too, I contend that these representatives of the Invisible worlds and the *mundus imaginalis* are here as our guides and for the purposes of initiation, helping us to prepare for the deep changes that are upon us, aiding us in healing our pain and our environmental collapse, and leading us toward a deeper compassionate gnosis of the heart, emblematic of the union of spirituality and sexuality, image and instinct.

In this sense, these experiences have a long and venerable history on our planet. They can be seen to belong to indigenous and shamanic cultures, which have visionary and mystical traditions, as well as to the death-and-rebirth mystery traditions that have always belonged to the esoteric and Gnostic side of our religion and culture, in both the East and the West. Like Jungian analyst and quantum physicist, Arnold Mindell, I want to draw attention to how a profound change in our worldview is leading us, as he writes in his book *Quantum Mind*, "over the Edge to the Universe," until our extraterrestrial and other dimensional encounters become more familiar to us.

Jung and UFOs as Collective Synchronicities

In his writings, Jung often humorously lamented his interest in the odd. In a letter on October 17, 1957, to Martin Flinker, head of the Librairie Francaise et Etrangere in Paris, who had asked Jung what he was working on now, Jung acknowledged his intrigue with "what is off the beaten track and is usually ridiculed or simply shrugged off with a joke,"[14] and wrote that he was interpreting the myths surrounding the reports of UFO phenomena that he had studied for many years. He adds that his UFO interests were another expression of his life-long attention to the manifestation of archetypal forms in all of life (biology, physics, art, mythology and parapsychology, as well as in the symptoms and dreams of individuals), adding: "The intimation of forms hovering in the background not in itself knowable gives life the depth which, it seems to me, makes it worth living." In other words, as Leviton indicates, ETs and UFOs are here to help us risk transforming our awareness to soulful depths of imagination and creativity.

Throughout his life Jung had been fascinated with the marginalized, the heretical, the idiosyncratic, and those things likely to be overlooked or dismissed in order to find the mysterious depths of meaning for which the human soul searches. In fact, Jung felt that it took heretics—a word that has come to have negative connotations but that actually means those who are "able to choose," conscious beings, in other words—to move our psychological understanding forward.[15] From this daring perspective, Jung considered the possibility that synchronicities were not only isolated, unpredictable events that happened to individuals alone, but that they were occurring on a collective level in the form of the "flying saucers" phenomena.

---

14 C. G. Jung, *Letters 11*, 1975, p. 397.
15 See also Jung, *CW 18*, par. 1539: "The reformers and great religious geniuses were heretics."

Jung makes the suggestion that UFOs are more than just projections of the collective unconscious in a more or less *mandala* form, a circular or cylindrical pattern representing a living symbol of compensation in a world that is increasingly disoriented and divided. He also saw them as actual physical facts, due to the measured traces of their presence on radar screens. Therefore, these "sightings" would be an example of synchronicity, an acausal meaningful confluence of both psychic and physical reality in a world desperately in need of transformation and spiritual awakening.

Jung had already remarked on the relationship between synchronicity and activated archetypes due to an intensification of feeling (and the associated move out of rational consciousness) related to key important moments in life. In this context, the "key moment" is a collective and cultural one, even cross-cultural. The constellating archetypes belong to the evolution of consciousness—the "dying" and "renewal" of archetypal constellations—related to a shift in the ages. This transition signals long-lasting changes in the collective psyche, as well as creating the associated (synchronistic) change in our cultural myth. Jung suggests that the universal phenomenon of UFOs, therefore, pointed to the activation and visibility of a "living myth," sparks or fragments of a new story, of a new worldview, that was coming into being right in front of our eyes. As with individual synchronicities, this cultural "psychophysical parallelism" as he calls it, invites us to realize something new, and to come up with a creative response to the changes before us. In this way, we can begin to prepare ourselves for the emerging "incomprehensible." John Mack's and Stephen Greer's work, for example, represents such a creative response, as does the research of those like Michael Glickman, John Martineau, Colin Andrews, Karen and Steve Alexander, Freddy Silva, Andy Thomas, Lucy Pringle and others, who wonder deeply about the crop circle phenomena which, like UFOs, are harbingers of a radical change in our cultural myth. Moreover, all those who in individual ways are contributing to the new vision of reality constellating in our midst (such as Barbara Marx Hubbard, for example) are part of this cultural creative change. Jung elaborates further on the new myth and its cultural expression by looking back in history.

UFOs and Cultural-Historical Considerations

In *Memories, Dreams, Reflections*, a few paragraphs after he has spoken about his alchemical vision of Christ, Jung hints at this relationship between archetypal constellations and the specific historical persons and events that become appropriate carriers of the transpersonal energies as they incarnate into time and space.[16] The alchemical vision, by drawing Jung's attention to the world soul alive in everything, led him both forward and backward; forward in terms of becoming more aware of the soul in matter and the matter in soul, and backwards regarding the incompleteness of the Christian myth, associated with the image of the fish (symbolic of unconsciousness) and the *imitatio*, imitation of Christ. This myth found its expression in faith and belief and in the creation of institutional religious systems (unconsciousness in general) rather than from gaining personal knowledge through experience of a transcendent reality.

UFOs can perhaps now be regarded as a collective alchemical vision uniting psyche and matter and initiating our direct experience of a transcendent reality. The "green gold" of Jung's vision is an expression of the world soul—*anima mundi*—and is also carried by the symbol in alchemy of the giant figure of the Anthropos, a kind of "perfect being" who animates the whole cosmos. Jung comments that this ancient archetypal image of the Self—also to be found in Jewish, Egyptian, and Gnostic thought—was given expression in the idea of the Son of Man or Son of God fantasies, already constellated in the zeitgeist of the beginning Christian era. This "perfect being" was "condensed" in Jesus, who must have been of exceptional character to represent the unconscious expectations of the age so well. These expectations reflected the unconscious hope for a spiritual value to prevail against the deified Augustus, ruler of this world. Jung goes on to say how we today are at precisely the same crisis.

Jung writes that the pressing issue of a spiritual life embodying values and meaning becomes central when individuals are threatened by personal dissolution in a predominantly materialistic culture, in other words, when they are robbed of their cultural independence and spiritual autonomy. This was true at the beginning of the Christian era with the "crushing power of

16 C. G. Jung, *Memories, Dreams, Reflections*, p. 211ff.

Rome" bearing down on the people of the empire. It is now also relevant for our own times as individuals hope for the Second Coming of Christ or express other apocalyptic fantasies or expectations of redemption.

The difference in the unconscious expression of this problem is that, according to Jung, the Son of Man fantasies prevalent before the emergence of the Christ figure have become replaced with symbols appropriate to the technological age. These symbols include the worldwide extraterrestrial rumors and, since Jung, the Marian visions, crop circles, and all kinds of anomalous experiences, along with the associated redemption fantasies or expectations that often accrue to these "sightings."[17] Central to the essence of Christianity, alchemy, and to contemporary times is the mystery of incarnation, how God becomes human (Christianity), and how humans become divine. The post Christian challenge today is to move beyond *imitatio*, belief, to *creatio continua*, self-realization and the birth of the divine within (individuation) and an ongoing creative life.

The shadow aspect, possession by this same UFO/Anthropos/Self archetypal content, is what is being lived out in the religious and ideological wars of today and in the pressure toward increasing impersonal "globalization" that obliterates cultural and individual differences. Perhaps this shadow aspect is present in the creation and terrible use of the atomic bomb in 1945. $E = MC^2$ does point to the psyche-matter connection in so far as it indicates the fact that matter is energy. And while its destructive use has been all too disturbingly apparent, it has awakened us to these dangers, which might support an upwelling of new creative attitudes about matter, energy, psyche and spirit. Perhaps, though, until we can accept the UFO as a new creation, we will continue to birth destructive creations. In *Mysterium Coniunctionis* (CW 14), Jung comments on the devastating effects of the "death" of the old gods and the outpouring of chaos, "lust for murder on a collective scale," that ensues when the task of making conscious again the "eternal images" in the human soul is not realized. He writes presciently:

Once the symptoms are really outside in some form of sociopolitical insanity, it is impossible to convince anybody that the conflict is

17 See, for example, James R. Lewis (Ed.), *The Gods Have Landed: New Religions from Other Worlds* (Albany, NY: SUNY Press, 1995) for this literalizing or fundamentalist tendency in relation to UFO phenomenon.

in the psyche of every individual, since he is now quite sure where his enemy is …. When [the individual] no longer knows by what his soul is sustained, the potential of the unconscious is increased and takes the lead. Desirousness overpowers him, and illusory goals set up in the place of the eternal images excite his greed.[18]

It is not surprising, therefore, that after the opening paragraphs of Jung's "Flying Saucers" essay, he focuses on the necessity for individuation "as the answer" to the spiritual hunger of humankind threatened with dissolution in the face of mass material mindedness that characterizes our times. From that perspective, Jung resorts primarily to psychological interpretations of the UFO phenomenon. In this regard, Jung speaks of UFOs as representations of the *anima*[19] (images of the strangeness of the collective unconscious, and the bearer of the Grail) assisting us in cultivating our relationship to the mysteries of life. Further, he sees them as symbols of the archetype of the Self, our numinous energies emerging at a time of disorientation and collapse.[20] In other words, during the Age of Aquarius, our task is a psychological one: to become aware of the Self/Anthropos/UFO as the larger personality within each of us and to realize its cosmic significance as that which gives us a feeling of being united to all humankind, which von Franz calls "inter-human Eros."[21]

The new alchemical myth of the union of matter and psyche leads us in the direction therefore of individuation and self-realization, of gnosis as direct knowledge of the eternal images, and in this endeavor makes us conscious of the eros wound of Christianity, a wound given creative expression by the Grail legend. The Grail myth, which is also associated with alchemy, tells us the "cure" of the Fisher King is related to the central alchemical theme of the *coniunctio*, the conscious realization of the union of instinct and archetype, sexuality and spirituality, cosmos and psyche. This realization leads to the establishment of a new third element, the subtle or resurrection body, the soul in matter, an achievement of compassion through *imaginatio*

---

18 C. G. Jung, *CW 14*, par. 510.
19 C. G. Jung, *CW 10*, p. 376, See Dream and par. 713ff for commentary.
20 *Ibid.*, pars. 619ff, 779.
21 Marie-Louise von Franz, *Jung His Myth in Our Time* (New York: Putnam's Sons for the C. G. Jung Foundation for Analytical Psychology, 1975), p. 138.

SONGLINES OF THE SOUL

vera, a development requiring our participation and, hence, the necessity for a continuing creation based on personal experience rather than just an imitation of Christ. Jung saw that the history of Christianity during the two thousand years of Pisces had not yet achieved its promise; it had remained too one-sidedly spiritual and had primarily lived out its shadow in extraverted aggression, not in the "higher value" of personal spiritual integrity, wisdom and love. In fact, the love that Christianity talked about, though it also found a flowering in the lives of twelfth century mystics such as Hildegard of Bingen, remained largely unconscious, certainly on the collective level and remains a challenging task for us today.

"Flying Saucers" and Jung's Doubt

Jung begins "Flying Saucers" with the bold promise to interpret the psychological consequences of "incomprehensible coming events" related to a whole new age—a new worldview and god-image—on planet Earth. However, the "Flying Saucers" essay disappoints in the end because, although Jung concludes that the erratic and unpredictable appearance and disappearance of UFOs is connected with alchemical images of mercurial transformations of matter into spirit and vice versa, he does not adequately pursue the implications of his opening remarks about the possibilities that UFOs are not just projections, but also might be *real* and therefore "something thoroughly out of the way." Therefore, he does not speak of the potentials beyond personal differentiation and development—as central as this is— toward real encounters and a new *psychophysical* basis of reality, relating to the evolution of consciousness *and* matter toward the recovery of the subtle body and subtle worlds. Psychological explanations are not exhaustive as Jung himself acknowledged. We are left with the heretical task of continuing to reflect on the significance of UFOs and to see how they are opening us to future developments and longer lasting changes in our understanding of reality, changes suggested by real events such as Steven Greer's close encounter.

When Jung wrote that UFOs were an example of synchronicity, albeit a collective one, he alludes to the breakthrough of the background subtle *unus mundus* world, which is a key feature of synchronicity. However,

UFO encounters take us further, to a domain of experience where the *unus mundus* world of soul becomes the *mundus imaginalis*, the Other world, the world where beings and landscapes have depth and extension but in a subtle form, as I described in chapter I. Sadly, this important distinction between the *unus mundus* and the *mundus imaginalis* has not been developed in Jungian psychology. The *mundus imaginalis* is as ontologically real as our three dimensional world, but in another dimension of consciousness, perhaps the fourth or fifth dimension of consciousness. As Corbin says, we get there via a break with consensual reality (through meditation, dream, or vision, or perhaps spontaneously), but we do not know or cannot say exactly the moment when that happens. Although Jung himself knew that synchronicity and UFO/ET encounters moved forward into contemporary spiritual experiences the non-local connection of psyche and matter described by the alchemists in their writings and visions, and he himself had direct experiences of these psychoidal shamanic domains in meditations, dreams, and visions, he falters at the moment when he comes to write about their strange nature and cosmic significance. Jung, therefore, does not explicitly explore the radical implications of synchronicity on an individual and collective level. He fails to describe fully the new myth of an Other world and its urge for us to reunite with the Cosmic Soul and to awaken the heart through Eros.

UFOs and Feminine Mandala Symbols of the Self

Exploring the radical implications of Jung's work, it is also important to stress how the primarily "masculine" Anthropos/Self image in Jung's description is balanced in the new myth by spherical and mandala symbols expressed by UFOs. These "circular forms" are in fact an ancient symbol of the creator, the cosmos, and the world soul that eventually replace actual deities with a geometric structure pointing to the unitary ground of all being that also resides in the innermost depths of the individual human soul. Historical expressions of this archetypal symbol can be seen from the representation of the Buddha as a twelve-spoked wheel, to Christ's representation in the center of a mandala surrounded by the four evangelists seen often, for example, on the façades of European Cathedrals, to the long history of the spherical nature of unitary reality (dating from the pre-Socratics), to the mystics' vision of God as a spark or circle whose center is everywhere and circumference nowhere. However, this circular divine ground was conceived primarily as pure spirit, with the ordinary human being and matter not included in the symbol. Jung also rediscovered the mandala as a centering ordering principle in his own psychological work, but here it is to be found embedded in nature as well. This nuance is important as it points in the direction of a more feminine mandala symbol, a creative matrix to the ground of being found in such images as the lotus and golden city of Buddha in the East, and in the West by the image of the garden of Eden, the temenos, or the fortress. These feminine symbols point to a god-image that is closer to nature and matter. Jung's golden castle painting described in chapter 2 (already linked to his interest in the development of the subtle body), his Liverpool dream (recounted in *Memories, Dreams, Reflections*) in which the city is arranged radially around a round pool at its center, with an island in the middle crowned with a gorgeous flowering magnolia—a dream that led to his discovery of the Self as an archetype of orientation, meaning and healing, the dream of the giant round jelly fish hidden in the forest (that decisively confirmed his decision to study natural science as a young man), and his experiments with mandala drawings all point in this direction as well. So do the Grail vessel, and the Renaissance revival of interest in matter which contains correspondences with God and the cosmos, and with which in contemplative effort we can interact.[22]

This inclusion of a feminine counterpart or Sophianic wisdom—(personified by a kind and loving wisdom figure in the Old Testament equal to the creator, or the "woman clothed with the sun" in Revelation)—that can reach deeply into the suffering of our world and its environmental and population problems is central to seeking the transformation of aggression in creative ways toward conciliatory and peaceful ends, giving birth to a new image of the divine. Many of the contacts between humans and ETs in UFO encounters result in an increased awareness of ecological considerations. Sometimes, invisible guides, inhabitants of ET craft, or other light phenomena, show these experiencers places of extraordinary natural

---

22 Marie-Louise von Franz, *Jung His Myth in Our Time*, espy. pp. 141–152.

beauty contrasted with devastated areas of the earth. And in many cases these experiencers become committed to educating themselves to become deeply concerned spokespersons for the threatened environmental collapse and ecological issues of our planet.[23]

Not only is the round mandala structure represented by the majority (though not all) UFOs, it can also be seen in the worldwide crop circle phenomenon, images of great beauty and harmony ranging from geometrical to galactic patterns. These images symbolize the descent of spirit into matter, the alchemical union of psyche and matter. As I explore in chapter 6, observers have also given many accounts of the relationship between UFOs and the crop circle mysteries, and how contemplating them has resulted in their entering into altered states of consciousness that seem to take them into subtle or psychoid realms, reminiscent of what Jung writes about when he describes the mercurial activity that is associated with UFOs and the transformation of spirit and matter in the alchemical *opus*. Reason alone is inadequate to the task of preventing or conquering our aggression. Only a greater power, such as is offered by the subtle body intensity of a UFO encounter, or being confronted by and receptive to the mystery of a crop circle—events that signal a union of masculine logos and feminine wisdom—can hope to achieve this.

These Eros images of the Self that ask us to balance our achievements in rational consciousness with our abilities to experience a deep subtle reality of imagination, feeling, vision and intuition, take the eros wound of Christianity beyond eros love as only inter-human love to a profound (what I call) "inter-galactic Eros," a reawakening of our relationship with our extraterrestrial and galactic neighbors, of experiences of unity consciousness and the revitalization of the Cosmic Soul. Joy Parker, writer, teacher, and healer offered me a fine example of this inter-galactic eros. She told me that one of the central dreams of her life that she experienced several years ago was about the flying saucer people landing and uniting all of humankind through story and ritual, two things that they understood from their own culture. Below is her description of her dream-vision.

---

23 John Mack, *Passport to the Cosmos* (New York: Crown Publishers, 1999), pp. 96–99.

DREAM VISION:
INTER-GALACTIC EROS AND THE SONGLINES OF THE SOUL

Joy writes: *This is a dream I had on December 26, 1996, that changed my life.*

Aliens had invaded the earth. They were so advanced beyond us that they had, in essence, conquered the planet without actually trying. We were afraid of them, yet we had to interact with them. I remember thinking, "They are our future. They will change our culture in such a way that we will become more and more like them." In our efforts to communicate with them (I mean this literally—they could speak and understand our languages), we discovered something important. Out of all the many achievements that human civilization had accomplished over the thousands of years of our existence, there were only two things that the aliens really valued and appreciated: storytelling and our ability to do ceremony. The aliens were great ritualists and their entire culture was based around ritual. They were especially drawn to Native American rituals, because these were closest in spirit to their own. Overnight, everyone on the planet who knew anything about ritual was suddenly taken very seriously and elevated to a level of great importance, and everyone was trying to learn how to do ritual.

We were preparing to sit down with them, those of us who knew anything about Native American rituals. I had my birth bundle with me. I also decided, intuitively, that it would be appropriate for me to take a bag of herbs and sprinkle them in front of our elders and the alien elders when they spoke. The bag of mixed herbs for the bath that Wolfram had put together seemed like the right ones. They were inside of the woven bag from Guatemala that Amalia, the Mayan midwife, had given to me at the weaving workshop.

I sat to the right of a human elder. A bowl of sweet steaming fragrant herbs and flowers was passed around for everyone to inhale. The young woman who passed it to me said something frivolous and I firmly and curtly reprimanded her, telling her that what we were doing was sacred. I wanted everything to be properly done and everyone to learn to behave with proper respect.

There were about eighty of us sitting in a large narrow rectangle, forty humans on the left side and forty aliens on the right. I thought of them as alien "monks" because they had bald heads and seemed more of the masculine gender than the feminine. Physically, the aliens were not too much different in appearance from humans.

The aliens began singing together at one point, and I was filled with a wistful longing and a quiet excitement. I thought, "It may be true that they are taking over our planet and our culture, but our future will be a culture filled with ritual, and I long for that." I saw a vision of the future in which ritual had healed our planet. There would be no more war, or rape, or racial hatred, or battering, or cruelty to children, or separation between people and nations, and I was filled with the deepest and most powerful sense of joy that I had ever experienced. It was as if we had been saved. The human race was not going to destroy itself. We were going to make it.

The language in which the aliens were singing was too strange for me to pick up the whole song, but I caught a repeating phrase near the end of the song and sang it with them.

One of the things I remembered when recording this dream were the words of Black Elk following the vision he received as a child. He said that a vision is not real until we take it out into the world and act upon it. I realized that I needed to begin to create healing rituals for the community of which I was a part. At the time I was reading a book by Gloria Naylor called Mama Day in which she described a Candlemas ceremony that took place yearly on February 2. Since I am of Irish ancestry, celebrating Candlemas seemed the right thing to do, so I invited about fifteen people to meet around a fire circle on the beach and asked them to bring white candles in jars to protect them from the wind. I told them about my dream as the sun was going down, then I lit my candle from the fire. Using my candle, I lit the candle of the person on my left with the ritual words, "Lead on with light." Each person in the circle shared something with the group, then they lit the candle of the person next to them, repeating the ritual phrase. I could see the spiritual hunger on each person's face as they spoke of their hopes and dreams for peace and passed on the light to one another.

Since then I have, as instructed by the dream, shared it with as many people as possible. I will never forget sitting in a Native American sweat lodge with Richard Sparrowhawk, then the spiritual leader of the Lakota. After I had shared the dream, he looked very thoughtful, then said, "Yes, that confirms something for me." But my favorite memory is when I shared the dream with Bob Roberts, founder of the prison aftercare program Project Return. Bob said, "It's not just a dream. Ritual really can heal the world if we believe it is possible." Since ritual and ceremony are capable of healing our hearts and our communities in ways that we can't even imagine, I do believe this is true.

To this day, I am convinced beyond the shadow of a doubt that our "salvation" from our self-destruction is possible and that ritual can cure the world's ills.

This powerful story of sharing and ritual also takes place in a context of song, where the singing of the aliens evokes the longing in Joy's soul for a healing of our planet and its peoples, and a vision that this will be so. The fact that aliens and UFOs will actually be helping our transition to the new age is confirmed by author, teacher, healer, and spiritual ambassador to and from many of the world's indigenous peoples, Drunvalo Melchizedek, in his book *Serpent of Light: Beyond 2012*. Concerning a Maori (Waitaha) prophecy told to him in Aotearoa (New Zealand) he writes: "[August 15, 2009] will be the beginning of a new human dream, a dream almost identical to the Mayan belief that the heavens will open and our brothers and sisters of the universe will reveal themselves."[24]

In a letter to Miguel Serrano on September 14, 1960, responding to questions about our contemporary problems, Jung (ten months before his death) comments that we must each "follow that will and that way which experience confirms to be your own, ie., the true expression of your individuality," and that this can only be accomplished by contact with others from whom we can discriminate ourselves. Jung laments here that we do not know ourselves because we are "cosmically isolated," even though collectively we are dreaming of interstellar travel. Returning to the possibility that UFOs are real, and that we need a new myth, he suggests that extraterrestrial contact might help us learn about ourselves, which is something we are desperately in need of as we stand at the brink of worldwide wars and unimaginable brutality that could annihilate us all. Furthermore, Jung observes that our dreams of traveling to the moon, Venus and Mars, and "the lore about Flying Saucers are effects of our dimly felt but none the less intense need to reach a new physical as well as spiritual basis beyond our actual conscious world." Recovery of the ancient idea of the subtle body as this new physical and spiritual basis could perhaps help us discover a much-needed new religious attitude and understanding of the self.[25]

---

24 D. Melchizedek, *Serpent of Light: Beyond 2012* (San Francisco/Newburyport, MA, Weiser Books, 2008), p. 254. See also www.onelotus.net, under "Live Broadcasts" where Drunvalo writes: "Even the ETs and the UFOs are essential to our new understanding, according to our indigenous friends."
25 C. G. Jung, *Letters 11*, pp. 592–594.

UFOs as the New "Annunciation"

Stephen Greer, in the opening to his book, *Extraterrestrial Contact*, stresses the importance of the potential transformational aspects of UFO encounters and their relationship with ancient mysticism, visionary Gnosticism, and quantum physics. In describing the death of his long-time assistant, Shari Adamiak, he relates her final days, when she would go out into the Joshua Tree wilderness to experience what she loved most: " the oneness with the stars, the universe and the communication with those peoples from other planets visiting our turbulent world." He goes on to describe,

> Fighting weakness, pain and increasing paralysis of her right arm and leg, Shari went into the desert each night, undeterred by the growing obstacles posed by her physical condition. And there, through the crossing point of light, we saw the depths of space and the people and spacecraft from Other worlds, who await our own coming of age as a people. Nothing would keep her from this purpose ....Awestruck, we witnessed a Light—a Presence—so beautiful, emanating from the center of creation. No words can depict it; it was beyond anything the intellect can grasp. An infinite brilliance, golden white in the center and becoming more peach, pink and magenta as it expanded infinitely before us, suffused us in a sea of love, joy and beauty unlike any experience of my life. It was the experience of the consciousness of God—pure light, unspeakable love and peace. And permeating that Spot were millions of voices joining as one, singing a melody too sweet to recall. And the refrain was: "We are all One in Spirit."[26]

Such wondrous and mystical descriptions of extraterrestrial life and its respectful intersection with our own, impress me with their deeply spiritual sensibility and feeling evocation. When I first read this account of Greer's tribute to his friend and colleague, Shari, I was moved to my core, stirred to my depths by some profoundly mystical and transforming truth that goes beyond anything I can rationally defend or articulate. Something invisible that I recognized resonated like a vibrating string in my soul, echoing sounds and songs

---

26 Stephen Greer, *Extraterrestrial Contact* (Afton, VA: Crossing Point, 1999), A Tribute, p. ix.

from the heart of the soul of the world. In moments like this, some ancient memory stirs again and I feel myself linked in a chain of being that throughout the history of our earth has known these links to the star nations.[27]

The golden white, pink, and magenta colors associated with the consciousness of God—Love—remind me of the angel in Fra Angelico's incomparable *Annunciazione* in the museum at Cortona, Italy. This angel, too, is a radiant figure of gold dressed in an exquisitely beautiful magenta-pink robe with golden borders and finely spun details—colors that are remarkably vibrant even after almost six hundred years. This stunning figure that dominates the painting quivers with the light coming in from a high museum window to the left, almost appearing to lift off the canvas as you move from one side of the picture to the other. The angel's features, like those of Mary, become curiously darkened with this move from left to right, transforming the figures from light beings to images of a darker nature. Mary becomes almost like one of those Black Madonna statues so prevalent in Europe. At the same time, with this transformation of the light, the shimmering gold, so dominant in the painting seems to become ever more scintillating. The painting is truly and magically alive. The angel's gestures (one hand toward Mary, the other pointing up—or is it an admonition to secrecy?) are authoritative. The words of this messenger flow out in three streams to Mary's heart (compassion), throat (authentic voice and creative center), and the transpersonal connection with the divine, the crown chakra above her head. Are these levels of consciousness seeking to be awakened in humanity now, and are our messengers from Other worlds seeking to aid us in this initiation?

Today, with the UFOs and so-called ET visitors, we are once again being addressed by the divine influx, but not necessarily in ways that are recognizable in a conventional way or ecclesiastically orthodox manner. Yet, with the UFO/ET encounters, meetings with guides—like Mary's with the Angel—are quite commonplace. The late Harvard psychiatrist, Dr. John Mack, gives many examples from his interviews with "experiencer participants" and careful reports of their encounters, collected over nine years, in his book, *Passport to the Cosmos*. For instance, Will, a forty-five year old divorced father of a teenage son, first encountered nonhuman entities

---

27 C. G. Jung, too, writes of a moment of déjà vu in which an utterly alien event seemed extremely familiar and natural, on a train ride to Nairobi in Africa, *Memories, Dreams, Reflections*, pp. 254–255.

during an out-of-body experience when he was electrocuted at age fifteen after grabbing a high voltage wire while climbing a tree. These beings encouraged him to return to his body, though he did lose his arm. In his interview with John Mack, Will told of an extraordinary encounter he'd had in 1980 while sailing from Bermuda to New England. He was awakened at three in the morning by a strange humming sound and, going up on deck, he saw a "city of lights" with multiple levels somehow strangely illuminated from within, hovering over the water off the starboard side of his boat. As he grappled with how he was ever to describe such a strange event, Will reported that the light and vibration shifted. Suddenly he found himself lifted in the air, almost as if he were inside a tunnel of some kind. Then he found himself crossing a threshold and arriving at the space craft. Once inside, Will became a different being than the man he was on the boat. With tears, he described "tall figures ...translucent ... beautiful ... luminous." They had a bluish tint and when he looked into them all he could see was light or light structures.[28] For Will, part of the emotional intensity of this and other encounter experiences relates to his rediscovery of another way of knowing based on direct perception. He describes it as an inner or intuitive way of perceiving, "another voice" to which we often do not listen. While this voice is "a state of remembering that has always been within us," today, he adds, we are being invited to reopen this window into deeper wisdom.[29]

Although visitations may occur at times of personal crisis, this is not the only time they occur. As with Mary's angelic visitation in Fra Angelico's painting, experiencers are encouraged—via direct experience through teachings, often of a telepathic or "immediate" nature—to speak the truth from their hearts, from a sacred source of knowledge beyond personal interest or gain, and often on behalf of humanity as a whole.

Of course, many indigenous cultures openly claim "visitations" as part of their heritage, what they call their connection with "the star people." In their cultures human-alien or Other world contact has been recorded in many ways, in petroglyphs and paintings as well as in texts, among various peoples and religious traditions across the globe from the beginning of time. Wallace Black

---

28 John Mack, *Passport to the Cosmos* (New York: Crown Publishers, 1999), p. 67.
29 *Ibid.*, p. 31.

Elk, a Native American elder, speaks matter-of-factly about "disks" and telepathic communication with the "little people," and laments how the American scientific attitude has lost touch with the "star nation people," and with the knowledge, power, and gift that accompanies such contact.[30]

The West African teacher, Malidoma Somé, from the Dagara tribe, who is an initiated elder and who became the head of his family following his father's death, tells of a visit by the "supernaturals" at his grandfather's funeral. These *Kontombili* had trained his grandfather in his work as a healer and medicine man. Somé writes:

> Within the world of the Dagara, so closely aligned with the worlds of nature and the worlds of the spirit, these beings are commonly seen—just as angels and other heavenly apparitions were once commonly experienced by devout Christians in the West.

He goes on to describe their appearance at the funeral:

> Approaching Grandfather's paala from the north came a strange group of beings, short red creatures who looked like humans. They had pointed ears and were two feet tall at most, with genitals so long they had to roll them around their necks, and hair so long it touched the ground ....
>
> Ignoring the crowd, these bizarre beings moved toward Grandfather's paala and gathered around it in a semicircle with an air of solemn homage .... Though they looked tiny and helpless, the Kontombili are the strongest, most intelligent beings God ever created. Grandfather told me they are part of what he called "the universal consciousness.[31]

In the Christian West we do not usually think of angels looking quite like this. But neither do the various descriptions of extraterrestrials often fit the usual human-looking winged beings that we see on mediaeval paintings.

The Kontombili are similar, however, to descriptions of the legendary tribe known as the *Menehune*, a powerful group of herbalists, healers, and

---

30 *Ibid.*, p. 10.
31 Malidoma Somé, *Of Water and the Spirit* (New York & London: Penguin Arkana, 1994), pp. 68–69.

medicine people, on the island of Kauai in Hawaii. In South African Zulu culture there are the *Mantindane*, givers of deep knowledge to humankind; in Australia, the *Wandjinas* are considered a powerful extraterrestrial race among the Aborigines; in Brazil there are the *Ikuyas*, which are beings who are considered direct messengers of the Great Spirit, and who can manifest in various forms—such as balls of light or animal forms—and who come from "nowhere," which would mean "they are everywhere."

As we learn from Henri Corbin, "Nonwhere" is one of the descriptions of the intermediate realm known as the *mundus imaginalis*. As I have pointed out in previous chapters, for Corbin the *mundus imaginalis* is an ontologically real realm. The metaphor "from the stars" therefore might too easily fail to acknowledge that UFOs as collective synchronicities are actually real. My claim in this book is that whatever they might *mean*, they are expressions of a real Other world.

In the Old Testament there are "messengers of God," and reports of flying machines with wheels going up and down. Even the Star of Bethlehem was seen to move and stand still, leading the wise men to a particular spot, and Jesus himself was considered amongst Gnostic Christians to be a high master teacher and healer "from another race."[32] In Jung's story of Orfeo Angelucci (which Jung includes at the end of his essay "Flying Saucers: A Modern Myth"), this "extra-terrestrial" identity of Jesus is confirmed. Orfeo is told by the voice from the UFO, that Jesus was in reality the "Lord of the Flame," "an infinite entity of the Sun" and not of earthly origin. In his sacrifice, Jesus became part of the *anima mundi*, the oversoul of humankind, and in this he differs from other cosmic teachers.[33]

The Immortal Guides of the Soul

From these examples we see that otherworldly guides (whether they are called angels, star nation beings, or orbs of light) who bring healing, wisdom, messages, and more advanced knowledge are, in fact, quite common cross culturally and throughout the course of history. As we have seen, there are many

32 Stephan Hoeller, *Jung and the Lost Gospels* (Wheaton, IL: Theosophical Publishing House, 1989), p. 43.
33 C. G. Jung, *CW 10*, par. 797.

examples from our own history in the Western world. For example, the alchemists readily spoke of their *daimon*, good angel, or spirit guides, and these subtle figures were key participants in the imaginative and meditative aspects of their devotions. Jeffrey Raff in his book, *Jung and the Alchemical Imagination*, draws particular attention to a figure in alchemical texts he calls the ally, a figure that connects the sojourner to the psychoidal or transpsychic realm. The ally is a potent subtle body entity, not an "inner" personification of a complex, but a real figure who *is* what he or she signifies. This description follows Corbin's view of the reality of the *mundus imaginalis* and its inhabitants faithfully and precisely. For Raff, one of the key features of the ally, who bestows power, guidance and knowledge on his or her human partner, is the blissful or ecstatic feeling often associated with encounters with them.

Contact with Guides, Spiritual Entities, or Beings of Light are invariably recounted in Near Death Experiences, and often take the person who has "died" on journeys to different places in the cosmos, or to different realms of consciousness, from "hell"-like environments to more "heavenly" or enlightened realms. These soul twins or helping guides may also afford the occasion for a full life review, after which they point out that the individual has not yet completed their human incarnation. At this moment, the individual is either encouraged to return, or he or she realizes that their death at this time is premature. In these cases they agree to return to their body and the NDE terminates. These experiences (like the UFO/ET encounters) are always described as "hyperreal." Those who have them claim that they are not imagined, nor do they experience them as dreams. Like Jung's own NDE, they have an "objectivity" about them that is psychocosmic and suprasensible. For this reason, they often have a profoundly transformative effect on the survivor. If you wish to read more about NDEs, go to www.near-death.com, a site which includes many accounts.

In the Sufi mystical tradition, too, the initiate makes contact with his or her "guide of light" through contemplation and prayer. This guide is known by many names—Heavenly I, Eternal Partner and Companion, "Perfect Nature." It is the personal angel or soul twin who helps us to understand the vertical, transcendent realms. In this way, the guide aids us in our recollection of our origin and true destiny in the concrete spiritual universe, what Suhrawardi calls the "heavenly Earth of [the mystical city of] Hurqalya." The angel, or suprasensory guide, also known as "sun of the mystery, heart or high knowledge," awakens us to our subtle organ, the "resurrection body" hidden in the visible physical body. Through our Perfect Nature we become reunited with our star, which is "the face we had before we were born." Meditation on our angel, the heavenly entity who rules and guards us, illumines the subtle rays of light and organs of wisdom found in the body and also in celestial Earth and, as Suhrawardi notes: "teaches [us] what is difficult, reveals to [us] what is right."[34] We are related to our invisible self as a lover is to his or her beloved, and there is an intimate reciprocal relationship between the two that Corbin describes as a paradoxical bi-unity—two figures that are united as one. We cannot become the substance of love without a thou, "without the Figure who makes [us] able to see [ourselves], because it is through [our] very own eyes that the Figure looks at [us.]"[35]

Medicine men or Clever men of high degree in the Aboriginal culture, too, in their initiatory rites come to know their guides as the "spirits of the dead, whose home is among the stars."[36]

In many traditions, cross-culturally, angels are known as messengers who act as intermediaries between the divine and human realms. From the Kabbalah of Judaism, in which types of angels are clearly differentiated, through Egyptian, Hindu, and Greek mythologies, from the "thunderbirds" and "Kerubim" of the Sioux, to the nineteenth century watercolors of William Blake, angels appear, either alone, or in choirs as they preside over arts and especially over music. There are warrior angels, fallen angels, angels associated with Hindu Tantra and Greek paganism, angels of death, sexual bliss, child-like angels, and the muses of inspiration. In *The Divine Comedy*, Dante gives perhaps one of the most sublime expressions of how angelic vision transforms the ordinary into the beautiful and beatific, and how the visionary eye is inseparable from the erotic and spiritual unity of love.[37] Even on the level of popular culture, there is an increased interest in angels as guardians and invisible guides.

---

34 Henry Corbin, *The Man of Light in Iranian Sufism* (Boston & London: Shambhala, 1978), p. 17.
35 *Ibid.*, p. 9.
36 A. P. Elkin, *Aboriginal Men of High Degree* (Rochester, VT: Inner Traditions, 1994).
37 See especially, Peter Lamborn Wilson, *Angels: Messengers of the Gods* (London: Thames & London, 1994).

Although traditionally angels mirror our wholeness and inherent divinity, and are the sources of wisdom, deep knowledge, and guidance from realms beyond the ego, it seems as if we in the West have lost touch with these visionary and imaginal beings, and with the "parallel" domains or other dimensional universes from which they come. Yet, simultaneously, particularly since the end of WW II, the latest versions of human-alien or "angelic" contact have been heating up. Since then increasing numbers of people claim to have some kind of connection—whether through sightings, encounters or repeated experiences—with the star people.

UFO Encounters and Initiation

I mentioned earlier that I realized that my own UFO encounter had been an initiation. The traditions of initiation have always played a part in the underbelly of official religions. These traditions keep gnosis (direct knowledge of the source) alive as a "golden chain" that flows beneath orthodox views. In all mystical traditions, in many of the alchemical traditions, and in virtually all shamanic traditions cross-culturally, the initiate is always subjected to trials and tribulations on the journey of becoming a *mystes*, or enlightened being. Initiation, from the earliest recorded history going back thousands of years to the caves at Lasceaux up to the contemporary psychology of individuation described by Jung, involves intense psychophysical experiences relating to symbolic death, journeying to other planes, rebirth, and illumination. This path presents engaging challenges, which can sometimes be quite severe, in order to create the strength of body that allows for knowledge of unseen forces, communication with the world of nature, spirits and gods, and access to cosmic as well as physical geography. The initiating crisis—be it a devastating illness, psychological depression, fainting spells, grief, constitutional vulnerabilities, visitations, or ancestral lineage—leads through sometimes horrible torments and a necessary solitude to the awakening of profound insight, healing ability, and a unifying timeless vision of the beauty and interrelatedness of the whole of creation in its visible and invisible forms.

The initiate returns with power and gnosis that is not his or hers, but is to be used in service to the community and to the wider creation of which each individual is a tiny seed or spark. She or he returns with a song, a song that rises from the depths of her or his nature and of the cosmos itself. She or he embodies the mystery of that Other world in her or his physical form, and seeks to resolve all polarities—the rational and intuitive, the ordinary and the visionary—in the knowledge that we are One. He or she is a poet, a dancer, a fierce warrior, an artist in life. In summary, she or he is a technician of ecstasy and the sacred, a witness to the whole of Being.[38] Having suffered the processes of transformation, she or he becomes the inspiration for transmutation in others, by her or his presence, her or his word, her or his song, her or his healing ability, her or his access to uncanny knowledge, her or his trust in the invisible worlds, and her or his wisdom. The UFO encounter leads us—at least potentially—toward the recovery of this ancient knowledge and gnosis. However, rather than leaving this effort to the relatively few, as our culture has done in the past, I think that more of us might risk creative, positive change in a conscious manner—quantum leaps of the soul!—as a way to support the emerging new myth. The devastation has gone too far, be it in our destruction of the environment, or in our insistence on allowing aggression and greed to be the defining values of our culture. Our modern world is filled with individual souls who lead quiet lives of desperation, yet who long to return home, to remember their long forgotten birthright that we too are stones, andgels, trees, and stars.

Individual vs. Collective Synchronicities and the New Myth

At the beginning of this chapter I noted how individual and collective synchronicites as signatures of the new myth share characteristics but are also to be distinguished. Both individual synchronicities and UFO encounters as examples of collective synchronicities occur spontaneously and unpredictably and are meaningful. They both point to an acausal and non-local relationship between psyche and matter which leads to an altered state of consciousness that is subtle, numinous, and transformative. Both are founded on an archetypal constellation that urges union. Both lead to "new creations"

---

38 Mircea Eliade, *Shamanism* (Princeton, NJ: Princeton and Oxford, 1992).

that involve the co-creative force of consciousness, and that signify a new myth related to *creatio continua*, eros, the redemption of the feminine, and a reconnection to nature and the cosmos.

Sightings of and encounters with UFOs are reported as spontaneous events, and the associated meetings and experiences of the "abductees," "witnessers," or "experiencers," occur usually against peoples' will or in spite of their intentions. They "happen" in an unpredictable manner during the day or at night, outside or inside a car, during sleep or when people are awake, even though some individuals report an anticipatory or uneasy feeling beforehand.[39] As such, these events indicate acausal correspondences between mutually independent psychic and physical events and the attendant elasticity of time and space that creates an altered state of consciousness, time, and landscape.[40] Perhaps we can imagine these encounters as spontaneous productions of the psychophysical psychoid archetype, world soul or *anima mundi* associated, as Jung cautions us to notice, with the tectonic shift from Pisces to Aquarius. Like the appearance of sophisticated crop circle formations overnight or during the day, UFO encounters "just are." They are not caused, they "just happen."

The "new creation" with UFO initiations, however, also differs from individual synchronicities. With UFO encounters there is an intensification of experience of a deeply subtle psychophysical nature. The "new creation" ups the ante from a unique and individual transformative event that predominantly involves a spiritual creation through meaning (as in an individual synchronicity), towards an intensified and potently transformed reality that is perhaps better served by the word transmutation, even transfiguration. Here the creation is both psychic *and* material, a psychophysical creation, a new body, a subtle body creation. The individual recounts not only a distortion or an altered sense of time in which past, present, and future, are experienced as one, but also a feeling of moving or shifting into a different and heightened sense of space, a place that feels intensely real, even "hyperreal," but is definitely not a dream experience.[41]

---

39 John Mack, *Passport to the Cosmos*, pp. 13, 75.
40 C. G. Jung, *CW 10*, pars. 655–656.
41 Mack, *Passport to the Cosmos*, pp. 53–56.

The initiate travels from "here and now," which still feels more or less familiar, to "there," to a new outside, an outside that is *really real* but no longer in any sense familiar or ordinary. In writing of the intensified reality of this other intermediate world, Corbin refers to it as a domain where interiority becomes the threshold to a new outside, a spiritual landscape where beings have extension and dimension but of an immaterial, subtle kind. This is a world where space is the outer aspect of an inner state. Like my own UFO encounter experience, recounted in Part Four of this book, the new "there" can seem like an alteration of the same space that one is occupying, but now it is felt as if it is in a different dimension. Other experiencers sometimes speak of "vortices" or "gateways through which they seem to pass from one dimension to another."[42] Too, in a similar vein to William James' account in *Varieties of Religious Experience*, these other dimensions seem as close as our faces. They lie all around us, are nearer than we think, and merely require a shifting of ordinary or rational consciousness to access them. [43]

However, in my experience, and as Corbin points out, you cannot quite pin point the moment of change or even how it happens. Yet, it is not possible to pass from the sensible world to the Other world without a break with ordinary reality, like that provided, for example, by a near-death encounter, or an intense meditative practice. Moreover, when the beholder of this other realm returns, he or she knows that they have been elsewhere, but it is impossible for them to describe to anyone else how to get there. This is different from individual synchronicities in which you know, more or less, when the epiphany, the "aha" moment happens.

A UFO encounter actually indicates the possibility of a journey to a parallel world, to the *mundus imaginalis* itself, which is beyond a sense of union with the background potential *unus mundus* world that I described as a feature of synchronicity in previous chapters. This is what accounts for the conviction on the part of the "experiencer" that he or she is not dreaming but actually awake in another world that feels intensely alive and inordinately strange. The initiate is moved beyond here and now toward what I would like to call Presence, an intensified psychophysical reality. This move to Presence is a move out of history, because it is a move out of time as past, present and future, and out

---

42 Mack, *ibid.*, p. 58.
43 William James, *Varieties of Religious Experience* (London: Penguin, 1982), p. 388

of myth, because it is no longer only a symbolic reality. In this double move it is simultaneously a move to another world, a *psychocosmic* landscape, a celestial earth, that is at once both symbolic and nonsymbolic. Here, as the twelfth century Sufi mystic, Suhrawardi describes, in a stage between waking, dreaming and sleeping, we meet, with "exquisite freshness and subtlety," frightening forces that threaten to destroy, dismember, or distract us, or angels and celestial powers. Moreover, for Suhrawardi, such encounters are not a result of daydreaming, but of direct encounters in a "world of pure figures" of forms disclosed in an objectively existing realm.[44]

Jung comments time and again that the "face" that the unconscious shows toward us depends very much on our attitude toward its reality. This appears to be true of the type of experience the UFO initiate undergoes. In these encounters, much depends on the nature of our consciousness and how familiar we are already with the waters of descent. All initiatory journeys involve frightening as well as beneficent encounters, and sometimes for those individuals who have repeated encounters, there is a move from initially terrifying to more fruitful and life-changing exchanges. Mack writes about how the phenomena changes and evolves according to the level of consciousness of the experiencer. He observes that initial indifferent contacts have led to meaningful connections over time, and even to profound love and ecstatic union beyond earthly forms of love.[45] Suhrawardi also speaks of encounters in the Other world happening to "masters" or initiates.

I would suggest that the nature of the UFO encounter depends on the extent to which we have been able to move from logos consciousness to eros awareness, and that one of the main purposes of the encounter phenomena is to initiate us to an opening of the heart chakra, to the compassionate life that unites us with all creation and leads us to live a creative life devoted to the harmony of the whole. A key feature of encounter experiences is their intensity, including intensely emotional states that have led people to compare them with kundalini awakenings. These intense feeling states move the sojourner beyond thinking and ordinary feeling to profound levels of passion and vision, in which they "are addressed" by concerns beyond their own personal interests, and are often led to change their life's work to a

---

44 Dan Merkur, *Gnosis* (Albany, NY: SUNY Press, 1993), p. 224.
45 Mack, *Passport to the Cosmos*, pp. 13, 18–19.

vocational destiny beyond what they could ever have predicted. Beyond the invitation to a creative idea or psychological content that *happens later*, which is characteristic of individual synchronicities, the "calling" in the UFO encounter is a galactic one, an illumination emanating from the heart of the cosmos *in the present*, and often involving concerns of planetary proportions such as our ecological crisis and even earth's place in the galactic community. Experiencers are offered disclosures explaining how our actions here on earth effect levels of being far beyond our own personal sphere of action and even beyond our own planet. From being isolated individuals working on ourselves we awaken within the current limited dream that we think of as being awake and become planetary citizens working on behalf of the whole, supporting the non-local nature of reality at a deep fundamental level. Here we move beyond both our addiction to suffering on the one hand and to a materialist view of reality on the other, and we learn to radiate a sense of well being, happiness and joy that comes from our exposure to the imaginal domains and galactic dimensions of the soul.

UFO Encounters, Cosmic Consciousness, and the Heart: Orfeo Angelucci's Story

In the Epilogue to his "Flying Saucers" essay, Jung includes the story of Orfeo Angelucci's extraterrestrial journeys and close encounters reported in his (Orfeo's) book, *The Secret of the Saucers* (1955). Though Jung himself was ambivalent about the "reality" of Orfeo's account, he was clearly drawn to it, and I am including the tale here for two main reasons. First, there are, notably, many interesting parallels between Angelucci's 1955 account and the many first-hand accounts reported by John Mack in the 1990s, especially the fact that Orfeo himself tells his story as "objectively" real events that occurred while he was awake though partially in an altered state of consciousness. Apart from the fact that the story recounts a mystical version of an encounter experience which, as I have said, is less visible in much of the UFO literature, other similarities with Mack's accounts include: repeated encounters; anticipatory sensations and feelings before the encounters ("feeling unwell," "a prickling sensation in the upper half of his body"[46]); different colored lights; telepathic communication and communication using TV screens; "strangely familiar" beings with "large shining eyes," "star beings," and beings of "supernatural perfection"; the dissemination of cosmic knowledge; the feeling of the everyday world becoming "an abode of shadows" upon one's return to it; ecological concerns and the desire for healing; a vocational change; feelings of great humility in the face of illuminating knowledge; altered states of consciousness; and missing time. The second reason to include Orfeo's story is a key emphasis on compassionate love. This story thus marks a fitting concluding account to our UFO chapter.

Although Orfeo's consciousness is altered, and time and space seem to have an elastic quality operating quite differently than they do under ordinary conditions, his travels in UFO ships allowed him mystical glimpses into the nature of the universe and a "great compassionate consciousness" that conveyed to him "the mystery of life" as he wafted into "eternity, into a timeless sea of bliss" to strains of the music of the spheres.[47] A universe of different levels of spiritual achievement was revealed to him, constructed more by cosmogonic love than by the impersonal and unfeeling scientific experiments often associated with the saucer people known as the "little Grays."

According to Angelucci, it is his physical weakness that has given him the spiritual gifts that make it possible for the heavenly beings to contact him. With deep compassion and via telepathic communication, these "etheric entities," who only manifest materially when appearing before humans, tell Angelucci of the special importance of humankind in the galactic community, and that we have been "under observation for centuries." Yet our current separation from the knowledge of the true mystery of our being, and the fact that each one of us is divinely created has endangered Earth. "For all its apparent beauty earth is a purgatorial world among the planets evolving intelligent life. Hate, selfishness, and cruelty rise from many parts of it like a dark mist." We have not kept pace morally and psychologically with our technological development, and, therefore, "the inhabitants of other planets were trying to instill into the earth dwellers a better understanding of their present predicament and to help them particularly in the art of healing."

---

46 C. G. Jung, CW 10, par. 792.
47 Ibid., par. 796.

Angelucci weeps with emotion, at recognition of our impoverished state, and with deep sorrow at this revelation of our present condition.

Further, the beings reveal that everyone on earth has a spiritual dimension that exists beyond our material existence outside time and lives in unity with the oversoul. As is taught in our own esoteric spiritual traditions, they confirm that "the sole purpose of human existence on earth is to attain reunion with the "immortal consciousness." Under the penetrating eye of compassion, Angelucci experiences his mortal limitations, as he is baptized in the "true light of the worlds eternal," while remembering all of his previous existences. He understands "the mystery of all life," and fears death is near as he is wafted into "eternity, into a timeless sea of bliss." Later he experiences "missing time"—an entire week has passed. During his absence he has traveled to a small planet whose description fits with many of the mystical lands in other traditions: beautiful flowers, smells, colors, nectar and ambrosia, noble spiritual beings, and the music of the spheres. He is linked with this world as a star being and undergoes the celestial marriage as a union of his erotic and spiritual selves.

Angelucci returns to this world and undergoes a complete change of vocation. He leaves his job as a mechanic for Lockheed Aircraft Corporation in Burbank, CA to becoming a spokesperson—like many current day experiencers—for the gnosis revealed to him by the Saucers and their inhabitants.

This close encounter, like the others I have recounted, speaks of a transforming experience that takes one out of ordinary reality to a cosmic landscape peopled by etheric beings, spiritual guides. It opens one's perception to encompass an immeasurably larger picture of our world, its relation to a wider galactic community and purpose, and its invisible domains that take on form for our convenience. In this Other world that we so often access only through our vulnerabilities and illnesses (as was the case with Angelucci), or through meditative techniques whose aim is to open us to nonordinary states of consciousness, we participate through our *imaginatio vera* in the powerful sacred realities which are both profoundly symbolic and profoundly real. These encounters, long recorded in the esoteric traditions of both East and West, are returning to our world. The wisdom they bring can help make the precarious journey from an incomplete and flawed vision of reality to one that once again reunites us with the angels and guides of the soul, and the vast expanse of mystical, healing, and sacred cosmic knowledge that it brings us. We have only to give our quiet, reflective, and humble attention to the gifts that are being offered to us at this time. If, as it seems, one of the main themes of encounters with our galactic neighbors is initiation into and preparation for humanity's next evolutionary phase of development toward wisdom and the realization of our divine nature, as well as changes in our feeling and moral identity and how we see the world and its relationship to the larger cosmos around us, then how the spiritual hierarchies and the presence of ETs at more advanced levels of development are here to mentor and assist us requires much greater attention.

Finally, we cannot ignore Orfeo's name and its link to the poet Orpheus; even Jung acknowledges that in his essay. We have mentioned before how Orpheus and his songs awakened those who heard them to their own true destiny, their true nature and vocation. The songs of Orpheus awakened the soul to its cosmic journey back home. His work inspired "anamnesis," that is, the recollection through "un-forgetting" of the soul's original commitment to incarnation in this world made in the mystical lands before and between lives. Orpheus is the poet who inspires the individual to recollect what she once knew but has forgotten, to remember the songlines of her soul, the destiny paradoxically both chosen by the soul and bestowed by the divine before birth.[48]

Furthermore, Orfeo's last name Angelucci also requires a comment. In Greek, the word "angel" is a messenger of the gods, connecting the invisible with the visible worlds. Orpheus as a shaman-poet travels between worlds. And yet Orpheus is no Christian angel of light, for he unites above and below. The myths tell us he must descend and be dismembered in order to recover his true vocation. In this respect, Orfeo as a re-presentation of Orpheus overcomes the failed Christian story where the angel is separated from the dark side. With Orfeo as an Orphic figure and as Angelucci we encounter the angel in the modern guise of the UFO. And, as we have seen, UFO encounters invite us into that imaginal world where spirit and instinct, the light and the dark, the above and below, are one.

---

48 See Robert Romanyshyn, "Anyway why did it have to be the death of the poet?" The Orphic Roots of Jung's Psychology," in *Spring: A Journal of Archetype and Culture*, 71 (New Orleans: *Spring* Journal, Fall 2004), pp. 55–87.

The Subtle Body as a New Creation in the New Myth

Although Jung does indeed write that individuation has to do with the establishment of the immortal or resurrection body, and his alchemy studies support this claim, this notion is not popular with those who study Jung's ideas. What I wish to stress, however, is that the new paradigm of reality includes the paradox, already suggested by the twelfth century Sufi Gnostic and visionary, Ibn al-Arabi, and echoed in the writings of contemporary shamans (Olga Kharitidi and Malidoma Somé, for example) that visions are both symbolic and nonsymbolic simultaneously. My claim is that the UFO sightings (and associated phenomena) are real expressions of a subtle Other world, and that through direct and immediate experience they are stressing the alchemical union of psyche and matter toward a subtle body reality, a new psychophysical reality, a third body comprised of new life, indeed, *a new creation never produced before*, arising out of "meaningful coincidences" on intense levels. Such experience is to be realized through devotion and personal effort. This is an idea that I will thoroughly explore in later chapters.

We might anticipate, too, that this new archetypal constellation will also be associated with an intensification of "irrational" elements, those indispensable ingredients of transformation already noted in chapter 4. To most people, UFOs and crop circles are "irrational" enough. But Steven Greer gives an excellent example of how these "irrationalities" can also create an "irrational" response. He reports being with a group of people in England searching for crop circles. One night, the group witnessed an extraterrestrial craft with otherworldly lights on it, spinning counterclockwise and making a beautiful and unusual pattern. Suddenly, one of the women in the group became "completely terrified...and came completely unhinged." As Greer attempted to get in closer contact with the craft, and the spaceship moved closer to the group, the woman said, "Don't do that." Greer replied, "But this is why we're here." The woman admitted that she didn't think that the saucers would actually come and believed that there might be a far-off sighting, but nothing more. With her fear, the craft backed off, which Greer says was an act of compassion. After this, he realized that people really needed to be prepared for these encounters.[49] As I know from my own experience,

---

49 Steven Greer, *Hidden Truth Forbidden Knowledge* (Crozet, VA: Crossing Point, n.d.), p. 89.

however, there is nothing that completely prepares you for the totally foreign and "irrational" experience of a close encounter.

With such potencies in the air, much will depend on the position and attitude not only of the ego as it comes in contact with these forces, and how aware it is of its own unconsciousness, but also how developed the *imaginatio vera* is, the spiritual imagination located in the heart. Perhaps we can already see both destructive and creative potentials relating to these archetypal dominants activated around us. On the one hand, there is an acceleration of war, violence, fundamentalism, and terrorism accentuating the destructive pole of irrationality that "acts out" and keeps the opposites polarized because the *coniunctio* is unconscious, the spiritual principle has been replaced with power, and there is no conscious relation to an Other. On the other hand, we see an increased interest in the healing and creative arts, the union of science and spirituality, and the desire for divisions between people and nations to be transcended toward a common purpose. We are also witnessing new ways in how we are being addressed by the anomalous and paranormal, the concern for ecological priorities, and the flowering of a new kind of soul life that depends on a personally meaningful relationship with the divine.

What might we call this new worldview, this new story, this new myth? I don't know. Jung's "myth of meaning" just does not do it for me! Jung's myth takes synchronicity into account, but stops there. It does not deal with the broader and more intensified implications of UFOs and other phenomena. It does not address the fullness and range of a multidimensional consciousness that reaches from the depths of the earth to the far reaches of the stars. It does not approach adequately the reality of an intermediate psychophysical subtle world as a domain that lies beyond the collective unconscious. It does not include Eros in its widest sense as the organ of access to the subtle world and to balancing the mind with the felt experience of the heart. Perhaps the "myth of continuing creation" suffices for the present moment.[50] Or, the myth of the songlines?

In a lyrical moment, Joseph Campbell calls myths the "songs of the universe."[51] They are truly the "music of the spheres," creating tunes to

---

50 E. Edinger, in *The New God Image* (Wilmette, IL: Chiron Publications, 1996), uses the term "continuing incarnation."
51 Joseph Campbell, *The Power of Myth* (New York: Doubleday, 1988), p. xvi.

which we do not yet know the words. We are perhaps too much in the midst of accelerated change to be aware of what is happening. However, our souls remember, and deep within the orphan in us all, the ancient memory stirs of Other worlds, other domains of consciousness, and other inhabitants of those long forgotten realms. UFOs arrive as reminders of these ancient memories. They initiate us into the mysteries, to the necessity of transformation and transmutation. Perhaps we are being invited to remember the songlines of our souls, to rediscover our ancient relationship with the larger cosmos, to reconnect as individual selves with other dimensions of reality, and to re-cover the mysteries through descent and renewal. In these critical times, our lives may depend on this humbling and awe-filled re-creation.

Chapter Six

CROP CIRCLES:
STAR CODES/EARTH DREAMS

[Crop Circles] are the new temples …. They are harmonic creations of light, sound,
and magnetism … unlocking ancient memories and reminding us
that we are not egocentric, but cosmocentric.[1]

C rop circles—mysterious and non-repeating patterns that form in fields of wheat and other grains and plants—unlike UFOs and Marian visions are visible to all and visited by thousands of people each year. What extraordinary force is at work here? Once again, our view of the universe and what constitutes reality is being shaken. Like UFOs, crop circles are another excellent example of synchronicity on a collective level, rising out of the psychoid archetype, and pointing to the spiritualization and meaning of matter itself. The living spirit of their multiple designs manifests itself on earth and they provide a stunning example not only of the union of spirit and matter but also provide venues of non-ordinary states of consciousness for those who visit them. Furthermore, these "star codes" and "earth dreams," as I like to think of them, appear quite spontaneously (often within a matter of seconds), usually (though not exclusively) in the hours between 2 and 4 in the morning. These spontaneous epiphanies, like UFOs, are another example of creations out of the world soul and hence are expressions of the myth of continuing creation. What are these amazing creations? Who or what is behind them? How are they "speaking" to or communicating with us? Are we listening?

1 Freddy Silva, *Secrets in the Fields: The Science and Mysticism of Crop Circles*, (Charlottesville, VA: Hampton Roads, 2002), p. 309.

The phenomenon of crop circles has been explored and taken very seriously for almost three decades by a whole host of people from scientists and philosophers, psychologists, cosmologists and astronauts, dowsers and students of earth mysteries, to journalists, metaphysicians, farmers and interested lay people, particularly in England where the majority (up to 95 percent) usually occur each year. But these enigmas, which have appeared every spring and summer since the early 1970s (now in up to 50 or more countries), actually have a much longer and more ancient history that can be traced all over the world. For example, a Zulu holy man and traditional healer, Credo Mutwa, reports that circles in corn or mullet have appeared in Africa for over four thousand years. These circles were viewed as sacred and as communications from the "star gods." Rituals honoring the star gods and the Earth Mother were performed in the fields set apart for the appearance of these disk shaped spirals in the stalks. Crop circle-like paintings have also been found in Aboriginal, Hopi, and Dogon cave art, and circular and spiral designs resembling the contemporary ones are carved on other petroglyphs, for example, on the kerbstone at Newgrange in Ireland, and on pottery and temples from around the world.[2] Such symbolic representations that point to encoded hieroglyphic and mythic messages that, like dreams, also aim to address our deeper natures suggest that we approach crop circle enigmas as we might our nightly dreams. In this way, we can allow our emotional and spiritual selves to respond to these marvels as well as opening our minds to their many-layered meanings.

Beginning most recently in the 1970s and 1980s with simple circular forms and concentric rings, some forming the design of a Celtic cross (which is a symbol for the four elements of earth, water, wind, and fire in equilibrium), crop circles developed to include a shaft, linear, or key pattern, eventually producing complex alchemical symbols based on sacred geometry, like the one at Barbury Castle, a Neolithic earthwork, in July 1991. Although to the naked eye this crop circle initially looks triangular in shape with central rings and circles at the apexes of the triangle (one is actually a stepped or ratcheted spiral), this glyph is a tetrahedron (a four-sided pyramid) important in both alchemical, Qabbalistic and Hermetic symbolism, that contains a hidden pentagram as well as two other geometric figures.

---

2   Lucy Pringle, *Crop Circles: Art in the Landscape* (London: Frances Lincoln Ltd., 2007), Introduction, pp. 5–7. Freddy Silva, *Secrets in the Fields: The Science and Mysticism of Crop Circles*, pp. 147–148.

The tetrahedron is a geometric shape underlying the physical universe and represents the way energy transforms itself into the creation of matter. It contains a formula for the inner transformation of changing the lead of our unconsciousness into the gold of illumination. The pentagram, a five pointed star, symbolizes the archetypal human (head and four limbs, five senses) as mediator between heaven and earth, as the one who can reconstitute with awareness the unity of above and below, cosmos and earth.

I shall return to the sacred geometry of crop circles below, but here we already have a taste of the multi-dimensional nature and subtle complexity of these glyphs and how they are restoring our connection to the mysteries of creation and of the cosmos, how our study of them can inspire us to expand our consciousness in keeping with the shift in the ages.

After Barbury Castle, which represented quite a leap in crop circle evolution, the circles continued to increase in complexity to include insectograms, "curly men," organic designs such as scorpions and bees, then double helixes, spirals, and a wide variety of fractal designs, and complex sacred *mandalas* recognized in various spiritual traditions.

Two of my favorite patterns are the so-called "Julia Set" and the famous Milk Hill crop circles.[3] The former, a fractal pattern which appeared quite unusually in broad daylight near Stonehenge on July 7, 1996, is a beautiful one thousand foot spiral design that looked like a base clef or a cross section of a nautilus shell. The latter, which appeared in August 12, 2001, was  eight hundred feet in diameter and was made up of 409 circles (some identify 410), looked like a pinwheel or, as I prefer, a spiraling galaxy. There are also stunning star, moon, and flower designs, dolphins, angels, butter-

3   All of the photographs in this chapter have been provided by Steve Alexander, a highly renowned photographer and reseacher of crop circles. Over his 20-year career, his photography has been featured in newspapers, magazines, books and documentaries world-wide, including the BBC and National Geographic. With Karen Alexander, he publishes *The Crop Circle Year Book*, which are considered to be the most important crop circle documents available. For more information, see www.temporarytemples.co.uk

flies, the seven chakras, and yin/yang patterns, not to mention those whose potential "wormhole" design suggest to some crop circle researchers that the circles are "traces" left by three and four-dimensional "subtle objects" passing through our atmosphere and earth, and are portals or gateways to other dimensions or parallel universes.

Subtle Energies and Stars

Circle researchers have discovered that the crop circles are often placed near or on the Earth's "geodetic energy lines," or at nodal points where these lines cross. Those who study and explore these energy lines are called geomancers and dowsers. The art and science of geomancy (the study of subtle earth energy) and dowsing (a remote sensing ability facilitated by copper rods or hazel twigs to get information from the morphogenetic field or visionary landscape of the earth) are very ancient. Since the 1960s, when interest in the electro-magnetic energy patterns at sacred sites was revived, there has been a resurgence of research into understanding their significance. Sacred sites such as stone circles, temples, and later churches were always built on such energy lines or crossings, facilitating access to the Other world and heightened states of consciousness. The electromagnetic currents, sometimes referred to as "ley lines" or "telluric currents," and also known as the "fairy paths," are similar to the Aboriginal idea of the songlines. Along the geodetic energy lines, which are not only "paths" linking sacred sites and megalithic monuments together, but also arranged in radial, spiral, and concentric ring patterns especially at nodal intersections where churches and older temples were built, the veils between the worlds are known to be thin allowing for entrance into the imaginal world to be made with greater ease. Knowing that many crop circles are placed on or near these energy currents, sometimes also called "serpent" or "dragon" energy, and near sacred power sites, helps in appreciating how people are known to have non-ordinary experiences in the circles or experience other kinds of unusual physical and/ or psychic and spiritual activity.

Moreover, the sacred sites and their enhanced geodetic energy were aligned to star constellations, and stellar influences were linked to human awakenings according to the "right timing" of the evolution of human con-

SONGLINES OF THE SOUL

sciousness. Some researchers, such as Freddy Silva, even suggest that the crop circles are reactivating the sleeping ancient megalithic monuments, such as Avebury or Stonehenge, and their dragon energy—even that the circles and sacred sites are "communicating with each other—to assist in Earth's Great Awakening and in helping ordinary people achieve mystic consciousness and experience alternate forms of healing.[4] To the Hopi, the circles are related not only to cosmic influences and earth changes related to their calendars but also to the return of the Star Nation people themselves.[5]

Though there are the usual "hoax" theories supported by governments and fuelled by the media that accrue to paranormal phenomena—and naturally, some are indeed man-made (though ways have been discovered to distinguish genuine patterns from hoaxes)—the sheer numbers of crop circles, the increasing complexity of their designs over the years, and occasionally their huge size (some of them reach four thousand feet in diameter) make it hard to believe that they are all human created. In fact, serious circle researchers do not subscribe to this point of view. One of the amazing things about actually going into any formation is the incredible detail of the lay of the crop and its precision of design. Sometimes the crop flows one way on top but in another or opposite direction underneath. The flow creates a river effect and you almost have the sense of being carried along in its energy. There are large sweeps of laid crop but also tiny narrow bands of only several stalks, all contributing to the integrity of the design. Moreover, there are delicate standing tufts with swirling patterns of wheat around them. Seeing the beauty of and marveling at these specifics, it is impossible to believe that humans in the dark of night could manage to create these aesthetic complexities and, furthermore, it is difficult not to see and feel some benign intelligent intentionality behind these works of art. There is a feeling that the subtle and no doubt powerful energy behind their creation haunts their presence.

It is hard not to wonder at their presence among us. For example, biophysicists, who have explored the circles from a complex electromagnetic perspective, and have noted altered soil samples and have measured the microwave changes in the crop stems that suggest intense heat, do not dismiss their mystery, even though they cannot explain their patterns and

4   Freddy Silva, *Secrets in the Fields*, pp. 235–236.
5   *Ibid.*, pp. 305–307.

designs. What intelligent design seems to be behind these wonders? Science researcher Nancy Talbott, who witnessed powerful "tubes of light" that have often been seen descending from the sky to the earth just before a new formation is created, has said that after this extraordinary experience she feels certain that the circles are created by a powerful agency beyond us. What possible form of communication is being addressed here? Are we being given new knowledge and are we being initiated into a dimensional shift of benign and unimaginable possibilities at the transition of the ages? In a crop circle in Litchfield in 1995, an ancient Celtic "Torc" pattern (a bracelet of interlocking semi-circles) appeared. This torc pattern represents in physics a combination of forces that create motion and within this pattern a previously unknown geometric theorem was later discovered.[6]

Crop Circles and the Sacred

In addition to the above, there are two other paths to understanding these mysteries, one sacred, one symbolic. Astronomer, geometer and author, John Martineau compares them with sacred geometry and sacred art. In fact, Martineau was among the first to recognize the geometric foundation and ordering principles underlying so many crop circles. He particularly noticed the importance of the pentagram or five-pointed star. John Michel, a well-known English metaphysician and writer about earth mysteries sees crop circles as "symbolic geometry, or geometry of meaning."

For Martineau, crop circles obey the rules of sacred art and architecture. In their stunning, inspiring beauty, and in the precision of their design they balance line and curve like the high art and design of mediaeval stained glass church windows. Also, like these windows that filter light and play with the tension between light and dark, the way the wheat bends, swirls and remains upright balance light and shadow. Moreover in this context of the sacred in its artful beauty and architectural form, crop circles seem to be the manifestation of the divine on earth. They matter in the double sense of this term. They effect us and even transform us, and in doing so they honor the integrity of the materials through which they appear. They are "green, clean, and holy" as Martineau says. In addition, some crop circle researchers have

---

6   *Ibid.,* p. 70.

described crop circles as temporary cathedrals. In this image, they endure, perhaps through their effects on us even as they perish. Like the sacred sand paintings of Tibetan monks, or like the Egyptian god Osiris who symbolized the inexhaustible power of plant life, who appeared and disappeared, died and was reborn every year, crop circles are mowed down every year at harvest time only to appear again.[7] Sometimes a ghost echo of the formation remains even after it has been mowed down. This echo can be viewed, for example, after a dusting of snow in the following winter.

Martineau suggests that the crop circles are the finest expression of innovative sacred art in our times, and that no modern artist compares with the crop circle designs. I think that his view of their beauty is key, for the effect of the impact of actually looking at the pictures of the circles, no matter what their origin, changes us, allows us to marvel, to witness the holy, to remember what we have lost, to feel appreciation and gratitude, and to recover a feeling of reverence toward the greater whole. The wonder of these creations is that as collective synchronicities they are, unlike UFOs and Marian visions, available for anyone and everyone to explore on the many crop circle websites.[8]

Epiphanies of Beauty and the Presence of the Goddess: Aphrodite/Venus

Crop circles as epiphanies of beauty and harmony remind us of the ancient goddess Aphrodite/ Venus. If we look at some of the stories surrounding Aphrodite's origins in Greece (the Roman Venus), we learn that she is the "golden crowned" goddess who arises out of the ocean, out of the frothing sea foam. She also emerges as the daughter of Heaven as it separates from Earth and therefore belongs to the beginning stages of creation. Aphrodite is an image of beauty and sensuousness joyfully experienced as sacred and divine. Desire (Himeros) and love (Eros) follow in her footsteps. Sandro

---

7   See the DVD: William Gazecki, *CropCircles: Quest for Truth* (OpenEdge Media, Inc., 2002).

8   www.temporarytemples.co.uk; www.cropcircleconnector.com; www.michaelglickmanoncropcircles. com; www.lucypringle.co.uk; www.silentcircle.co.uk. Pictures can also be seen in: Steve and Karen Alexander, *The Crop Circle Yearbook* (Gosport, Hampshire, UK: Temporary Temple Press). Other great DVDs on crop circles are: Robert L. Nichol, *Star Dreams* (Genesis Communications Corp., n.d.); *Crop Circles: Crossovers From Another Dimension* (UFO/TV, 2006).

Botticelli's painting *The Birth of Venus* (c. 1485) has her standing with long flowing hair on a half shell, one hand over her heart, the other hand, her left hand, over her genitals. As goddess of love, she inspires both animals and humans with erotic longing for the other. Where she walks flowers spring up, so she awakens the earth.

Aphrodite as love through beauty belongs to our desire for reunion with our deepest nature, with our beloved, and with the wholeness of being. Crop circles inspire this same desire for connection. Images of fertilizing rain and swelling moisture accompany the goddess, and such erotic wetness is also to be found in the annual ritual bathing of Aphrodite in the spring on her island of Cyprus as the seasons move toward renewal and rebirth after the cold winter months. Water immersion also links Aphrodite to the Sacred Bath, which is a theme I discuss in Part Four, chapters 12 and 13, on healing, eros consciousness, and water therapies. A beautiful fifth century B.C. sculpture envisions both the goddess's birth from the foamy sea and her relationship to the sacred bath in the wavy folds of the garments worn by both the goddess and her attendants as they lift her out of the water.[9] Interestingly, the majority of crop circles in the UK are placed on or near water sources, particularly on and around the aquifer or underground water table in southern England.[10] Water is fundamental to life, is related to lunar tides, and to the cycles of death and renewal.

Aphrodite/Venus as symbolic of the reconciliation of earth and heaven, desire and love, renewal and return are embodied in the crop circles that appear each year in spring and early summer as the fertilizing rains and warm sunlight help transform the wheat from virgin green to mature gold. In this unification, Aphrodite heralds the new creative vision of the world that we are being invited to see no longer with a single, rational, scientific eye, but rather with double, imaginal, symbolic, transformed, moral vision.

One of the lovers of Venus/Aphrodite was Mars/Ares, the red planet and god of war and aggression. They had three children: Terror, Fear, and

---

9   See for example, Anne Baring and Jules Cashford, *The Myth of the Goddess: Evolution of an Image* (London: Arkana Penguin, 1993), pp. 349–364.

10 Freddy Silva, *Secrets in the Fields*, pp. 120–121. Together with the chalk beds associated with the aquifer, the region creates a low magnetic field that conducts electricity and is associated with the ability of crop circles to form in this area.

Harmony. Surely we have had enough of war, the terror and fear that accompany it, and its horrifically destructive consequences. Now is the time to bring back our earthy passions, to transmute our rage and aggressive instincts in service of asserting our creative abilities, and to seek a more harmonious response to our own and the world's problems. Crop circle patterns, if we allow ourselves to be so moved, can help and inspire us each to discover our vision for and new role in the emerging new age.

Aphrodite belongs to the lineage of the ancient goddesses of heaven and earth, going back not only to Cyprus and Crete but also to Innana-Ishtar in Mesopotamia, and Isis in Egypt. This line of female personifications of the sacred is seen predominantly in sculptures of Aphrodite when she is accompanied by dolphins, swans, or a goose or dove, and sometimes with the planet Venus (visualized as a star) or a crescent or full moon. There have been several dolphin, stellar, moon, and bird formations in the crop circles. Dolphins are known for their playfulness, sensitivity, great intelligence, songs, healing abilities, their connection with the star Sirius, and their unfathomable ancient nature. I always think of them as guardians of our planet especially when we consider that our "planet" is actually (like our bodies) mainly water.

While dolphins are connected with water, birds have always been connected with air or Spirit and have particularly been seen as messengers between the heavenly and earthly realms. The dove is not only linked with Aphrodite/Venus and is present in alchemical imagery as an emblem of the goddess who watches over the work of transformation, it is also preserved in Christianity as the missing feminine element in the Holy Spirit who descended as a dove at Christ's baptism and reappeared at Pentecost. We are in times when we need to return to the origins of Christianity and embody its original intent, which was not institutional orthodoxy but the task of each through direct experience to make the sacred immanent and present in their own lives, to discover what truly heals by being fully ourselves, and to learn the art of compassion and the nature of our cosmic destiny.

While it was not formed of images of the goose or dove, the birds of Aphrodite, I was privileged to be in a bird formation when I visited some crop circles in Wiltshire in August 2008. It was a large creation of stunningly beautiful design in mostly golden wheat made up of a pattern of swallows with their distinctively shaped "forked" tail and pointed wings. Swallows are known for their cheerful warble, extensive migration patterns, and nesting habits in barns and stables close to humans. They signal both the arrival of spring and hence the rising tides of sexuality, new creative expression and possibilities of love and, at the close of summer when they depart for southern spheres, the slow withdrawal of energy as golden summer turns to auburn autumn. The swallow, then, can be the spiritual guide for the flow of our own soul's energy, its outgoing and introverting rhythms, attentively following our nature's organic cycle rather than the imposition of collective norms and values.

In Egyptian mythology, the swallow is sacred to Hathor, a manifestation of the Great Goddess who, in her associations with joy, lovemaking, and music (cosmic harmony), is sometimes related to the Greek Aphrodite. However, Hathor is also the Mother who provides spiritual nourishment and is often depicted as a cow-headed figure with horns and a solar or lunar disc between them, or as a celestial cow whose body is strewn with stars, or as a female figure with cow ears. She has a beautiful colonnaded chapel at Queen Hatshepsut's magnificent Temple in the stunning natural and sacred setting of Deir el-Bahari, and a healing sanctuary at Dendera, the main seat of worship of Hathor, with its sacred lake and sanatorium built around a central bath of magic water. Hathor also has a destructive side often symbolized by the raging lioness goddess Sekhmet who has parallels with the Hindu Kali of India, and who as Bastet, a cat goddess in Egypt, images the more domestic aspect of the feline goddess. Hathor, meaning "House of Horus," plays a part in the Egyptian funerary texts where she appears as solace to the soul on its underworld journey, and as one watching the "weighing of the heart" ceremony of the deceased. "Transforming oneself into a swallow," suggesting an attunement to the divine manifestation of the energies of Hathor indicates the realization of a high degree of esoteric knowledge. From an esoteric perspective, the Hathors are considered to be inter-dimensional beings who claim to exist in the fourth dimension of our universe and who hail from the Sirius star system—a star system (which together with the star Regulus in the Leo constellation, and the central star in the belt of Orion) is related to Egyptian cosmology. The Hat-hors, masters of sound and energy, have been involved with our planet for aeons and are intimately connected with events here on earth as we transition into a new age.

The swallows formation created in rare fashion over two nights in South Field, Wiltshire, July 22–23, 2008 consisted of twelve swallows of six each in a pattern of three rows of birds—one bird in the first row, two in the second, and three in the third—linked together with the same arrangement of the other six swallows "flying" in the opposite direction. At the center where the row of three birds on each side "met" was created a line of nine alternating almond-shaped "vesica piscis" designs. Interspersed between the birds were six "plume" shapes, reminiscent of Aphrodite's shell perhaps, with a further three variations of this pattern. The "vesica piscis" ("vessel of the fish") or "mandorla" (mystical "almond") as it is also called due to its shape, is created by two intersecting circles of equal radius, and has been noted in many other crop formations. As an alive space where two meet, in mythology this almond shape is a common yoni symbol, on

the one hand suggestive of female genitalia or the vulva, on the other symbolizing a gateway and the fertile energies of the goddess birthing creation. In sacred art and architecture, the "vesica piscis" depicts divinity and is the painted shape that houses Christ or the Virgin or sometimes the infant Jesus in Mary's womb. The two sides of the almond shape also point to duality or the tension of opposites and hence to the creative principle becoming conscious in matter. Too, the "mandorla" refers to a flame signifying the manifestation of soul. The way the "mandorlas" are created in the crop also suggests images of quarter moons and further emphasizes the centrality of the feminine dimension of the divine—including such values as intuition, feeling and imagination—manifesting herself in nature.

A second crop circle that I visited also represented this lunar wisdom. The formation consisted of three inter-locking circles that drew attention at first to the underlying "vesica piscis" motif inherent in the design. In addition, there were two sets of prominent "eyes" that suggested "owls eyes."

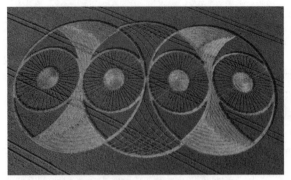

The owl is perhaps most popularly known as the bird of Athena, Mother-goddess of Athens, and the goddess of wisdom and crafts, whom the Greeks claim was born from Zeus's head a fully-grown woman and adorned in armor, after he had swallowed her mother Metis. The owl has been considered the familiar of witches, conductor of souls to the land of the dead, and is a bird of wisdom associated not only with the wisdom of the goddess but also with oracular powers. The owl was a totem of Lilith (sometimes considered the first wife of Adam in the Old Testament) and other triple goddesses of the moon. Writer and healer, Barbara Hand Clow speaks of retrieving a past life as a young priestess who belonged to the Owl Clan, which served the sacred sanctuary at Avebury Stone Circle since the Paleolithic era. This retrieval was pivotal for her in her developing relationship with the crop circles and initiated her first journey to Avebury in this lifetime.[11]

Moreover, in addition to Athena, there are ancient Mesopotamian "Eye-Goddesses" whose staring owl-eyed images have been found throughout the Middle East. Furthermore, the image of the Eye itself has always been associated with the all-seeing divinity, or is a symbol of the faculty of intuitive vision and illumination. The Eye in dreams can often convey a sense of "being seen" from the deep wisdom of the soul within while at the same time our consciousness can look back at its own mysterious ground. Too, there are many myths where universes are born and die with the opening or closing of the god's or goddess's eye.

Beauty is ephemeral and this "death-in-life" theme is also imaged in Aphrodite's association with the bee. The bee goddess appears in ancient Crete where the "Melissae" were attendants and priestesses of the goddess and were associated with mantic knowledge of hidden truths and the mysteries of death and renewal. This is an appropriate image for our era of

11 Barbara Hand Clow, *Alchemy of Nine Dimensions: Decoding the Vertical Axis, Crop Circles, and the Mayan Calendar* (Charlottesville, VA: Hampton Roads, 2004), pp. 168–170.

change as the patriarchal myth collapses all around us and we are called to see the earth and cosmos anew, recovering our ability to see spirit in matter, the earth around us penetrated by the subtle imaginal worlds, and to do so while awake and in full consciousness.

The buzzing sound of bees has been heard in relation to crop circle formation, and in ancient times their buzzing presence was regarded as the "voice" or "sound" of creation. At Delphi, the oracular site devoted to Apollo, the Pythia or main oracular priestess was called the Delphic Bee.[12] In this context, we might regard crop circle designs as contemporary oracular portals, the patterns "speaking" in a pre-verbal symbolic language that requires our tuning in and meditative presence in order to decipher their communications.

Demeter the Corn Mother and Persephone the Corn Maiden

We cannot talk about crop circles without mentioning Demeter and Persephone. In Greek mythology, Demeter (Roman Ceres) is the corn; she is the earth goddess of harvests and the ploughed fields, and Persephone, her daughter, is the maiden or Kore in whom the new seed is continually reborn. This story, in which the Kore is abducted into the underworld while gazing on a narcissus flower and united in marriage to Hades or Pluto, is then sought for by her grieving mother until her rage at her loss induces Zeus to bring about their reunion. This myth was already prefigured in ancient Crete where frescoes of the goddess holding sheaves of corn (circa 13th B.C.) remind us of later reliefs of the Grecian goddess of the harvest (circa 3rd B.C.) and of the earth that gives food. Likewise, the mysteries of descent and ascent at Eleusis (where Demeter arrived from Crete) were also anticipated in earlier Cretan feminine images that suggest a movement down into the earth, and a return from below, in the presence of a flower. Here we see once again the age-old theme of the relationship of death and regeneration which, in our time, has become severed. Could it be that the mystery of the crop circles themselves are reminding us of this enduring archetypal pattern and its significance not only in agriculture but also in the human soul?

There are many myths surrounding Demeter and we cannot follow all their threads. I will limit myself to the most essential elements and their

---

12 Anne Baring & Jules Cashford, *The Myth of the Goddess*, pp. 118–120.

significance for our musings on the phenomena of crop circles. Symbolically, mother and maiden belong together—the mother finds renewal in her daughter, the daughter becomes a mother herself. The Kore is thus an image of the new seed or spirit of life born out of loss and grief of the old in the mother in a cycle that repeats eternally. Demeter and Persephone unite above and below, the living and the dead. The myth suggests that the life of vegetation and of the death and renewal of the human spirit are analogically linked. In a sacred world—one that we have lost—the new plants and the return of the goddess-daughter emerge as one.

The Eleusinian mysteries were honored for two thousand years, up until about the fourth century AD. They relate to an initiation to a vision, a ritual surrounded by secrecy and silence that both women and men could attend. In the Lesser Mysteries, held at the end of winter, a pig, the animal sacred to Demeter, was sacrificed, symbolizing the "death" of the initiate and "rape" of Persephone. The rite involved purification, fasting, blindfolding and handling of sacred objects. In the Greater Mysteries, that took place in the autumn, purifications and celebrations were accompanied by sacrifices and honoring of Iacchos/Dionysos, not the god of wine and dismemberment, but the mystical child and image of perpetual renewal. The culmination of the ritual was achieved in three stages: enacting the abduction of the Kore, the sorrowful wanderings and enraged agonies of the mother, and the final rejoicing and reunion of the mother and daughter. These processes signified the terrors and unknowns of initiation that led inevitably to a vision of light and renewal. It seems likely that the rituals and drinking of potions led to a transpersonal revelation in which death and life are experienced as one. Even though there is no male consort of the goddess in this story, the central mystery of the ritual drama still seems to have been (as from Neolithic times) the Sacred Marriage and birth of the child. This was enacted either concretely with hierophant and priestess and/or symbolically to effect union with the divine before or as the occasion of the return of the Kore from the underworld.

Separation and reunion of mother and daughter is at the heart of this myth. This eventual reunion of mother and daughter forges a new pattern in human consciousness whereby the relationship of the above and below worlds are kept open and a new perception of continuity becomes possible that links "life-in-death" and "death-in-life." When mother and daughter are so intimately bonded such that the unbearable loss of the daughter causes sterility in agriculture and threatens the very environment upon which we depend—(or alternatively, we women can think of our own complex and often fraught relationship to our mothers and daughters and the possibilities for transformation of these dynamics through the myth)—birth and rebirth are inextricably linked and duality is finally transcended. The "birth of the child" becomes the spirit of renewal from the descent into the underworld, through Persephone's marriage to Ploutos/Hades (Latin Pluto), names which actually mean "wealth." The "death" then becomes the "riches" of the harvest or the "treasures" of soulful depth and sight.

The Mystery of Wheat

The mysteries of Osiris no less than of Eleusis point to a long tradition of the mystery of "ears of wheat." At the temple of Philae in Egypt, Osiris lies in a sarcophagus (a symbol of transformation through death, rather than a coffin) from which ears of wheat are rising watered by a priest. Underneath, the ankh, sign of eternal life, alternates with the scepter of divine prosperity. The inscription reads: "This is the form of the unmentionable, secret Osiris who is speeding upward." Osiris here is the life force of the wheat that withdraws from the surface of the earth and returns to the earth each year. "Cut wheat" as also considered a mystery, even a symbol of the god; the emblem of Eleusis itself was the "ear of wheat" and is found on the architecture of Eleusis. The cut wheat, like Osiris and the "death" of Persephone, is that which dies yet paradoxically returns each year. Somehow here we see symbolized the mystery of an individual life that is born and dies at one with the source of all life that is eternal. This symbolism also finds its way in the Christian tradition where the wafer or bread is also the body of Christ. Perhaps too we are reminded of Jesus' saying in the gospel of John 12: 24-5, where he too hints at the mysteries of life, death and rebirth: "Except a corn of wheat fall into the ground and die, it abideth alone; but if it die, it bringeth forth much fruit. He that loveth his life shall lose it; and he that hateth his life in this world shall keep it unto life eternal."

It is unlikely in our day that we will reinstitute the mysteries of Eleusis, but the pattern of human suffering, of deep losses, sorrowful wanderings, and (if we are lucky) happy reunions and new realizations that the myth of Demeter and Persephone points to, are elements of our psychological and interpersonal lives to which we can all relate. If we can bring such a mythical eye to the yearly patterns in our wheat fields and appreciate the unfailing abundance and generosity of nature sprouting forth anew each year no matter how we humans disregard the fragile ecosystems of which we are apart, perhaps we could be moved into our own depths and find there the deep mysteries and complexities of our own being and of Being itself. Perhaps, too, if we pause long enough, we might be able to sense ourselves as not only a life that begins at some point and will end in time, but also as a stranger to ourselves who participates in the great round of death and regeneration, a cyclical eternal return symbolized by Demeter, the Mother and her Kore. Perhaps such a vision could change us and we could, knowingly, participate in the great death and renewal that is part of our cultural experience at this delicate time.

Journal Entry: Crop Circles as Portals-Gateways

The following meditation recorded in my journal in the presence of the Milk Hill "spiraling galaxy" hints at their being a portal or gateway to alternate states of consciousness for wisdom and healing. I began with these simple questions: "What are you?;" "Who are you?;" Why are you here?" Such questions suspend for a moment the rational biases that would dismiss the mystery of crop circle phenomena. In this context the meditation is also a good example of "tuning-in" as a possible way of coming to understand these mysteries.

We come at this point of enormous earth changes on your planet to remind you that you are not alone in the cosmos. Earth—Gaia—herself is ascending to a new level of consciousness and human consciousness needs to align itself also to a higher level. We have great love for your planet and its peoples but the ages are ending and a new level of awareness is needed. You have lost your orientation and have lost a sense of the whole, the sacred. There is no time to lose. When you wake up to who you truly are both as individuals and as a whole you will grieve the losses and, like one of our circles, see that you are a cell in a larger body, that each circle reflects the whole and the whole is in each part. "As above so below" the ancients said. You are becoming aware of this again.

You humans also need to rediscover your joy and delight. The earth and cosmos are beautiful. The orchestration of the many levels of being and consciousness, when in alignment, also bring happiness. We seem to be such a mystery to you only because you have forgotten the mystery. The mystery is awesome for your human self but not for your divine self because in your essence you are one with all Being and have co-created this reality since before the beginning. Even just contemplating our spiraling wheels will help balance the emphasis on the left brain achieved in your world with recovery of a right brain appreciation for the deep feminine wisdom of Sophia—who, quite literally, manifests herself in our circles—the interconnectedness of all being, the visionary and intuitive consciousness, and the silence and passion of following what is true.

The time you are in with its suffering is a labor, a painful labor before the birth of a new era which will stretch for the next five hundred thousand years. You are just at the beginning of this aeon. Do not despair; our circles bring love and bring hope. It is not the end; it is the nigredo that dismembers old forms before the birth, or rather the rebirth of the new. You are privileged to be here now; indeed have chosen this incarnation in order to be bridge builders between the dying Piscean age and the emerging Aquarian age when a new relationship to the cosmos and its many citizens is awakening to you. Deep in your hearts and souls you know this relationship to the many other beings in the galaxies. We are trying to help you awaken to the recovery of this knowledge. The surface consciousness "forgets" or "denies" but the deeper self has galactic consciousness. Look at the many crop circles in a meditative way and you will remember this vaster reality. It is a home-coming. We are waiting for you. Let the circles be your friends and allies, your angelic invisible presence taking form, the twin in that Other world that helps guide you here. Slow down and allow yourself to feel our love and our guidance at any time, and especially when you get pushed off your center!

You can also imagine our circles as spheres and use them as a galactic gateway above your head in meditation, seeing the gateway as the link between your local and universal self. If you can put aside doubt let the guidance from cosmic consciousness flow through and down even as your consciousness can rise up and travel "out." Always at the end of the meditation bring the energy of Oneness into your heart and imagine it flowing out to those near you and then around the planet itself. Do not despair; all is not lost. You are simply and wondrously witnessing the ending of an old cycle and the beginning of a new one.

Laura Smith, a Pacifica Graduate Institute doctoral student, was drawn to the image of "The Towers," a radial one-point perspective formation of three groups of four towers around a central twelve-pointed star, from Uffington on July 8, 2006. At the time of her meditation on this circle, Laura was reflecting on her identification with a driven and somewhat unfeeling life style, and was trying to recover her more sensitive, intuitive and receptive qualities buried deep in her psyche due to a traumatized past. Gazing at this incredible three-dimensional glyph, with beautiful woven and flowing patterns, she writes:

I am the masculine with the feminine center. I radiate out from the center, not yet in perfect harmony with the feminine but on my way there. I am strong, powerful, thrusting, fierce, pulsating, POW! Yet the center, the feminine, is perfectly contained, holding. My power radiates out of her. The feminine is from whence I came; I leap and thrust out of Her. I arise from the feminine, allowed to be an individual but still part of the whole. Everything in the universe births from a single feminine star.

Laura writes that as she was "receiving this information," Cyndi Lauper's song *Time After Time*, a song that speaks of the imbalance between masculine and feminine energies, though they seek integration, was playing in her head. The song felt like "an uncanny yet appropriate accompaniment to the image." Laura goes on to say that Michael Glickman in his book, *Crop Circles: The Bones of God*, comments on how this circle appears to be a warning. The towers resemble skyscrapers or power and the risk of a catastrophic fall, perhaps anticipating the events of 2008, the collapse of banks and of the housing market? On the other hand, the theme of 12 +1, the twelve towers and the central circle, equals the number 13, the number prominent in the "swirling galaxy" formation, a number associated with both transformation and the presence of the goddess. As in the meditation above, that suggests that a contemplation of the circles can help balance the left and right sides of the brain, Laura is aided in balancing her powerful achievements with a central containing ground of being, her "feminine star."

The well-respected English psychic, Isabelle Kingston also relates a "tuning-in" to the crop circle creators whom she knows as The Watchers. This "extra-planetary intelligence" conveyed to her very similar insights about the purpose of the circles long before they were of much public interest or research. According to the Watchers, the appearance of circles marks places of power connected to the subtle and elemental energies of sacred sites that draw cosmic power and are part of an awakening and healing process of our planet as it labors to create a new reality. The Watchers use the metaphor of music to describe this awakening; they say that the circles are like a score of music between the Earth and the cosmos and that what is essential is to feel what is going on rather than trying to read the score. Here are some excerpts from her telepathic communication with the Watchers: "There is a new code of understanding being transmitted. It is a blue-print of a new energy-coding coming on to the planet . . . . You have been given the task to unlock ancient doorways . . . . Within you, you have the blueprint to raise consciousness, to see the unseen, to link telepathically . . . You have all walked on this Earth many times but you know you came from other civilizations, other planets. You must protect your world for many will follow . . . . The Aboriginal people understood the dimensions of the Dreamtime, and although the information is lost . . . [it] can return at the point of the change-over [consciousness shift]."

As in the message above, Isabelle conveys from the Watchers the centrality of love, the fact that we are not alone in the universe, and the need for humanity to take responsibility for its fate: "Amidst all its struggles, humanity does not seem to want to accept that love great and powerful is encircling the world and being transmitted . . . . Your Earth cries with tears, and we feel the pain and sorrow of humanity's misunderstandings. We have not the will to change the world—this, my friends, is your work. Do not always look upward, for there is much to love below."[13]

In the spring of 2008 I was reminded of this possibility of crop circles as portals to Other worlds and other ways of knowing. At that time I visited a small and little-known ancient Asklepeian healing sanctuary called Lissos, in a hidden valley on the southern coast of Crete. I was astounded to dis-

---

13 Freddy Silva, *Secrets in the Fields*, pp. 272–276

cover later that on the mosaic remains of the temple sanctuary floor, which I had photographed, there was a design that was almost precisely the same image as a crop circle pattern—a beautiful four pointed star, or "stretched" square formation surrounded by a circle—from Etchilhampton, England, in 2006. There is a suggestion that the star design at Lissos and in the Etchilhampton formation is similar to the Mayan symbol for the planet Venus.[14] Perhaps, once again as in ancient times, we are being asked to consider our relationship to Other worlds. The design also points to our galactic connection, that our earth is intimately unified with the greater cosmos, and that we are an embodiment of the stars originating from elsewhere.

Crop Circles and the Flower of Life

Another mosaic from the temple sanctuary at Lissos on Crete suggested another connection to crop circles. I had a photograph on my desk of this exquisite mosaic created in a circular mandala pattern. A four-petal flower design was placed at the center of the circle, and radiating out from this center were groups of two, three and four "petals" in the slightly more stylized shape of diamonds, that also approximate a "mandorla" or "vesica piscis" shape. Actually the groupings of four on the circumference were only "implied;" they were "cut" in half and looked therefore more like triangles. Interestingly, these shapes were all in a dark color, but I realized later that the spaces between them replicate the pattern precisely albeit in a lighter

---

14 Steve and Karen Alexander, *Crop Circle Year Book* 2006 (Gosport, Hampshire, UK: Temporary Temple Press, 2006), p. 25.

contrasting shade. This design intrigued me for months and I would keep looking at it and wondering about it, trying to decipher its secret.

Then in the spring of 2009 I came across an ancient symbol called "The Flower of Life" and its accompanying description in a book called *Serpent of Light: Beyond 2012* by Drunvalo Melchizedek. Drunvalo had already published two volumes on the secret of this flower glyph, which he found initially on a six thousand year old Egyptian wall at the Oseiron at Abydos and then found subsequently all over the world, mostly in ancient places. In *Serpent of Light*, he briefly describes the Flower of Life as "the creation pattern for the entire universe and everything in it, including all living creatures." He adds "it's even the creation pattern for aspects of the universe that are not considered things or matter, such as emotions and feelings."[15]

Soon afterward I came across a further description of The Flower of Life in Freddy Silva's chapter on the geometry of crop circles in his remarkable book *Secrets in the Fields: The Science and Mysticism of Crop Circles*. Silva writes that for the Egyptians sacred geometry was the source of mathematics, the laws of physics, and the morphogenetic structure behind the physical world. This "code" and its philosophy were attributed to the Egyptian Thoth, god of learning and measure. Thoth revealed to the ancient philosophers and priests "the secret formulae for spiritual, mental, moral, and physical regeneration," and these cosmic truths were taught to the initiates of the Mystery Schools. The main emphasis in the Mystery School training was on the geometric symbol of the Flower of Life (or, Flower of Amenti), also called the "infinite grid of  creation." It is constructed from "a circle divided into numerous repetitions of the vesica piscis. The process repeats sevenfold and rotates outward to create a "cell;" with every eighth division, a new outward expression begins and the process repeats ad infinitum, creating a matrix." Though in two dimensions it appears as a group of circles, it actually represents a three-dimensional series

15 Drunvalo Melchizedek, *Serpent of Light Beyond 2012: The Movement of the Earth's Kundalini and the Rise of the Female Light, 1949–2013* (San Francisco/Newburyport, MA: Weiser Books, 2007), p. 32.

of spheres within spheres. The Flower works as a hologram, each circle containing the pattern of the whole, and referencing the division of the human cell while simultaneously working as a metaphor for the unfolding process of nature, mythically represented by the seven days of creation in Genesis, and musically by the octave of the music scale.

The information encoded in this glyph is enormous and I cannot go into all the details here. The main point is how several crop formations are related to this ancient design. Silva writes: "The Flower of Life is the culmination of a number of outward rotations, each a form in itself. The first is the Seed of Life." Within this glyph there are a series of pathways called the Tree of Life in Kabbalistic teaching, a system of Jewish mystical thought that leads the seeker to knowledge and wisdom. From the Seed of Life comes the Egg of Life, "a pattern that combines the harmonics of music with the electromagnetic spectrum and underlies all structures in biological life." The Flower of Life unfolds from this Egg. In *The Emerald Tablets of Thoth* (quoted in Silva's book), an inscription beautifully reads: "Deep in the Earth's heart lies the flower, the source of the Spirit that binds all in its form. For know ye that the Earth is living in body as thou art alive in thine own form. The Flower of Life is as thine own place of Spirit, and streams forth through the Earth as thine flows through thy form."

It is thought that the Cathars and Knights Templar also were familiar with the Flower of Life and it was, in part, the secret knowledge of the life force code it contained that they refused to surrender to the Catholic Church's Inquisition for its possible misuse by them. Crop formations appearing in 1994, 1996, and 1997, including the Seed of Life and Egg of Life as well as others based on hexagonal geometry (a circle can naturally be divided into six parts), made Silva realize that they could be superimposed over the grid of The Flower of Life. In other words, the crop circles were pointing to this ancient Egyptian knowledge, this universal code of life and its manifestation through all the dimensions of existence, planetary and human.[16]

Is it possible that the Lissos "flower" mosaic that I had photographed and contemplated for many months is a version of this Flower of Life with its numerological and replicating patterns? Did the ancient Greeks also include

---

16 Silva, *Secrets in the Fields*, pp. 183–186.

teachings about its mysterious and cosmic body of knowledge to Mystery School initiates based on the Egyptian code? Was this design carefully placed on the floor in an ancient Greek temple and healing sanctuary that may itself actually go back almost six thousand years, used for healing? Was healing itself related to the spirit of the Earth as well as the recovery of cosmic mysteries such as we see in crop circles today? Though the Lissos temple has fallen into neglect and is no longer the site of dream incubation rituals, yet its beautiful symbol calls to us still from across the centuries to help awaken us to its timeless wisdom. This connection between temple dream incubation rituals and crop circles is a theme in Part Four of this work.

This contemplation of crop circle formations and their symbols hints at the possible "hieroglyphic" communication of these vital signs. These earth dreams touch our depths before they stir the surface; they point to the spirit becoming alive in nature and in us. The circles educate us to move beyond polarity to a consciousness that can appreciate the unified whole of creation. The crop codes suggest that our imagination, intuition, and feeling can be activated as a profound guidance system to co-create a new reality by reflecting on these visitations from other dimensions of consciousness. They also suggest that we are being seen from the deep wisdom of the cosmic soul and that this deep wisdom is sending its love and energy to encourage us as we make the huge yet necessary transition from one age to another.

Crop Circles and the Imaginal Landscape of the Soul

Comparisons have been made between the crop circles and ancient stone circles such as those at Avebury and Stonehenge. Were these ancient ritual and astronomical observatories once made of corn or wheat? Interestingly, the major crop circle activity is in the vicinity of the landscape of Wiltshire, southwest of London, in the Stonehenge, Avebury, and Silbury Hill ("Hill of the Shining Beings") areas, places where there still remain chalk white drawings of horses, thousands of years old, etched on the side of hills. The Druids and Celts believed that these horses carried the souls of the dead to the Other world. On the other hand, the white horse has also been associated with the winged Pegasus who issues in the new era.

I remember as a child my family driving through Wiltshire on our way to Devon in the West Country for the summer holidays. Along this route, I would always feel a shift in the landscape, and experience a mystical connection to something strange and sacred that would deeply affect me. Looking out the car window at night, I saw how the moon seemed to be moving along with us, accompanying us like a guide through the uncanny atmosphere of this part of southern England with its rolling farmland and occasional groups of trees on hilly mounds. Glastonbury in Somerset (also in this general area), of course, is the site of the mystical land of Avalon, the lore surrounding King Arthur, Guinevere, and Merlin, and is a current day mecca for all sorts of spiritual revelations and metaphysical tourism. Avalon is a celestial city of the heart as we will see in the chapter on mystical cities in Part Four.

We know that the ancient idea that the earth, Gaia, is a living being— ("For know ye that the Earth is living in body" as the Egyptian Thoth text states)—is returning to us today. In the same way that we have subtle levels to our body, earth, too, is enveloped in a subtle imaginal geography and, throughout this book I have given examples of how our eye of vision and imagination, located in the heart, can access this landscape. Since Plato, our planet was visualized and described as being made up of grids or templates with geometrical properties that linked the physical world to its spiritual origins. More recently geomancers and dowsers have mapped this energy grid or network of so-called "ley" lines—what the ancient Chinese called "dragon paths"—that often follow ancient pathways and link sacred sites together. We are electromagnetic beings that respond to these forces in the environment all around us, and we are slowly becoming more aware of this fact.

Plato saw that the subtle energetic grid of Gaia comprised a dodecahedron, made up of 12 five-sided plates or pentagons related to the fifth element (beyond earth, air, fire and water) of what was then called "aether." This subtle life energy is now being re-evaluated by today's physicists, cosmologists, and psychologists. Each plate or "face" distributed equally around the planet is also called an Albion plate. The English poet and visionary William Blake, in his famous poem *Jerusalem* (1804), referred to a giant original and ancient archetypal human figure whom he called Albion sprawled, as it were, across the whole earth. This figure is often imaged as a "rotundum" and, as geomancer and clairvoyant Richard Leviton describes in his book, *Signs on the Earth*, this rotundum is a vast spherical form containing all the dimensions of reality and the enormous store of collective and mystical experience. Albion, viewed from the point of view of the *mundus imaginalis*, is a hologram of our galactic history including the influences and energies of major stars and star beings associated with our planet.

I have already noted how Jung felt that in our time we are being encouraged to make this larger spherical shaped Anthropos or Self—also symbolized by the UFO—more conscious. Today, according to geomantic vision, Albion, having slumbered for aeons, is now on the verge of waking up, apparently already stirring in France and England, Spain, and Portugal.[17] This suggests that as Gaia awakens, that is, becomes conscious, we too can assist in her evolution by accessing the holographic field and walking in her imaginal domains, increasingly being enabled to perceive "the mysteries and epiphanies of higher space-time."[18] As Earth wakes up, we also awaken! The fact that the figure of Albion is connected with Great Britain and its sacred geography is important for crop circle phenomena for, as we know, the circles' major center of activity is in the Glastonbury, Stonehenge, Avebury, and Silbury Hill vicinities. Crop circles are the visible signatures on the earth of this awakening cosmic field of intelligence and we have an obligation to listen in to how we are being educated as we extend the range of our consciousness and imagination into expanded dimensional realities.

Crop Circles and Inter-dimensional Dialogue

Many researchers comment on the unusual interactive nature of crop circles, for example, how experiments in meditation and imagining particular patterns have resulted in just those patterns appearing the next day or shortly thereafter. There is a playful element, therefore, a sense that a dance has been initiated, and that we are in the "early stages of a universal, intercultural, intermingling," with other civilizations not based on planet earth, or as architect and crop circle researcher, Michael Glickman, says, "other consciousnesses, intelligences,

---

17 Richard Leviton, *Signs on the Earth* (Charlottesville, VA: Hampton Roads, 2005), pp. 209–210.
18 *Ibid.*, p. 123.

or parallel dimensions, that are interested in making contact with us."[19] My own meditations on the circles are in harmony with this view.

The circles have also been seen in relation to balls of light of various colors or tubes of light, which have been videotaped and authenticated, UFO sightings, or close-encounter activity. There is actually a hill called "Golden Ball Hill" in Wiltshire that marks the ancient nature of the balls of light phenomena.

ET/UFO researcher and author Dr. Steven Greer relates how in the early 1990s his research group, Center for the Study of Extraterrestrial Intelligence or CSETI, got permission to stay on a farm in Alton Barnes in England where they practiced their protocols for contacting extra-terrestrials. This time they visualized an actual shape—an equilateral triangle with a circle at each apex—while performing a special meditation process with the intention of sending this shape into Universal Mind and to the ETs. The next day, this exact shape appeared in a crop circle nearby. On another evening when the group was engaging in its contact protocols, a craft with counter-clockwise circulating lights shining down on them appeared from above the clouds. Later that same night, the group saw a 100 foot space ship above a field, with beautiful multi-colored lights—red, green, blue, yellow—spinning in unusual patterns, and of an intensity that he describes as not of this world.[20]

Writer and researcher, Barbara Hand Clow, feels the Circlemakers (as she and several others now call the creators of the glyphs) are related to her communication with the Pleiadians since the 1980s. For her, the circles represent downloads of information from these star beings which are related to her research into superstring theory. Clow suggests that the appearance of crop circles points to the possibility of a multi-dimensional activation of consciousness from our roots in the earth to more subtle levels of being. She also has experienced direct communication with the circles, recounting several examples of synchronistic drawings that coincided with the appearance of precisely that design appearing in the fields. One striking example is her sketch of the 1991 Barbury Castle circle right before it happened.[21] Strangely enough,

---

19 Gazecki, *CropCircles: Quest for Truth.*
20 Stephen Greer, M.D., *Extraterrestrial Contact* (Afton, VA: Crossing Point, 1999), chapter 32, pp. 210–231.
21 Barbara Hand Clow, *Alchemy of Nine Dimensions*, p.174.

though distant in time, my daughter Sarah's drawing on January 26, 2002 of a symbol she titled "soul life" has an uncanny resemblance to a crop circle called "The Revelation of Pi" that also appeared at Barbary Castle, on June 1, 2008. Pi is an infinite and irrational number, so indeed points to the soul—more on pi below in the section on sacred geometry. I only chanced upon my daughter's drawing as I was reviewing the final draft of

my book. The similarity of these two "Pi" glyphs show how close crop circles are to products of the creative unconscious, and indicate that matter itself has a spiritual depth, has soul.

The circle, found in crop circles and in the shape of the circulating lights of extraterrestrial craft, is a major symbol of unity cross culturally, and one of the primary symbols of divinity. Like the spiraling arms of the galaxy, Navajo, and Tibetan sand paintings, Cathedral rose windows, Islamic geometries, and the alchemical image of the tail-eating serpent, crop circles are natural earth *mandalas*, symbols of wholeness, images of the Self in matter, signaling to us that it is time to integrate our science with our religious longing and unite our earthly and heavenly natures, making planetary and ecological decisions from a position of centeredness, wisdom, and compassion, rather than limitation, crudeness, and division. In this context, looking at the circles helps activate the right hemisphere of our brains bringing our intuitive and imaginative natures into greater harmony with our left brain analytical and reflective abilities.

Healer, physicist, cosmologist and mystic, Jude Currivan, tells the story in her book, *The 13th Step*, how in May 1998, sitting on the top of Silbury Hill looking down at a newly formed crop circle in the shape of a golden disc made up of an inner and outer circle linked by 33 curling "flames"— also called the "Beltane wheel" due to its appearance three days after the Celtic solar festival of Beltane—she was gradually guided to a series of sacred journeys to awaken the healing energies of other etheric golden discs

(that the crop circle had mirrored energetically and symbolically), placed at various key sites around the world. Following and trusting in her guidance the journeys, beginning in Egypt and culminating in the UK through the dreaming landscape of Albion, became an initiation of inner and outer transformation, which she felt was helping individual, collective and galactic shifts of awareness at this critical time in our planetary and cosmic history.[22]

Crop Circles and Sacred Geometry: The Mystery of Number

Most recently, crop circles have been studied in relation to the universal laws to be found within sacred geometry and the symbolism of numbers—pentagram, Star of David, golden mean or phi, heptagon and octagon, even nine-fold to twelve and thirteen-fold forms. Sacred geometry refers to the timeless and inherent underlying structure of energy as it enters matter and motion in the universe and on earth. It governs proportion that creates order and beauty. The alchemical sign for uniting spirit with matter appeared in many alchemical pictures that depict the task of "squaring the circle." This "squaring of the circle" is represented in the four-pointed star with circle in the background that I mentioned above both visible at the healing temple sanctuary of Lissos on Crete as well as in the 2006 Etchilhampton crop circle. It serves as a reminder that we can marry heaven and earth in our human form and live our temporal lives from the point of view of the awareness of the timeless and spiritual dimensions of reality, of the marriage of masculine and feminine, logos and love.

The mystery of number and geometry ("measure of the earth"), shape and proportion express universal constants found in the designs of flowers, galaxies, temples and cathedrals, and in the human body itself. Going back to philosophers such as Plato and Pythagoras these mysteries were thought

22 Jude Currivan, *The 13th Step: A Global Journey in Search of Our Cosmic Destiny* (Carlsbad, CA: Hay House, 2007).

SONGLINES OF THE SOUL

to be reflections of the divine creator and so they were incorporated in the designs of sacred spaces, buildings and gardens. Jung's collaborator on the psyche-matter problem, quantum physicist Wolfgang Pauli, who felt he embodied both the scientific as well as the mystical view of the cosmos, wrote that the mathematician Kepler (1571–1630) found geometry to be "the archetype of the Beauty of the universe," and that mathematical proportions "were implanted from all eternity in the soul of man, made in the likeness of the Creator."

Furthermore, as Jung has demonstrated in his psychology of the unconscious, numbers are as much *discovered* (2+2+2=6 is an *a priori* truth) as *invented* (for the purposes of counting for example), and so stimulate the imagination embodying an archetypal numinosity. Indeed, Jung felt that although this ancient spiritual force of number (found, for example, in the I Ching, the Kabbala, the horoscope, as well as Pythagorean mysticism) was not currently valued in mathematics or academic psychology, it was nonetheless the common ground shared by psychology and physics. So number as an ordering principle could form a bridge between the archetypal, imaginal world and the tangible, physical world. Perhaps we might even say that number creates an eros or love bond between psyche and matter. We are witnessing this erotic bond in the harmonious beauty of the crop circles.

For example, the *mandala* shape of the circle (in all its variations) represents Oneness, wholeness and unity and also, qualitatively, has an ordering and centering or healing and meaningful purpose. If you visit a Greek temple or enter a European cathedral without knowing anything about the principles of sacred geometry, you intuitively sense the spiritual and emotional effects of its measure, size, proportion and design. Crop circles based on these principles have the same impact on the body and psyche. Once seen or visited they change the way you feel about and perceive the world. They can activate a deep and sometimes obscured longing in the soul. Uncannily, they even seem familiar as if we know what they are even if we cannot describe it very well.

While much has already been written on the sacred geometry of crop circles especially in the work of prominent researchers Karen Alexander and

Michael Glickman,[23] I want to give a few examples of how number is not only a quantitative measure but also a qualitative difference, which, as such, has the property of uniting different parts of ourselves, the literal and symbolic, the functional and metaphoric. For example, the circle, which represents the monad or one, wholeness, unity or the divine, the center from which everything else evolves, has the interesting characteristic of Pi. Pi is a ratio between the circumference and the diameter of the circle. It is an irrational number whose value can never be completely known for its decimal places stretch into infinity without resolution. By definition, therefore, a circle includes the idea of no beginning and no end, or infinity, and hence it has a connection to the unfathomable mystery of an eternal creation that also has no beginning and no end. Commenting on the "Pi" formation of June 1, 2008, as a "true historic marker" and the "outstanding formation of the year," Michael Glickman also writes of Pi as the mathematical constant used in all calculations relating to circles and is key to "squaring the circle," the alchemical symbol for the union of spirit and matter, or marriage of Heaven and Earth. Too, the central point of a circle, though we may represent it by a compass or pencil point, cannot be seen and is really only known by inference. This may remind us of the old mediaeval scholastic definition of God as "a circle whose center is everywhere and the circumference nowhere." The crop circles remind us of these eternal and esoteric truths and therefore through their shape awaken us to the sacred in nature as well as in ourselves.

John Anthony West in his book, *Serpent in the Sky: The High Wisdom of Ancient Egypt*,[24] describes how the French Egyptologist Schwaller De Lubicz recovers the fact that the pyramid builders also knew how cosmic laws, processes, functions, and principles were included in their myths and simultaneously expressed by number and the relationship between numbers. Number, therefore, was imbued with symbolic meaning for the Egyptians as well as for the Greeks. So, for example, the number 2 represents the division of the circle into a dyad so that, symbolically, creation can come into being. If there is

---

23 See, for example, Steve and Karen Alexander, *Crop Circles: Signs, Wonders, and Mysteries* (Chartwell Books, Edison, NJ, 2008), and Michael Glickman, *Crop Circles: The Bones of God* (Berkeley, CA: Frog Books, 2009).

24 John Anthony West, *Serpent in the Sky: The High Wisdom of Ancient Egypt* (Wheaton, IL: Quest Books, 1993). For my discussion of sacred geometry I have relied on this and the above books as well as Silva's *Secrets in the Fields*.

only unity there can be no difference. Geometrically, 2 is created by two intersecting circles and this makes the "vesica piscis" that I noted above in the swallows and the owl formation. This archetypal expression of "twon-ess" first appeared in the crop circle phenomenon in 1996 and speaks of our descent into physical manifestation and the experience of opposition and polarities. "Twoness" in dreams often indicates that an unconscious content is becoming more conscious.

The number 3 holds the tension of opposites between the unity of one and the difference that two makes. It creates a third reality that both incorporates and transcends division. This third force cannot be understood rationally, for only the principle of relationship by love, affinity, or desire can, via the heart, understand Three. We can imagine this perhaps as the Mother and Father principles creating the Child, the Child representing a new creative potential and hope for the future. We have a felt sense of this when conflict acknowledged consciously eventually resolves itself in a new approach or attitude that can move our lives forward in some unforeseen way. Three-ness is an equilateral triangle or a three-fold unity as expressed in numerous universal mythologies of the trinity, and there are stunning crop circle designs expressing both these possibilities. At Avebury Trusloe in 1998, a true triangle shape appeared with three small circles at the apex of each point, while in 2001 at Liddington Castle in Wiltshire, a forma-tion appeared in wheat that used three interlocking circles that looked like crescent moons enclosed within a unifying circle. At the center a circle is circumscribed by a triangle with curved sides. Patterns such as this have been used in the "trefoil" designs of European church and cathedral windows emphasizing the trinity or three-fold nature of God.

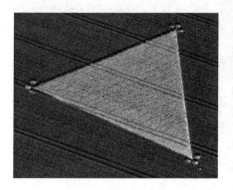

Four brings depth and material substance to reality. Four can be geometrically expressed as a square or as a cube, like in a lump of sugar. "Fourness" is found in the four elements (earth, air, fire, water), the four seasons, the quadratic expression of the self either as the four functions of consciousness (feeling, thinking, sensing and intuition) or as a *mandala* expression of wholeness (such as Buddhist representations of a holy city). Four is also the "squaring of the circle" pointing to the mysterious connection between one and four, and between our spiritual and physical natures. Four is also the cross, the cross of matter upon which we are all pinned and limited and, but eventually, through our consciousness, redeemed. Crop circles have used numerous examples of four—squares, cubes, grid patterns, Celtic cross designs, and four times four circles linked together in different ways.

Five is the pentagon, the five-sided figure, and pentagram, the five-pointed star. In Egypt the ideal of the realized individual was to become a star, to become Ra. There are myriad five-pointed star designs in crop circles perhaps alluding to our potential to become stars, to become fully realized human beings. To the Pythagoreans, five related to the "creation" of matter, to its "happening," to the life principle itself. It was also the number of "love" because it represented the union of the male number three

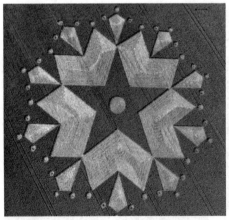

and the female number two. Five-ness gives expression to the human body with a head, two arms and two legs, as well as five fingers on each hand and five toes on each foot. Five is the quintessence, the four plus one, the expression of our physical form and its subtle body or eternal essence.

The geometry of the pentagon figure and the pentagram star is also the generator of the Golden Section or Divine Proportion. This is a ratio called "phi" that relates to the patterns of all living things from plants to the structure of human bodies. The ratio and proportions of the Golden Section are thought to underlie the designs of what we find most beautiful and have therefore been included in the structure of sacred spaces for thousands of years. The pentagram, too, is linked to the generation of the so-called Fibonacci sequence, a series of numbers that demonstrates an elegance in the way nature propagates its forms, and which can be found in the Golden Spiral. An example of this spiral can be seen in the Stonehenge "Julia Set"—a swirling nautilus or shell shape—mentioned earlier. This shell-like form, looking a bit like a G or treble clef, was also produced in a circle near the Pewsey Vale white horse in 2002. The clef also points perhaps to the musical strings underlying all creation.

Interestingly, Leonardo da Vinci's famous picture of Vitruvian Man unites both the five-fold human form with the squaring of the circle, suggesting that human beings as physical bodies that house the immortal soul are the mysterious mediators between heaven and earth. Moreover, in the construction of temples or cathedrals as the meeting place of gods and men, or the union in stone of the sacred and human, both the squaring of the circle and the Golden Proportion principles of sacred geometry were employed to evoke an emotional and spiritual response in the pilgrim. In so far as they embody these principles, crop circles serve the function of pointing to these archetypal foundations to human experience and the deep changes that can come if we make ourselves vulnerable to their appeal. The circles remind us that life itself is a fundamental universal principle, and not an accident or an afterthought. Recovering this view of life radically alters the way we see ourselves, each other, the planet, and our life in the universe as a coherent and meaningful mystery, no longer to be disregarded and squandered but rather to be honored and treasured.

The hexagon and hexagram geometry contains the double triangle or six-pointed star. It is known as the Star of David or the Seal of Solomon, a mystical symbol in alchemy that refers to the union of above and below and the balance of our celestial and terrestrial natures. The upward pointing triangle is solar and symbolizes life, spirit, the linga and the masculine principle, while the downward pointing triangle is lunar and symbolizes the waters, the body, the yoni and the feminine principle. These pairs of opposites that include both our essence and substance aim for integration within an individual and a culture. The Seal of Solomon also points to the realized union of the upper and spiritual chakras of humankind with the lower and physical chakras at the heart center where access to wisdom, balance and love become available. This double triangle, that values spirit and matter equally also yields to the intermediate subtle world of the imaginal, *mundus imaginalis*, and its parapsychological or magical epiphanies that are coming into prominence as we move into Aquarius.

John Michell found the seal of Solomon encoded in the ground plan at Stonehenge, and beautiful six-pointed stars made of stone are placed in the ground outside the cathedral at Orvieto in Italy. These examples suggest that the Seal of Solomon has been honored since time immemorial. According to Freddy Silva, thirteen of the forty crop formations reported in

1997 were hexagon-based. It was his devotion to deciphering these hexagon-based circles that led him to the revelations of the Flower of Life mysteries discussed above. There was also a beautiful Seal of Solomon crop circle surrounded by a "necklace" of hexagrams and diamond-shapes at Avebury Henge in July 2005. Moreover, six is also symbolized by the double trigrams of the Chinese *I Ching*, and in Egyptian mythology six creates time and space and is the number of the material world in which we live and die and yet, from the mystical point of view, can transcend. Six underlies temporal divisions such as twenty-four hours in a day (twelve day hours and twelve night hours) and twelve months in a year. The six-sided cube, which is a symbol for volume, is often the "throne" upon which the Pharaoh sits or out of which the Pharaoh is seen to emerge. The Egyptian temple both symbolizes and is time and space. Once again, the crop circles are communicating to us these ancient and enduring universal truths.

Seven or the heptagon and heptagram points to the colors of the rainbow, the notes of the musical scale, the major chakras of the subtle body, the days of creation, or the seven deadly sins. Seven cannot be divided equally into the 360 degrees of a circle so it produces an "irrational number" that points to the reality of dreams, intuitions, the unconscious, numinous experiences, and the deep emotional self. Seven also relates to the phenomenon of growth, which is not a continuous process but rather takes place in quantum jumps. Seven also refers to stages, or sequences, or cycles of change. For example, the mystic alchemists felt that the seven "operations" or stages of the opus (*solutio, calcinatio, sublimatio,* etc.) represented a cycle of transformation, which the initiate would repeat until the work was completed. Furthermore, Egyptian pyramids are built on the principle of seven, a combination of a square base symbolizing the four elements of matter, and triangular sides alluding to the spirit. Beautiful heptagon formations such as the circles at Danebury Ring, Hampshire, East Field, Alton Barnes, and Tawsmead

Copse, Wiltshire began to appear in July and August 1998.

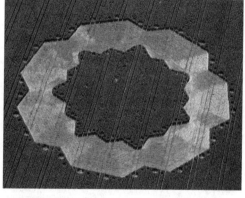

I will end this brief discussion of sacred geometry with the number 8 but, as I have said, crop circles have been created with up to thirteen-fold forms, these higher numbers referring to worlds of possibility and potential also required for acts of creation. Too, as we consider number symbolism, it should be remembered that each number itself not only has specific functions and characteristics, but also includes all combinations of functions leading up to it. Seven is 4 and 3 (as in the pyramid) but also 5 and 2 (opposition united by love), 6 and 1 (manifestation in time and space of the source point of creation). With 8, the octagon (an eight sided figure) and octogram (an eight-pointed star), we have the completion and renewal of a cycle, the simultaneous ending and beginning of a unity or phase of consciousness either individual or cultural, symbolized by the theme of "the death and rebirth of the king" in alchemy or Egyptian mythology. For example, an Egyptian text referring to the myth of creation states: "I am One, who becomes Two, who becomes Four, who becomes Eight, and then I am One again." (The fertilized ovum is a biological expression of this ancient dictum). It is Thoth (Hermes to the Greeks), messenger of the gods and god of writing and knowledge who gives humankind access to the mysteries of the created world, which is symbolized by the number Eight.

Eight is also a lunar number as the different phases of the moon from dark to full to dark again are usually divided into eight periods. Divinities of the Moon speak to rhythms and cycles, water and healing, our psychic and oracular consciousness, death and transformation. Moreover, octagonal geometry underlies much Islamic art and architecture and is mirrored, for example, in the Wheel of Dharma and the idea of the eightfold path of enlightenment in Buddhism. These profound mythic, philosophical, mystical and universal truths are being communicated to us by the Circlemakers. They are calling us to our depths, reminding us that we could recover a rich heritage and coherent understanding of ourselves at this time of death, transition, and renewal by exploring the whole of ourselves through the separate but interrelated disciplines of science, art, religion and philosophy.

Most importantly for our discussion, 8 is the sounding of the octave, the seventh note in a musical scale that "resolves" itself simultaneously as an ending (the "eighth" note) and a new beginning (the "first" note of the new scale), a note that repeats itself at a "higher" or "lower" frequency. With the octave we have resonance, harmonics, and potential music. Crop circles with their underlying number symbolism and beautiful artistic expressions

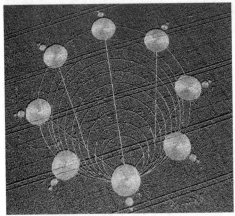

can be considered visual epiphanies of the music of the spheres or the underlying strings of creation. They are symphonic glyphs speaking to us in the notes of the cosmic soul, appealing to our hearts to change our lives. Robert Fludd (1574–1637) the English Paracelsian physician and philosopher who was interested in the correspondences between the celestial world and nature, in his *De Musica Mondana*, shows a picture of the relationship between the planetary harmonics and the musical scale with God's "hand" at the top tuning the cosmos visualized as a sort of stringed instrument.

There are many lovely examples of eightfold crop circle designs: the octogram at Bishops Cannings, Wiltshire, June 2000; the mandala "star" pattern at Lane End Down, Hampshire, in July 2001; the "underbelly of a space-ship and lights" formation in Huish, Wiltshire, August 2001; and the "figure eight" or infinity symbol on August 8, 2008 at Milk Hill, Wiltshire. These circles call to the songlines of our souls inviting us to a wider range of frequencies, to harmonize with our destiny, and to find creative expressions of the subtle imaginal vibrations that are calling us into the future.

Crop Circles and Sound

Crop circles invite us to "resonate" with their earth dream messages. This has led circle researcher Freddy Silva to link the principles of sacred geometry found within their multiple patterns with vibration, sound—what he calls in his book *Secrets in the Fields* "acoustical alchemy."[25] Silva first explored this musical thread in his conversations with Professor Gerald Hawkins, astronomer and author of *Stonehenge Decoded*, who discovered diatonic ratios—perfect intervals of the music scale—beginning in some of the circles in the early 1990s. Sound as trilling, droning, crackling, humming, and other unusual sounds—even celestial chords—have been heard just before formations are created. In both Eastern and Western cosmologies, sound was always imagined as the source of creation. "In the beginning there was the Brahman, with whom was the word" (The Rig Veda), or "In the beginning was the Word, and the Word was with God" (John I, verse I). Sound and geometry were linked as far back as 4000 B.C. and this link was taught both at Egyptian Mystery schools and encoded in their stone temples. The importance of sound and its relation to creation is so significant cross-culturally that early mystic-philosophers (such as Pythagoras) considered the study of music to be integral to an understanding of the mysteries. I have already referred to Fludd's illustration of "The Celestial Instrument" describing the relationship between earth elements, astrological forces, higher spiritual energies, and the musical scale. The channeled material of Isabelle Kingston noted above also suggests a musical link between earth and the cosmos. In religious traditions cross-culturally the sounding of the OM or AUM, for

---

25 Freddy Silva, *Secrets in the Fields*, chapter 11, pp. 204ff.

example, or other kinds of chanting is used to align the practitioner with the cosmic source and thereby spiritually center the individual.

Are the unusual sounds heard in tandem with crop circle formation related to high frequency emissions involved in their creation? Silva reports that while he was entertaining this possibility two glyphs appeared that pointed to this sound theme, one so-called "ratchet" glyph (Stockbridge Down, 1995) suggesting a connection with Pythagoras' "lambdoma," a circular diagram defining the exact relationships between musical harmonics and mathematical ratios, and the other (Goodworth Clatford, 1996) a sonic "cymatic" rose pattern in barley in which the plants were unusually bent six inches from the top. Moreover, the mathematical ratios in the lambdoma show how octaves ascend and frequencies accelerate and therefore point analogically to the multi-dimensional nature of reality to which we are being invited.

Today, matter is no longer considered a "thing" but a pattern of energy orchestrated by invisible frequencies and magnetic fields. The study of cymatics explored by the Swiss scientist Hans Jenny and others illustrates this relationship between frequency and physical form. Sound emitted as frequency through water, powder, oil and sand creates geometric and harmonic shapes. Raising the frequency increased the complexity of the patterns from simple circles to complex tetrahedrons and mandalas. These studies suggest a visual connection between crop circles and sound. Furthermore, the increasing complexity in the design of the crop circles over the years and especially since 2000 suggests that the frequency with which they are being created is also increasing. Experiments measuring frequency discrepancies in and around crop circles have been carried out and seem to confirm this rise in frequency. Without going into further details here, I will say only that it is now proposed that the tubes of light sometimes seen in relation to the appearance of crop circles, and shown in a photograph in Freddy Silva's book, "step down" from the eighth dimension into the seventh where sound occurs. The light to sound movement then passes through the sixth dimension of geometry drawn by gravitational forces and electromagnetic fields into the earth where geodetic energy combines to create the formation. It seems to me that some form of intelligence and consciousness from a wise and loving source must participate in this process. The planet is evolving, awakening, raising its vibration and we too are being invited to awaken and to raise our vibration and expand our consciousness.

Ancient sacred sites located for their enhancing magnetic or geodetic properties often near water, from Neolithic places of veneration to Egyptian pyramids, temples and Gothic cathedrals, were built on cosmic principles involving sacred geometry, planetary and musical harmonics and, when the beneficial and centering affects of song or chant were added, were designed to heighten awareness and expand consciousness. Crop circles may perform a similar task. From this point of view, crop circles are expressions of the harmonics of creation, those invisible frequencies now understood to underlie all physical matter, and are considered temporary (and contemporary) temples designed for the purpose of mental, physical and spiritual regeneration through enabling altered states of consciousness, and to help reunite above and below, cosmos and self.

Crop Circle Dreams and the Great Awakening

A dream that I had a year after first visiting the crop circles, on September 23, 2009, picks up on the musical theme. In one scene in the dream, Michael Glickman is in a beautiful English church ringing the local church bells while also drumming; his actions are related to responding to the crop circle phenomena. In another scene there is a large party being planned for the end of the crop circle season. I go up to Michael and a woman standing with him and say something like "the crop circles are activating and energizing me." They reply by asking me what does this feeling make me want to do? I say it makes me want to dance! Then I begin to dance, expressing myself in large gestures and movements. I feel alive and free. This dream points to a kind of Dionysian ecstatic joy that comes from interaction with the crop formations, a less rational more feeling approach to them that points to rhythm (drums), dance and gesture as three forms of ritual energy expression to embody my relationship with the sacred.

Crop circles signal the emerging shift in consciousness that seeks to link us with the hidden mysteries of our being here. One crop circle researcher, cultural historian, and psychotherapist, Jonathan de Vierville, had a "big" dream in August 2003 that coincided with his early interest in the formations and the New Cosmological Story of the Universe articulated by Thomas Berry and Brian Swimme. Not all the details in the dream are shared, but key themes include the following: A major cosmological initiation and transformation process was underway. This was a deep secret concerning a global mind change and one had to be prepared and ready to receive the new vibration. The dreamer felt an electrical impulse that came through and over his head. This blue-white light also moved through his body, up his spine and out through his head changing the constitution and character of his body, brain and being. He was energized but calm. His task was to take this energy "through the justice courts to where it belonged."

This extraordinary dream is unequivocal about the galactic and planetary awakening that is occurring. It is a path to a new consciousness as we transition to a new stage of human evolution. The dreamer's experience recalls the increasing number of stories of *kundalini* spiritual openings that re-form and "re-wire" us into a new being, not only mentally but also energetically, altering the nature of our subtle form. The dream hints also at the ethical claims made upon those who are given this gift: to change one's life (the "justice courts") in service to this planetary initiation and to bring precious gems of knowledge into everyday life.

Key crop circle researcher, Karen Alexander, has dedicated herself to this change in planetary consciousness indicated by the crop circle manifestations. Speaking in 2010 at the Crop Circle Conference held annually in the UK that she and her husband Steve organize, she mentions how our imagination, contemplation, and unconscious—especially as revealed in dreams—is also a significant aspect of the crop circle phenomena that helps deepen us into its mystery. In her lecture, she recalled a dream:

I was traveling to a European country with my husband, daughter, and friend Michael Glickman, to give a talk on crop circles. We got off the bus and were taken to an inn. We were eating, drinking, laughing and talking about the crop circles. I notice a window and look out of it to see a beautiful green meadow; the conversation around me faded away to quiet. In the meadow was a beautiful shrine. I got up and went to the back door. I noticed I was wearing a white dress which was grubby and, though I tried, I couldn't get it clean. I walked out the back door, into the meadow, and looked toward the shrine. A priest walked by, dressed in scarlet, heading toward the stone shrine. He stood facing it and pulled his garments over his head and onto the shrine so I couldn't see what he was doing. I watched fascinated. I looked down at my shoes and saw that I was not on grass, but on flowers, only flowers. Looking back at the priest I wondered what he was doing. Was he praying over the bones of a saint, I wondered? The priest took down his robes and came over to me. He stopped and reached out with his hand and put something in my hand: it was a communion wafer, but the wafer, amazingly, had a crop circle design on it. The design was the stunning cross formation with Celtic knot (or lovers knot) inscribed on it from Etchilhampton in 2008. I was awed that I had been given this crop circle wafer. The priest walked away, and I looked down and suddenly saw that my dress was now all white— the grubbiness had gone.

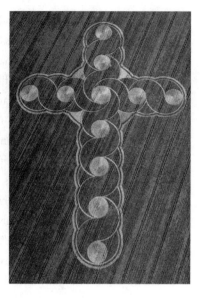

Reflecting on the dream, Karen wondered why she had not put the wafer in her mouth. Months later, she had another dream. She asked, "what is this?" (meaning the wafer with the cruciform and Celtic motifs from the first dream). A voice says, "it is the leaven of the wise." In alchemy, this "leaven of the wise" is one of the many symbols for the Philosopher's Stone. Karen felt that she was being told that the crop circles are the philosopher's stone. The goal of the alchemical opus was to produce this stone; it was imagined as an incorruptible subtle essence, sometimes called the celestial or resurrection body, produced by the great work and effort of transforming matter into spirit, and spirit into matter. Perhaps, Karen thought, she was being told that the crop circles are indeed spirit incarnate in matter. In this dream, Karen ate the wafer.

In life, Karen views the cross as a symbol of the inherent cost of spiritual development and of the conflicting demands that arise in such a path. Dedicating herself to this development both personally and collectively has cost her personal friendships and other hardships. However, the cruciform glyph with its lovers knot inscribed in the arms of the cross was a reminder to her from the wisdom of the dream that the sacrifices involved in the individuation process must be made willingly and in full consciousness, no matter how hard the path may be at times. The formation spoke to her of the passion, compassion and ultimate heartbreaking beauty of this act, an act that arises out of love. Also, in the dream, the fact that she is standing on flowers (not grass) is emphasized. This recalls the presence of Aphrodite and flowers springing up in her path. Karen's vocation is rooted deeply in the feminine ground of the earth.

The numbers 7 and 4 in the formation (7 referring to the reality of dreams and the alchemical operations or stages of transformation, and 4 symbolizing that which gives material substance to reality) = 11—a number that in the East is connected to the Tao, a number therefore that refers to the breakthrough into a new dimension of reality where the microcosm and macrocosm are unified as One—were also powerful echoes of the underlying message of the formation. She has become more aware of the shadows of this path and of the shadows in the crop circle community itself and believes this is the greatest challenge yet to the phenomenon. From her dreams and years of research, she hopes that the integration of the shadow will lead to a deepening picture of how we are being addressed by the crop circles and their alchemical message of transformation and transmutation.

A Great Mystery

Crop circles signal the emerging shift in consciousness that seeks to link us with the hidden mysteries of our being here. To many crop circle researchers they seem to be a co-creation of the living Gaia or the angel being of the Earth through their appearance in crops, and-or expressions of the mythic or collective unconscious through their cross cultural symbols, and-or a recollection of the four great Liberal Arts that often provided the educational foundation for the ancient Wisdom Schools through sacred geometry, number, music and cosmology, and-or the presence of extraterrestrials through lights in the sky or UFO and encounter phenomena found in tandem with their creation, and-or the manifestation of other dimensional intelligences perhaps, for example, from devic and elemental forces accessed through the earthstar chakra referred to in chapter 2 to enlightened beings who reside on other planes of reality. In addition, their placement in the sacred landscape of Great Britain draws our attention to the reality of the genii loci or spirit or etheric guardians of places and therefore to the subtle energies or blue prints of nature and ourselves that exist before physical matter congeals into form. People have reported healings, insights, emotional responses, physical effects (not always pleasant), deep peace, and profound inspirations from being in the circles. Certain groups have been called to perform sacred ceremonies within their enclosures. Exposure to their subtle guidance can deepen our vision of why we are here at this time of course correction on planet earth and if we are humble enough to pay attention and to listen.

The annual appearance of crop circles is arguably the most mysterious and enigmatically miraculous creation of our time. You would think we would be ecstatic, deeply grateful, and enormously humbled to witness the divine in action! Together with the Marian and Black Madonna visions as well as extraterrestrial and star nation visitors they are signatures of the new millennium and the new emerging myth and vision of reality that is demanded of our times. Crop circles are spontaneous manifestations of the cosmic soul and hence give us confidence that new creations and possibilities for our world are forever emerging into time and space. Moreover, for those with eyes to see and ears to hear, we are invited to participate in creation's unfolding if for no other reason than the fact that these wonders seem to evoke so many creative responses in so many different people. Indeed, we might say that the appearance of the circles suggest that the cosmos itself is an act of imagination, "true imagination" as the alchemists say, the manifestation of a spiritual and visionary power that we, too, can access with the eyes of the heart. With our imaginations we can create sustainable alternatives of reality based on wonder, awe, beauty, and sorrow for what we have done and lost, and hope for what we can still recover if we attend to the dreams of the Earth encoded in the appearance of crop circles.

Earth has an evolutionary destiny and we are called through our hearts and higher chakras to receive the help we are being offered from the galaxy and other dimensions to assist in overcoming the sorrow of separation so that we might embody the galactic gnosis of unity consciousness. The circles call us to our Source, to the inner voice of wisdom that can guide us to our highest truth and deepest expression of who we truly are. While fear and doubt threaten to constrict our calling, we can no longer afford to live by our destructive practices and their mournful consequences on our psychic and physical life. A new found integration of knowledge and intuition, reflection and action must be found in order to follow the guidance that comes from far distant realms in the universe as well as from the very earth beneath our feet.

Crop circles, like synchronicities, seem to express a kind of longing, a yearning of psyche toward matter, body toward becoming fully ensouled so that our world will begin to thrive within a cosmology radiant with mystery and complexity, more wondrous than we at the turn of the twenty-first century can possibly imagine. Or is it simply a matter of remembering how we once lived? Sometimes I have dim remembrances of another kind of world that I can not quite place. But I sense it is returning. Our deep knowing is being awakened by these healing forms. As we spiral down to our truest nature with the circles as our guide, we find once again the divine ground of our human life. Here, though the rational mind may dither and doubt, our vision and imagination restore us to our wholeness. Crop circles are marvelous epiphanies of the *mundus imaginalis*, that other third domain of spirit and matter from where the music of the spheres echoes in harmony with the songlines of the soul.

Chapter Seven

A NEW VISION: AS ABOVE SO BELOW

When male knowledge joins with female transformation,
then the great magical union is created, and its name is Wisdom.
Wisdom means both to know and to transform.[26]

[The alchemist] Ruland says, "Imagination is the star in humankind, the celestial or
supercelestial body".... Imagination is therefore a concentrated extract of the life forces,
both physical and psychic .... a realm of subtle bodies.[27]

Thus far in *The Songlines of the Soul* I have unfolded a new vision of reality, a new worldview, a new myth of continuing creation at the ending of one astrological age and the beginning of another. The main focus in these chapters has been to identify the signatures of this new myth and to give many examples of its emerging presence in our midst. So, for example, I have shown how epiphanies of the imaginal world of the soul as a subtle Other world, located between the world of the intellect and our world of the senses, occur in individual synchronicities, visions and dreams. From this starting point, I went on to show that the signatures of this new myth unifying spirit and matter in a subtle world also appear collectively, in the universal manifestation of UFO and ET encounters, Near and After Death Experiences, other anomalous events such as the Marian visions, and in the beautiful annual creation of Crop Circles.

The twin phenomena of UFOs and Crop Circles are especially relevant as two important signatures of this new vision. For too long they have been

---

1   Paulo Coelho, *Brida: A Novel* (New York: HarperCollins, 2008), p. 47.
2   C. G. Jung, *CW 12*, par. 394.

treated apart from each other. On one hand, because of the relatively scarce evidence of their material aspects, UFOs are too easily dismissed as only psychological projections. On the other hand, because of their worldwide material manifestations, Crop Circles are often safely reduced in terms of natural scientific explanations. Divided in this way, spirit and matter are kept apart. But, as I have tried to show in this book, Crop Circles can be regarded as material manifestations of UFOs, and UFOs as psycho-spiritual manifestations of Crop Circles, heralding a new age where spirit and matter are one. Crop circles and UFOs: As above, so below! This union of above and below, sky and earth has been symbolized mythically by the image of the "plumed serpent;" in Aztec mythology, for example, the image is a combination of the Quetzal bird and the snake. Alchemy speaks of a *coniunctio*, a marriage of opposites that gives birth to a new creation.

I have also argued that understanding the new mythic constellation of a continuing creation that unifies above and below, spirit and matter provides a context for our consciousness being expanded to include other dimensional realities—what we have called the paranormal—and a preparation for our world being visited by civilizations not of our Earth—encounters. Signatures of the new worldview are pointing to a revitalized connection with the cosmos and a new view of our home planet. This in turn shows us a new way of being in the world, a path characterized by eros, wisdom, and the feeling imagination, a way of being that we must try to adopt if we are to continue on this planet as custodians of our Earth. I believe that each of us is called to this benign, co-creative, and loving possibility.

As I was approaching the final revisions and edits on my manuscript, just before it was time for me to send it out into the world, I had the following dream. As a way of closing this part of the book I would like to share some relevant parts of this dream.

The dream takes place in France, the quality of light suggesting somewhere in Provence, which for me is the landscape of love, the imaginal world of the grail, and the place where my soul feels at home. I am with my daughter and we have parked our car in the lot beside an old church or chapel that we are about to visit. We go inside and it turns out that we are there because it is a shrine to Mary Magdalene. I am in a side chapel looking at a painted wooden statue of Mary and her child. (It is not clear if this is the Magdalene or Mary the mother of Jesus; I believe it is the latter). I am feeling very emotional and am crying, feeling sadness and loss.

Then Carl Jung comes up to me and seems to indicate that there is something more important than the statue that he wishes to show me. He takes me outside and says that the shrine really has to do with a "previously undiscovered star" and points up to the sky, which though covered with clouds clears as he points upward, and we see the brightly shining star together. (It is like a big secret between us. I am overwhelmed by what he is showing to me; it feels very significant.) Then he points to the path that leads from the church straight out into the distance. Jung says, "this path is the "dragon path" and it links with the other sacred shrines," implying shrines to Mary Magdalene, though he doesn't mention her name, it is just understood between us. In the dream I know that "dragon path" is the Chinese description for the invisible energy lines that link holy places together on the planet. (It should be said that although I had been exploring the invisible imaginal geography of the earth, linked to Corbin's ideas of "celestial earth," I was not conscious of having read yet about the dragon paths. Synchronistically, however, the following day I opened a book by John Michell and there was a whole chapter on dragon paths! Michell also calls the dragon paths the "Earth's Imagination"). By pointing to both the star and the dragon path, Jung is showing me something even more important than the chapel and the statue in the chapel. That is the idea conveyed in the dream. The dream wakes me up at 2 A.M.

I was deeply moved by this dream and by the presence of Jung and what he was showing me. The "star" is a new understanding, a new revelation, the new worldview and a new hope for the awakening of humanity associated with 2012-2013 and the Hopis and Maya. The "dragon energy" is the creative energy of life which in alchemy guards the treasure. The star as a new constellation, or as a messenger, is linked to the dragon paths which also points to the alchemical dictum of "as above so below," the relation of spirit and matter and its new conjunction in a subtle imaginal world that is breaking through in our time in, among other ways, crop circles. It seemed as if the attempt to advance our understanding (for me, beyond what Jung made explicit in his lifetime) is for the sake of "my daughter," that is, for the next generation. The linking of the sacred sites are the places where the stars are grounded as it were, holy ground, "celestial earth," the spiritualization of matter—Earth's imagination—and the redemption of the feminine, of *anima mundi*, of eros and love.

In the dream, the statue of Mary the mother as a symbol for the feminine is enclosed in a church structure and so she cannot advance psychologically. Perhaps this is why I am weeping. However, the dragon paths link shrines to Mary Magdalene, and her constellation as an archetype of the feminine in our time is not confined by patriarchal limitations and an overly spiritualized view of the feminine. The Magdalene also has a strong presence in France for she is honored in many churches and shrines. She links spirit and instinct and, like the crop circles, is representative of the spirit of the Earth, chthonic matter, and not a Heavenly Queen. As an initiate of the mysteries, she embodies the visionary imagination inviting everyone to be who they truly are, creative co-participants in the new unfolding myth. Moreover, Mary Magdalene is in the lineage of Aphrodite/Venus, Ishtar and Isis, for whom the star is the pre-eminent symbol.

In *Part Four: Mystical Cities and Healing Sanctuaries*, we move onto a deeper consideration of the Earth's Imagination, "celestial earth," and the expression of the *mundus imaginalis* now become the mystical cities of the soul. In this next part, we explore the features of the new emerging consciousness in more detail and consider implications for healing and for embodying the new knowledge.

Part Four

❧

Mystical Cities
and Healing Sanctuaries

Chapter Eight

PRELUDE TO THE JOURNEY TO THE OTHER WORLD

There are only two ways to live your life. One is as though nothing is a miracle.
The other is as though everything is a miracle.

ALBERT EINSTEIN

Like wingless birds, we swept into a city of cathedrals. These cathedrals were made entirely
of a crystalline substance that glowed with a light that shone powerfully from within.
I was awestruck. This place had a power that seemed to pulsate through the air.
I knew that I was in a place of learning.[1]

We are journeying deeper now into *The Songlines of the Soul*. We have our map, the outline of the emergence of a new myth in our time. As we have seen, the signatures of this new myth unfold through individual synchronicities and in certain visions and are expressed collectively in UFO sightings and ET encounters, Near- and After-Death Experiences, other kinds of shamanic or mystical experiences, and in the worldwide phenomenon of Crop Circle formations. All these expressions of the World Soul are forging a new view of our Earth and a new relationship of our Earth to the Cosmos. We are in the process of course correction on our planet, from being cut off from the vast expanse of Universal or Cosmic Mind—a fracture that has lead to fear, the need for control, and violence to ourselves, to others and to the planet—to an awakening of unprecedented proportions and a "new field of organization" that is beginning slowly but surely to radically transform our worldview. Fields of non-local conscious-

---

1   Dannion Brinkley, *Saved By the Light* (New York: HarperPaperbacks, 1995).

ness and communication are opening up and leading us to greater wisdom. The age of miracles and a return to the Mysteries is upon us. We are reinventing ourselves. What an incredible time to be alive!

So far, in describing the irruption of a subtle background world into this world, I have used various kinds of terminology that have been used historically in discussions of these ideas, such as Jung's recovery of the mediaeval alchemist's *unus mundus*, Henri Corbin's recovery of the Sufi *mundus imaginalis*, and Wolfgang Pauli's sense of a background "psychophysical" dimension behind this one. I have also noted William James' description of parallel worlds of consciousness that intersect with our own. Further, I have shown how mystics, shamans, poets, and artists throughout the long course of history have experienced these Other worlds directly through their imaginations and have regarded them as ontologically real. The Tibetan and Egyptian Books of the Dead also describe worlds beyond physical existence, experienced in post-mortem *bardo* states, familiar also now to many NDEers. In many traditions, too, there are references to Other worlds, fairy lands, magical kingdoms, or lands beneath the waves or beyond the sea, underwater cities or secret places under rocks or inside mountains. Today, we tend to think of these Other worlds as symbolic descriptions of psychological states, but I am making the bold claim in this book that they might also be "real" as well.

Such a claim is not without evidence. In its uncovering and recovering of other dimensions or parallel universes in OB (out-of-the-body) travel, afterdeath, and near-death experiences, modern consciousness research points in the direction of the existence of Other worlds. In the field of transpersonal psychology, holotropic breathwork sessions created by Stan and Christina Grof are designed specifically to assist individuals to reach deeply into the multi-layered dimensions of psychic life beyond our immediate and local circumstances. A variety of designations are used in these more recently explored fields for the different levels of experience that have been uncovered through lengthy research.[2] Holotropic means "moving toward or in the direction of wholeness," and Stan Grof's written publications are important in identifying the dramatic and profound changes in sensory perceptions,

---

2 For COEX systems and BPMs, see Stanislav Grof, *The Holotropic Mind* (New York: HarperCollins, 1993).

emotional states, thought processes, and psycho-somatic manifestations characteristic of these holotropic states. Grof notes that these states—that reach beyond archetypal and mythological realms to encounters with spirit guides, extraterrestrials, and inhabitants of parallel universes—form a bridge to the oldest forms of healing in the world, including aboriginal, indigenous and shamanic practices, and he laments the limitations of conventional psychotherapy that often do not honor these non-ordinary states of consciousness, and usually deal inadequately with the effects of altered states of consciousness on the physical body.

Philosopher and theologian, Christopher Bache has used Grof's breathwork technique and described his profound experiences in his book, *Dark Night Early Dawn*. Though he does not refer specifically to Other world cities, his stories describe his archetypal *rite d'entrée* into the Other world in a particularly stark and moving way. Such accounts suggest undeniably that in the new worldview we need to move from an egocentric and personal worldview through a transpersonal worldview toward an ecological and cosmo-centric view of consciousness and reality that is even transpsychic.

Travel to Other worlds or dimensions of consciousness, whether found in descriptions of UFO encounters or in accounts of spontaneous "journeys" to times past or times future,[3] have many analogies in modern scientific and psychological ideas. These experiences parallel Bohm's theoretical descriptions of the implicate order, Jung's psychoid archetype or transpsychic realm, and the quantum physicists' description of the non-local and holographic qualities of reality. Two major features all these types of adventures have in common are the expansion and deepening of the participant's cosmic knowledge and the experience of profound levels of love. Most often they experience these states directly and instantaneously. These experiences occur in a heightened state of metaconsciousness, a broadly expanded awareness that leads to greater honesty, compassion, sensitivity, and wisdom, and to the realization of the interconnectedness of all levels of being, personal, collective, archetypal, imaginal, and transpsychic. The profound transformation that usually results from these far journeys is also accompanied by the recognition that the new knowledge is needed here and now, in this

---

3   Michael Talbot, *The Holographic Universe* (New York: HarperCollins, 1991), pp. 224–228.

world. By becoming the embodiment of this gnosis, we not only help fulfill our own destiny, and perhaps assist others with theirs, but we also aid the unfolding of the Divine's delight and hunger for awareness of Itself in an ongoing reciprocal continuing creation.

Perhaps by now it should not be so surprising that in many spiritual traditions, these subtle landscapes to which we travel in non-ordinary states of consciousness emerge as precise locations with actual names. They are designated as Pure Lands or as the Mystical or Luminous Cities of the Soul. In this book, I wish to recover the ontological reality of these other dimensions of consciousness, these Celestial Cities that are parallel worlds that have a psycho-spiritual, psycho-cosmic or imaginal geography. Henri Corbin whose work I discussed in detail in Part One describes this imaginal landscape as "Celestial Earth." In exploring these mystical metropolises, and the "libraries" and "schools" often associated with them—which the Rosicrucians called the Invisible College[4]—I will give examples not only from religious traditions and the historical record, but also from contemporary accounts. Some of these modern accounts tell of startling, spontaneous visits to these luminous locations and their "institutions of advanced learning."[5]

I wish to suggest that these parallel worlds exist within what Ervin Laszlo calls the metaverse, places beyond ordinary time and space and, therefore, beyond history. In this book, I am claiming that these places are more spiritually evolved than our own, and that they are now intersecting with us for four major purposes.

First, they are appearing now to help us re-member who we truly are and to awaken through deep feeling and imagination our moral conscience.

Second, they are helping to educate us about the heart by giving us a direct experience of the heart's openness in order to vastly expand our knowledge beyond intellectual thought.

Third, they are facilitating life as a continuing act of creation in which we participate.

---

4 Jeffrey Mishlove, *The Roots of Consciousness* (New York: Marlowe & Company, 1993), p. 62f, p. 163f. See also, Nicholas Goodrick-Clarke, *The Western Esoteric Traditions, A Historical Introduction* (Oxford: Oxford University Press, 2008).

5 Mishlove, *ibid.*, p. 272.

Fourth, they are resituating our broken lives within not only a mythic and transpersonal but also a trans-human and subtle imaginal context, rich in the beauty, love, and sorrows, of compassion.

These extra-ordinary or suprasensible experiences are in the process of initiating not only individuals but groups—perhaps even the species as a whole—in increasing numbers into a new vision and myth of reality for the purpose of the evolution of consciousness on this planet. And such events, which shatter our old worldview and the currently deficient vision of our culture, often take the form of some version of the death and rebirth initiatory pattern, a journey that opens us to a hidden reality.

The twelfth century Sufi mystic, Suhrawardi, confirms that the Other world—meaning the ontologically real imaginal world of visions and mystical journeys—is not to be explained in rational or logical terms, but rather apprehended through the subtle organ of knowledge, *imaginatio vera*. This subtle knowledge often manifests through dreams, and indeed this work was seeded with a dream of Suhrawardi told in chapter I. For Suhrawardi this subtle way of knowing involves in his tradition a curious paradox: the "other world" is understood as being spatially both within a person's earthbound body *and* also as a distinct region of the cosmos. While this paradox is difficult for the mind to grasp, it is nevertheless reflected in the words that modern people use to report the felt experience of these other domains. This paradoxical experience of altered states of time and space experienced both in the body yet seemingly also in an unknown and unfamiliar "elsewhere" has been reported by credible witnesses time and again throughout our long history right up to the present. Descriptions of these journeys show that they require a break or discontinuity with consensual reality, a rupture of the laws of the physical world. You cannot say precisely when this happens or how you got there. Thus, you cannot adequately describe how to find the path to anybody else. This is the great paradox of such experiences.

As we move forward in *Songlines of the Soul*, I am imagining the future as a present reality, and in so doing I am leaving Jung behind. Jung's psychology of individuation and his later work on UFOs take us to the threshold of this new future. In the new paradigm, we must differentiate between the *unus mundus* world and the *mundus imaginalis*. The latter term is a more explicit way to affirm that these Other worlds are ontologically real and as such manifest themselves as the mystical cities of the soul, which now are increasingly calling us to attend to their presence, to those actual journeys to and encounters in these Other worlds. These Other worlds, which we experience here and now but which are beyond the here and now, present us with gifts of knowledge, love, wisdom, compassion, beauty, and an inspiring vision, but are to be incarnated in our world. These gifts from direct experiences of these indispensable qualities are required of our times.

In addition to showing the multiple ways in which the psycho-geographies of the *mundus imaginalis* as the mystical cities of the soul have been described and experienced, I will also elaborate on the healing potential of these subtle landscapes. In essence, we need a second path beyond Jung's description of individuation, to a kind of Individuation 2, a psycho-cultural-cosmotherapy that leads us beyond finding meaning only in our suffering. Fundamentally we need to change our lives. Though we always need to be aware of our shadows, we can also move toward increasing levels of happiness and joy rooted in a deep sense of the interconnectedness of all Being and our multi-dimensional wholeness, and embrace the power of our imagination to help create a new vision for a new century. The next three chapters explore the mystical cities of the soul, our sojourns there, and the features of consciousness that are awakened by exposure to their subtle landscapes. The following two chapters are devoted to the Asklepeian Healing Sanctuaries and their echo in contemporary spa culture—especially water cures and hydrotherapies—as a paradigm for how we might restore a more holistic way of living the new myth in our bodies and incarnating the Songlines of our Souls.

Chapter Nine

MYSTICAL CITIES AND MUSICAL NOTES

*Different names are now given to the ancient place in which the sacred knowledge is kept.
Belovodia is one of them . . . . Tantric Buddhism . . . gave the place of initial knowledge
the name of Shambhala.*[1]

L ike towns in our space-time earth, the great cities of the soul have
actual names in the various traditions: Shambhala in Tibetan Buddhism; Avalon, the mystical kingdom often associated with the
Arthurian and Grail legends; Hurqalya, "Na-Koja-Abad," or "Land of
Nonwhere" in Sufi mysticism; Belovodia and Olmo Lungring, the trans-
historical metropolises in Bon Buddhism. In fact, Bon Buddhism distinguishes itself from other kinds of Tibetan Buddhism by tracing its roots
back 17,000 years, to the founder's birthplace, Olmo Lungring, "a place not
considered in this (historical) dimension."[2]

Mystical Cities and the Features of Subtle Geography

Clairvoyant, researcher, author and teacher, Richard Leviton, in his book, *Galaxy on Earth,*[3] explores through geomancy (the study of the subtle or imaginal
body of the earth) the visionary geography of sacred places on the planet. He
identifies eight types of celestial cities, sometimes linked with the golden city
of Mount Meru, home to the chief Hindu gods, Brahma, Shiva, and Vishnu,

---

1 Olga Kharitidi, *Entering the Circle*, (San Francisco: HarperSanFrancisco: 1996), pp. 213 & 214
2 Tenzin Wangyal Rinpoche, in Marvin Spiegelman, Ed., *Psychology and Religion at the Millenium and
Beyond* (Tempe, AZ: New Falcon Publications, 1998), p. 111.
3 Richard Leviton, *The Galaxy on Earth: A Traveler's Guide to the Planet's Visionary Geography* (Charlottesville,
VA: Hampton Roads, 2002). See also his websites: www.world-mysteries.com and www.blueroomcon-
sortium.com.

and at other times, known by familiar names Avalon and Shambhala. Leviton observes, significantly, that these celestial cities have affiliations with the Earth's inner heart chakra, the *Ananda-kanda*, and are known for various distinct qualities that help facilitate spiritual purposes and initiations.[4]

The cities comprise features of a visionary geography that make up a "light pattern library,"[5] features which are called by such names as grail castles, stargates, labyrinths, domes, mithraeums, soma temples, and vibrating stones, as well as many other terms. We also receive hints of these light patterns through myths associated with actual places on Earth that act as guides to the esoteric imaginal events that are forever happening in the *mundus imaginalis*. We can educate ourselves into accessing these landscapes through ritual, imagination, visionary dream, and meditation, and thereby assist in the healing of our planet and ourselves toward our unfolding destiny as guardians of deep cosmic remembering and the evolution of consciousness.

Leviton adds that just as in Chinese or Hindu models of consciousness the body is connected to a universal energy field through subtle organs such as chakras, and the flow of chi through an auric field that extends beyond the physical plane, the earth herself has a multi-layered spiritual body that is imprinted by cosmological forces, and literally strewn with stars. Our planet is truly extraterrestrial in this sense. Particularly at sacred sites, the veils between the worlds are permeable and provide doorways through which we can penetrate into the subtle mystical terrains. It is also fascinating to note that civilizations from other star systems can use these thresholds to travel to our realm.

Various accounts, which confirm and clarify my own intuitions, strongly suggest that mystical cities are linked with and sourced by star systems connected with galactic, planetary, and human evolution. These star systems include Sirius, the Pleiades, Arcturus, Orion, Canopus, and Ursa Major, among others, and each has contributed to seeding knowledge here via

---

4 Leviton, *The Galaxy on Earth*, p. 45. I am not going to explore what Tibetan Buddhists describe as the various Hell Realms or Dante's marvelous details of Hell and Purgatory for I feel that these shadow areas have been well covered in Jung's psychology. Moreover, collectively we still seem to be driven by hatred and greed or, alternatively, superficial pleasures and the limitations of a mindset that is not awakened to our wholeness. This book assumes knowledge of the necessity to integrate shadow characteristics and to make complexes conscious. I have said enough, I hope, in my text to convey the knowledge that it is often the "death of the ego" and the suffering that ensues that initiates us—at least potentially—into our true radiance.

5 *Ibid.*, p. 37.

the imprint of subtle energy formations in the astral body of our Earth, knowledge designed to be "opened," "activated," or "remembered," at the appropriate time. Each of the cities is also linked with various deities of different qualities, or Celestial figures, who are also imagined as Guardians of the cardinal directions, east, west, southeast, and so on. These seeds of new knowledge, which are a signature of the new myth for a new century, can also be found in the sacred geometry and hieroglyphic symbolism of pyramids and stones, and more recently in crop circles.

According to Leviton, there is also a link between the deities, guardians, and subtle celestial figures called the Ray Masters of the Great Bear constellation who, like cosmic messengers, form bonds with actual historical representatives whose purpose is to help activate the influx of cosmic consciousness to the planet when the *kairos* or right moment permits. The Ray masters also assist humans in achieving contact with the astral dimensions of consciousness for initiatory purposes. Jesus, for example, was entrusted with disseminating Christ consciousness on this planet, while the Buddha taught the Middle Way. Both Masters sought to teach the centrality of kindness and compassion. The Ray Masters travel to and from the mystical lands, and are known in Hindu myth as the seven Seers or Rishis. They are also linked with various Sanctuaries where their specific types of consciousness are pooled and distributed. Apollo, for example, "god" of prophecy and dreams, used the oracular center at Delphi as one of his prime manifestations on Earth. The Marian apparitions, increasing in our own times, are actually a composite of several "female" Ray Masters, and Lourdes in France is one of the major intersecting points on our planet for this holy and "royal" lineage. Today, countless individuals are making contact with these messengers.

In my own experience, I have had a particular affinity with the Lady Nada who has found expression throughout history by means of individuals such as Mary Magdalene, once scorned by the official Church quite erroneously as a prostitute, but now coming to be recognized in her rightful station as Initiate in the High Feminine Mysteries and the favored disciple and lover-consort of Jesus. During these turbulent times the Magdalene is emerging into history as a Sophianic presence, especially in connection with the Grail myth, and as an expression of the need for a recovery of a healing and embodied eros. The Lady Nada has also been envisioned through Goddesses such as Venus/Aphrodite and the Egyptian Isis or Hathor, and also through the Celtic Brighid or Saint Bridgit. She is linked with the throat chakra, the power of vibration, sound, music, and the spoken word to effect change. She is influenced by Pleiadians and related to the color royal or navy blue of the lapis lazuli stone. She, who awakens the songlines of my own soul, has appeared in the imaginal landscapes of active imagination and in my dreams as The Lady Melissa. She is a priestess of the sacred bee, devotee of Aphrodite, and linked with the death-rebirth mysteries of Dionysus.

The cities, though they exist in their own right, are also aligned and connected with sacred sites distributed throughout our Earth and have found earthly form in association with the Mystery Schools, Sacred Colleges, and Healing Temple Sanctuaries in ancient Egypt, Greece, India, England, and Mexico, as well as other sacred places on the planet, including oracular shrines such as the one found at Delphi. My own experience suggests that these Sanctuaries, Schools, and Shrines were located at domains where the veil between the human, etheric, astral, and cosmic planes once was particularly permeable, and in some cases still is permeable. Contact with the mystical cities was even cultivated by these Schools as part of a training to remain in contact with the guidance and wisdom of our stellar psychopomps during the search for the elixir of life and the establishment of the immortality of the soul before death.

A recurring motif used in the description of these cities from ancient times to the present is that they are extraordinarily beautiful, with their own forests, mountains, minerals, food and light sources, water courses, lakes, buildings, Temples, libraries of knowledge, as well as all sorts of inhabitants, angels, and subtle beings of light. Corbin mentions that although we have primarily lost contact with the *mundus imaginalis*, the very thought of these cities causes our hearts to resonate with longing, evoking the myth of the "lost continent," mostly remembered in connection with the submerged "sacred island" of Atlantis such as Critias describes in the unfinished Platonic dialogue of that name, a fabled account that originated (significantly) with priests in Egypt.[6] In modern times this longing can be seen in the Disney movie *Atlantis*, and in the appeal of Graham Hancock's films, *Quest for the Lost Civilization* (a search for an

---

6   Republic, Book X, in *Plato: Collected Dialogues*, Ed. Edith Hamilton and Huntington Cairns, Princeton, 2002, pp. 1214–1224.

SONGLINES OF THE SOUL

Ur civilization much older than current scholarship suggests), and *Underworld* (an exploration of ancient underwater cities). Even though these are quests for actual historical civilizations rather than a recovery of subtle geography, they nevertheless give expression to this nostalgia, a term which means a longing for home in those who have been exiled from home, which perhaps accounts for the popularity of these searches in the modern imagination.

While a comprehensive exploration of the mystical cities as features of a visionary geography in and of themselves is well beyond the range of this chapter, I will focus on four of these mystical landscapes: Shambhala, Avalon, and Hurqalya, and a brief mention of Olmo Lungring. I focus on them because each has struck a particularly powerful chord in my own experience. In addition, I will also explore the Grail castles—a myth so key for our times—and a recent dream of what I later discovered to be a Soma Temple also known as a celestial city.

Shambhala

Shambhala, mostly associated with Tibetan Buddhism, is also known as the Western Paradise or Blessed Isles, and is considered one of the most important "Buddha fields" mentioned in the Mahayana Buddhist tradition. It is presided over by Amitabha, a high Bodhisattva who founded this paradisiacal realm, and who is considered the teacher of Avalokiteshvara, the "archangel of universal compassion … the "God of Sensitive Concern." The female goddess or archangel of universal compassion is called Tara. Like the visions of Mary in the West, reports of Taras growing out of the rock in Pharping near Katmandu have been recorded by China Galland in her beautiful book, *Longing for Darkness: Tara and the Black Madonna*. Galland asserts how much we need Tara's wisdom and how out of her compassion she is appearing in our world as a new vision constellates in our time. The Dalai Lamas are believed to be incarnations of Avalokiteshvara, and, we would add Tara as well.

Shambhala, the City of Sukhavati meaning the domain of the "Blissful," is considered the seat of spiritual governance and the preeminent home of the spiritual hierarchy concerned with Earth and human evolution. It is also the land of ascended humans and celestial beings. One can be reborn there, awakening in a lotus flower, and live a blissful life until reaching Nirvana. Shambhala is flooded with the radiance of its own inner light, and filled with healing fragrances, bejeweled trees, exquisitely colored flowers, the bubbling sounds of rushing water. It is home to celestial music and enlightened teachings.

Do modern people still journey there? The answer is a resounding yes. Echoes of Shambhala are found in a beautiful account shared by an NDEer who reports arriving in a heavenly pasture with flowers of brilliant rainbow hues, colors that seemed to be filtered through a diamond prism. For him, time was altered in such a way that his experience could have lasted seconds or an eternity. While there, he experienced this "place" as if with another kind of consciousness than his everyday mind. It seemed like it existed in another universe more vital and alive than anything he had known on Earth, yet at the same time this city was strangely familiar, as if he had always known of its existence. Here he heard music so beautiful it could not be captured by earthly composers, yet its soothing warmth seemed to emanate from a source deep within him. Words failed to capture the awesome and sublime beauty of this rebirth experience. He writes: "It was as if I was in the center of a lotus flower which was unfolding its beauty around me in every direction." He was met by a golden, radiant androgenous being of immense love who seemed extremely familiar to him, as if it were the "source of my life and perhaps even my creator." This being filled him with inexpressible joy and love.[7] It is this joy and love that we so desperately need to bring back to earth.

Some aspects of Shambhala are portrayed as the magical city of Shangri-La described in James Hilton's Lost Horizon published in 1933. Interestingly, Hilton suggests toward the end of his book, that the worlds of imagination and their inherent wisdom begin especially to activate during times when untold darkness threatens to shroud our planet. This was true on the eve of World War II when Hilton was writing, and it is even more true today. This idea would certainly be in keeping with many reports of UFO/ET contacts, considered by some as visitations from the mystical cities since the ET's disclosures and warnings are often about the ecological and spiritual devastation of our planet, and our need to begin caring for and honoring the earth, rather than continually raping and exploiting it.

---

7   Kenneth Ring, *Heading Toward Omega: In Search of the Meaning of the Near- Death Experience* (New York: William Morrow, 1985), pp. 64–65.

According to Leviton, Shambhala is home also to blue-skinned Sirians with pointed heads, who are present there to impart and teach their wisdom. He suggests that the best time to travel to Shambhala is during the first full moon in May, the Celtic Wesak, as that is the time of an annual mystical celebratory event there.[8] One can access Shambhala through one of 1,080 apertures distributed over the planet. These "doorways" can be accessed, for example, at the sacred sites of Delphi, Glastonbury, and Mt. Kailish in Tibet, as well as through meditation techniques or psychic visions wherever you are.

In his book, *The Jewel Tree of Tibet*, Columbia University professor and Tibetan Buddhist Robert Thurman offers one such meditative path toward enlightenment, love and compassion through silence and imagination by accessing "jewel beings," that is, angels, mentors, and bodhisattvas who, as friends, can become our teachers on the path to freedom and the acknowledgement of our vast human potential. Focusing our attention on the Noble Country, we can retreat from narrow and habitual ideas about ourselves, and open to an expansion that refuels our energy and creativity, allowing us to cultivate sensitivity for others and the ability to love more fully.[9]

The opening to the *Mentor Devotion*, the sacred Tibetan text—thought to be authored by the Fourth Panchen Lama believed to be the incarnation of Buddha Amitabha—that Thurman uses for the teaching of this meditative technique already gives us a hint of our own potential radiance, not in some mythical future, but here and now, a now that is an infinite moment. To touch on this experience, read the following while slowing down and going into a space of silence:

> *Through the great bliss state,*
> *I myself become the mentor deity.*
> *From my luminous body,*
> *Light rays shine all around,*
> *Massively blessing beings and things,*
> *Making the universe pure and fabulous,*
> *Perfection in its every quality.*[10]

---

8   Leviton, *The Galaxy on Earth*, p. 68.
9   Robert Thurman, *The Jewel Tree of Tibet* (New York & London: Free Press, 2005), pp. 1–7.
10 *Ibid.*, p. 10.

Perhaps for a moment, we can release ourselves from a feeling of inadequacy and feel empowered and challenged to change our lives, awakened to our true selves, feeling the suffering of others as our own, and a deep desire to alleviate it. Thurman writes of the Buddha's vision: "that you in your deepest being, your deeper, deeper reality of cells, of subatomic energies, your reality of your deepest sensitivity is, in fact, freedom—no matter the theatre of pain you have fascinated yourself by, gotten caught up in, or are habitually obsessed with."[11]

Toward the end of his book, Thurman moves from exoteric meditation teachings to the esoteric teachings of the Tantras, thought to accelerate enlightenment in this lifetime. Turning to the commitment of the adept, initiate, or meditator to achieve buddhahood for the sake of all beings, Thurman writes that the bodhisattva is ready to be "patient and enduring; ... to practice generosity for three incalculable aeons of lifetimes; ... to practice justice and sensitive, ethical interaction with others ... ; ... to practice tolerance and to bear with the injuries of others, sacrifice the self, and leave the victory to others." Having been loosened from the grip of a solid, separated, and alienated self that is the core of self-centeredness, the bodhisattva is "always joyful, even when suffering .... because they have felt the essence of reality as freedom, even though they haven't fully experienced it."[12] This state may take many, many lifetimes, perhaps tens of thousands, but in each we make an incremental step toward freedom.

Continuing, Thurman adds that once knowledge of the illusory basis of reality is understood and mastered (and his book, *The Jewel Tree*, gives a full description of what this entails), you are free to build a new world on the basis of wisdom. "*Tantra* (meaning "continuity") *is the art of building such a world of wisdom.*" He goes on to describe this perfected world where everything—lotus, dragonfly, waters—is itself a teaching of liberation, freedom and enlightenment. But one of the main keys to attainment of this state is mastery of the subtle body, what Thurman calls a virtual reality, through imagination. Through practice within the transformed space of the Jewel Tree *Mentor Devotion* meditation, and by paying attention to the deeper knowledge in dreams, you can anticipate being "a much vaster

---

11 *Ibid.*, p. 15.
12 *Ibid.*, p. 223.

type of sensibility and being." Knowing that the self is not fixed but malleable, particle and wave in one, you can understand that you are merely imagining yourself to be in the body you now have. Therefore, you can also re-imagine yourself in another, completely different world all the while remaining in the same body.[13]

The Tantra practices take place in mandalas that have the form of magnificent palaces, beautiful magical environments, and alternative universes; in other words, in the mystical cities of the soul. There, "you train as an architect of worlds of enlightenment, as an engineer of the embodiments of enlightenment." Basically, however, all the practices aim to expand your mind and imagination. Thurman comments, "I think it's the most amazing, most subtle, spiritual psychoneurology that the world has ever seen." He adds, "But I believe that most mystical systems—including Hindu Tantra, Taoist Tantra, Kabbalah, Sufi Tantra, Christian mysticism [including the spiritual practices of Teresa of Avila and Hildegard of Bingen]—are all in the same ballpark."[14]

One of the key practices is consciously rehearsing the experience of death, *The Tibetan Book of the Dead* is in fact more accurately translated *The Book of Natural Liberation Through Learning in the Between State*, or *bardo-realm*. One of the major lessons of this text is that there are no dead people; death is really just a transition or doorway into another existence. The book contains instructions on how to navigate the moment of death and the after-life journey, and if we prepare for this moment in advance, in this life, we will not be shocked by it, and we will be able to celebrate death as a release into a new birth, into another embodiment in which we can develop even further. In the after-death body we gradually separate from our physical denseness and become a body made of subtle energy shaped according to how the mind is used to experiencing itself. Apparently, we go through several different stages, through smoke and heat, stillness, luminance and moonlight, radiance and sun light, dark light, and a state of transparency and true freedom. This latter state is very creative, healing, and powerful. Yogins learn how to navigate these states consciously, so that they can guide their subtle bodies toward a positive rebirth, unless they feel called to remain in one of the Buddha lands.

---

13 *Ibid.*, pp. 224, 228–229.
14 *Ibid.*, pp. 229–230.

We can also learn this navigation system through the Tantra practices. NDEers also refer to these different levels. Here is a brief example, reported by NDE researcher Kenneth Ring:

> This is a woman who, in 1975, while in her twenties, had three cardiac arrests within a period of four hours as a result of anaphylactic shock. During this time, she knew "with certitude" that she was dying. Her experiences during this life-threatening episode were extremely profound and revelatory, but here I have to confine myself just to one phase of her NDE that occurred toward its end. At this point, she felt that she was "rocketing through layers upon layers of realities, seemingly to the heart of the universe itself," and she was terrified. She thought she had gone too far and would be lost forever. Then: Oh my God. I was "picked up" as if by an ENORMOUS pair of hands, and as I looked up I found myself looking into a gigantic EYE, out of which flowed a tear of all consuming, profound ineffable love and compassion, and I KNEW without a doubt, that I was looking into the heart of my self, who is all selves, whatever it is that God is. And I was brought into the EYE, and was home.[15]

Interestingly, Thurman writes of one of the most beautiful representations of Avalokiteshvara as a being with several heads, many arms and eyes, and an eye in the palm of each hand. His arms symbolize his power to reach with his compassion into the heart of every being. His helping hands are sensitive (the tear in the example above) to what we really need because he has infinite powers of sight.[16]

In our culture we do not talk about death. Death is feared, often terribly feared, and more often seen as an end rather than as a liberating event. By avoiding death we become better consumers, better producers, and better voices for the party line and status quo. Thurman makes some wonderful comments about the need to have a transformative view of death. If we can live in the now (which, if you think about it, is really all we have), live as if every day and every moment is our last, then we can be really free. He goes

---

15 www.near-death.com/experiences, articles.
16 Thurman, *The Jewel Tree of Tibet*, p. 240.

SONGLINES OF THE SOUL

on to describe some of the creative possibilities of living in the present that death as a teacher offers: "If you live in the immediacy of death awareness, you're going to be insubordinate, individualistic, seeking some sort of freedom, liberation, bliss, being compassionate. You're not going to be easily coercible."[17] You are not going to want to consume and engage in wars; you are going to want to be free to live your own spiritual and creative, one-of-a-kind meaningful life!

That is why here, in this body, we can use any difficulty, any suffering, even the most terrible and negative emotions of which we are capable, as vehicles for disentangling ourselves from unexamined views toward embodying greater wisdom and compassion. Jung too always said that the shadow is 90 percent gold. His insight was the same as Thurman's. We have the power to transform, through understanding our suffering and distress, from paying attention to our dreams, and from *imagining* patience, justice, tolerance, generosity, sensitive ethical interaction with others, and bearing with their suffering, in the Noble lands and mystical cities that call us to a higher vibration.

The biologist Bruce Lipton affirms in the following examples that we are increasingly becoming aware of the fact that we are much more than we have heretofore allowed ourselves to be. He observes:

> A child walks across hot coals. A woman lifts a car to save her trapped child. Congregants of the Free Pentecostal Holiness Church drink toxic doses of strychnine during exultation without harmful effects. We can walk on fire, drink poison and lift a thousand pounds. Yet, we have fallen victim to the myth that we are vulnerable and frail organisms whose limitations are programmed in the genes. Facing crises in health, home and heart, to survive we must recover the true powers with which we were endowed.[18]

So it is to address current health crises, limited and limiting views of self, interpersonal relations, environment, and a war-ravaged world—in

---

17 *Ibid.*, p. 239.
18 Bruce Lipton, *The Biology of Belief: The Science of How We Create Our Lives* (Carlsbad, CA: Hay House, 2011). "The path toward self-empowerment is now offered by leading edge science that is synthesizing a grand convergence of the Body-Mind-Spirit trinity. A renaissance in cellular biology has now described the nature of the communication channels linking the mind and the body. This new science reveals how our thoughts, attitudes and beliefs control our abilities and create the experiences of our lives."

other words personal and planetary suffering—that we seek the wisdom to awaken from illusion to reality in the mystical cities of the soul.

As I was rewriting this chapter, I was sent an email notice about a gathering in honor of Hopi prophecies, and the showing of a documentary film on the Hopi water run, with a guest speaker, Kymberlee Ruff, MFT, who is Cherokee. The notice said:

> [Kimberlee] recently received the great honor of being made an Honorary Hopi elder by Chief Grandfather Martin Gashweseoma, The Keeper of the Sacred Tablets of The Fire Clan. There are people who have heard the message and the warning of the first Prophecy Rock from the Hopi Nation. The first Prophecy Rock spoke of the two possibilities of WW III: one nuclear and one non-nuclear that will end in the Great Peace. There is a Second Prophecy Rock that until recently, only the Initiated knew of. The second Prophecy Rock speaks of the message of Hope for the future that will follow the Peaceful Ending: "The Emergence of Shambhala." The time has come to share the message of Hope that the second Prophecy Rock brings. Kymberlee has been given permission from Grandfather Martin to share this message with the people. For the first time, the Grandfather Martin has allowed the Prophecy Rocks to be filmed and shared with the world. The Hopi believe that we are in the Eleventh Hour and that *"We are the people we have been waiting for."*

Although no further explanation of "The Emergence of Shambhala" was given, I was astounded to read that the Hopi people protected a prophecy regarding the Tibetan kingdom, one that, until recently, was known only to the initiated until now, and that they speak of Shambhala as a symbol for a hopeful and peaceful future. This experience has confirmed my intuitions about the mystical cities and their purpose of helping us to imagine a world of peace, unlimited freedom, and healing.

Avalon

The mystical city of Avalon is the name by which the Celtic myths referred to the Other world. Avalon, the "Isle of Apples," the Summer Country is the imaginal domain most often associated with the Arthurian legends in Glastonbury, England. Avalon is also the paradisiacal realm in the astral plane where Morgaine (Morgan le Fay) presides with her eight priestesses. She is reputed to have taken her brother King Arthur there after his death for recuperation until his next incarnation. It is also the place to which the magus Merlin—the medicine man and bard of Celtic mythology associated with the Grail and Arthurian legends—retired until a more favorable time arrives for the reception of his shamanic and alchemical knowledge. In her book, *Jung, His Myth in Our Time*, Marie-Louise von Franz proposes that Jung is the reemergence of Merlin in our time, and makes this claim through pointing out the many similarities and affinities in their character, including their laughter, their connection with deep streams of knowledge and healing, their stone refuges in nature, their observation of the stars, and their poetic and visionary sensibilities.[19]

But it is not just Merlin who is returning, it is also the mystical city of Avalon itself that is drawing back its veils and emerging into our consciousness today. This mysterious realm is also known as the Celestial City of Gandhavati, city of celestial musicians, located in the northwest area around Mt. Meru in Hindu cosmology. Avalon is also known as the City of Vayu, Lord of the Wind. Lastly, it is home to the Apsaras (celestial dancing maidens), and the Nine Muses of Greek myth. Avalon is also known as Venusberg, which hints at its special relationship with the divine feminine and, especially at Glastonbury, with the grail vessel and its relation to the mysteries of the goddess. In our day, the figure of Mary Magdalene, who arises as a compensation to the "light" and "virginal" aspects of the goddess in the Christian West, is being restored to her rightful place in the grail lore, which was preserved in the unconscious depths of the psyche and hidden in secret sects in the shadows of Western culture. In this context, the

---

19 Marie-Louise von Franz, *Jung His Myth In Our Time* (New York: C. G. Jung Foundation for Analytical Psychology, 1975), ch. XIV, pp. 269–287.

Magdalene can be seen as the figure associated with the emergence of higher spiritual wisdom from Avalon into modern history.

The Magdalene, who is still revered in many parts of France, including Chartres, Vézelay, Stes Maries-sur-Mer, and Ste. Baume, belongs to the lineage of the feminine counterpart of the divine, which stretches back to Sophia, the Wisdom-Eros side of Yahweh, and her beautifully erotic expression in the Old Testament "Song of Songs." Before Sophia the line reaches back to Aphrodite/Venus arising out of the watery amritic origins on her half shell, and even further back to Isis, who was both the Egyptian goddess of the dark underworld and death, and queen of the upper Heavens.

These feminine images of the goddess emerge too in individual dreams. For example, Marie-Louise von Franz tells of one of the most powerful dreams of her life which she had as a young student, and which concluded with the birth of Aphrodite out of the sea-foam, symbol of the birth of the Self in feminine form.[20] Another dreamer, a creative wood designer who suffered from a destructive mother complex, eventually dreamt of "Mary Magdalene (like Venus-Aphrodite), arising out of the sea," a numinous event which provided a profound level of healing to his wounding and undermining mother problem. Theologian Jean-Yves Leloup argues in his book *The Gospel of Mary Magdalene* that the recovery of the visionary imagination and the body as a sacred vessel for the divine, is central to the figure of Mary Magdalene, and is the task of the twenty-first century.

Avalon, also known as Venusberg and the "Temple of the Golden Apple," which held the fruits of higher spiritual wisdom, can also be accessed through Delphi in Greece, one of the major oracular shrines of the ancient world. This sacred grove was dedicated to Apollo, god of dreams, prophecy, and incubation, and to the inspirational Muses who were associated with the nearby sacred Castalian Spring. In his work on pre-Socratic philosophers' training using dream incubation techniques, Peter Kingsley draws our attention to Apollo as the god o f divine messages. He stresses the importance of exposure to that transformative world in a meditative state that is neither precisely sleeping nor waking, and our need for this oracular and poetic wisdom tradition which we have lost, much to our peril today.

---

20 *Ibid.*, pp. 205–207.

Kingsley has also found references to Avalon as a mythical land of immortality located in the far north around Scandinavia. This area was known as a major source of amber, a substance connected to the sun and sacred to Apollo, god of dream incubation. Directions for getting to Avalon, tantalizingly, tell us to go north, and then just keep going north![21] Perhaps this seems less problematic if we remember that for the Sufi initiates, the direction north also belonged to the initiatory journey of a mystic to those realms that are neither precisely dreaming nor waking, to a cosmic north, a spiritual north, to Hurqalya, "Earth of Visions."

The Greek word for amber means "the shining one," and this gives us clues as to other sites where Avalon can be accessed. Silbury Hill near Avebury in England is also called the "Hill of the Shining Beings," and is the site of many crop circle formations in recent years. Much later, as I have already noted, Avalon became associated with Glastonbury but even the "glas" (*glez* in ancient Scandinavian) refers to "the shining one." Amber is also the color of the second sexual chakra, and is perhaps a reminder of our radiant, playful, and erotic nature, a creative matrix that comes palpably alive in reconnecting with our expanded Self. In Delphi, too, there is reference to the "shining ones," and to the "northerners," a mysterious group of beings from "beyond the north wind" who are associated with the founding of this oracle center, according to one legend.[22] The mountainous beauty of Delphi and its magical landscape has always attracted me and on one occasion when I was there with a friend, a thunderous downpour greeted us, only to give way late in the day to a gray-pink sunset and to strange familiar voices echoing secrets from the stones of the ancient Temple precinct.

As explored in Part Three, it appears that by means of the UFO phenomena the "shining beings," perhaps once regarded as celestial guides, are now returning to help us. In the same way that indigenous cultures have their relationship to the star nation people, and the man or woman of light in the Sufi tradition found their guides of light, or ancient philosophers entered into processes of incubation to discover their immortal guides, the shining beings are arising once more. They are returning once again to help

---

21 Peter Kingsley, *Reality* (Inverness, CA: The Golden Sufi Center), pp. 268–269.
22 Leviton, *The Galaxy on Earth*, p. 206.

restore our connection to our galactic neighbors, and to reconnect us with a wisdom greater than that of which we currently seem capable. The mystical cities are opening up their borders once again in a time of crisis so that we may find our way home.

Dreams can be portals to the reality of these Other worlds, direct experiences of their own autonomous presence and power. One of my own dreams just four days before the catastrophe of 9/11 illustrates this point.

We are living in a community in the forest. My husband and children are present, as are many others drawn together by some common purpose or commitment to a spiritual or transpersonal principle. We are interacting with the animals (tigers, lions, bears, birds, and so on) as if we live closely with them, although I am observing that maintaining the appropriate attitude toward the animals (especially the ones that are physically stronger than us) is a difficult challenge. We need to maintain the necessary respect and fear and not become too uncomfortably familiar with them; after all, they are animals and not human.

It is now dusk, close to night and darkness. We are in a round circular clearing in the forest. There is much activity. Then suddenly beings begin to appear from "the subtle visionary world." We all stop what we are doing, become silent, and marvel at what we are seeing. This is remarkable (I think to myself) because it is not an individual vision, but a collective one—many people at once are witnessing the mystical and visionary realms. The beings are floating toward us just above our heads as if in a procession. Out of an apparent "nothingness" they manifest themselves in a form so that we might behold them. At the head of the procession is a figure that I somehow know is called "The Little Buddha." He is wearing a long white robe and holding something in his hands (a candle perhaps?). I think to myself that he looks like an angel. As he passes over our heads, I can look up under his robe and see a light emanating from him that is also giving off heat. This is a blessing on us, causing some kind of transformation or healing. He is followed by other "mythic" beings who are coming to tell us that their story is not yet finished. One of these is a woman in richly colored garb. In the dream I know which myth they are talking about, but cannot recall it on waking. It might be the Grail myth, or something to do with Philemon and Baucis, or even the children from "The Lost Domain," (the withered world of imagination found, lost again, and searched for in vain described in Alain Fournier's novel, Le Grand Meaulnes).

The other disclosure in the dream is that figures of myth have an ontological reality in the imaginal world and only become mythic or representative in historical time. They want us to know about their living reality. After the procession has passed over us, it turns back in a U pattern and goes into the trees, eventually dissolving at great speed into a star in the night sky. I look at this star that is burning particularly brightly, and draw the analogy to the Star of Bethlehem. I wonder if the unfinished myth has to do with Christianity. There is also some link in my mind with the appearance of these beings and UFO behavior.

In the next scene, some time has passed. Several members of the community are now sitting around with their arms folded. I think to myself that this gesture suggests that these people are forgetting—or may have even already forgotten—the aweful, numinous, visitation from the Other world. They are acting as if nothing happened. How can they be forgetting already? I feel alarmed. Such visions bestow a responsibility. We must finish the myth, help live out its completion. We must witness the events we have seen.

In the final scene, it is much later. We are now living in a city. Everything seems dark. There has been an almost complete forgetting of the collective vision. Society is corrupt. Spiritual life has been replaced by alcoholism, and social and moral collapse is rampant. No one remembers the gods or the divine realms any more. The feeling of loss and separation is overwhelming. This grievous feeling wakes me up.[23]

This dream, with its numinous images, made a powerful emotional impact on me. I felt deep gratitude and inspiration for being granted such a vision. What immediately struck me was the reality of the "angelic" figures from the subtle visionary world of the *mundus imaginalis*, that "lost domain" of the worlds of imagination and their imaginal inhabitants, recalled for us in Fournier's novel.[24] Figures of myth and legend, such as Philemon and Baucis from Greece, or the Grail personalities in the West that we appreciate symbolically in historical time have real existence in that Other world. Could these figures be the "shining beings," including Morgan le Fay, Merlin, Mary Magdalene or the Muses from the mystical city of Avalon, making themselves visible to assist us in the continuing evolution of life on our Earth? Moreover, the dream suggests that it is not just me but many others also, linked together by a common spiritual purpose or temperament, who are witnessing through near-death, close-encounter experiences, shamanic ordeals, or altered states of consciousness the miracle of the irruption of another world in this one.

The old story told by the Roman poet Ovid concerning Philemon and Baucis mentioned above describes the kind of attitude that one needs in

---

23 Author's dream journal, September 7, 2001.
24 See also, for example, James Hilton's novel *Lost Horizon*, and Colin Wilson & Rand Flem-Ath, *The Atlantis Blueprint: Unlocking the Ancient Mysteries of a Long-Lost Civilization* (New York: Delta Trade Paperbacks, Random House, Inc., 2002).

relation to these subtle worlds. Philemon and Baucis are humble folk who are living in an age that has forgotten the gods. Two gods, Jupiter and Mercury, disguised as weary travelers, enter their village in search of hospitality. After being refused they arrive at the cottage of Philemon and Baucis who are the poorest of the poor. But Philemon and Baucis usher the strangers across their threshold, rinse the dust of the road from their feet and welcome them with drink and food. Indeed, they even offer them their single prize possession, the goose of Aphrodite, the goddess of love. In these gestures of hospitality toward the strangers, the strangers drop their disguise and reveal their numinous presence. This moment is a transformation of consciousness. Indeed, in the tale this transformation of consciousness shows itself as a transformation of their being. Philemon and Baucis become eternal. In his commentary on this tale, Jungian analyst Wolfgang Giegerich says that it is love that makes the difference. It is Eros that transforms them, and it is Eros that opens the numinous in the ordinary.[25]

Reflecting on this dream I realized I could make no sense of it in relation to anything that was currently going on in my life at that time. The closest I came to understanding "why" I might have dreamed it on that day was that my husband was leaving for Ireland that afternoon for three weeks, and I felt that the dream was encouraging me to use the time during his absence to get back to my creative work, which was so involved with the imaginal worlds of the psyche. I knew that I would miss him, yet the wonder aroused by the dream in a curious way made me feel less alone. Dreams do not always have a reason in causal terms. They can appear acausally, synchronistically.

How could I know that four days later the world would change forever when the planes hit the World Trade Center, and that this pearl had dropped vertically as it were from the world behind this one, "like a stone out of heaven," as a message of both comfort and warning? In retrospect, I wonder if this dream is related to, and presaged, the events of September 11 and the situation we are now in of increasing fear and demise. We are, indeed, in end times, as the final scene of the dream depicts, the stage of kali-yuga characterized by consumerism and depravity. The *disiunctio*, the terrible separation from

---

25 Wolfgang Giegerich, "Hospitality towards the gods in an ungodly age: Philemon-Faust-Jung," in *Spring: Journal of Archetype and Culture*, 1984, pp. 61–75.

the sacred, is almost complete. The dream from its vantage point outside of time, in a fateful moment both personally and collectively, has helped me to find the orienting attitude in an increasingly disorienting period in our history, one that fills me with sadness and overwhelms me with sorrow. I felt addressed by the *daimon*, the inner guide of the soul who, though a stranger to our modern times, keeps us linked to the songlines of our destiny, held and preserved in those imaginal realms beyond time. The dream constellates the anamnesis, the recollection of the original commitment to bear witness to the Other world and its mysteries, lest I too forget and, overwhelmed by the horrors of our times, fall into lethargic and hopeless sleep.

In the first part of the dream, human beings and animals are living in close contact with one another as if the group, united in some common purpose, is in touch with the deep unconscious and instinct in a kind of participation mystique. Yet, though there is guidance from such a rich instinctual source, there is also a cautionary sense of its power and perhaps its dangers. The human and animal worlds coming together are slightly wary, yet not really threatening to each other, as would normally be the case. There is no hunted and hunter, no predator and prey in this imagery, which is in stark contrast to the situation in the world and the horrific events of September 11.

There is, too, a hint of the profound connection of archetypal vision and deep instinctual processes in the body. These domains are not separate from each other, which is what the symbolism of the Magdalene emphasizes. In our times we must allow our bodies to stretch—slowly and carefully—to include and withstand the numinous awe, the *mysterium tremendum*, of transpersonal reality. This capacity might help birth a sorely needed new vision for our time, one in which extraverted action can be balanced by introverted devotion to some kind of meditative path of individual choice. While spiritual leaders like Gandhi, Mother Teresa, or Thich Nhat Hanh represent very visible examples of such a vision, many of my students and patients as well as other individuals also live such a life as I have illustrated in these pages.

In the next scene, we are in a round, circular clearing, a *temenos* in the depths of the forest. The circular temenos is the sacred "space" in myself and in the group that is receptive to spiritual and visionary guidance. We see a procession of beings and we all marvel at them and stop what we are doing. This may be an injunction to stop all that is unessential and pay more attention to this guidance. I keep forgetting, falling off track, wandering off course—this is no longer acceptable given the gravity of our times. I feel as if the beings from Avalon and other mystical cities are making a special effort to be seen by all of us. This is both a privilege and a responsibility, since witnessing the vision and trying to "hear" what is being communicated obliges us to reflect on and ponder the meaning of these visitations.

The angel or Little Buddha gives a healing blessing that transforms us all. The heat suggests that we are close to the Source, which is often associated with fire imagery. The beings tell us that their story is not yet finished. In the dream I know what myth they are talking about, the one that connects Buddhism with Christianity and the Grail legends. As I worked on the confluence of these symbolic hints in reflection, research, and active imagination, what emerged as the unifying factors were the deeply introverted state of eros awareness, love, as well as the neglected worlds of imagination.

Buddhism points to the possibility that each being is sacred and can realize by effort their own divine nature. Each individual is potentially a Buddha and can reach enlightenment. In fact, the Buddha achieved just that. He became an illuminate. Christianity offers the same possibility, but this has not yet been recognized because in Christianity not only is that myth not yet finished, it has never truly begun in the sense of being able, collectively, to achieve kindness and loving wisdom. To the extent that we follow the example of Jesus as an *imitatio*, we restrict ourselves to being "true believers" which precludes real change. Moreover we have lived out the dark destructive shadow of Christianity as evidenced by all the wars fought on its behalf. We have not yet achieved, through introversion, knowledge of our own heart of darkness, our own shadow, a necessary precursor to the development of wisdom, conscience, and heart knowledge as an embodied reality within the individual and culture.[26]

This time of crisis is pregnant with the realization that the teaching of Christ—loving your neighbor as yourself—must be realized more consciously, not through belief but through compassion. For example, could we

---

26 See, Jung, *Memories, Dreams, Reflections*, pp. 279–280.

even consider the possibility of loving an enemy who has committed such atrocities as the airplane attacks on U.S. soil? Could we sacrifice the natural instinct for revenge by first acknowledging it (without acting it out) and then transforming it to devotion to a higher spiritual value? This is the Star of Bethlehem, the new birth, the new revelation—a difficult, but important challenge. For example, compassion in the face of personal and cultural destruction is provided by Buddhist monks in Tibet at the time of the Chinese invasion in 1959. When the soldiers murdered many of their comrades and destroyed their monasteries, driving many of the monks and the Tibetan people into exile, the monks refused to return the hostilities either in word or action. Buddhism stresses compassion that is a feature of the heart. Tantric Buddhism especially focuses on transforming via meditation instinctual energies in the body into the wisdom of the heart. This yoga practice is gaining ground in our time, demonstrating the response on the part of many people to find peaceful and alternate ways of harnessing and transmuting their energies, anxieties, and stress, so that cosmic consciousness that is surrendered to an experience of love, even momentary bliss, might be achieved.

The Grail stories, which are intimately connected to Avalon, erupted in the twelfth century. Though these stories got lost in the thirteenth century, the agenda for the education of the heart in Western consciousness was laid down in them, and has now returned to instruct us in the wasteland of our spiritually bankrupt times. We have not achieved heart gnosis as the true relation between people, the relation between men and women, and the relation between nations too often shows. Furthermore, the degradation of the planet and the continuing disregard on a collective level of the powers of the unconscious psyche, especially our power shadows expressed as domination over others instead of empowerment and inter-relatedness, demonstrate all too readily the failure to achieve this gnosis of the heart.[27]

Though the Grail stories emerged in the West, they incorporate themes that unify pre-Christian, Christian, and post-Christian elements, and complex imagery from diverse cultures and traditions. These include alchemical lore and classical myth, Arabic poetry and Sufi teaching, Celtic mythology and Christian iconography. The ancient cauldron of the Goddess is filled with the

---

27 Lindzay Clarke, *Parzival and the Stone from Heaven* (London: HarperCollins Publishers, 2001).

blood of Christ and awaits redemption and renewal through human quest and efforts via the question that in itself reveals the compassionate response lacking in our times: What ails thee? And whom does the Grail serve? Only heart gnosis can heal wounds and fertilize our modern wasteland.[28]

Most important, like the teachings of the Sufi mystics and Jung's emphasis on the reality of the psyche, the Grail stories emphasize the power of the creative imagination and of the visionary imaginal realm in the transformation of consciousness. Imagination is a spiritual power in its own right, an organ of vision that gives us access to the suprasensible "angelic" world of the soul, and opens us to the perception of hidden things. Imaginal sight exposes the figures in my dream as real, and not "just imagination." They remind us of Hildegard of Bingen's mystical treatises, Plato's teacher Parmenides' vivid account of his journey to the underworld, his encounter with the goddess, and participation in the death and rebirth mysteries,[29] the journeys into hell through purgatory and into paradise in Dante's Divine Comedy, Jung's mystical experiences, and the experiences of all the visionaries who have actually encountered and talked with people or angels from the invisible world.

The grail, like the alchemical philosopher's stone, is that imaginal reality that symbolizes the inexhaustible vessel of the source of life continually pouring into creation, an appropriate image for Jung's theory of *creatio continua*. It brings the feminine, Sophianic wisdom of the goddess back into our culture by attuning us to that eros awareness that comes into being by exposure to the dream and visionary worlds. By our conscious participation, we can rediscover the grail anew and actively participate in the continual creation of life. The Invisible or Enlightened Ones from the *mundus imaginalis*, from Avalon, help us with this ongoing creation, and thereby keep us linked with the songlines of our destiny.

Of central value for us is the linking of this source of creation with the human heart, and our embodiment of it in an enchanted world from which we have become estranged. The events of September 11 have brought this separation all too grievously to our attention.[30]

---

28 E. C. Whitmont, *Return of the Goddess* (New York: Crossroad, 1992), chapter 11.

29 Peter Kingsley, *In the Dark Places of Wisdom* (Inverness, CA: The Golden Sufi Center, 1999).

30 See Anne Baring & Jules Cashford, *The Myth of the Goddess: Evolution of an Image* (London: Arkana Penguin Books, 1993), for a description of the great separation.

We cannot penetrate into the imaginal geographies of our souls by force. Access to these worlds involves a fundamental shift toward hospitality and love as illustrated by the story of Philemon and Baucis. This fundamental shift in attitude can also be described as an attunement to a different octave of experience, suggesting the connection between mystical cities and musical notes. One finds this connection between these mystical landscapes and music for example in Old Testament prophets who used harp playing to open inner vision, in the shamans who beat the drum and sang ritual songs to assist them on their journeys, in the songlines of the Dreamtime that characterize the Australian Aboriginal connection to the land, and in the beautiful notion of the music of the spheres that lasted well into the seventeenth century. Indeed, this sense of the music that echoes the numinous, mysterious and imaginal dimensions of nature is returning. No less a physicist than Michio Kaku says that the equations of physics are the symphonies of nature.

The mystical city of Hurqalya, which is the subject of the next section, is also connected with music. It is "in Hurqalya" that Pythagoras was able to hear the music of the Spheres, the cosmic music, with subtle ears, beyond the material organs of sensory perception. Sounds, therefore, which are not created by sound waves traveling through the air, can be heard by the active imagination. They constitute the archetypal image of sound. Behind the ordinary reality of each thing that exists lies its non-ordinary expression, and so the physical world is transmuted, via *imaginatio vera*, to its psycho-spiritual activity in a corresponding subtle world of color, extension, scent, and resonance beyond the dualism of spirit and matter.[31]

If we wonder about this connection between mystical cities and musical notes, we might realize that music plays such an important role in these experiences because it is connected with a lowering of mental, rational thought and an opening to a direct path to one's deepest feelings. Avalon where the Muses reside opens to the rhythms of the heart. These resonant harmonies between the songlines of the soul and the music of the spheres are the basis of our vocation to the mystical cities of the soul.

---

31 Henri Corbin, *Spiritual Body Celestial Earth* (Princeton, NJ: Princeton University Press, 1977), p. 88.

Hurqalya

According to the Sufi mystics, the mystical cities are to be found on the bound-ary of time. These timeless worlds are located in the "Eighth Climate" and the Celestial Earth, also known as the "Earth of the Emerald Cities," just beyond the cosmic mountain of Qaf. Sometimes the cosmic Qaf is known as the emerald mountain that surrounds our universe, though its green vault looks like a blue dome to us. Hurqalya, which is the name of this mystic country as a whole, also includes the two immense cities of Jabarsa and Jabalqa, which resemble each other somewhat. Like the Heavenly Jerusalem, these cities have dimensions in a subtle space, and are laid out as a mandala, the symbol of harmony and wholeness. Mt. Qaf gives them their light, yet the minerals in their soil and the walls of their towns secrete their own light too.

Entry into Hurqalya, or "Nonwhere" as it is also called, is by way of the soul's longing and desire. There we will find mountains transfigured to their essence as places of revelation and illumination, mountains of the dawns that are made of rubies and mirror our awakening intelligence, mountain seats of the diamond palaces of Archangels, mountains from which flow the heavenly Waters of Life. Marvelous flowers, animals, and trees surround this wellspring, home of the virgin goddess or angel of the wilds. Here too can be found the immortal elixir. As Jung says about union with the *unus mundus* world, in this world of the archetypes, of autonomous imaginative forms, all ills can be healed. This "Earth of Truth" includes Heavens and Earths, paradises and hells, in a subtle state, perceived according to the spiritual state and imagination of the pilgrim who arrives there, since the soul in this place is both subject and scene. In fact, as Corbin notes, *Hurqalya is the Earth of the soul, because it is the soul's vision.*[32] We can never eradicate this celestial Earth, but we can betray it.

Jabarsa and Jabalqa are to be found in the lower regions of the interme-diate realm. These two cities are both immaterial universes whose substance is light, but whereas Jabalqa contains all the archetypes of the universe, it is located in the East, and is a more subtle world that contains the mystery of what is possible. Jabarsa, a world of autonomous images is located in the West, and is the world to which people go when they leave earth, a

---

32 Corbin, *ibid.*

darker world containing the forms of all completed works and of all moral behavior, a world made up of the mystery of the impossible and irreversible. These two worlds together comprise one descending and ascending whole, and initiates are encouraged to meditate on both at the same time, as the human heart is the organ of gnosis of all these worlds.[33]

Echoes of these celestial cities, and different levels or divisions to be found there, have been recorded in the literature describing Near Death Experiences. Pioneer NDE researchers, Drs. Lundahl and Widdison, note in *The Eternal Journey*, how the cities of light are contrasted with a realm of bewildered spirits, a place devoid of love, a place of earthbound/lingering spirits, the sphere of wasted and misused opportunities. For example, the authors describe an experience recounted by an NDEr:

> Those living on the higher realms of the city radiate the brightest light, being so resplendent that their glory must be cloaked so others of lower degree can look upon them. Visiting the higher levels is possible, but the spirits of lower realms must be prepared or covered so they can stand in the presence of greater glory ... Some new arrivals are taken to a place of orientation where they rest, adjust to their new condition, and prepare to take their place in the city of light.

Summarizing many of these kinds of experiences, the authors write:

> Individuals who have had an extensive visit to the Other world report that its structure is very complex. In the previous chapter it was noted that individuals acquired new senses in the spirit world, one of which is the ability to "know" others' thoughts and desires. This enhanced sense seems to be a factor in the ultimate placement of each individual in the spirit world .... There is evidence that a type of judgment occurs at the time of death. This judgment involves a review of a person's life and results in their placement in the spirit world .... Sometime after the judgment the person is assigned (in many cases this assignment is self-imposed) to a specific place or level in the Other world—a place where his or her spirit feels most at ease. Eadie "understood that there are many

---

33 *Ibid.*, pp. 160–163; p. 192.

levels of development, and we always go to that level where we are most comfortable."[34]

Another NDEer, Jan Price, who, when she almost died of a heart attack, was met not by a being of light but by her beloved dog Maggie (recently deceased), writes in her remarkable book *The Other Side of Death* of meeting a wise guide in a vast and beautiful Temple of Knowledge. Inside the Temple, there are painters, musicians, and dancers, and Jan realizes that the musical background for this visual feast came from a "celestial choir," an orchestra of voices singing the praises of the Creator. The guide explained to her, telepathically, that different levels of consciousness created different experiences, but that everyone was of equal importance and could never cease to exist, and could progress to higher and higher levels of being. He showed her the different levels of cities where, according to your current achievement, you feel right at home:

> Taking form before my eyes was the skyline of a great city. I could see three different dimensions of it simultaneously. The first had a dinginess pervading the atmosphere. There was a gloominess, and everything was gray, even the inhabitants, though I sensed that somewhere beneath the discoloration pulsed life and beauty. It brought to mind the lowest levels of existence in the world from which I'd come. Evil walked the squalid streets with malevolent bearing. No one here was up to, or expected, any good.
>
> The second dimension was of the same panorama, but brighter and more colorful, and had a familiarity. Hope lived amid despair. There were neighborhoods with neat houses holding reasonably contented folk; shabby rows of dwellings housed those more discontented. Expansive lawns separated palatial homes from those of less grandeur. Within each sector was happiness and horror, love and hate, joy and sorrow—the dualities of life on a less than harmonious plane. It was a life accepted by many in the land I'd left behind as the only way life could be. Some knew better, more than just a few, and the hope that lived amid despair would at some time blossom into a better way of life.

---

34 Drs. Lundahl and Widdison: http://www.near-death.com/experiences/experts11.html

Last in the trinity was a city of light, like John's holy city in the Book of Revelation. I saw the same skyline as before, but this time it was pure gold—with colors like precious gems, transparent glass, crystal clear. All who walked through the city brought glory and honor into it. Harmony and order prevailed, and the residents lived joyfully, creating that which brought forth beauty and fulfillment— a place of perfect peace, the peace that passes understanding.[35]

Jan realized that what she was observing took place on both sides of the veil, and that a change on the densest level caused a ripple effect, changing the next level. Whether in physical form or on the other side of death, an altered perception benefited all. She knew that our deeply held beliefs not only affect our own life experience but that of others. "We are intricately connected to all that exists throughout eternity." The Wise One explained that the creative energy or unlimited Spirit of God was always expressing itself through us and everything else. He sent her into the innermost part of the Temple to receive knowledge that she would remember bit by bit when she returned to her body, as more understanding was needed on Earth. Jan, in fact, created an organization to explore the mysteries of ageless wisdom, and to integrate their truths with metaphysical spirituality. She also became a writer and teacher of meditation.

Well-known psychic Edgar Cayce induced his NDEs by hypnosis and made over fourteen thousand journeys to the Other realm. Here, he describes several levels in which he moves from gray, grotesque forms (hell realms) toward a lively landscape of light, beauty, and music, and on to the Hall of Records, similar to the Temple of Wisdom noted above:

I am conscious of a white beam of light, knowing that I must follow it or be lost. As I move along this path of light I gradually become conscious of various levels upon which there is movement. Upon the first levels there are vague, horrible shapes, grotesque forms such as one sees in nightmares. Passing on, there begins to appear on either side, misshapen forms of human beings with some part of the body magnified. Again there is change and I become

---

35 Jan Price: http://www.near-death.com/experiences/animals01.html

conscious of gray-hooded forms moving downward. Gradually these become lighter in color.

Then the direction changes and these forms move upward and the color of the robes grows rapidly lighter. Next, there begins to appear on either side vague outlines of houses, walls, trees, etc., but everything is motionless. As I pass on, there is more light and movement in what appear to be normal cities and towns. With the growth of movement I become conscious of sounds, at first indistinct rumblings, then music, laughter, and singing of birds. There is more and more light, the colors become very beautiful, and there is the sound of wonderful music. The houses are left behind; ahead there is only a blending of sound and color. Quite suddenly I come upon a Hall of Records. It is a hall without walls, without ceiling, but I am conscious of seeing an old man who hands me a large book, a record of the individual for whom I seek information.[36]

The emerald itself in "Emerald Cities" refers to the subtle crystal deep in the invisible heart center of each of us that is the access point for the mystical cities of the soul. It is this inner emerald stone, "the heart within the heart," that is currently in the process of being activated as part of our human evolution on planet Earth. Several versions of the grail myth link this stone, which "fell from heaven," with the achievement of the treasure of the grail itself, and often times in esoteric lore, this heart is associated with the movement of the planet Venus. There is also an emerald city associated with the great Mayan center at Chichen Itza, Mexico, where a link between the Pleiadian star system and Venus has been observed. Too, what is known as the prime holographic emerald, a double-terminated six-sided gem said to be at the origin point of Earth's visionary topography, is located in what is now a small church with a huge two-thousand-year-old tree within its precinct, near Oaxaca in Southern Mexico.[37]

Hurqalya is a suprasensory interworld, external but not physical, an "earth of visions" outside ordinary time and space. This earth of visions is also the earth into which we are resurrected after death in our subtle body form, as

36 Edgar Cayce: http://www.near-death.com/experiences/cayce01.html
37 Leviton, *The Galaxy on Earth*, p. 166; pp. 54–55.

has been suggested by so many NDE reports. Jabarsa and Jabalqa are also said to lie just beyond Mount Qaf, a cosmic mountain "locus" for all spiritual pilgrims that marks the boundary between our world and the Other world. At this juncture—"at the entrance to the Chinvat Bridge," on the third day of our death, we meet the celestial "I" from whom we originate. Jan Price gives a beautiful account of such a meeting during her NDE. She writes of the joy and love she experienced when she encountered the consciousness of God. Through this experience, she came to realize that the Kingdom of Heaven was not only within her but that she was within it. She realized she could never be separated from God.

> Now, before me, shimmering, iridescent light began to take a particular shape. A woman of breathtaking beauty appeared as I watched in awe, and even after the full materialization from pure light to visible, substantial form was complete, nothing was static. I continued to see a "quivering" of her structure, as though looking at a fluid, rippled reflection in a pond. Her movements were of pure grace as she positioned herself directly in front of me. Her hair was dark, her face pale, yet with color.
>
> "Look into my eyes," she said with a gentle but commanding smile. As I did, I felt myself being absorbed. I was no longer just the entity I knew of as me, but more, so much more. The eyes I stared into were mine, the eyes of my soul. In deep humility, I accepted that which I was shown. "Oh my, I am all of that—so beautiful, glorious, wise, loving, kind, powerful. I didn't now. I had no idea."
>
> As though looking into a kaleidoscope, I saw myriad lifetimes and experiences. Oh, the wonder of me. This powerful creative energy could take on any form it chose, and right now it was expressing as a woman called Jan, so of course I would perceive it as feminine.

The power and beauty of this meeting filled Jan with gratitude, with the realization that her former view of life was impoverished compared to the wonder of Reality. Her "true self" told her to let go of obligation and duty, and live for the pure joy of being.

"Take my hands," she said, and the sound of the voice was like music. As we made the connection, waves of ecstasy washed through me, and I took on the fullness of this magnificent being that I am an extension of. No longer was I observing this shimmering radiance. I was it. The glory I had in the beginning, I thought, I have now and ever will have. Complete in my individuality, I understood the old admonition, "Know thyself."

According to the Sufis the cities of the soul are accessible also by suffering the dark night of the soul, "the death before you die." All mystical traditions speak of this journey of conscious sacrifice as the way to the Self, to the gods who need us to remember them. Knowledge of the earth's visionary geography and of meetings with the loving guide of the soul can help facilitate this pilgrimage.[38]

As is evident from this brief taste of Persian mysticism, the Sufis have a highly differentiated view of celestial geography, angelology, and spiritual practice that aims at the development of the subtle body. NDEs confirm these views. Meditative exercises aim for realization of the resurrection planes, the earth of visions, and the recognition of our soul guides that can help us awaken to our true and "perfect" (whole) nature through refining and clearing the darkness around our hearts. Corbin clarifies that entry to celestial earth refers not to a geometric landscape with spatial coordinates, but rather to a qualitative space, an origin point of presence "at the center," also referred to as Eran-Vej. This is the "place" where psycho-spiritual events always take place. No matter where an event takes place in physical time and place, an archetype-Image (a personification or "angel") transmutes such an event back to itself as center in such a way that the sacred space is *always* at the center of "the luminous wheel." Such a central space is *situative*, that is, carries its space along with it, instead of being *situated* in an actual physical space. For example, each and every Mayan village and ancient city was built around this center point, "the navel of the world." Once a year as the culmination of the initiation ceremonies of the adolescents, they would raise the World Tree by placing

---

38 Corbin, *Spiritual Body Celestial Earth*, p. 74.

it into this sacred hole. A great deal of other ritual work was—and is today—done in this location.[39]

Understanding this perspective allows us to see, for example, that the UFO encounter takes place in a geographical point that has been transmuted to its hierophanic or sacred "space" via the "angel" as memory of the center, the central luminous hub where the timeless and time-bound wheels interlock. The organ of active imagination (*imaginatio vera* or visionary imagination) consecrates the space as a "holy place," as the Earth of Visions. This "takes place" in the soul, not in actual geographic space. This soulscape finds extension in the mystical and luminous cities of our psycho-cosmic dimension where our mystical selves recall the memory of such places and our embodied souls are fully at home.[40]

Corbin suggests that whether we experience the mystical cities as beautiful and luminous or horrific and destructive depends upon the nature of our imaginative faculty, which can be creative or demonic, but never innocuous.[41] Hence, a UFO encounter or NDE will be either traumatizing or mystical depending on how much we have suffered consciously through the dark night of the soul, and how much we have educated our consciousness toward eros and an expanded, open, view of the world as multi-dimensional. This latter statement is not a judgment. It is simply a reflection of the fact that until we can stretch ourselves beyond the narrow confines of a consciousness reduced to rationality (ideas) and history in the ordinary sense (that is, chronological time and sensory measurement), we will inevitably experience the imaginal worlds as imaginary. Hence, we will see the landscapes of the mystical cities through a deformed consciousness, one that has eclipsed the visionary imagination which opens us to the (qualitative) intermediary and intermediating world of the soul, and to hidden things.

---

39 Martin Prechtel talks about this in *Long Life Honey in the Heart*; and Joy Parker Freidel in her book co-authored with David & Linda Schele, *Maya Cosmos: Three Thousand Years on the Shaman's Path* (New York: William Morrow & Co., 1993).
40 Corbin, *Spiritual Body Celestial Earth*, pp. 22–24.
41 *Ibid.*, p. x.

Olmo Lungring

Olmo Lungring is a subtle location at the source point of Bon Buddhism, and it is connected with the Andromeda Galaxy, whose center of consciousness and guidance is Sirius. It is imagined as a large blue disc, about one hundred miles in diameter, resting motionless above the holy Mount Kailash in Tibet. Leviton describes it in the following manner:

> Inside are hundreds, perhaps thousands, of caves, each containing a multidimensional being of pure light. Perhaps they are stars; or maybe rishis; or living crystals; or maybe something altogether different, formless, indescribable. These are the Og-Min, the original Bon-po sages who came from a higher dimensional reality.[42]

According to esoteric Taoism, access to these heavenly astral caves or positive starry energy holes in the universe—which are places of captivating beauty—bestows immortality. As there is no sense of time there, it is thought that a few minutes, subjectively experienced, could translate into centuries for those who return to the human world.

These mythical kingdoms and mystical cities have long been known about in various esoteric traditions throughout history, though their precise locations remain vague because their "place," their "where," is beyond physical geography in a psycho-cosmic landscape. The Sufi mystic Ibn al Arabi says that visions are both symbolic and non-symbolic simultaneously, confirming the ontological reality of mystical experience as also taking place some-*where*. And Olga Kharitidi stresses the fact that these subtle lands really exist, and must be distinguished from archetypal fantasy or legend, unreal or merely symbolic "as if" descriptions of certain psychological qualities and characteristics.[43] These sorts of descriptions are similar to journeys that shamans make to Other worlds, for healing, soul retrieval, and to deliver messages from the divine to the human realms.

In the examples I have given of the mystical cities, we see the outpouring of history as a two-way flow from an invisible background, an implicate realm, into this world of time and space, and then back again to the etheric

---

42 Leviton, *The Galaxy on Earth*, p. 414.
43 Olga Kharitidi, *Entering the Circle* (San Francisco: HarperSanFrancisco: 1996), p. 211.

and imaginal dimensions. Nothing is ever lost. We remember and forget according to the divine timing, according to the seasons of the glacial evolution of our consciousness. Yet part of the profound awakening today is the reality of the mystical cities of the soul, which hold our secret past and are opening up their doors to new vital revelations.

Grail Castles

In addition to the accounts of the mystical cities, there are other particular features described as belonging to the imaginal landscape of these subtle domains or of this celestial starry landscape. One such feature of this subtle geography that is significant for this book is the Grail Castle (of which there are 144 on earth, according to Leviton). Grail castles have different names such as Munsalvaesche (in Wolfram von Eschenbach's *Parzival*) believed to be located at Montsegur deep in the mystical landscape of the Pyrenees mountains in southwestern France, or Yima's *var*, literally "enclosure," mentioned by Corbin as a "hyperborean paradise," a city "including houses, storehouses, and ramparts...luminescent doors and windows that themselves secrete the light within."[44] Within this subtle geography of the Grail Castle, we enter a different octave of experience, a higher frequency involving deeply felt emotional states. Entering a Grail castle can open us to deep memory, cosmic knowledge, healing, an abundance of food and drink, and wondrous hospitality. Imaginal travel marks our progression to a qualitatively different world, and though the elements are changed, yet the melody remains the same. So on the mythic level a Grail castle leads us to the Grail legend, the wounded Fisher King, and the recovery of the healing balm of feminine eros. On this level, however, we remain within history and a symbolic interpretation of events. On the esoteric level, we are invited into a direct experience of ancient initiatory events, which involve vision quests in the service of death, transformation, and renewal. On this level we go beyond simply knowing *about* something and are *awakened* to cosmic and spiritual truth.

The Cathars were a Holy Spirit sect in the twelfth century that included both men and women, and whose main and final outpost was Montsegur.

---

44 Corbin, *Spiritual Body Celestial Earth*, p. 24.

Although, there were many strongholds throughout Languedoc in south-west France such as the mediaeval walled city of Carcassonne, Montsegur was said to be an access point for an etheric Grail Castle. The Cathars at Montsegur practiced a rite of passage or spiritual baptism called the *Consolamentum*. It was thought that behind their doctrines of dualism, which were perhaps only a convenient spiritual façade, they practiced clairvoyance and development of psychic abilities, comparable perhaps to shamanic initiations. Eventually, they were extinguished as heretics during the Inquisition and the sect was destroyed. Their extinction was a loss because they clearly understood that the world had become a wasteland and that the Rich Fisher King had become wounded because we had forgotten our vast past and the Sacred Marriage, symbolized for them by Christ and the Magdalene.

The wasteland is the absence of the Grail, sometimes depicted as a sacred stone that fell from heaven in the war between the forces of darkness and the forces of light. This stone was under the protection of those neutral angels who, refusing to take sides and striving to hold the universe together, became its guardian. However, Anfortas, the last Grail guardian-King betrayed his sacred charge in his mad desire to do the will of a lady with whom he had fallen in love and wished to possess, but who refused him. In battle with her enemy, he was wounded in the thigh, and now awaits the one who can understand the healing power of the Grail and can ask the question that must be asked to restore prosperity and wholeness. The story shows that the loss of the Grail occurred as a wounding to eros, to love. Sensitivity to the values of the Grail requires a mature heart that can hold the opposites of our shadows and love together. Nothing is more difficult than love. Love requires a compassionate presence that knows about suffering firsthand, and that unites our willfulness with a humbling attitude that honors the wisdom of contemplation and the effort to be wholly ourselves. Anfortas is everyone who is wounded, who is separated from the sacred, who has not yet learned to love, and who longs to celebrate the Sacred Marriage within the self, between the self and the beloved, and between the self and the cosmos.

The Cathar adepts or initiates were given techniques to access the grail castles. Opening up their crown chakras and using the subtle organ of their true or spiritual imagination, they would gather at a round table with many others on a similar search. At the center of this table stood a golden chalice. The chalice, like the stone, is also a symbol of the grail, signifying the process of recovery of our initial wholeness. It is particularly a feminine symbol. Staying close to that in-between state that is neither sleeping, dreaming, nor waking, the participants would awaken to the vast cosmic memory that is the Grail. They would awaken to a living library of great riches, which reveals the history of our galaxy, to an awareness of why one is here now as a soul, to an understanding of what other incarnations one has undergone, and where all this great movement of deep time beyond time is going. The land of spiritual superabundance—where, as we are shown (by von Eschenbach) in Parzival's first visit to the Grail castle, every desire is granted—is also the fabled Celestial City of Lanka over which Kubera, Lord of Riches, presides in the Hindu myths.[45] The Grail is the attainment of the union of opposites, a stone within a vessel that bestows a creative abundant flow that restores the deep mystery of life because we have asked the right questions: "What ails thee?" and "Whom does the Grail serve?"

Moon or Soma Temples

Another feature of the subtle geography of the imaginal landscapes of the soul is the Moon Temple. This feature, like the grail castle and the mystical cities are realities that belong not only to the past. They are living realities. To illustrate this point, I close this section with a description of a dream in which the image of the moon temple arises. The dream, which I called in my journal "Journey to the Land of Liberation," went as follows:

DREAM: JOURNEY TO THE LAND OF LIBERATION

In July 2001 a colleague and friend of mine died quite suddenly and unexpectedly. The initial shock gave way to deep feelings of sorrow and loss. One night, about two weeks after her death, I could not sleep. I was particularly concerned about the effects on the soul of dying so suddenly, without preparation, before her time as it were. My friend was in her late 50s and there had been no indication that her death was imminent. I eventually fell asleep in the early hours of dawn.

---

45 Leviton, *The Galaxy on Earth*, pp. 355–359, 57–58, 414.

I dreamed I was in a small airplane that was taking off. Suddenly the plane went almost vertically up, "breaking through" a fine level of cloud that was like a very thin sheet of ice that shattered as I went through it. It was like going into another dimension. Then the plane went into a stall, and I thought, oh, no, now I'm going to die. The plane started falling toward the earth. Although I was terrified I was simultaneously quite calmly thinking what the point of impact will be like? As the plane came close to the ground, everything started to slow up. Suddenly, I was by myself, and my "seat" became a kind of force field surrounding me. There was no crash. As the plane was about to touch the earth, this "force field" became a "vehicle" for transportation. I took off—the feeling of liberation and freedom was both profound and exhilarating. A great primordial shout of joy came out of my throat. I realized that I could fly and travel anywhere I wished to go, yet at the same time, "this steady hand surrounding me," was the thing I depended upon to "hold" me. At one point, I had the feeling of "taking my seat belt off" and feeling such tremendous joy, and an enormous feeling of Life. The feeling in the dream was that this was really happening—it was a genuine experience in another dimension of consciousness.

I realized with full certainty that "death" is only an ending from the ego's point of view, but from the soul's (or spirit's) point of view, it is a tremendous liberation filled with much joy (which was why my friend was laughing so much). Simultaneously I knew that this fear really comes from a kind of constriction of consciousness, when we think in limiting ways, telling ourselves that "death is the end." I realized that the point of what I was experiencing was to bring this joyous feeling into my life here and now while I am in this physical body. I awoke feeling filled with life and joy and certain of my friend's happy state—as if I had been given a very real message of assurance from the other side, perhaps even given this dream as a gift from my friend herself. I now knew, beyond that shadow of a doubt, that death is most certainly not an end, but a doorway to another, much less constricted level of reality and freedom.[46]

In this dream I am taken to a "place" beyond ordinary time and space. This "place" has that quality, associated with the landscapes of mystical cities, of a locus deep inside me that emerges to become a new "outside," a real space in which I feel a liberating and fulfilling sense of joy. While I did not know it at the time of the dream, these sensations of liberation and joy are characteristic of a moon or soma temple. This realization of experiencing something that had been experienced before by others was

---

46 Author's dream journal, June 21, 2001.

both calming and very reassuring, because the dream came as I was struggling with deep sadness over a colleague's sudden death. What seemed
strange to me was that every time I thought about her death, I could only
"hear" her laughing.

The thin sheet of ice through which I passed is echoed in Sufi thought
by reference to the crystalline structure that separates this world from the
lowest level of the imaginal realm of Hurqalya. The feeling of liberation and
joy suggests the subtle feature of a moon or soma temple, which is another
of the eight celestial cities of Mt. Meru, known as Kantimati. Soma is the
ambrosia or mead that is the drink of "non-death" or immortality. It is the
amrita, "stored in the Moon in a sacred vessel from which the gods drink
every month," a drink that bestows freedom from death and the prover-
bial "Fountain of Youth." In words that are surprisingly close to my dream
reality, Leviton writes that this drink produces "an ecstatic experience that
brings the Earth closer to the sky," and he further quotes Eliade who speaks
of soma as revealing "the fullness of life, the sense of a limitless freedom…
the possession of almost unsuspected physical and spiritual powers."[47]

Soma temples offer the possibility of eternity of consciousness, of
resuming an unbroken awareness—the Ocean of milk—from which we
originated, that we once knew, and often forget here. I am miraculously
reassured that my friend in her physical "death" returned to these celestial
origins, and is most likely continuing her journey from there. Her gift to
me in my sorrow is that I too can dip into these streams of joy and freedom
while still in my body here and now, even while knowing that such experience is sourced in one of the Pure Lands of celestial Earth.

We are linked by threads in a vast network and web of being to which
we are once again awakening. This web is a subtle vibratory structure whose
undulations echo the songlines of our souls. The modern transpersonal
traveler, like the shamans and prophets of old, are accompanied by chanting, gonging, and galactic music to open up their inner vision.

---

47 Mircea Eliade, *A History of Religious Ideas, Vol. 1, From the Stone Age to the Eleusinian Mysteries*, trans. Willard
R. Trask (Chicago: University of Chicago Press, 1978), pp. 210–212.

Morphic Fields and Waving Trees

To close this chapter I want to consider briefly some very contemporary expressions that further amplify the imaginal landscapes of Other worlds.

Rupert Sheldrake's ideas of morphic fields suggest that these fields are the organizing patterns of Earth prior to the establishment of its physical body. These fields are what the Aboriginal peoples call the "Dreamtime," and to them this dreaming is both more real than our physical world and something that existed prior to it. David Bohm's notion of the explicate order unfolding from the implicate order of which it is a part, is relevant here. His understanding is that our tangible reality is really a kind of illusion on the surface of a much deeper and more primary level of existence that gives birth to everything in our world. This idea is not very far from the ancient Indian belief that our world is the dream of Brahman, or from Blake's poetic vision of "heaven in a wild flower." It is also very similar to Jung's notion of the ego resting on a Greater Personality, our consciousness resting upon the collective unconscious, or of the human psyche as "the greatest of all cosmic wonders, and the sine qua non of the world as an object." We rest on and are non-locally connected to the organizing fields of these parallel worlds. The West African teacher and "Keeper of Rituals," Sobonfu Somé, from the Dagara tribe, known as being an unusually "magical" people, even says that trees communicate with each other through this subtle energy bond.

"There is a web of connection, life, and light," Sobonfu explains, "a web of feminine energy that goes from the earth, to the moon, and to all the other dimensions." This web is a form of consciousness of oneness that links all of life together. "Different energies flow into this web; ... it contains wisdom, knowledge, and a healing energy for the whole world." We can connect to these energies by connecting to the web. Sobonfu also affirms that women have special access to this web because the web itself is a form of feminine energy. "Anything that works non-hierarchically, like a web, can be considered feminine."

Sobonfu feels that women, through their particular gifts, have an energetic power that enables them to honor life, to value each individual, to connect with others and the earth, to feel, and to "be" in silence. Because of this, they play a vital central role in bringing forth the kind of feminine healing energy that we need to take the next step in our human evolution. This next phase includes "making a conscious connection to a greater wholeness, a great web of life, light, and wisdom that connects us all, and connects our world here on earth to other planets and other dimensions."[48]

Moreover, not only do humans connect to the web, but also animals connect and are especially sensitive to it and hence can be attuned to their environments in ways that we are not. We should learn this. Plants, too, are conscious of the web of light. Trees, as Sobonfu shows, are like antennae that direct energy from the earth to the moon—the source of feminine wisdom and energy—and to other planets, to Other worlds. "Trees do inter-dimensional traveling through the web, and communicate with trees on other planets without moving." Sobonfu explains that her grandmother was a visionary who helped her to see in multiple ways—for example, that trees, although they look still actually have a lot of activity going on. It was her grandmother's role to help others see, accept, and prepare for the future.[49]

The mystical worlds often appeal to us through the resonant image of the "lost continent," such as Plato's Atlantis to which I have already referred, a loss that appeals to the nostalgia in our hearts, for we know deep down of the existence of these realms. They are our Source, and we travel there in altered states, in unusual encounters, and in between incarnations. These intermediate worlds are external worlds, but not the physical worlds of ordinary space-time. They are the imaginal locus of the concealed god's Presence, revelation, and creative emanations as Sophia, Wisdom, Soul or Angel of the World, also known as the Shekhina of the Kabbalists. They are the complex subtle dimensions of the deep psyche that must be experienced directly to be known at all. Shamans learn to be in this third space by sitting quietly in the natural world and paying attention to every tiny living thing going on around them.[50] This kind of stillness activates the knowledge that wasp, snake, and wind are the manifestation of the gods, the clothing the gods and goddesses wear in order to be remembered, and that the smallest of the small is interwoven with the majestic spiraling of the galaxies with no separation.

---

48 Sobonfu Somé, in *The Unknown She*, Ed., Hilary Hart (Inverness, CA: The Golden Sufi Center, 2003), pp. 240–242.
49 *Ibid.*, pp. 239–240.
50 See Martin Prechtel, *Secrets of the Talking Jaguar* (New York: Jeremy P. Tarcher /Putnam, 1999).

Chapter Ten

MYSTICAL CITIES: THE HISTORICAL RECORD AND SOME RECENT ACCOUNTS

Whoever reaches Shambhala or is reborn there can never fall back to a lower state of exis-
tence and will either attain Nirvana in that lifetime or very soon thereafter.
Lamas add that Shambhala is the only Pure Land that exists on earth. When I inad-
vertently suggested to the Dalai Lama that it might be only an imaginary or immaterial
paradise of the mind, he immediately replied, "No, definitely not:
Shambhala has a material existence in this world."[1]

Opening to the mystical cities helps our consciousness evolve toward a "vaster type of sensibility and being," as Robert Thurman suggests. Taking our cue from the experiences of close encounters or NDErs, or practicing meditations that take us to Temples of Wisdom and the guides of our soul in the form of animals, luminous beings or a wise "friend," we too can awaken to knowledge and a broader spiritual dimension not bound by any specific religious tradition. This awakening, often induced by a direct encounter with love and an unconditional acceptance of who we are including both our strengths and our faults, can help us feel both more confident and inspired. Such an experience can lead to our feeling more compassion for others and to an intense desire to see world conditions change, and to work toward such a goal.

In the last chapter, I mentioned how Sobonfu Somé speaks of the centrality and importance of women and feminine energy in this evolution of consciousness and culture. One of my favorite stories about the contribu-

---

1   Edwin Bernbaum, *The Way to Shambhala* (Garden City, NY: Anchor Press/Doubleday, 1980), pp. 9–10.

tions women have made to the world through the means of their visionary imagination and their courageous forays to the mystical lands of the soul while in an altered state of consciousness is to be found in this remarkable life account of the fifteenth century writer, Christine de Pizan.

Christine de Pizan and the City of Ladies

Christine de Pizan was born in Italy but lived in France. In 1405, this gifted and highly respected mediaeval poet and prolific writer wrote a hauntingly inspirational book called *The Book of the City of Ladies*.[2] According to this biographical account, in a moment of dark despair about being a woman in a misogynist society, Christine was visited in a waking vision by three majestic and noble women of great beauty and wise demeanor from another mysterious realm who informed her that, because of her deep desire to acquire true knowledge, she had been chosen by God to construct a city—The City of Ladies—with the celestial guidance of these three women. The names of the Ladies were Rectitude, Reason, and Justice. Christine describes her vision:

> I sat slumped against the arm of my chair with my cheek resting on my hand. All of a sudden, I saw a beam of light, like the rays of the sun, shine down into my lap. Since it was too dark at that time of day for the sun to come into my study, I woke with a start as if from a deep sleep. I looked up to see where the light had come from and all at once saw before me three ladies, crowned and of majestic appearance, whose faces shone with a brightness that lit up me and everything else in the place. As you can imagine, I was full of amazement that they had managed to enter a room whose doors and windows were all closed.

The Ladies tell Christine not to be alarmed for they were there to comfort her and to help her get rid of the misconceptions that were clouding her mind. They assure her that "it is in the furnace that gold is refined," and that it is "the very finest things which are the subject of the most intense discussion."

---

2   Christine de Pizan, *The Book of the City of Ladies* (London & New York: Penguin Classics, 1999), and pp. 7-8, for the quotes that follow.

The construction of this city was to be accomplished by Christine writing a book in which she would refute the derogatory accusations against women, and confirm their strengths and gifts by telling stories of heroines from the past and present, women who have distinguished themselves as poets, mystics, royalty, politicians, pirates, warriors, artists, teachers, mothers, lovers, and healers. Throughout the stories the virtues of women's compassion, constancy, fierceness, creativity, ingenuity, innate intelligence, and love would shine through. Christine's book, written six hundred years ago, remains an inspired and inspiring gem for women today who, in their commitment to heal their wounds and find true knowledge, continue to help build this mystical city. Christine was told that her City of Ladies would be made with strong foundations, and that its great walls, lovely moats, and lofty towers, would remain indestructible for all time. Christine de Pizan's story concurs with accounts written by others who also claim that mystical cities can be built with knowledge itself. Both Raymond Moody and Kenneth Ring have reported cases in which NDEers reported that "the buildings of higher learning they visited were not just devoted to knowledge, but were literally *built out of* knowledge."[3]

THE CALL OF THE DIVINE FEMININE

One of my students, Candy Kleven, told me a very moving story of how she overcame the pattern of a destructive life through her own fortitude and desire for knowledge. She had spent most of her life rejecting the Divine Feminine by repressing, suppressing, abusing, cursing, even hating her femininity. Her self-loathing echoed the life she was raised in: growing up with a distant, disinterested mother, a sexually abusive father, enduring two painful violent rapes, turning to a life of prostitution, and later an abusive marriage, Eventually the pain of the "hole in her soul" lead her to study Eastern philosophy, and her strong desire to "claim her true nature" led her to reconnect with the divine feminine through means of an intense dream that took her to another world filled with soul guides who imparted important messages to her about her future work. Here is what she wrote about her life:

3   Michael Talbot, *The Holographic Universe* (New York: HarperPerrenial, 1991), p. 273; Kenneth Ring, *Heading Toward Omega* (New York: William Morrow, 1985), p. 72.

I needed to become more conscious, and to salvage all the different parts of myself, to discover a sense of my own value. Gradually, through my studies of the different expressions of the Divine Feminine, found in Hindu, Buddhist, Greek, Egyptian, Sumerian, Polynesian and other traditions, I found resources that initiated a longing in my soul to become a vessel for the ancestors to speak through me about the sacredness of life, the values of feeling and intuition, strength and vulnerability, fierceness, intelligence and compassion. I knew deeply that, as Jungian analyst Christopher Whitmont writes, "through reverence for the sovereignty of the Goddess in her repellent no less than her beautiful aspect, the quester thereby receives her boon and may drink again of the ever-flowing waters."[4] I feel convinced that my path is a quest to discover, understand, accept, and embody the Divine Feminine and drink from her sacred waters evermore.

One night, I was visited by a powerful and numinous dream that took me to another dimension of existence:

It was dark as I walked up an old wooden stairwell. I had a sense that I was about to go to no place or another world. I found myself in a magical chamber filled with images of the Hindu Gods and Goddesses, and my guru Sai Baba along with his guru Shirdi Baba. I was stunned with no words to say, and no place to hide; they knew me, and every part of me.

I stumbled into another world where the images were so real, almost animated. It was as if they were talking to me without moving their lips. They were beaming with golden yellow and white light. They were also telepathically relaying messages I couldn't understand; yet instinctively, I knew they were talking to me—not to my worldly physical self, but to my spirit, my unconscious, my soul. Their eyes were gentle and their smiles illuminating as I felt them caressing every part of me, while at the same time saying, "Welcome. We have been waiting for you for a long time. You are to be a harbinger of our world and many will come when you accept your fate. We are here for you. We love you and we have chosen you." I did not ask any questions. There was no right or wrong, good or bad in that moment. There was only love, peace, and joy.

In that moment it was as if I was an extension of the divine. I felt my individual self vanish as I stood there in the presence of the divine. I felt the rush of fear, feelings of unworthiness, and pangs of pain from the events in my life for which I had not yet forgiven myself. These feelings surfaced and were wiped out immediately as I profoundly understood that in my past there were moments of understanding who I truly am and what I am supposed to do. Those feelings lasted for a split second as if the past, present, and future were one.

---

4   Edward. C. Whitmont, *Return of the Goddess* (New York: Crossroad, 1992), p. 171.

I came back to my physical self and sensed a smell of musty old books. I realized that there were ancient books all around the room. There were large, brown, hardcover books with gold and black inscriptions and colorful vibrant images. I was overwhelmed. I thought, "Oh my god, these must be holy texts. (I am feeling goose bumps while I am writing this). Why have they been hidden? What am I to do with them?

As I started questioning myself again, I felt the pull to our physical world. It is so very hard to explain this phenomenon and very difficult to find words to describe this feeling. It is as if I journeyed to my Self, and now had to return to my self. I was aware of the feeling, the place where you drop down into the unknown to the numinous where the "I" disappears and the "we" is felt and embodied. So magnificent and so real! It is more real than this world we live in now. I felt all my senses heighten as I was whole and an extension of yet another bigger whole.

I looked on my left and I saw the Goddesses; they were beautiful, loving, and magnificent. Their divine feminine presences balanced the room and as I understood immediately, the world. They wanted me to know that they were here for me and that I am to trust what is happening. "There is a lot that you do not understand yet, just trust that what you are to do is for the good of all." I looked at them only briefly since their brilliance was so intense that I felt I would vanish if I looked into their eyes for more than a glimpse. I also felt unworthy in their presence. Lovingly, with only seconds to look and bow to them, I knew what they were asking from me. I also knew that this was just the beginning. There are many tests that I am to go through.

In that very second, I claimed my fate of being a caretaker of the holy chamber. I went to the back room where I was to live and found an old dilapidated shower. I was dismayed at the sight and thought it challenging to bathe there. It was so out of place from the context of what I was experiencing that it did not make any sense. I could not understand what it signified.

I started opening the sacred space to the public and people started coming. There were women dressed in saris singing bhajans and men praying to the Gods and Goddesses. More and more people started to come and we had to put up tents outside as a waiting room area. Hundreds of crowds came, men and women from all religions, races, and creeds. They had their personal conversations with the Gods and Goddesses in the room. What was happening was beyond me, much bigger than I was. I was being led and was only a tool, a servant to the Divine.

Suddenly, I was in an open space. It felt like spring. There was a river, with a flowing current in the landscape and the fragrance of flowers, green grass, and trees permeated the atmosphere. There were tables set for a celebration and I felt a keen sense of excitement. What was happening? There was to be a wedding ceremony and I was the bride, yet it was not a marriage to a man. At that time, I woke up filled with awe, joy, and confusion. Who was I to be married to? Wait, I was already married to a man I dearly love [my new husband], why am I getting married again?

"I stayed in bed for awhile and as I started to come back to this world, the movie Field of Dreams came to me. I remembered the famous line: "If you build it, they will come." Yes, that is what I was supposed to do. I was to build the temple within, create the space for the Gods and Goddesses, while living a life of devotion to the Divine Feminine within me. From the Goddesses, I would be able to draw Eros, courage, strength, and grace to do this work. Writing my dissertation on this is part of the vocation. Returning to my life of singing and song—though now with different lyrics—is another aspect of what calls me forth.

"I realized that the Hindu Gods and Goddesses visited me because I am being asked to light the holy fire, their temple, within me. I do not know what it all means, and I will continue to ask for guidance and blessings. What I do know is how important it is for me to get back to my true nature and be true to my heart. The Hindu Gods and Goddesses have always been with me, even when I went astray. There was Brahman and Saraswati, Vishnu and Lakshmi, Shiva and Parvati/Sati, Krishna and Radha, Rama and Sita, with Kali and Durga. I am here for them once more, now with awareness."

∽∝∽

This visionary dream is another stunning example not only of the fateful and vocational call from the Other world, but also of the collective nature of the event, that, as Candy writes, "what was happening was much bigger than I was." She is playing her part in a much broader "course correction" taking place on our Earth, supported by the Holy Ones in the mystical cities beyond time. Two aspects of the dream remained a mystery for Candy. One was the old dilapidated shower, and the other was the marriage to the "unknown one" by the river. What did the mystery of water have to do with her initiation? Turning to a dictionary of symbols, Candy read the following, which felt meaningful to her. Water is illustrated as:

> a source of life, a vehicle of cleansing and a centre of regeneration
> …. To immerse oneself in the waters and to re-emerge without
> having been utterly dissolved in them, except by dying a symbolic

death, is to return to the well-springs and regain fresh strength from that vast reservoir of the potential.[5]

She knew she was being asked to bathe in the cleansing waters and die a symbolic death to be reborn and connect with the divine. She was being initiated into sacred space, and asked to participate in a ritual of redemption, regeneration, and rebirth.

Candy's deeply moving life story speaks of lingering feelings of self-doubt, self-condemnation, and lack of compassion toward herself. Perhaps, in the presence of the holy, we always feel unworthy and inadequate. Sometimes, she fears that her experience seems grandiose and inflated; indeed, we need a humble approach to the awesomeness of the divine. But truthfully, she believes that feelings of deficiency could also be an excuse to live unconsciously, to continue to repeat the past. They could be "hideous justifications to give up my dharma and settle for an unfulfilled life."

As with Christine de Pizan, Candy fully explores her suffering about being a woman in a misogynist family and culture, and opens herself to the possibility of change. In her lucid dream, a journey to the mystical lands of the soul, that seem entirely real—even more real than here—and where past, present, and future are experienced as one, she receives support and guidance from the immortal messengers. These representations of her larger Self speak to her soul telepathically, confirm her vocation, offer her wisdom from the Books of Knowledge, Sacred Texts, and initiate her into a path of devotion to recover the divine feminine in contemporary times. Her painful past, far from being a hindrance to her calling, fills her with the necessary compassion to be a vehicle of lost and ancient values. Like the training of the shaman, it is our suffering, the ordeal of our wounds and the death-rebirth mystery that accompanies this ordeal, that singles out an individual to be a healer, mystic, or visionary. Candy's dream is initiatory; it is the beginning of other events to come that will challenge and deepen her experience, and allow her to live in different worlds simultaneously. From having known the profane aspect of the Sacred Prostitute, Candy can now be Her devotee, recovering feminine sexuality and living in

---

5 Jean Chevalier & Alain Gheerbrant, *Penguin Dictionary of Symbols* (London & New York: Penguin Books, 1996), pp. 1081–1082.

harmony with her own deepest truth, as a way of being in service to the Goddess of Love.

In addition to Pizan's mystical City of Ladies, there are in the historical record, many other examples of journeys to, or visitations from, other places not to be found in ordinary reality. Here is a sampling.

The Invisible College as a Mystical Domain

The suggestion of an invisible and indestructible hall of learning and knowledge that "shall forever remain untouched, undestroyed, and hidden to the wicked world," is perceptible in the writings of John Dee (1527–1608). Dee was a philosopher and mathematician who had the largest library in England. He encouraged the founding of a royal library, and was court philosopher and astrologer to Queen Elizabeth I. Dee was also interested in the occult and mystical traditions, and his philosophy, linking Hermeticism, alchemy, and the Cabala, served as a basis of Rosicrucian teachings (the "Fraternity of the Rosie Cross"). He was part of a hidden brotherhood of scholars, most of whose works were published anonymously.

Sir Francis Bacon (1561–1626), was also part of this secret brotherhood and perhaps the founder of the order of Rosicrucians, though he did not associate with this order publicly. His commitment to "advanced learning" eventually led to the founding of the Royal Society in 1660, and many believe he was the secret author behind works attributed to William Shakespeare. It was a posthumous publication, *The New Atlantis*, which revealed his connection with The Invisible College, called Salomon's House, a building with wings which existed nowhere, yet connected all members of this esoteric group. Higher initiates were invisible teachers, the so-called R. C. Brothers, who taught their advanced knowledge to worthy adepts, who themselves became invisible.

Thomas Vaughan (1621–1666) writes of access to this esoteric knowledge in paradoxical terms, and as acquired through an "alchemical" journey of death and renewal to "an invisible mountain in the center of the world," (a mountain both small and great, soft and stony, near and far, surrounded by beasts, guarding a treasure, reached by one's own labors and effort), to find the treasure, the Tincture, the pearl of immortality. The journey is accomplished by unwavering courage and determination, dependence on God, and also with the help of an unknown and protective Guide that one meets on the way and who will lead the initiate to the mountain at midnight. Following all sorts of difficulties and trials, and a great Wind, eventually the adept will experience a great calm, see the Day-star, and experience the Dawn. In unmistakable alchemical metaphors, the mystic finds the Tincture, which is likened to pure gold. This, like the achievement of the grail, is described as a divine gift healing all ills and bestowing immortality.

Other members in the lineage of the perennial philosophy and Rosicrucian movement included Robert Fludd, student of John Dee. Isaac Newton (1642–1727) was also a member of the Invisible College. Newton, an eminent scientist and alchemist (though this latter fact is not well known), was deeply interested in the occult and esoteric, and is known to have been a Grand Master of the secret Prieure de Sion.[6] More recently, Jung's colleague, the physicist, Wolfgang Pauli, in linking the study of physics to the psychology of the archetypal unconscious, imagined himself to be recovering this ancient Hermetic alchemical union of psyche and matter and to be part of this esoteric line.

Perhaps the success of Dan Brown's *The Da Vinci Code* reflects the intense desire on the part of large numbers of people for the restoration of the invisible domains, the Invisible Ones, and those mysterious lands where we learn the esoteric secrets of cosmic knowledge. Brown's book recovers this lineage, linking the search for the grail with the Mary Magdalene traditions, acknowledging the keepers of this underground knowledge in secret societies, and referring to the significance of the Rose Line and its symbolic "guidance" via the sacred feminine imaged by Venus and Isis. This gnosis is revealed by a search for the "bloodline" and birthright of the soul, "outcast" and lost for too long, and now returning, born out of a nostalgic longing in our hearts.

Emanuel Swedenborg's Accounts of Mystical Cities

Emanuel Swedenborg (1688–1772) was a mathematician who spoke nine languages and had many other interests, including designing prototypes of the airplane and submarine. A mystic, he also meditated regularly, entered deeply altered states of consciousness where he conversed with spirits and

---

6   Jeffrey Mishlove, *The Roots of Consciousness* (New York: Marlowe & Co., 1993), pp. 60–64, 163–164.

angels, and visited realms that suggest the mystical cities. Passing through a dark tunnel, he entered extraordinarily beautiful landscapes beyond time and space where he experienced peace and serenity and luminous light and light beings who emitted deep feelings of love. In describing one mystical city, Swedenborg wrote that it was a place "of staggering architectural design, so beautiful that you would say this is the home and the source of the art itself."[7] Similar to the accounts of many NDEers, he writes that he observed the newly deceased arriving in heaven and watched as they submitted to their life review, a process recalling the book of knowledge called by Swedenborg, "the opening of the Book of Lives." He describes how our life's achievements are recorded in the nervous system of our spiritual body, and how an angel or guide could review this accomplishment by examining every aspect of this "resurrection" body. Communication was direct and telepathic, yet contained vast amounts of information far beyond what we humans know. In these afterlife realms spiritual knowledge also took the place of food as a source of nourishment. Interestingly, his accounts of these cities even included the subtle bodies of people from other planets.

In Swedenborg's view, our universe is being constantly co-created both as a wave-like flow from heaven and a wave-like flow from the soul or spirit of individuals here on earth. This wave-like flow pattern is similar to Jung's view regarding the ego's relationship to the unconscious and David Bohm's view of the relationship between the implicate and explicate orders of reality. Swedenborg also believed that in spite of the subtle dimensions of the mystical cities, "heaven" was actually a more fundamental level of reality than our own physical world, and that the two were not really separate and that our world could be imagined as really a more dense or frozen dimension of that Other world.[8]

The Hindu holy man, Sri Yukteswar Giri (d. 1936) also experienced these luminous landscapes through yogic practice. He describes an exquisite land much larger than our material world, constructed of intensely vibrant colors. There, we will find all those with whom we have been in relationship

---

7   Dole, in Emanuel Swedenborg, *The Universal Human and Soul-Body Interaction*, ed. and trans. George F. Dole (New York: Paulist Press, 1984), p. 44. See also, E. Swedenborg, *Life on Other Planets* (Swedenborg Foundation, 2006).
8   Michael Talbot, *The Holographic Universe*, pp. 257–259, 272.

through all of our various incarnations, and we will be able to acknowledge the indestructible nature of love and relate to all equally. Telepathic communication or "seeing" is possible through any aspect of the body. The materialization of food or flowers is accomplished through desire, healing through willingness, and feasting through imbibing the ambrosia or mead of new or immortal knowledge.[9]

Another Indian sage, Sri Aurobindo (1872–1950), also wrote about the spiritual country within us, which is found by silencing the ceaseless chatter of the conscious mind. He writes of an advanced multicolored vibrational reality peopled by nonphysical beings who can take on any form at will to make themselves more accessible to a particular consciousness. In this luminous landscape we can absorb knowledge in vast amounts directly and perceive large extensions of space and time all at once. Here we know that all separation is illusion and that all things—both spirit and matter—not only have consciousness and are alive, but also are interconnected and whole. However, he warns that we must be wary of being imprisoned by our ideas and theories or equating these with some ultimate truth, for the ineffable refuses to limit itself to any particular expression. Rather, it invites us to proceed from illumination to illumination, from soul state to soul state.[10]

Contemporary Accounts of Mystical or Luminous Cities

In my previous book, *Eros and Chaos*, I tell a story of a meeting I had with what I call a Being of Love. While my physical body was asleep on an airplane, I entered an altered state of consciousness—not a dream—that seemed to give me access to a parallel realm of being. There I met with this being and other emissaries from the realms of cosmic love. Likewise, in my dream just before September 11 (recounted in the previous chapter), the figures who appeared assured me that they came from an imaginal realm located somewhere in the stars. Since recording these strange events, I have become increasingly aware of other individuals' accounts of these other lands.

---

9 *Ibid.*, p. 262.
10 *Ibid.*, pp. 263–265. See also, Robert McDermott, *The Essential Aurobindo* (Lindisfarne Books, 2001).

Olga Kharitidi and Belovodia (Shambhala)

In *Entering the Circle*, an autobiographical account of her altered states of consciousness, Russian physician-shaman Olga Kharitidi makes several references to a place she calls Belovodia, which she acknowledges has various names in other traditions. For example, she writes that in Tibet and in Tantric Buddhism, this place is called Shambhala. As I note in the epigraph at the beginning of this chapter, Shambhala is clearly a real place, not just an imaginary utopia of the mind.

Olga Kharatidi writes that these sacred lands were associated with a belief in a time wheel, and that initiates—or as Suhrawardi calls them, the "People of Love," *fedeli d'Amore* (a phrase reminiscent of my own description of the Being of Love)—in their ritual ceremonies were supposed to be able to access the portals or doorways by which these mystical cities could be reached.[11] We know that time has both quantitative and qualitative possibilities. In my UFO encounter, which is described in the next chapter, I experienced a synchronized union of these two aspects of time. I felt as if the eternal realm were breaking through into three-dimensional time and space, or alternatively, as if I were stepping through a hole from here into eternity. Mystical visions and unions in general are often characterized by such synchronizations.

In Olga's shamanic experiences in altered states of consciousness and dream, she becomes increasingly curious about the phenomenon of Belovodia and to what extent this is not just a mythical or legendary city, but a real subtle realm that resides in a parallel stream of reality, which can intersect with our own. Through her encounters with her Siberian shaman-teacher Umai and others, she is awakened to the possibility that each person has access to Belovodia/Shambhala, and that the journey to this place is made while escorted by a guardian or spirit twin who resides at the entrance to this realm, and who is associated in the deepest way with the essence of one's being and with the full realization of one's destiny here. Her description of the guardian is reminiscent of the guardian, ally, angel, or "Man [Woman] of Light" described in Sufi mysticism.

This kind of journey is intimately connected with self-knowledge. It follows all Gnostic, mystic, and visionary traditions based on illuminative

---

11 Olga Kharitidi, *Entering the Circle* (San Francisco: HarperSanFrancisco, 1996), p. 217.

SONGLINES OF THE SOUL

insight that hold to the maxim: "He or she who knows him or herself, knows the All." Such an experience is not primarily orchestrated through the ego self, but in an altered state via the Heart Self, which is the gateway to Belovodia/Shambhala. The heart with its beating vibration is the place in the physical body that links to both the heartbeat of the earth and to the subtle realm of Belovodia as a distinct region of the cosmos. The sacred knowledge of love and its mysteries lies at its center. This insight is echoed in my own account of the recovery of missing time in the next chapter, and comports with what Leviton observes about the celestial cities being attuned to the heart chakra center, the *ananda-kanda* of the Earth, and of humans. Writing of this center he states that it is "said by Hindu tantric models of the chakras to have eight petals and to hang like a pendant below the main, outer heart chakra, the Anahata."[12]

Olga tells us that when she was starting her manuscript, she went in search of her shaman-teacher Umai for permission and advice. Umai told her that: "the Altai name for the Great Spirit was Ulgen, which was derived from Ulgar, the Altai word for the constellation known in English as the Pleiades."[13] Here again is the hint that the mystical domains that we can access via the heart are linked with various star constellations. Every sacred site, from the Egyptian and Mayan Pyramids, to the stone circles of England and France, to the Nazca lines and other ancient temple sites around the world, make this connection, since these structures functioned, at least in part, as astronomical observatories of the nighttime sky, and were constructed perhaps to facilitate inter-dimensional time travel. The stars we see in the night sky serve to remind us of one of the deepest mysteries of our being here on this planet. This link with the star people suggests not just the immortality of the soul or the journey of the soul following death, but the transformation of our consciousness, here and now, on this Earth, toward a vastly expanded sense of our destiny as star lords and ladies with a job to do within the context and integrity of our relationship with the galaxy as a whole.

The mystical cities are opening up their borders once again to help us to manifest our essence, not just to change our life, but to "become" the experience of heart-felt spiritual radiance.

---

12 Richard Leviton, *The Galaxy on Earth* (Charlottesville, VA: Hampton Roads, 2002), p. 45.
13 Olga Kharitidi, *Entering the Circle*, p. 223.

A Journey to a Universe of Light

Author, mother, naturopathic practitioner, counselor, and organic farmer Penny Kelly, writes of a kundalini spiritual awakening in the late '70s that arose quite spontaneously and involved powerful orgasms and blissful states not only when she was making love, but also in the middle of her work day! She then began to find herself in other times and places, able to anticipate events, hear the thoughts of others, including plants and animals, as well as seeing lights around people. Leaving her job as a tool engineer for an auto company with no context for what she was experiencing, she spent the next few years suffering a complete crumbling of her perception of reality.

For almost three years she could not sleep at night. On one such sleepless night, Penny writes that she was visited on the roof of her house by three Beings made of light that flew toward her from the western sky. They extended greetings and an invitation to go with them. Drawn up out of the core of her body-mind, she felt her ordinary reality being replaced by "an intensely felt *knowing* and an exquisite feeling that came with its own vision and sound—and threatened to disintegrate me altogether."

Penny was then taken to a universe made completely of light. She notes that what was shocking to her was not the light but the fact that it looked exactly like our earth with people, plants, buildings, animals and landscapes—"except there were no wars, no crime, no sickness, no accidents. Greed, fear, anger, and corruption did not exist. People were extraordinarily beautiful. No one was overweight, poor, unkempt, or disabled. Everyone was made of light, as were the flowers, rivers, trees, houses, schools, and buildings." Love seemed to orchestrate everything and was palpably alive; even the stones seemed conscious and responsive. She was taken on a tour and told that this was her real home. Earthlings had tried to reproduce this real home on earth, but had failed miserably. Comparable to other stories where the initiate is shown a Book of Knowledge but forgets its contents upon waking in ordinary consciousness, Penny was told very important things by her guides many of which she could not recall upon returning to her rooftop. However, though she was visited again on several occasions, she never forgot the impact of the journeys and the exquisite beauty and overflowing love that was part of the universe of light, "one of the heaven worlds."

Through her kundalini experience, Penny "awoke" to her Self, to the divine I AM at the core of her being. Through this transformation she dissolved her conditioned values and learned to listen to the still small voice at the center that was the Teacher of Life and Truth providing guidance in the present Now for the unfolding of her hidden potential. She questions: "What would your life be like if you unfolded the full potential of your human design?" Perhaps we would begin to move from our world today that is filled with war, famine, and illness to one that is closer to the mystical world of light that Penny visited where fear, pain and corruption did not exist. Over time, Penny's life transformed completely. Not only does she teach about the transformation of consciousness and offer counseling services to others, she also writes about the evolutionary potentials of *kundalini* energy in human experience and actively works toward a sustainable future on a global level.[14]

NDEers Travels to the Luminous Cities

Consciousness researcher Kenneth Ring records how the near-death experience sometimes includes travel to cities of light.[15] For example, a client of his named Darryl who experienced an NDE described it this way: "I moved closer to the lights and realized they were cities—the cities were built of light... I stood in the square of a brilliant, beautiful city....The building I went in was a cathedral. It was built like St. Mark's or the Sistine Chapel, but the bricks or blocks appeared to be made of Plexiglas. They were square, they had dimension to 'em, except you could see through 'em and in the center of each one of these was this gold and silver light." Darryl goes on to describe how this building of light was a source of direct learning and knowledge, and that he was bombarded with information.

Another client named Stella speaks of finding herself heading—at tremendous speed while passing other life forms—toward an "immense" city of light supported by a beam of light coming from within it. From the midst of that city, a laser was aimed at her, gently drawing her into the city. She describes a clear gold street where objects had definition and clarity, yet

---

14 Penny Kelly, "Kundalini: Unfolding the Human Design," in *Kundalini Rising: Exploring the Energy of Awakening* (Boulder, CO: Sounds True, 2009), pp. 37–46.
15 Kenneth Ring, *Heading Toward Omega*, pp. 71–74.

everything seemed to blend together as well. Stella's account bears a remarkable similarity to other descriptions of the mystical cities:

> The flowers and the flower buds by that street—the intensity, the vibrant colors [were] like pebbles that have been polished in a running stream, but they were all like precious stones, rubies and diamonds and sapphires...and [had] a strong fragrance of roses.

As she begins to meet others and hear unknown languages that she can understand, she realizes that she is approaching a place of knowledge beyond anything she can describe in human terms, and begins to cry as she knows that she cannot proceed at this time and must return to life.

A client named Jayne does not arrive at a city of lights, but like some UFO experiencers, finds herself in an extraordinary natural setting, "on a green plain." She writes:

> I had a body again...And this was a beautiful green meadow, with beautiful flowers, lit again with this glorious radiant light, like no light we've ever seen, but there was sky, grass, flowers that had colors that I'd never seen before...Just utter glory in color. And I walked along and I saw that there were people up on a little rise in front of me. So I started walking toward that rise to talk with these people and when I had just about gotten up there, I could see a city.

Ring emphasizes that individual values change dramatically in the wake of such powerful, direct, and moving experiences. NDers often experience psychic and often visionary changes. For example, they develop compassion for others, move toward a quest for greater meaning in their lives, and experience spiritual transformations that often take them beyond their former orthodoxy.

UFO Encounters and Mystical Cities

As Carl Jung recounts in the Epilogue to his "Flying Saucers" essay, we can encounter mystical experiences with "friends from Other worlds" in sometimes breathtakingly beautiful and galactic settings. Similarly, John Mack, in

Passport to the Cosmos, gives several examples of contactees" mystical encounters with beings in landscapes that, like Orfeo Angelucci's, suggest a visit to the mystical cities of the soul. For example, Mack reports that an individual named Will went aboard a huge "City of Lights," which involved a complex process of changing his physical body into a more subtle one and going through some kind of threshold. He had this visionary experience in the middle of the night while sailing on the ocean somewhere between Bermuda and New England. There he encountered tall bluish luminous figures that moved him deeply by their beauty, which was strange as these beings were not recognizably beautiful in earthly terms.[16]

The experience of Nona—mother of five children and married to another client of Mack's—reminds us of the "hidden valley," "green valley," or Pure Lands theme in Tibetan lore. She describes a night time journey—"not a dream"—with another woman to a magnificently beautiful Brazilian rain forest environment (a possible "UFO base," she adds) in which balls of light and an illumined landscape, whose source was unknown, contributed to a sacred and powerful feeling among this luscious growth. She remembered being in a valley or gorge surrounded by mountains and standing on a metallic platform, which was pushed up from deep within the Earth till the tops of trees were at her feet.

When Nona told her account to the Brazilian shaman and anthropologist, Bernardo Peixoto, he recognized the natural "bowl" clearing as a specific place of power in the Amazon basin known to other native people who also had seen "lights swirling over the tops of trees." Nona further comments on her experience: "When they show you these environments, you can actually see the life-force in flowers and in the leaves and the water. It's like colors you've never seen before... In the rain forest you could see the life existing within a leaf, within the tops of these trees. There were earth spirits dancing all over the tops of those trees."[17] It is the intensity of color, the vision of the life force itself, and the presence of spiritual entities that hint at a comparison with descriptions of the mystical landscapes. Here there is the suggestion that these luminous lands are easily accessible through ordinary reality if we could but see with "eyes that see." Philosopher and

16 John Mack, *Passport to the Cosmos* (New York: Crown Publishers), pp. 66–67.
17 *Ibid.*, pp. 97–98.

theologian Henri Corbin speaks of *imaginatio vera* as the organ of visionary sight, the mode of "seeing" that transmutes physical reality to its subtle essence or "angel."

Sometimes for experiencers, these scenes of extraordinary natural beauty are contrasted with devastating earth visions of death and destruction that appear on monitors or TV-like screens. One of the effects of these visions is to convey with tremendous feeling the bleak outcome of our continued polluting of our natural resources and environment. Mack writes of Jim, a residential real estate broker of Italian-American background, who conveys how difficult it is to bear "the sorrow of the truth [of] these awful scenes."[18] Jim's encounters have led him to become a political activist on behalf of the survival of the planet. Nona adds how exposure to the exquisite life and beauty of the earth is something she tries to live each day. Many experiencers, whose own suffering seems to embody and parallel the Earth's own distress, become environmentalists working on behalf of restoring harmony and balance to our fragile ecology.[19] Many, too, become drawn to indigenous spirituality and Gaia consciousness because these traditions so deeply honor our connection to the Earth and to every living inhabitant on it. It is as if when we see with "Hurqalyan perception," we peer into the subtle beauty of our world as a realm in its own right, and find ourselves in the mystical cities of the soul.

Internationally known Mexican photographer Carlos Diaz's leadership in ecological issues began with an encounter that occurred shortly after he had taken some spectacular UFO photographs near Mexico City. Many experiencers report receiving knowledge in "libraries," either through books or balls of light storing vast amounts of information, usually recovered in incremental amounts due to the fact that receiving this information all at once would shock or overwhelm them. Subsequently, Carlos reports many teachings in which he is either instructed verbally by non-human beings who can nevertheless take on human form, or taught through direct knowledge, sometimes on a space ship or from inside a strange sphere of light inside caves where his vision expands. There the intimate connection of every living animal, plant, or person, from the tiniest to the largest, becomes apparent to him, as well as

---

18 *Ibid.*, p. 97.
19 *Ibid.*, p. 99.

the interconnectedness of living and non-living matter to the whole order of creation. Like the alchemists' *lumen naturae*, Carlos describes in great detail the different kinds of light in the natural world, which he calls "the light of this life," and how these various lights intersect with one another, from insects and turtles to leaves, sand, and the ocean itself, as a multicolored diamond display. Once again, he experiences a deep love for the planet as a remarkable and rare womb of life in the universe, along with deep sorrow in the company of those who do not share this profound vision of a living Earth made up of intersecting, simple, yet complex eco-systems that we must help protect.[20]

Spontaneous Journeys

Some modern-day experiences of the celestial cities, unlike UFO encounters, NDEs, or shamanic journeys, are simply spontaneous travels to these other domains. In Part I of this book, I related a story told by my husband, Robert Romanyshyn, called *The City in the Clouds*, a spontaneous experience he had while recovering from an operation for the removal of a benign pituitary tumor. This evocative account of an emerald and diamond "musical" city that we help to construct by gathering the sparks of beauty in this world reminds me of Christine de Pizan's epiphany of the celestial ladies who assured her that writing her book on behalf of the real truth of women's nature would help build the City of Ladies for all time. Once again, love, sorrow, beauty, and truth are the gems of our truest identity. If we work diligently and with devotion in service to realizing our particular contribution to this deepest reality of which we are made, we help to build the mystical cities of the soul, indestructible for all eternity. Perhaps it is worth noting, too, that the pituitary (and pineal) glands are also related to the third eye, so that my husband's operation, on a psychic level, was perhaps related to the opening of this visionary organ.

In this second story Robert tells of a different kind of city, one beneath the sea. Once again, as Henri Corbin notes, we can observe how our experience of these domains depends very much on the state of our own consciousness, how our imagination is opened to what the soul needs to apprehend.

---

20 *Ibid.*, p. 100f.

The City Beneath the Sea:

I have always had a fear of being in deep water. I had made many attempts both to overcome this fear and to understand it, and I had with much difficulty learned how to swim. But even in this context I could not bring myself to swim in water which would be over my head if I stood up. In addition I could not put my face in the water while swimming and then turn it to catch a breath, which limited my swimming to the length I could travel in one breath. Every time I tried to enact this rhythm I would get confused between holding my breath while my face was in the water and breathing while it was out. The result inevitably was that I would inhale water and panic. I would struggle to stand up, gasping for air, trying to breathe in as much air as possible.

My wife and I were on a cruise ship. The weather had been mild and warm and the combination of sun and relaxation over the course of a week made it easy for me to slip into states of reverie. One of the pleasures of the cruise for me was to stroll around one of the upper decks, and on one of these occasions I found myself near the front part of the ship. This part of the deck for some reason was empty, which was uncommon because the ship was crowded and I had not previously found myself alone in such a quiet place. I stood by the railing, looking down, mesmerized by the flow of water beneath the ship. How long I was there in this state I could not say, but suddenly I began to gasp for air, as if I had just managed to break the surface of the water. The feeling in my body was exactly the same as the feeling of panic I would experience when I inhaled water while swimming. Shocked by this identity, I had what felt like an out-of-body experience. For what felt like a very brief moment I saw myself leaning over the rail watching someone rising out of the waters of the sea. I then "saw" a watery city at the bottom of the sea and I felt in my body that the someone rising from the sea was "me" in some earlier life when I had lived in that city and had departed from it. The bodily sensation of gasping for air was what that earlier someone had felt when, for the first time, "he" had breached the surface of the waters and taken his first breath.

As I walked away I had the uncanny feeling that my bodily feeling of panic in deep water was the memory of that earlier life and specifically of that moment of leaving the water and the city beneath the sea to live in the air. I felt that these bodily experiences were the "cellular" memories of that earlier existence.

∽

The next example is an account of a woman, Kathy Atwood, whose descriptions of the luminous cities are interesting because they are not related to extraordinary events of any kind, such as UFO encounters or NDEs. On the contrary, she has had these experiences quite spontaneously throughout her life, since she was a child, and this suggests to me that, quite possibly, many others like her know of these realms. Often children have some sort of experience with figures and guides from other realms that, unfortunately, we turn into imaginary (meaning "unreal" or "made up") events. Hopefully, this misunderstanding will gradually be corrected as we learn more about these kinds of experiences and confirm the landscapes of the transpsychic and the mystical cities of the soul. Kathy describes herself as a contemplative, philosopher, and explorer of consciousness and quantum physics, areas of study that she entered in order to find a context for, and to understand, her own "ineffable" and many anomalous experiences. Because, like many others, she felt she would not be taken seriously, it took years for Kathy to bring herself to speak of her unusual "journeys."

THE LUMINOUS CITY OF LIGHT

I didn't know of the existence of the City of Light until I found myself there, quite unexpectedly, quite spontaneously. I was in the shower when suddenly I was on the threshold of the most remarkable architectural structure I had ever encountered or could even have envisioned. I simply arrived there, seamlessly. There was no means of travel detectable and no time passed, it was instantaneous. Directly in front of me, as I arrived, was a Being that I know but do not know here in time. He was responsible for my being there, for my arrival. I had entered at an arch in this very broad and very long architectural structure that continued to the left and served as a walkway. At one end was a very large, very ornate circular structure wherein wisdom and knowledge abide, a sort of ethereal library or university. The walkway continued around it. Directly in front of me I could see through the archway the most incredibly divine landscape. What set this apart from any earthly experience was the luminous nature of everything. It was as if everything were actually constructed of light: the structures, the plants, the grass, the material of the walkway. The structures were not to protect or guard against any adverse elements; they existed solely and purely for aesthetic purposes.

On the other end, to my right, was a Great Hall. There were large double doors and they were open and through them I could see many people gathered at the front of the Hall and beyond a long stage upon which two Beings were standing. However, only one was addressing the group. I knew, without seeing, that the Great Hall was full of people. I knew that I was part of that group assembled and that we were meeting about the Earth Project. Then,

I was back in the shower. After I recognized that I was back in my shower I began weeping uncontrollably. I was weeping because these are "my people" and for the first time I did not feel like an interloper on foreign soil.

Following this initial encounter my nighttime activity changed. Most nights I would be there, engaged in some form of education, tutorials as I came to think of them. I was being tutored in the circular structure, the library that contained knowledge. I was never aware of leaving to go there, but I was often aware of returning and feeling my entry back into my physical body.

The aftermath was a very interesting and somewhat difficult time. I had seemed to split between a timeless and temporal self. One part of me knew that place, and had known that place, intimately well; the other part of me was absolutely amazed and had no idea that the likes of that existed — anywhere. The final arbiter was always the absolute REALITY that I had encountered. It was more real than any place or experience, so much so that this world appeared dreamlike and insubstantial and seemed, as Ralph Waldo Emerson states, merely "a tent in the night." There was also a profound and abiding sadness about being here, on earth, in time. Truly I had been in a heaven. Not only was this place an architectural and natural paradise, but it possessed an essential ethereal "atmosphere" of wholeness, harmony, and gentleness, an atmosphere where negativity and evil simply could not abide. By contrast, this earthly temporal experience seemed lacking in all those qualities.

I was comforted and validated by reading Michael Talbot's book The Holographic Universe *that refers to the civilizations of the subtle realms and observes that those who are privileged enough to visit them—such as NDEers, yogic adepts, and ayahuasca-using shamans—universally report seeing many vast and celestially beautiful cities there as well as libraries and schools for the pursuit of knowledge. It gave me "permission" to begin integrating both my sense of the time-bound world as well as those timeless dimensions of the luminous cities of light and higher learning.*

Journeys to the mystical cities of the soul take us beyond the psyche as we know it; they expand our vision of reality to something much vaster. Many have suggested that such experiences point to a collective awakening or shift of consciousness on a planetary and cosmological level to a direct experience of the world behind this one. Perhaps we could call it the fifth dimension and perhaps it involves the beginnings of a collective opening of the third eye, the eye of vision and creative imagination. Such experiences open us to the beauty, majesty, and miracle of creation. Here we see into the mystical essence of reality. We often re-discover those to whom we belong on a deep soul level. We no longer need to have a fear of death, and indeed, our fears in general are dissolved. We are inspired to live creatively, to become activists on the part of our vulnerable planet, and to have courage to speak up on issues that are not popular in most government and cultural circles. In summary, our education is expanded way beyond what we learn in school, and our sleepy conventionality is challenged as we are given a vocation to become spokespeople for the Invisible Realms and Invisible Ones. Furthermore, we are often opened to deep feelings of love, of the sacred Presence in every cell, and our intuitive capacities are stretched to marvel at the complexity and wonder of being here at all, something that cannot be adequately described in words.

THE KINGDOM

My final example comes from Deanne Jameson who first encountered what she calls "the Kingdom" during a time of grief and loss. Deanne and I met after she had read an article that I wrote for *Spring Journal* on the creation of the subtle body (connected to the individuation process), and the possibility of journeys to the subtle worlds suggested by some of Jung's visions, anomalous experiences such as NDEs and UFO/ET encounters, and Corbin's descriptions of the mystical cities of the soul from the Persian mystics.[21] Deanne felt powerfully and intuitively that her "visits" to the Kingdom were in alignment with these accounts of the Other world. She has kindly given me some examples of her experiences in the Kingdom, a story that reveals like some of the examples above an unfolding and deeply felt "dialectic of love" between herself and the Beloved behind it all. What is rather unusual about her account is that it represents an ongoing creative encounter with the imaginal Other world that now spans many years.

As Deanne began dealing with the deep depression that accompanied a painful divorce and the realization that she had been living a life too far from the source of her being, the unconscious broke through with dreams, visions, and spiritual insights. She read mystical texts, opened to alternative healing

---

21 Veronica Goodchild, "Psychoid, Psychophysical, P-Subtle! Alchemy and a New Worldview," in *Spring Journal: A Journal of Archetype and Culture, Spring 74, Alchemy* (New Orleans: *Spring* Journal, 2006), pp. 63–89.

modalities, dreamt of indigenous cultures, and discovered Jung. But she still felt she lacked a substantial foundation beneath her capable of being open to the mystery she had so long denied in her life and her new insights were not lifting her depression. On the verge of giving up and going back to the "real world," she suddenly and spontaneously experienced an opening to an Other world. Sitting at her computer poised to write her last despairing insight, she found herself instead in a house in the woods. Deanne continues:

"An old fashioned Key was weighing down the pocket of my long blue dress. I was in the imaginal house and at the same time at my desk, fingers flying across the keyboard, as if recording the experience. At the back of the cottage was a locked door I'd never seen before; the key in my pocket fit the lock. I opened the door and descended three steps to a barren landscape, a small abandoned stone arena to my right. Lifting my eyes to the horizon I saw only emptiness. I stood there, not knowing what do. I didn't want to go back to a life on the surface that had become unbearable and frightening, as I knew deep down there was something terribly wrong. Yet I didn't know how to speak of it to any one without sounding crazy and revealing the emptiness at the core. And so I waited; I waited a long time. Eventually a cloud of dust appeared; as it got closer I saw a small boy with large dark eyes, riding a donkey. When he arrived at my side, I climbed on the donkey's back and without speaking we turned from the back door of the house in the woods and for three days and three nights traveled through a desert, provisions magically provided when we needed to stop and rest.

"Eventually we arrived at a walled town where alone and on foot, I entered through a passageway carved into the thick stone walls, into a lovely town. Winding cobblestone streets led to a lively outdoor marketplace at the center. The inhabitants were preparing a celebration, which I learned later was a celebration of my arrival! As I made my way through the marketplace, the crowd backed up giving me passage to a small Moorish style palace. Alone, I stepped through a small gate built into the palace façade, and into an interior courtyard whose stillness startled me. When I shut the gate, I closed off the animation in the town and the rest of the world. Except for the gentle splash of fountains, an occasional bird song from somewhere else in the palace, the silence here was full and deep, protective and comforting, and for the first time in years I began to relax into myself.

"At dusk, from deep in the palace the alchemist king, who became my beloved Joseph, appeared. He was bathed in an inner light of clarity, which permeates everything in the kingdom. This would be the beginning of our ongoing love encounter. As he would do almost every time we met, he held out his hand, waiting for me to place mine in his. With great tenderness and care, he led me to our

chamber deep in the palace. Thus began a transformative encounter that would reshape the kingdom and open me to dimensions of myself, the world, and Other I didn't know existed.

"Over time and with many forays to the kingdom, I found healing I hadn't been able to find in my ordinary life. As I became stronger Joseph introduced me to other parts of the palace, in particular a small room under the stairs. We had to bend down to enter the small circular room where, at the center, a woman sat before a spinning wheel. She was humming and singing to herself, delighted to see Joseph and already expecting me. I couldn't see the yarn, and remember thinking that either she's crazy or I simply can't see what's here. Of course it would turn out to be the latter. I wanted to ask her questions, but she indicated she spoke only through stories. Through such a story she revealed that she tended special sheep whose wool could be spun into magical tales. She's a tale spinner, she told me, a storyteller known as Generator Woman because her stories, tales and myths generate the energy in the kingdom. She would become a great teacher to me and, over time, like a sister."

What follow are further excerpts from Deanne's journal about the Kingdom, chosen for particular qualities that she learned over time by visiting it that substantially contributed to her healing and "awakening" process. Of particular importance was the exquisite feeling of participating in creation itself by interacting with the reality of her imaginal world and of the feeling that the Kingdom itself needed her to survive as much as she needed its landscape and figures to thrive. This echoes what we have heard so often in the examples in this book. In all the accounts of an encounter with the Other world what is emphasized is the co-creative and interdependent nature of these encounters: the participation of the imagination is foundational for the creation of reality; and the imaginal world itself needs us as much as we need it. Deanne weaves her stories with reflections about them.

"It's early evening when I reach the marketplace. Most of the stalls are closed, some still closing. There's a light on in the small room behind Generator Woman's stall. I knock lightly. She knows who it is and sings out for me to enter. She's folding her embroidered cloth tales and, without looking up, greets me as if she'd been expecting me all along.

"'You knew I was coming,' I state. (I didn't know I was coming, but she always does).

"'Always,' she says, then looks up smiling. "I always know you are coming—as you are always expected—so that when you arrive (though I do not know it ahead of time) I am ready for you."

"'I am always prepared for your arrival,' is how Generator Woman puts it. 'It is always a surprise, but not surprising.' (Or is it the other way around, always surprising but not a surprise, I wonder?) It is the next moment, yet every moment here is fresh and new."

As Deanne reflects on this aspect of her story, she writes:

"There's something wonderful to me about this attitude, this way of experiencing each moment in its fullness which prepares you for the next moment from fullness, that I can't quite articulate. It isn't as if Generator Woman is anticipating my arrival, waiting with one ear cocked, but when I arrive it is the most natural thing in the world, simply the next step. When the moment is right, she simply places her full attention on me in genuine encounter. Every moment is like that here in the kingdom, created from the capacity to meet and be met that then generates the next natural moment. Here in the kingdom the inhabitants have the capacity to engage with the not yet known and to expect the unexpected with hearts capable of weaving it into fresh perceptions. It's a deeply creative dynamic and so alive, this moment-to-moment meeting from wholeness.

What Deanne emphasizes here is how the inhabitants of the kingdom know how to live deeply in the present moment, in the Now. Again, as we have witnessed before in stories told in this book, time as past, present, and future seems to collapse into one, a kind of creative fullness that is neither precisely one thing nor another.

Continuing with her story, Deanne writes:

"The next day I wander the streets of the walled town, delighting once again in the activity and the energy of the place—everything animated, fresh and new, even daily activities met with open hearted good humor. It makes me think of Thoreau's 'infinite expectation of the dawn' as a way of life in the Kingdom. I feel the dawn's radiance in the inhabitants as well as the stones themselves, as it permeates and illuminates everything from within. Every morning, every moment is new, composed of what has happened with what has not yet happened and yet it is all happening at once.

"This is how I feel at times when I'm writing the kingdom while participating in its life. Dynamic patterns of wholeness come alive in me, realigning my body and psyche for an encounter with the Other, the Friend or Beloved, the Unknown; then, when I'm fortunate, opening me to the invisible, to a generative Source from which spring the living waters of the soul's imagination. It is an incredible feeling and privilege to be in the kingdom when new

things are really emerging, when I'm discovering and learning what I could never have thought of or known myself. In those moments I am also sitting at the computer keyboard, playing it like a musical instrument, with a felt sense of sourcing and being sourced at the same time, of being a part of making the Invisible visible, of participating in creation itself."

What seems so clear here is that Deanne does not experience herself as the creator of this story or the maker of the figures who belong to it. Rather, she experiences herself more as one who makes a place for the story to unfold, which is what the author Isabelle Allende says, without equivocation, in this excerpt from "Writing and Inspiration:"

> [T]here is something magic in the storytelling. You tap into another world …. I have a feeling that I don't invent anything. That somehow I discover things that are in another dimension. That they are already there, and my job is to find them and bring them into the page. But I don't make them up …. I am open to all the mysteries. And when you spend too many hours—as many many hours a day as I do—in silence and alone, you are able to see that world.[22]

The following passage from Deanne's on-going account comes at another time when she was sinking into depression and despair. She writes:

"And so I return to the kingdom. I think I will walk from the arena. I need time to myself, to leave the world of the surface behind, but halfway there Spirit, a black horse whispered into his magnificent true self by Hermes, arrives with Jade. (Hermes was the boy who, arriving on a donkey, first welcomed me to the kingdom. He is now an accomplished horse and animal whisperer who listens deeply into people's wholeness and whispers their essence back to them. Jade was a deeply wounded child who would not speak or be consoled but whose life in the palace kitchen, nurtured by alchemist chefs, taught her the magic recipes that reveal the interiority of things and open the heart. She has become the youngest master chef and her recipes inspire great creativity in everyone. Furthermore, she and Hermes are now married). I haven't really seen Jade alone in years; she's been busy becoming a young accomplished woman.

"Without a word I climb on Spirit's back and lean into Jade. Jade has become my strength now. I rest my head and my tense body on her back, close my eyes and let the rhythm and

---

22 www.isabelallende.com

motions of the beautiful Spirit rock me to sleep as we approach the walled town and make our way slowly through the winding streets to the gates of the palace. Jade takes Spirit back to the stable behind their house, where Hermes awaits her. This is a very important night, I can feel, here in the kingdom; all is quiet and there is a sense of honor and love that is holy. So on this holy night I enter the palace gates by myself. There is so much going on here in the kingdom, yet I am spent. I feel so empty; I have given of myself, tried so hard, but I am exhausted and once again feel I can't go on.

"I enter the familiar courtyard and sit by the fountains. Sensing my despair, people I've met over the years emerge from different parts of the palace—those whose lives have been profoundly altered and aligned through Joseph and my love encounter that has helped bring balance and deeper harmony to the kingdom. They gather near me in silence, acknowledgment and gratitude, as if their very presence could somehow begin to reanimate me. I can feel it, but no longer know whether this is something I desire; maybe this is as far as I can go.

"Joseph arrives and lifts me in his arms and carries me to our chamber. I lay on the bed, my body still cold, unable to warm itself. Those who have gathered retreat a little but stay close around the midnight oil, as if they are attending the night of a great journey—perhaps a death—I don't know. Is this it, then? Am I dying? Joseph lies with me and I let my body sink into his, melt into his warmth and in spite of myself my heart begins to warm. I thought maybe this was the end; that I had done all I could and now it was time for me to leave the kingdom to itself, without me, it doesn't need me anymore. I have helped breathe life into it but now I am lifeless.

"'That is why we are here, dear one. You are not leaving us. On the contrary, this is a new beginning. Now you are going to receive OUR GIFTS; we are going to minister not to your death but to your new life."

"At this very moment, somewhere else in the kingdom, in silence and without witness Jade and Hermes conceive their child."

One cannot read this part of her story without feeling moved about the deep sense of compassion and love that Deanne experiences from the Kingdom. It is this experience of love that arises from her sojourns in the Kingdom that makes her consider this place a landscape of the heart. This deep sense of love and compassion felt by Deanne is what so many others in their accounts of the Other world have also described. Love and compassion appear to give a coherence to her life, which as she notes she still finds amazing even after all these years.

Deanne, however, makes it clear that this coherent sense of life informed by love is hard to sustain. Once again, she feels the familiar fear often suffered in her ordinary life, still hoping to find the courage to live with greater ease in her outer life the ways of the discerning open heart found in the kingdom. And so she seeks out the kingdom because this is where she drops below conditioned and reactive realities. She writes:

"And yet the potential capacity for living from heart awareness when I'm not in the kingdom, desirable as is sounds, requires all the courage I can summon as it goes against years of conditioning and the outer collective values of fear and mistrust in the wisdom of the Imagination and Invisible Ones (though these old ways of the collective are, finally, collapsing around us). To live with this attitude of "infinite expectation of the dawn" requires radical trust in an invisible creative intelligence, a trust that builds from each new encounter with the kingdom."

Deanne has learned from her forays into the Kingdom. Making the difficult attempt to articulate her subtle process, Deanne describes how as she writes, it does not at all feel like "making it up." Rather, she experiences some kind of living pattern begin to move through her body, and without knowing exactly how she is doing this—(remember, Corbin says though we know it happens, we don't know the precise moment we slip into the imaginal world)—words and stories and images emerge as if in some very mysterious way she is translating these felt experiences of moving and living patterns into the co-creation of the imaginal world or, alternatively, they (the stories of the Kingdom) are translating themselves through her. These imaginal tales are disclosures that emerge in the process of writing/ discovering itself; they are epiphanies that erupt as from a living sacred text.

For Deanne, it is not one big encounter experience but a continuing dialectic of love, an ongoing revelatory exchange that, over time, is stabilizing itself in her body as a transformed way of re-imagining the world and how we might live in it as a new era comes into being. Deanne's writing is perhaps a contemporary version of Suhrawardi's mystical treatises, Hildegard of Bingen's visionary recitals, and Christine de Pizan's reciprocal relationship with the mystical city of Ladies. Deanne writes that the Kingdom is a place of dynamic coherence, where the inhabitants discover and cultivate unique gifts that serve the whole. A high value is placed on harmony and balance, on cultivating peace, not as something static, but as a way of life where parts are woven into a whole living pattern. The more coherent and balanced the kingdom, the more it attracts similar kinds of beings, which is why the travelers market place, for example, is now a portal for healers and wise medics from other dimensions, those, that is, with the capacity to heal and make whole. This evolution of coherence and devotion to the whole is the reason, Dianne adds, why the Radiant One, Queen of the Dawn, was after years of exile able to return to the fields outside the town, to permeate the fields and meadows with her radiance and to teach her healing magic to her young apprentice, Joy. Now too there are celebrations and festivals in the fields—perhaps even echoing the appearance of crop circles and the rituals individuals and groups are often inspired to enact in them—to honor significant events in the kingdom.

The feeling of participation in an ongoing creation, *creatio continua*, is a work of the heart, and with awareness of this phenomenon, we can—each of us—in our own small ways participate more consciously in such a miracle, bringing our hearts into this ongoing process as well. *"These moments,"* Deanne concludes, *"are thrilling and erotic, deeply intimate and personal, yet at the same time universal."* Moreover, she adds, *"My engagement with the Unknown or mystery has also changed how I think about death."* As with many experiencers, NDEers, those individuals who have reached deeply into transpersonal and transpsychic realms of consciousness or parallel worlds, and crop circle initiates, Deanne no longer fears death, but imagines it as yet another great journey, a part of the Mystery of our being.

Deanne's story confirms that creative moments are in some way openings to the Other world where we are not so much authors of the experience but agents in service to something other than ourselves. She helps awaken us to the fact that our being is the portal through which the wisdom of the mystical cities of the soul can flow and *that* illumination, as in the other accounts in this chapter, helps bring a new heaven to a new earth.

Chapter Eleven

MISSING TIME AND MYSTICAL CITIES

Forgetting what we think is important
may be a remembering of what is important.[1]

The phenomenon of "missing time" is often associated with UFO encounter experiences, and I will put forth in this chapter that these "lapses in memory" may involve a journey to the mystical or luminous cities of the soul. I was especially alerted to this possibility by the fact that what I have come to call my UFO encounter seemed to last only a minute or two at most. Yet, even allowing generously for travel time to and from the desert mountain location where my encounter took place, there was no way to account for the four or five hours I "lost." I have already noted that with synchronicities in particular, and paranormal events in general, we are opened to an experience of momentary timelessness and spacelessness.

Likewise, Ellie Arroway's galactic adventure in the film *Contact* lasted only a few minutes, clocktime. However, in the subjective sense, she journeyed for hours, exposed to the wondrous and poetic vision of the consciousness of God. This experience gave her an overwhelming and palpable feeling sense of the beauty and rich colors of creation, including (notably) sightings of the luminous cities—a mystical reality for which her scientific training had not prepared her. There is a curious altering of time during other-world journeys, depending on the perspective of the "participant," though, unlike Ellie, I could not consciously remember anything that happened to me during that lost time, at least not until much later.

---

1   Patrick Harpur, *Daimonic Reality* (Pine Winds Press, 2003), p. 185

In 1797, the poet Samuel Taylor Coleridge had a vivid dreamlike vision in which "images rose up before him as things...without any consciousness of effort," and which, he said, would have filled three hundred lines of automatic writing—a kind of direct channeling. Yet most of this poetry was lost when he was prematurely interrupted. This points to the precarious nature of these very real but evanescent "missing" events in relationship to memory. Nevertheless, Coleridge did manage to salvage his famous sorrowful fragment, "Kubla Khan," and held fast to the idea that primary imagination is an encounter with the sacred, a finite experience of the infinite creativity of the divine I AM.[2] Indeed, Ellie would have needed to develop an Orphic, poetic voice to describe her galactic vision, as her scientific one proves entirely inadequate.

John Mack in *Passport to the Cosmos* refers to only one missing-time event. An "experiencer participant" (as he calls his interviewees), Celeste, a homemaker with four children who resides in British Columbia, wrote to Mack recording an upsetting event that she and a friend had experienced in 1980 as undergraduate students in Rome. They both experienced thirty-six hours of missing time, and while Celeste vividly recalled being taken by non-human entities into an unfamiliar place where she was subjected to intrusive medical-like procedures, her friend had no such abduction-related memories associated with the event.[3]

Celeste dared not tell anyone about her experience, which was accompanied by a feeling of profound isolation as well as a feeling that her concept of life and reality had been shockingly challenged. She knew she would not be believed, or would be laughed at and, in any event, there were no frameworks or structures in our current worldview to make these kinds of events comprehensible. Celeste's loneliness also points to the necessity of widening our concept of reality to include the irrational and impossible as part of our foundation of reality, as I have repeatedly insisted in earlier sections of this book.

One way to imagine such a missing-time experience is to think of it as "deep" or "aeonic" time, such as when we "experience" long hours of

---

2   Samuel Taylor Coleridge, *Selected Poetry*, Ed. H. J. Jackson (Oxford: Oxford University Press, 1999), p. 101. And, S.T. Coleridge, *Biographia Literaria* (London: Everyman, 1817), 1965, p. 167.
3   John Mack, *Passport to the Cosmos*, pp. 43, 52.

sleep that seem to pass in no time at all, or lengthy dreams that take place in seconds—relatively "short" spans of time that, from another point of view, seem to involve a much longer duration of "time." Our consciousness apparently can participate in both perceptual "time frames." In terms of modern physics, we can experience time as both particle and wave, simultaneously.

Ten years after my encounter experience, I set out to try to discover what had happened during those hours that seemed like brief moments to me, a problem I could not rationally solve. The outcome of this search was unexpected to say the least.

My search led me to a general reflection on the whole archetypal pattern in these human experiences of altered realities, as well as the desire to understand the purpose of remembering and forgetting often connected with these strange experiences. Plato speaks to the importance of this universal theme in his theory of anamnesis, literally "unforgetting," a state of consciousness that suggests that we once knew something and then "forgot" it. Only later are we called by the soul to "wake up" and remember this deep knowledge, which then restores a connection to our truest and deepest identity. Reports of missing time, I believe, can be fruitfully understood within this arc of recovering what we once knew but have forgotten. Perhaps missing time associated with encounter phenomena speaks to the necessity today to awaken on a collective level to all the anomalous experiences that are entering our lives unexpectedly, as if "something" was trying to broaden our definition of ourselves as cosmic citizens.

The Myth of Er

Plato addresses the theme of anamnesis when he tells the story of the warrior Er, abandoned on a battlefield and left for dead, but who, at the moment his funeral pyre was about to be set ablaze, awoke from his death-like slumber with the memory of having journeyed elsewhere, and of having been told to be the messenger to humankind, to tell of that Other world he had visited.[4] Indeed, it seems that the soldier Er had what we now call a near-death experience, that he traveled to the world where the dead go before

---

4   Republic: Book X, in *Plato: The Collected Dialogues*, Hamilton, E. & Cairns, H., Eds. (Princeton, NJ: Princeton University Press, 1989), pp. 838–844.

a new incarnation, and returned with a tale of what happens in those *bardo* or post-mortem states.

Er describes that in the post-death landscape there is a Spindle of Necessity containing whorls within whorls, with a Siren attached to each whorl who utters a note, which combined with the eight other notes sung by the Sirens creates a single harmony. Also present are the three daughters of Necessity, the three Fates, Lachesis, Clotho, and Atropos, helping to turn the whorls of the Spindle, and singing in unison with the music of the Sirens. Lachesis sings of the things that were, Clotho the things that are, and Atropos the things that are to be. For those souls who are reincarnating, each one first goes before Lachesis. A "prophet" takes from the lap of Lachesis lots and patterns of lives of every variety of animal and human. The lots are thrown and each soul chooses a life, becoming attached, of necessity, to that life, yet also responsible for the quality of life and the character developed—whether toward justice or injustice—during it. Er adds that some souls choose hastily in reaction to habits, pain, or humiliation from a previous life, and that the choice of a life in which wisdom is gained through suffering is the sanest choice.

Then each soul goes back before Lachesis who gives each a "genius," a guide, to help with the fulfillment of the destiny. The guide takes the soul to Clotho to "ratify the destiny of his lot and choice," then to Atropos to "make the web of its destiny irreversible," and finally without a backward look the soul passes before the throne of Necessity. The last stop is on the plain of Oblivion by the river of Forgetfulness—Lethe —where one drinks a measure of water, the amount imbibed dictating the level of forgetfulness one will experience when born into the new life and destiny one has chosen. The amount drunk will also influence each soul's memory of the in-between world, and the nature of reincarnation itself. Er, however, was prevented from drinking the waters of forgetfulness so that he could tell this story when he woke up again "at dawn laying on the funeral pyre."

The songline of the soul is here imagined as a destiny, paradoxically both given and chosen, with different levels of remembering and forgetting the immortal state of one's soul, according to each individual's choice. Our day and age, on the collective level, seems to be characterized more by "forgetting" the deeper truths we knew before birth. However, those who journey to the Other world through visionary experiences, close encounters, or NDEs often return with the knowledge of some kind of "higher spiritual dimension." They experience there the understanding that death is not a finality, but only the door way to the certainty of reincarnation, there being only the movement from life to life. They often meet beings of light or wise guides who are only rarely associated with a major figure (such as Christ) of a particular tradition, though sometimes a familiar figure from one's own tradition appears. These experiences almost invariably lead also to the pursuit of a life of wisdom, often through a review of previous suffering as well as understanding the purpose of suffering, to a quest for a deepened spirituality or meaning, and to levels of "absolute knowledge" that could not be gained any other way.

Mellen-Thomas Benedict's After-Death Experience

After-death-experiencer Mellen-Thomas Benedict, "died" from terminal cancer in 1982.[5] He describes a life of increasing despondency over the nuclear crisis, the ecology crisis, and war, and writes that he thought that humans were so flawed they were really a cancer on the planet—the very disease that he himself "died" from. His life before he was diagnosed was, it seems, characterized by having forgotten the great mysteries and was filled with a negative and depressing attitude. Having never developed any kind of spiritual life, and having been told that his cancer was inoperable and that he had six to eight months to live, he began to study various religions, philosophies, and alternative healing strategies to prepare himself for his death. His soul was beginning to awaken. On the day he "knew" he was going to die, he said goodbye to his close friends and arranged with his hospice caretaker to be allowed to remain undisturbed for six hours. He wanted to be ready to experience what his reading had taught him about post-death experiences.

Although he says that he did not immediately remember the content of his After-Life journey upon returning to his body, he does describe the beginnings of a typical near-death (or after-death) experience: rising up from his body, seeing vividly all the things around him, and then becoming aware

5   I first read about Benedict's story in John Jay Harper, *Transformers: Shamans of the 21st Century* (Forest Hill, CA: Reality Press, 2006), p. 79, and then read the first hand account of his ADE on his website, www.mellen-thomas.com from which the excerpts below are taken.

of and turning toward a shining Light. He did, however, slowly recover the memory of a vividly real Other world of various levels and an encounter with the Light, a "higher self matrix" or "oversoul," which changed into different figures—Jesus, Buddha, Krishna, mandalas, and archetypal images and signs—and with whom he dialogued telepathically. Many of his questions about how the universe works were answered at this time, allowing him to realize that whatever beliefs you hold are the ones you get to examine after death with the "oversoul" or "source." The purpose of this examination, he learned, was to heal and redeem himself. The Light told him: "You were created with the power to do so [ie. heal yourself from cancer] from before the beginning of the world." Benedict saw that the Higher Self matrix comprises a grid of subtle energy around the planet where all the Higher Selves are connected. Human souls were revealed to him in all their magnificent beauty; no matter at what level of consciousness we may be, in our core and essence, we are a magnificent creation!

Benedict then "entered into another realm…deep in the Heart of Life" and was invited to drink deeply of the "River of Life," manna water that filled him with ecstasy. Requesting to see the rest of the universe beyond human illusion, he was carried by a Stream, accompanied by soft sonic booms, past the solar system, traveling faster than the speed of light, a journey which was, he realized, simultaneously his own consciousness expanding to take in all this knowledge. He flew through the center of the galaxy to a point of profound stillness, beyond all silence, to the Void. He comments radiantly:

> I was in pre-creation, before the Big Bang. I had crossed over the beginning of time/First Word/the first vibration. I was in the Eye of Creation. I felt as if I was touching the Face of God. It was not a religious feeling. Simply I was at one with Absolute Life and Consciousness. When I say that I could see or perceive forever, I mean I could experience all of creation generating itself. It was without beginning or end …. Scientists perceive the Big Bang as a single event which created the universe. I saw during my life after death experience that the Big Bang is only one of an infinite number of Big Bangs creating Universes endlessly and simultaneously

.... The ancients knew of this. They said God had periodically created new Universes by breathing out, and recreated other Universes
by breathing in. These epochs were called Yugas. Modern science
called this the Big Bang. I was in absolute, pure consciousness. I
could see or perceive all the Big Bangs or Yugas creating and recre-
ating themselves. Instantly I entered into them all simultaneously.
I saw that each and every little piece of creation has the power to
create. It is very difficult to try to explain this. I am still speechless
about this.

Continuing his description, Benedict adds:

It took me years after I returned from my near-death experience to
assimilate any words at all for the Void experience. I can tell you
this now: the Void is less than nothing, yet more than everything
that is! The Void is absolute zero; chaos forming all possibilities. It
is Absolute Consciousness; much more than even Universal Intelligence. The Void is the vacuum or nothingness between all physical
manifestations. The space between atoms and their components.
Modern science has begun to study this space between everything.
They call it Zero point .... There is more of the 0 space in your
body and the Universe than anything else! What mystics call the
Void is not a void. It is so full of energy, a different kind of energy
that has created everything that we are. Everything since the Big
Bang is vibration, from the first Word, which is the first vibration.
The biblical "I AM" really has a question mark after it. "I am—
What am I?" So creation is God exploring God's Self through every
way imaginable, in an on-going, infinite exploration through every
one of us. I began to see during my near-death experience that
everything that is, is the Self, literally, your Self, my Self. Everything is the great Self. That is why God knows even when a leaf
falls. That is possible because wherever you are is the center of the
universe. Wherever any atom is, that is the center of the universe.
There is God in that, and God in the Void. As I was exploring the
Void ... I was completely out of time and space as we know it.

Further on in his description, Benedict writes of his return to "this creation, or Yuga":

I rode the stream of consciousness back through all of creation, and what a ride it was! I passed through the center of our galaxy, which is a black hole. Black holes are the great processors or recyclers of the Universe. Do you know what is on the other side of a Black Hole? We are; our galaxy, which has been reprocessed from another Universe. In its total energy configuration, the galaxy looked like a fantastic city of lights. ... Every sub atom, atom, star, planet, even consciousness itself is made of light and has a frequency and/or particle. Light is living stuff. Everything is made of light, even stones. So everything is alive. Everything is made from the Light of God; everything is very intelligent. ... I could hear the Music of the Spheres. Our solar system, as do all celestial bodies, generates a unique matrix of light, sound and vibratory energies. Advanced civilizations from other star systems can spot life as we know it in the universe by the vibratory or energy matrix imprint. ...The Light explained to me that there is no death; we are immortal beings. We have already been alive forever! I realized that we are part of a natural living system that recycles itself endlessly.

Nearing the end of his journey, Benedict writes:

I don't know how long I was with the Light, in human time. But there came a moment when I realized that all my questions had been answered and my return was near. ... Every human has a different life and set of questions to explore. Some of our questions are Universal, but each of us is exploring this thing we call Life in our own unique way. So is every other form of life, from mountains to every leaf on every tree. ... We are literally God exploring God's self in an infinite Dance of Life. Your uniqueness enhances all of Life.

Though the details differ from Plato's account, and he drank from a River of Life (more like the soldier Er) rather than a stream of forgetfulness, Benedict's story persuasively describes a journey of "unforgetting" and wisdom gained through suffering, and the desire to see through illusion to reality, the realities of a between world, or subtle background world that is multi-tiered and vaster than anything we might imagine. In his journey, Benedict realized the truth of reincarnation, that we choose what we do with what we are given. He reports that after these extraordinary experiences he thought of himself as a human being for the first time, a human spark of God, which was a "blessing beyond our wildest estimation of what blessing can be"! Benedict actually thought that he would reincarnate into a baby so he was quite surprised when he found he had returned to his own body and saw his hospice worker crying over him. He reports that at first this world seemed more like a dream than the other one, but after three days he began to feel "normal" again, though he noticed right away that he ceased completely his previous judgmental attitudes. Although he was feeling good, he was after three months tested for cancer. The doctor, however, found no trace of it. Benedict knew it was a profound miracle though the doctor called it a "spontaneous remission."

Benedict has since devoted himself to telling his story and helping others "wake up" to the "little star of light" available to every soul. He says that we have access to new levels of creativity as we go along: "As I saw forever, I came to a realm during my near-death experience in which there is a point where we pass all knowledge and begin creating the next fractal, the next level. We have that power to create as we explore. And that is God expanding itself through us." Benedict asserts that we can get to this realm of the near-death experience in meditation, that we do not need to die to arrive there. The body is a universe of Light: "spirit is not pushing us to dissolve this body. That is not what is happening. Stop trying to become God; God is becoming you. Here." Benedict suggests that our world problems—over population, nuclear arsenal proliferation, environmental devastation—are so big that they are now "soul size." Paradoxically, these soul size problems are inviting soul size answers and so are enabling us to wake up on a global level to a shift in consciousness that will change politics, money, energy, and open us to the secrets of the wisdom of life and death.

The Song of the Pearl

There is a parable that reflects this deep archetypal gnosis of "forgetting" and "remembering," as part of our human story. It is recorded in *The Song* or *Hymn of the Pearl*, reported in the apocryphal Gnostic Acts of Thomas.[6] In this story, the initiate or sojourner travels from his royal "homeland in the East," divested of his robe of glory, into Egypt, to retrieve a pearl from the middle of the sea, guarded by a roaring serpent. Upon his return, he puts on the robe of glory once again and, together with his brother, becomes heir to the kingdom.

Having arrived in Egypt where he is a stranger, the traveler is warned to disguise his royal heritage by dressing as the Egyptians do so that his presence will not arouse suspicion. However, he is soon recognized as a foreigner, and eventually he is persuaded to adopt the local food and customs, which make him forget his mission. His parents, seeing what calamity has befallen their son and heir, write a letter to him, to remind him of his charge to recover the pearl from the sea. The contents of the letter, delivered by an eagle, serve to awaken the prince to the memory of his original commitment, which was also inscribed on his heart. He sings a song to the serpent that is guarding the pearl, mesmerizing it long enough with the names of his father, mother, and brother, to procure the pearl. After, he travels home with the letter, which had now become a light of love that drew him forward, and helped him to overcome the fears encountered on the long journey back to the kingdom of the East. The robe of glory that he had surrendered and forgotten now seemed a mantle of his own reflection, and when he donned it, the two became one, "rippling with the holy Gnosis." The King of King's voice arose from the mantle and celebrated the achievements of the prince. Then he was welcomed by his parents and, with great jubilation and music, he was finally admitted to the Divine Presence.

This symbolic tale points to a transcendent realm of unity from which we all come, descending into the body and material Earth realm (symbolized by Egypt) with a destiny: to recover a treasure guarded by a great serpent. This "roaring monster" signals the effort required to penetrate unconsciousness—alienation and forgetting—that seems inevitably, though

---

6   See Edgar Hennecke and Wilhelm Schneemelcher, Eds., *New Testament Apocrypha* (Philadelphia: The Westminster Press, 1963), Vol. 2, pp. 498–504.

temporarily, to attend our fall into time and the constrictive vehicle of the body. Some kind of wake-up call—be it a depression, an illness, a loss, a life transition, an unusual event, a dream or vision, a UFO encounter or near- or after-death experience, a homesick longing, or as in the tale, a "letter," a kind of magic messenger—signals the recovery of the destiny both chosen and bestowed in the land between lives, the Void, and returns to us the memory of that greater Reality, the treasure of our true authenticity, vastness, and depth. Though the soul always feels like a stranger (necessarily so, for we must first adapt to being here) until it can connect once again with its spiritual truth, *something* happens to begin the search to recover the divine essence hidden within our souls and bodies.

Myths like Plato's Myth of Er and parables like the Hymn of the Pearl are living realities that endure over time. For example, literature and mythology professor, Betty Kovacs, in her book, *The Miracle of Death*, echoes this theme of a journey. Her book is a profound account of her and her husband's awakening to a new cosmic and planetary vision for our times, a vision which arose out of the ashes of the anguishing loss of their only son. It describes an excruciatingly painful bodily-felt sense of our planet in crisis. In her deep sadness over our polluted Earth, she envisions an emaciated mother holding her dying child, whom a voice describes as the "Pieta of the earth." How had we come to this empty devastation—what we might call the wasteland of the Grail—she asks? A voice answered, "You forgot. You forgot." We have "forgotten" ourselves into a "terrible dream."

Awakening from forgetfulness, Betty describes the miracle of a collective longing to create a new reality. She "sees" in her vision a circular disc of radiant conscious light arising out of the southern sky and coming through the glass doors of the room she was in, to hover above her head. Out of the bottom center of the disc, a woman of light spiraled into Betty's body and began to sing through her,

> *"We are the Light,*
> *Circling around your planet*
> *Can you feel us?*
> *Your planet has called us*
> *And we are here."*

The Voice said that "they" were ready to connect to our planet, and that they had been drawn by all those on our planet who are longing for a more meaningful life and who are trying through love, grief, and longing to awaken and to create worlds of Love and Peace. At this moment, Betty says she felt energy flow through her into the Earth. Then the female form spiraled back up and into the disc of light, which moved back through the glass doors and toward the mountains to the North. Betty speaks repeatedly throughout her book of how the academic and rational mind eventually tries to dismiss the visit of the radiant being (as well as other direct dream and visionary experiences) as impossible, to make us forget again. Eventually, she realizes that it is the artist mind in her that "sees" the symbolic whole of reality that arises through the contemplation of our depths.[7] The artist mind can be likened to the Orphic voice of the poet who awakens us from our state of sleep into our cosmic destiny.

The poet William Wordsworth sings in this Orphic voice, when, in his ode "Intimations of Immortality," he captures this double aspect of our "forgetting and re-membering" natures:

Our birth is but a sleep and a forgetting:
The Soul that rises with us, our life's Star,
Had hath elsewhere its setting,
And cometh from afar.
Not in entire forgetfulness,
And not in utter nakedness,
But trailing clouds of glory do we come
From God, who is our home . . . .

Eventually, however, as the poet notes, the light of vision fades into the common light of day. But, if we are lucky, we find others who are on the search for truth and we pick up the quest and respond to the call for a larger vision once more; we open the letter! We trust our true imagination! We retrieve the lost pearl, a pearl of great price born from and created out of irritation, that is, difficulty, blindness, depression, and unconsciousness, so that eventually we

---

7   Betty Kovacs, *The Miracle of Death* (Claremont, CA: The Kamlak Center, 2003), pp. 151–157.

rejoin our time-bound life with the timeless mystical One world, and those celestial travelers called here by our longing to help recreate our world.

As in the field of depth psychology, where uncovering forgotten personal memories and experiencing the feeling-toned images associated with them is key to a healing prognosis, so re-membering and awakening to our deeper archetypal reality, past-life memories, and ancestral voices, is indispensible for recovering our depth of character, profound complexity, and creative capacity. I would claim that "missing time" experiences open us to these archetypal depths and are to be seen within this larger collective and universal potential. The narratives presented above and other similar stories refer to visits to the immortal guides of wisdom, who reside in the mystical and luminous cities of the soul, which are real places in the subtle body world where our soul's residence is revealed in its fullest clarity and essence.

The Mysteries of a Close Encounter

In May 1989, after a Nine Gates Mystery School training in which participants were working intensively with the different chakra centers of the body and their mythic parallels, a friend and I experienced an encounter with a UFO in the mountains near Joshua Tree Wilderness in Southern California. I have written more extensively of this experience in my book, *Eros and Chaos: The Sacred Mysteries and Dark Shadows of Love*. Here I would like to share key features of this experience and explain why they provoked such a profound change in my life. I also experienced four or five hours of "missing time" (not infrequently associated with encounter phenomena), which I was only able to recover ten years later. By sharing these experiences, I hope to show readers the transformative importance of these kinds of events on a personal level. However, this experience is not just about the personal, but about how these sorts of events address our culture in modern times, helping us to re-vision our world.

This encounter with what seemed like a round flying object with rotating colored lights on its underbelly, hovering next to a mountain peak near Palm Springs, was strange, powerful, and evocative for several reasons. There was, for example, the change in the landscape, the mysterious quality of light, the numinous awe created by the event, the altering of time and space, the period of so-called "missing time," as well as the earthquake of change that resulted from this event and that became even more intense after I was able to remember what occurred during the hours of "missing time." All of these features gave me a direct experience of the world behind this one, a glimpse into that quantum, imaginal landscape that not only transforms our constricted and divided view of the world, but also opens us to the creative forces of a world guided by love, a world in the process of birthing itself here.

The change in the landscape:

On a mid-May evening, having taken in the sparkling vista of the valley below from a small parking lot almost at the top of one of the magnificent mountains outside Palm Springs, my friend and I turned back to the car to drive back down the mountain. The wind was very blustery and it was quite cool. As there was much traffic winding its way up and down the hillside, we anticipated that it might take us a while to return to the home of our hosts.

Before we got back inside the car, however, my friend stopped rather abruptly and pointed toward the mountain peak. He asked me if I could see what he saw: what seemed like a large, circular object in the sky. It was hard to make out its exact shape, but it seemed to have rotating colored lights on its underbelly and to be hovering in midair just off to the side of the mountain top. The rotating colored lights could be easily seen against the darkness.

As I stood still, following his gaze to where he was pointing, a most remarkable event occurred: the whole landscape shifted, as if into a completely different vibration of reality. Although it was unmistakably the same geographical location, all at once the blustery wind ceased completely, and the busy stream of cars totally disappeared. We were now all alone in a very quiet "place."

The mysterious quality of light:

The darkness of the evening shifted to a dreamy moonscape, as if the land was now illumined by an unseen source. Everything around us was now quite brightly lit although it was still clearly night-time. The effect of the light on the land was like a full moon at night, but it was much brighter than that.

The numinous awe of the event:

A profound stillness and calm pervaded the place where we were, a silence so pregnant that for me it was as if that landscape had become the "still point of the turning world," that place that partakes intimately and seamlessly of both the real and the Other in a simultaneous eternal moment that has broken through the veil into time. Although at different periods throughout my life, from early childhood on, I had had mystical and visionary experiences, this was unlike anything I had known before.

It was as if all energy was focused in that moment between us and the spacecraft that held our gaze. It was as if that connection itself were opening up an unseen pathway between Earth and stars, between Earth and a long-forgotten relationship with the cosmos, a relationship that now was longing for rebirth and remembrance, at this end of a century, this ending of a millennium, this closure of an aeon. In that mountain landscape where a meeting between human and Other took place, in that reality that was neither the material world nor the spiritual realm, yet participating in both, in that crack between the worlds where psyche and matter, no longer split from each other, were re-membered back into the integrity of their original Oneness, their two faces merely different expressions, separate vibratory resonances of a single unity, a soft voice called out, addressing me in the vastness of its Silence.

The altering of time and space:

We did not know how long the visitation lasted. In memory, it was but a few minutes, maybe only seconds. When the door that had opened between the worlds closed again, the wind resumed its blustery force, and the busy traffic continued its course up and down the hillside. But when we returned to the home where we were guests, it was late in the night (actually about two in the morning) and everyone else was already in bed and asleep. When I looked in the bathroom mirror, I hardly recognized myself. The cells of my face looked as if they were glowing, on fire, and an energy full of rainbow light was radiating outward from my body. I couldn't quite believe what had just transpired, and might have been in danger of dismissing the whole event had it not taken place in the presence of another person. But now, right after the event, I felt intensely alive and full of a gentle, vibrating life force that, as if breathing itself through me, not only summoned me into new octaves of experience, but also filled me with a deep sense of erotic compassion.

This encounter experience took place on a mountain, often the mythic landscape of encounters between humans and the divine. What this revealed to me, as has been revealed to so many "experiencers" before me, is that there is a reality that defies the usual laws of time and space. The geographical landscape transmuted itself into another world, an external but not ordinary world, a still, subtle world of intensified, psychoid, psychophysical being, illumined by an unknown source of light. This is reminiscent of Henri Corbin's remarks about the Eighth Climate, which is outside ordinary time and space. In the Eighth Climate, no matter where an event takes place physically, the *imaginatio vera* can transmute the event into its qualitative soul essence, where there is a direct experience of the center where the wheels of time and timelessness momentarily intersect. Such a "space" is always "holy," and "takes place" in celestial earth, in the subtle world of the mystical cities, in the Earth of Visions, not in ordinary geography.

In myths and legends all over the world there are tales of journeys to other domains, magical realms and fairy lands, underwater cities such as "The Land beneath the Waves" or "Beyond the Sea," as well as Other worlds under the earth or inside mountains or hills. There are also references to a magical island called the "Island of Women" (reminiscent of the City of Ladies) because it was thought that such a magical place could only be inhabited by women. It is believed that these mystical domains are to be found here in the midst of our ordinary lives, but concealed by a misty haze, only revealed and made visible under certain conditions to particular people.[8]

The dream-like character of these worlds, like Parzival's first visit to the Castle of the Grail, draws attention to the altered state of consciousness that one usually experiences when drawn into these non-ordinary lands, and that also marks an underworld journey or descent to the unconscious. This feeling of strangeness also characterizes the ego or local self's dislocation and descent from a logos consciousness, rooted in the need for control, toward the fluidity and intensity of our own vulnerabilities required for the move toward eros awareness.

Other features described in the lore about these domains are a timeless and spaceless quality, suggesting that we are removed temporarily from the three-dimensional world with its sense of past, present, and future, and are now situated in an "always everywhere" world of non-local character in an eternal Now. We often have this experience in certain kinds of dreams, usually the "big" dreams that Jung describes as having an archetypal, transper-

---

8   Emma Jung & Marie-Louise von Franz, *The Grail Legend* (Boston: Sigo Press, 1986), pp. 66f.

sonal, transpsychic or numinous character. In such worlds we find that our activities and choices are orchestrated by desire, or alternatively inhibited by fear: our spiritual state defines the place and rather than our spiritual state being situated, it situates us. In this breach of normality we are near to those of like minds, and far from those with whom there is no resonance.

Similar experiences are described by the mystics and visionaries of all time (such as Dante, Hildegard of Bingen, and Parmenides) in their visionary tales, and in the journeys of contemporary shamans, for example, the Tzutujil Mayan shaman Martín Prechtel, the West African Elder, Malidoma Some, and Russian psychiatrist, Olga Kharitidi. We also hear of them in the accounts of near- or after-death experiences, *kundalini* awakenings, and, more currently, in the encounter experiences of contemporary "abductees" and "experiencers." What is key to all these experiences is the reality of the visionary world as an actual place, an external but not ordinary world; the exposure to a numinous union of the timeless with the timebound; the breakthrough of the *unus mundus* as a feeling of the eternal being present, here and now; the experiencing of energetic shifts in the body; and the opening of the heart with its sorrows to the mysterious beauty of creation.

Henri Corbin in his recovery of the visionary world of the Sufi mystics draws attention to the fact that a journey to the mystical cities, the home of the soul, is distinguished by two dramatic features: there is a break or discontinuity with ordinary space and time, and at the same time, though the beholder of this realm returns from this "elsewhere," it is impossible for them to describe the way to anyone else.

Lumen Naturae, Light of Nature

The shift in the atmosphere during my encounter was also accompanied by a change in light, as if the dark night had become illuminated by a brighter than usual full moon. It was as if I entered, via an invisible doorway, the spiritual essence of the place.

Mediaeval visionary alchemists had a name for this kind of subtle light, this night vision: *lumen naturae* or the "light of nature." This luminosity emanated from the powerful energies of the stars and was associated with the astral body, an invisible, subtle body with which we are born and that, by devotion to its development through spiritual practice, was established as a resurrection body that could survive physical death. The physician-alchemist Paracelsus felt that animals, too, were attuned to this light, and so the auguries of birds, for example, could be linked to premonitions guided by the spirits of the *lumen naturae*. The idea behind this notion is that there is a wisdom hidden in the natural world, a knowledge beyond the authoritative concepts of traditional thought, that is accessible in an instinctual, intuitive, or imaginative way, based on the authenticity of one's own experience. Paracelsus claimed that this light was particularly active during sleep and was revealed in dreams or visions. He also thought of this kind of illumination as dwelling in the heart.

My experience initiated me into the ancient reality of the *lumen naturae*, an altered visionary landscape that reconnects us with the Invisible, yet always present background world and its inhabitants, the Invisible Ones, those Star Beings who have already mastered the quantum world. They have come now as guides to remind us that we are eternal beings in transitory envelopes, here to help Earth at a critical juncture as She dies and is reborn into a new identity, one that reconnects Her to her subtle angelic form, and Her place in the universal community. As our own consciousness is awakened to the existence of those places where the time-bound touches the timeless, we too experience our galactic cousins and ourselves as part of a much wider family. No longer the dominating or dominated, we cross a threshold where our single being becomes one string in the symphony of creation. This large and beautiful vision opens the heart, stretches our capacity for humility, allows us to suffer grief for our current abuses of life, both personal and collective, and engenders the transformative energies of love. In strengthening and developing our subtle bodies, we have a felt and embodied sense of our life as an eternal flame, flickering briefly here as we witness and facilitate the mysterious forces of creation.

In addition to the certainty I feel about the occurrence of these kinds of experiences, my own interest in them has been primarily focused on their transformative potential, their aid in assisting us into a new worldview based on a *unus mundus* model in which human consciousness is a co-creative participant, one that has now been exposed to transpersonal wisdom and knowledge centered in the heart, a gnosis that arises from direct experience of the psycho-spiritual landscapes of soul in which body and spirit are experienced as one. Such I believe is the intent of so-called UFO encounter experiences.

This deeper wisdom cannot be gained, however, without a descent to our own deep illusions about ourselves and to an embodied awareness of all that we are not, a felt exposure to our sorrow and grief, our power shadows and ego ambitions. Therefore, encounter experiences are often first experienced as dark, forboding, and terrifying. In the same way, the underworld journeys in ancient death-and-rebirth mysteries demonstrate that encounter experiences must follow an initiatory pattern of descent and renewal if the process is to be sustained. This process cannot be short circuited, as mystics such as St. Teresa, St. John of the Cross, Julian of Norwich, and the anonymous author of *The Cloud of Unknowing*, clearly demonstrate. Moreover, if experiencers suffer their own process and move beyond their natural fears in the face of the unknown, they often experience a deepened relationship with a profound and compelling power, a power both erotic and spiritual. Experiencers also feel close to what we call the Divine, Source, Home, or infinite creative principle. In such cases, there is a striking similarity to the divinely erotic *unio mystica* of the visionary or mystic in which the individual feels penetrated by the Spirit of Creation and participates as one with all life and as a cell in the ground of all Being.

Jung recovers this same patterning in his description of the individuation process, a process which confronts us with the shadow side of our personalities before presenting us with an understanding of the deeper calling for which we are all here. During this process of recovering our divine heritage, it is vital to understand that the dark night of the soul, in whatever form it comes, is paradoxically a highly developed state of consciousness very close to the divine. The ability to completely surrender to one's own suffering *consciously* is often the prerequisite for grace and disclosures of the sacred. In turn, these exposures to the numinosity of transpersonal and even transpsychic landscapes, have the purpose of burning through our narrow illusions about reality and ourselves, and initiating us into an unimagined expanse of consciousness in which we feel called to set off on a different path in life—to work on behalf of ecological issues, to become a quantum healer, to leave a numbing conventional life. We devote ourselves to an ongoing creative path in which we are continually dipping into the quantum, archetypal, imaginal field for guidance, seeking to inspire others (regardless of our vocational "cover story") to remember their own deepest natures and truths.

Missing Time

The other key quality of my UFO experience, often associated with such experiences, was the feature of missing time. What, if anything, had occurred during that "space" of a few minutes that was, in fact, four or five hours of ordinary chronological time? Ten years later, a friend and colleague, a psychotherapist who assisted many clients in recovering lost and forgotten memories through meditation techniques came to visit. I decided then to see if I could recover those "hours" of missing time. What follows are some excerpts from the transcription of the tape-recorded session. In this session, I describe both my experiences of missing time and my growing awareness of their significance.

I am in a landscape bathed in a kind of white light although it is night and dark everywhere else. I see that there is a bridge of denser white light that leads from where I am standing up to the UFO craft. Everything is very still and quiet, and I know that I do not need to be afraid. I have a feeling that I know the inhabitants of the spacecraft. I arrive at the door and am greeted by two guardians, one male and the other female, dressed in long, white robes. "Welcome home, Veronica," they say. They are in human form although I cannot see their faces clearly. It is the benign, gentle, flowing quality of their presence that immediately makes an impression. When they speak my name, I hear the sound as a vibration in my body that seems to awaken a memory. I know that these people are my kin.

At this point my friend who is at some distance behind me makes a decision not to proceed along the bridge but rather to turn back. I continue on alone.

Standing at the threshold to the UFO craft I look inside and see an infinite expanse of space, although from the outside the vessel seems to have a definitely proscribed bell shape. Again I have the feeling that I know these people, and again I am completely overwhelmed with their presence because they vibrate an exquisitely beautiful energy field that is refined beyond anything that we have achieved collectively as humans on earth. The guardians invite me in, communicating with their eyes, and making bodily gestures as if their communication and language emanate from their whole bodies.

Once inside I am awestruck by the beauty of the environment. There is a large pool surrounded by lovely flowers, lush plants, and huge crystals. I wonder to myself if the crystals form some kind of computer system—perhaps providing access to the Akashic records? I feel surrounded by what I can only describe as a multicolored atmosphere in which a deep, dark, royal blue is the predominant color, though I cannot tell from where it is emanating. (I remark to myself that this dark, velvet blue is my favorite color since childhood). Through a window there is a wondrous celestial vision, as if the planets, stars, and different kinds of galactic material and events are much closer than we usually perceive them from earth. I feel calm and relaxed, and I feel myself to have moved into a state of consciousness that matches that of my hosts, a state of awareness that is compassionate, gentle, and keenly alive.

Other people begin emerging from the periphery into this space. They have human form and substance, though they seem less congealed or dense than humans, and they move with grace, and fluidity. Although there is activity going on, everything seems still like the pool. I have a momentary thought that if I truly surrender into this place I might not want to go back.

Someone is coming now, a woman. I know her face—it is my shaman teacher Ash*tiana Sundeer, though here she is in a different form, what seems like her stellar form. It is perhaps the beauty of the richly colored cloth she is wearing, together with an unusual kind of headdress that makes me think this. She's laughing and very funny: "I bet you didn't expect to see me here!" I have the immediate feeling that past and present are not longer separate—they have become one. Everything is "now," right here, in the present moment. Ash*tiana rehearses our history together in a telepathic and instantaneous way. This "present moment" is another piece of our connection, another teaching about this "time" in another dimension.

Now the focus shifts to my chest. This is the teaching for which I have come. My heart has to be able to open and expand. I feel a pain in this whole area as if constricted areas around my heart are beginning to try and stretch open. I feel a heavy weight on my chest almost as if I am being suffocated. The pain is completely real; I feel it physically as if I'm being crushed, or as if a large, invisible hand has reached into my heart and is pulling it open, stretching the muscles and extending that whole area out, out, out from my body. I can hardly breathe; the weight on me, and the expanding motion are extremely difficult and painful. I become fearful, and my fear wants to stop the expansion, contract the process. I don't feel capable of what is being asked of me.

Then a voice says, "We've been doing this for millennia." I start to cry, tears of joy, tears of sorrow and confusion, tears of recognition and remembering, tears of dissolution and surrender. How can this be? What follows are images, one after the other, of crop circles, dromenons and labyrinths, the circular patterns on the stones at Newgrange or the different shapes in the Nazca landscape, hieroglyphs on pyramids I've never seen, stone circles like my beloved Avebury, the sanctuary at Delphi. Out of these images and their cosmic connections the thought arises that these sacred circles are symbolic realities. They are the visible structures of a multi-dimensional subtle field, the doorways into the imaginal landscapes of the mystical cities of Belovodia, Hurqalya, Avalon, Shambhala. They are the earth's heart, access points to other streams of reality that intersect our own, gateways to our cosmic cousins and stellar neighbors. The circles are designed in alignment with those points in the earth's calendar such as the solstices and equinoxes and other "openings" such as the Pleiadian "high degree" days in mid-May and mid-November, when the tides of the cosmos enjoy a particular activation of energy and filter more easily through to Earth, awakening the heart center and its gnosis in an especially focused way. "This ship is Heart School," the voice continues, as if reading my thoughts. "The heart is the center, not only of the body, but of all things."

And then I see pictures of hierarchies, other levels of being that do not end. So what my visit to the Being of Love on the airplane (which I described in my previous book, Eros and Chaos) was to me, was also replicated for him and his kind on higher dimensional frequencies. Similarly, our human three-dimensional aspect seems awesome to two-dimensional, or one-dimensional reality. Then an amusing yet revelatory thought comes: that the origin of our universe is not a Big Bang, but a Big Heart!

The heart is then revealed in the fullness of its beauty, instinct, power, passion, and compassion, and its landscape is much vaster than I had previously imagined. It seems that the heart and its ray, perceived here together with its twin truth, are the benign yet potent forces that penetrate all the samskaras or complexes and karmic patternings and dissolve them, transmuting our earthly density and suffering into ever more refined levels of being and joy, if we can elect to put ourselves in love's way. It is not that the darkness ends, but that our relationship to the depths and the darkness that is also wisdom is continually deepened and refined to the extent that we are able to love. This deepening broadens the range of being that we are able to hold in our form, both subtle and manifest. We are simultaneously able to incarnate animal instinct and visionary gnosis with increasingly greater ease, but these gains are won through excruciating losses, both real and attitudinal. At the same time, we fall and fail continuously and must allow ourselves this vulnerability, this deeply human aspect of our being that only serves our rich complexity and potential for compassion. And there are always those who are farther along than us in their ability to hold this multidimensional range of being, and always those who are further behind.

Love is revealed as having nothing to do with the sentimentality that is so prevalent in our culture, especially in our media and politics. Sentimentality is, rather, to be linked with its twin, violence. Both are a kind of maya or illusion linked with an insensitivity to genuine feeling that, nevertheless, express themselves in brutally real ways in some dimensions, particularly on Earth. These cruelly devastating places need to be penetrated by love's gaze, that ray that can tolerate the wounding, grief, fear, and loss that are often violence's real face. The earth needs more of this vibration, this challenging and difficult work of loving, for this loving helps forge the broken linkages to our larger home. I find myself breathing in this knowledge and these images associated with the centrality of love in life, taking it in to take it back.

(At this point on the tape, when I listen to it later, there is a sound, an actual thumping, like a beating heart!)

Then I wonder: why was there a veil of forgetting surrounding this experience? Almost as soon as the question is posed, it is answered. A kaleidoscopic vision of the details and experiences of my life during the ten years since the UFO encounter ensues. Bracketed by two endings—a devastating divorce and the death of my father—I see how this period of my life falling apart and beginning to recreate itself marked the end of the first half of my life, and the clearing of the way for the next cycle to begin. During this time, not only major vocational and relationship changes, but also geographical relocations, had occurred. Although it was a period marked by crucial periods of suffering and being alone, from the perspective of its completion, now in this moment, I could see that it was a period that had to be lived, had to be fully incarnated. Also, in this particular moment from the perspective of its completion, I was able to view this time as a beautifully orchestrated series of events in service to my life.

I had set off in search of a memory, and arrived now in this beautiful environment where my kin are, where they have always been, where they never left, nor ever will. A voice conveys the following: "Remember this place, now, when you walk back down the bridge onto the mountain, back into your own life. The shift that you are realizing coincides with one that is happening on earth and to many others on earth. Allow this review and all those forces that helped inaugurate and complete this cycle to enter your heart with grace and compassion and trust. We are always with you. Jump into the river and let the waters of wisdom continue to guide you."

Then an image comes before my vision in the form of a gnosis: that our world and the entire universe is like a dance, that all the worlds, universes, planets and stars, in all the different dimensions both visible and invisible, both macroscopic and microscopic, are the "corps de ballet" of an exquisitely choreographed dance pulsating with lithe beauty and unimaginable integrity. In this cosmic dance, even the darkest of dark places belong to the wholeness of being and take their place as those shadows intimately involved in the invisibility inherent in all things that are continually coming into being and passing away. All being is in service to a mystery that we cannot know and do not understand. All we are given are the hints that belong to our part now in this time/space locale, seen and unseen, and these hints are the hand dealt with which we can choose to co-create or not. It is entirely up to us.

Now it is time to leave. I have a feeling of deep gratitude. Ash*tiana gives me a blue lapis lazuli stone, a stone that sparkles with gold stardust and the dark blue-black of intergalactic being, to take with me to wear on my heart as a reminder of this meeting and the commitment to continue to bring to earth-bound reality the lessons of the heart and its dark shadows that signal the way home.

Missing Time and Eros Awareness

I need to emphasize to the reader two key aspects of this experience of missing time. The first one is that this experience of missing time, the sense of penetration through the veil to another reality while remaining grounded in this world, is by no means unique. It is comparable to journeys to the *mundus imaginalis* or mystical cities of the soul shared by others, some of whose tales have been included in these chapters. In these stories there is often a description of the meeting with invisible guides and a sense that these normally Invisible Ones are part of one's soul tribe or group. There is an exposure to a celestial environment, or at any rate, a place of extraordinary beauty. In this domain there is a feeling that this place is being sourced by a light that cannot be located yet infuses the place. Jung had a very similar experience at Ravenna. Accompanying these sensations of light is a form of telepathic communication reported between the pilgrim and the invisible guide or enlightened figure, providing disclosures of knowledge beyond what is normally available to the ego self, and that are felt to come from a creative Source, a Book of Knowledge or a vast Library, knowledge that cannot always be recovered upon return, and may have to be sought in this life like the chalice of the Grail. Too, in the light of this expansive beauty, wisdom, and unconditional love, pilgrims to these other lands often experience a brief ambivalence about returning to ordinary reality. However, what is recovered in the *mundus imaginalis,* in the mystical cities of the soul, needs also to be lived here and now in an embodied way on this Earth so that the treasures from that domain can be brought here to help transform us and our troubled world; simultaneously, our own efforts help build the emerald cities for all time.

The second aspect of this account of missing time is the ten-year process of coming to a deeper and more complete awareness of this experience. I already mentioned that the recovery of the experience in the tape-recorded session was bracketed by two losses. But here I want to emphasize that the transformation that occurs in these experiences can fall away and be forgotten primarily because there is nothing (or at best, very little) in our culture that supports it. Indeed, if one looks at these experiences from a psychological point of view only, they are more often than not likely to be pathologized. What I have tried to offer in this book are other frames of reference for these experiences, and my own ten-year journey and beyond to integrate them into my life, love, and vocation bears witness to how difficult this journey can be. The transformation is both individual and collective, helping to change us as individuals and also helping us to revision our world, a world in a cosmos fuelled by love. In this regard, though the UFO encounter initiated me into a deeper sense of my own erotic life, linking spirituality and sexuality in a subtle mystery, on a broader level, this union has become an initiation to a much vaster vision of reality, a union of psyche and cosmos toward the subtle expression of an Eros Awareness that inspires compassion, wisdom, and the creative initiatives of the soul. This new vision takes time to realize and incarnate, so that over time it requires each of us to find the courage to truly change our lives in alignment with the new dispensation. My hope in telling my own ten year odyssey is that others will be encouraged not only to stay with and to tell their stories, but also to allow the stories to support the changes, however small, subtle and incremental they may be, they feel called to make in their lives.

"The Shift You Are Realizing Is Happening to Many Others on Earth"

One of the great joys of working on this book is to become aware of just how many people are being called into a new paradigm of reality, a new evolution of consciousness that reconnects us with our ancient cosmic destiny. I have given many examples of these types of experiences throughout this book. I would like to close this chapter with two final examples.

Stephen Greer writes that through the intercession of divine beings, through human prayer, and through our own efforts, an infinite progression of the soul—similar to the one revealed to me above—is possible toward celestial perception, cosmic awareness and, through the exercise of free will, the expression of our full potential.

Greer speaks of an infinite cosmos stretching from finer (astral, etheric) non-local resonance fields to linear material space-time events—a kind of continuum of reality and energy—integrated through conscious intelligence. Within this continuum, he says, "There are extraterrestrial civilizations that are in the several hundred thousand to several million years or more techno-logically evolved beyond us, who are in a state of consciousness where the entire civilization is in cosmic consciousness, God consciousness, or unity consciousness or beyond …. And some are just a little beyond what we have." Scientist, Buddhist practitioner, and devotee of the Egyptian Lion Path mys-teries, Dr. Charles Muses, also writes about the higher worlds in our cosmos where advanced beings practice a symbiotic rather than predatory ecology and live by love and wisdom in harmony with their whole surroundings.[9] And presumably some worlds are either similar to ours or even behind where we are.

Greer reports that some of these advanced civilizations use demateri-alization and re-materialization processes to travel vast distances, and some use the vibratory aspect of sound to create and materialize needs.[10] Even in the human record there are reports of humans who through the use of con-sciousness can bilocate their bodies, and appear in two places at once, and there are stories of yogis manifesting material objects "out of nothing." In his autobiography, *Of Water and the Spirit*, Malidoma Some speaks of people in his tribe who can bilocate. Greer seems to use this expansive vision in a creative and hopeful way to encourage each individual to discover their Dharma, "right livelihood," the optimal path or role, whether modest or great, that is consonant with our own unique nature.

Like the multi-tiered universe disclosed in my missing time vision, and similar to the NDE vision of Mellen-Thomas Benedict in the early part of this chapter, Greer reveals a mysterious, beautiful, and un-ending creation that evolves from a three-dimensional material cosmos to a more subtle one. His experience is that a highly organized inter-planetary group facilitates a benign interface of extra-terrestrial civilizations with our own emerging world, and that they anticipate with protection and care our own evolution to a more highly evolved state of consciousness.[11]

---

9   Charles Muses (Musaios), *The Lion Path: You Can Take It With You. A Manual of the Short Path to Regeneration for our Times* (Berkeley, CA: Golden Sceptre Publishing, 1989). See also: www.house-of-horus.de/Lion.
10   Steven Greer, *Hidden Truth, Forbidden Knowledge* (Crozet, VA: Crossing Point, n.d.), p. 284.
11   *Ibid.*, pp. 286–287.

Ervin Laszlo, former successful concert pianist, holder of a PhD from the Sorbonne, recipient of four other honorary doctorates, professor of philosophy and other disciplines in major U.S. and European universities, Nobel Peace Prize nominee, author of some seventy-four books, and Founder and President of the Club of Budapest (an international think tank that centers on the evolution of human values and consciousness as crucial factors in changing course), notes the following in his book *Science and the Akashic Field* (his recovery of an ancient term for a sort of non-local quantum "plenum," a subtle, in-formation field that cosmologists call the zero-point field):

> At this crucial juncture in the evolution of human civilization it would be of particular importance to cultivate our long-neglected faculty for accessing the in-formation conserved in the A[kashic]-field. We would not only develop closer ties to each other and to nature; we might also gain crucial insights into ways to cope with the problems of our technologically evolved but largely rudderless civilization.[12]

Laszlo goes on to suggest that other civilizations must surely exist in the billions of galaxies in our universe where technologically advanced civilizations must have at some point learned to live with potent developments in science and the issues of sustainability. What ways did they discover to "do no harm" to their home planets? The answer, Laszlo feels, must be in the Akashic field. We could learn to access their wisdom, much like the ancient philosophers did in their deep meditations.

Moreover, as many individuals report from encounters in non-ordinary states of consciousness, they are given experiences of profound unconditional love, the cultivation of which also inspires us to "do no harm" and to act with gratitude and wisdom toward each other and the earth, a sustainability of the soul. Near-death experience researcher Pim van Lommel refers to this extended consciousness as an indestructible and evolving field of information where knowledge, wisdom and unconditional love are present and accessible.

---

12 Ervin Laszlo, *Science and the Akashic Field: An Integral Theory of Everything* (Rochester, VT: Inner Traditions, 2007), p. 99.

I believe we are now on the threshold of a collective shift of consciousness. As we awaken and re-member who we truly are, we re-discover our hidden heritage and evolve our cosmic destiny.

The Songlines of the Soul is devoted to assist all of us in the process of truly awakening, to a recovery of what we once knew but have temporarily forgotten.

Chapter Twelve

HEALING SANCTUARIES
AND HISSING SNAKES

[Sacred knowledge] is becoming open to you again now, because the power and energy you have accumulated are capable of causing many different kinds of catastrophes. Belovodia is becoming accessible to your consciousness to protect you by showing you other ways to live.[1]

The soul comes "from the stars" and returns to the stellar regions.[2]

Throughout the course of this book, I have described some of the features of a new consciousness arising in our midst, an eros consciousness associated with a kind of direct knowing or *gnosis*, which can be found in imaginal experiences, synchronicities, UFO encounters and the like, as well as journeys to the mystical cities and landscapes of the soul. In his earlier work, Jung described a process whereby deeper soulful experiences could be nurtured through active imagination processes that sought to create a link between the personal ego and the deeper parts of the psyche. The new point or personality created by these imaginal processes established what Jung called the transcendent function referring to the reciprocal and healing effect of the unconscious on ego consciousness and the creation of a new third position or attitude that partook of yet transcended the separate positions. This remains a valuable way of seeking to deepen one's experience.

However, in his later work, Jung began to describe this resulting new and intensified consciousness as belonging also to spontaneous experiences

1 Olga Kharitidi, *Entering the Circle* (San Francisco: HarperSanFrancisco, 1997) p. 214.
2 C. G. Jung, "The Psychological Aspects of the Kore," in C. G. Jung and C. Kerenyi, *Essays on a Science of Mythology* (Princeton, NJ: Princeton University Press, 1969), p. 170.

arising out of a psychophysical or psychoid world where psyche and matter are one. This *unus mundus* subtle world that exists beyond the opposites becomes the primary goal of such experiences. For Jung, this cosmic ground of potential reality beyond time and space has a historical and cultural similarity to other spiritual traditions of the East and West. For example, it could be compared with various stages of the alchemical philosophers' spiritual search or with visionary states of mystics, and journeys to Other worlds in indigenous cultures or shamanic practice. Moreover, this emerging subtle reality was also to be found in the new physics of quantum mechanics and its properties of entanglement and non-locality.

This emerging subtle reality which I have extended to include the *mundus imaginalis* and the subtle domains of Avalon, Shambhala and Hurqalya, is associated with the movement in our time toward a new myth that is constellating as we are entering the final stages of what Indians call the *Kali-yuga*—the ending of a cosmic era, a time marked by darkness, destruction, and spiritual decadence—and navigating our way precariously from the age of Pisces to the age of Aquarius, the age of illumination, interconnectedness, and the individual's relationship with the cosmos. Grounded in physical reality, we are wired for transcendence! "By entering altered states of consciousness in which our everyday rationality does not filter out what we can apprehend ... [w]e [can] access a broad range of information that links us to other people, to nature, and to the universe," writes Ervin Laszlo.[3] The move from self-consciousness to an expanded cosmic consciousness—the next phase in the evolution of humanity—could, potentially, have momentous consequences for our civilization. Lazslo continues:

> It could produce greater empathy among people, greater sensitivity to animals [and] plants, and ... could create subtle contact with the rest of the cosmos. When a critical mass of humans evolves to the transpersonal level of consciousness a higher civilization is likely to emerge, with deeper solidarity and a higher sense of justice and responsibility.[4]

---

3   Ervin Laszlo, *Science and the Akashic Field: An Integral Theory of Everything* (Rochester, VT: Inner Traditions, 2007), p. 116.
4   *Ibid.*, p. 118.

How can we support the incarnation of this dawning awareness? This chapter and the one that follows explores this question, focusing more precisely on the nature of those "new creations" that are part of the new myth of continuing creation, and suggests ways of helping us to embody these subtle domains of experience. This work is only possible with a solid foundation under our feet. Insight into and differentiation of the shadow—self-knowledge—cannot be circumvented and remains part of the new ethics required of a relationship to the unconscious. But in addition to an analytic mode, we are being called to intuitive, imaginal, and inspirational ways of knowing and to an expanded view of reality. Perhaps we could also characterize this shift in psychology and medicine as a move from emphasis on a disease model and suffering (psychiatric "disorders") to prevention and wellbeing, and the search for meaningful experiences of the sacred. Analysis needs to be consciously supported by contemplative practices, and the silence and stillness that helps mine the wisdom within. Furthermore, with the exciting new developments in science and consciousness studies we can cultivate a curiosity and educate ourselves about the subtle body, the imaginal worlds, and the visionary geography of the world behind this one.

It is perhaps worth noting, however, that Jung was never in favor of too much "understanding" or "interpretation" when working with clients. Though he knew such an approach might be useful, especially to a new patient, giving him or her a temporary "orientation" in the beginning stages of the therapeutic process, he realized that his own interpretations had limitations, reflecting the erroneous idea that the doctor knows everything about the patient's emerging inner life in advance, rather than allowing the real situation to emerge at its own pace from the patient's psyche. This situation cannot be anticipated because the ego (of both doctor and patient) does not have this knowledge. The ego only has conditioned (already known) information, not information about new and unheard of possibilities. These unknown potentials and ideas are exactly what the psyche is aiming for in each specific individual as the personality unfolds. In other words, Jung was always on the side of the unknown and new creative potential.

New Features of Consciousness in the Age of Aquarius

In the new reality the new focus is on that world where psyche and matter are one, where the primary reality is the *unus mundus* world, a background unity to existence, which I have further explored as the *mundus imaginalis*, the imaginal world filled with beings and landscapes experienced as existing in a subtle state. This subtle reality includes an appreciation of the fact that time and space under certain conditions are compromised, giving way to non-ordinary or altered states of awareness. Visions, synchronicities, UFO encounters, NDEs, and other paranormal events—excursions into earth's visionary geography for example—are examples of these transpsychic levels of reality that connect us with mystic consciousness, an erotic rather than logos consciousness, which thrives, as Jung writes, when spirit and instinct are in "right harmony."[5]

The focus in these supportive strategies is not so much on interpretation but rather on *direct experience of another world while living in this one*. We can characterize this shift as a move primarily *from a psychology of images to a psychology of encounters* and *a consciousness that extends self-interest and awareness to one of compassion for others, for nature, and a commitment of care for the liberation of all beings*. Jung has described this state in a number of ways, but it can perhaps be summarized as being related to an experience of the Tao, of "thinking in terms of the whole," and the paradoxical awareness in the body of the subtle complexity of the union of time and eternity. As I describe in my own UFO encounter, for example, we have a felt sense of being both in the dreamtime and simultaneously present here and now. This experience can yield to a feeling of being fully alive, fully in the present moment that we might not always experience under ordinary circumstances. We are being invited to a higher differentiation of consciousness, to a world beyond conflicting opposites, a fifth dimensional or psychoid reality where world or cosmic wholeness and self-actualization go hand in hand.

In this non-ordinary state of consciousness and radical shift of perspective, we are exposed to time as deep time, and often have direct knowledge of things we do not ordinarily know and which seem to arise from some source of "absolute knowledge." In this state we are open and permeable

---

5   C. G. Jung, *Two Essays on Analytical Psychology*, CW 7, par. 32.

to the impossible, irrational, unpredictable, intuitive, and oracular. We are aware that our intentions, desires, thoughts, and soul's longing can have an effect if we choose to align our will with our heart's desire, and if we find ourselves open to the deep mystery of our subjective reality in ways that are occluded under ordinary conditions. In this state, we can use our spiritual imagination, our *imaginatio vera*, in the service of creative realizations. In this state we may become aware of visions and deep insights about the nature of reality, not only our personal and planetary reality, but the reality that relates to the unfolding history of the cosmos, and humankind's place in it.

Other feelings that may arise from this deeper state of consciousness may include deep sorrow that goes beyond our own suffering and extends to the state and suffering of the entire world. With the emergence of feelings of compassion, we are guided by our conscience to "do no harm"; violence toward self and other is no longer an option. When destructive impulses arise, we put forth every effort to make them conscious, to discover their meaning, and to find the appropriate channels for their energy. It might be time for a wound or vulnerability to surface, an attitude to die, a relationship to transform, a life to change, or a new creative project to be undertaken.

Recovering a sense of beauty is also part of the new consciousness: appreciating a piece of art or architecture, or nature in general—perhaps a crop circle in particular, or a momentary vision, for example, of light on water or light's penetration of a flower. Or perhaps we find ourselves appreciating the beauty of a child, a beloved companion, or simply the mystery and majesty of creation. Beauty is not just about what is pretty. Following Plato, beauty awakens the soul to love, to its own timeless condition, to its song. Beauty is a work of anamnesis, literally "unforgetting;" it is connected with memory therefore, memory of our origins beyond time, a reminder of our transcendence as well as our immanence. Along these same lines we might begin to sense with awe, as Steven Greer claims, our "oneness with the stars, the universe and the communication with those people from other planets visiting our turbulent world." There is a general deepening of the atmosphere around us as we appreciate these realities, a sense of something having transformed in a beneficent way. We now care both for ourselves and also for others, and experience the knowledge that a depth of experience is crystallizing within our essence, helping us to create the immortal body.

We may have a meeting with messengers or guides of the soul in the form of luminous figures, star nation people, our heavenly partner or soul twin, nature beings, extraterrestrial, alien or humanoid beings, strange creatures or animals, daimons, angels or other forms. Finding ways to foster a connection with these immortal friends of the soul through meditation, active imagination, creative acts, or direct telepathic communication can awaken the soul on deep emotional levels to illuminations and gnosis of cosmic or planetary significance. This connection can lead us to new insights, offer us wise counsel in the face of difficulties and challenges, and enable profound healing experiences in the body. Such encounters may reveal knowledge of our many incarnations on this planet, in many different guises, and how our present life is fulfilling our arrested dreams from other times in which we lived, or from our own biological, cultural, or spiritual ancestors—the karmic factor, as Jung suggests.[6] Such visitations may deepen our capacity for intuition, telepathy, and clairvoyance. As Jung claims, we are each being invited to realize our mystic, shamanic, and indigenous nature, that unitive layer of consciousness that resides beneath our historical conditioning and archetypal structure in a transpsychic subtle world reality.

The wild soul is calling out, calling for us to sing our song as the new myth breaks through, calling for new vision, for new creations, for the embodiment of subtle knowledge centered in the compassionate heart. Our journeys to the celestial landscapes of the soul, the mystical city of ladies, to Avalon, Hurqalya, Shambhala or Belovodia, can also be supported especially by esoteric and oracular practices such as astrology, the *I Ching*, or card readings such as the *Goddesses Knowledge Cards, The Wisdom of Mary Magdalene Cards, The Mayan Oracle: Return Path to the Stars, The Tarot*, the *Tao Oracle, or Water Crystal Oracle*.[7] All these experiences open and strengthen the heart, fill us with gratitude, connect us to our vocation, and urge us to creative endeavors that support our incarnation in this lifetime, and our contribution to both shifts in the collective unconscious and to culture in the world.

---

6 *Ibid.*, par. 118, and note 15.

7 See, for example, Wilhelm Baynes, *The I Ching or Book of Changes* (Princeton, NJ: Princeton University Press, 1977); Susan Boulet, Paintings, Michael Babcock, Text, *Goddess Knowledge Cards* (San Francisco: Pomegranate, 2003); Sharon Hooper, *The Wisdom of Mary Magdalene* (Sanctuary Publications, 2005); Ariel Spilsbury and Michael Bryner, *The Mayan Oracle: Return Path to the Stars* (Rochester, VT: Bear & Company, 1992); Angeles Arrien, *The Tarot Handbook* (Sonoma, CA: Arcus, 1987); Ma Deva Padma, *Tao Oracle* (New York: NY: St. Martin's Press, 2002); Masaru Emoto, *Water Crystal Oracle* (Hillsboro, OR: Beyond Words Publishing, 2005).

This move toward perceiving the psychophysical and subtle world as the primary reality inevitably leads us to a different view of the body. At this point, the body can no longer be regarded as only physical. Rather, while our physical forms are essential vehicles while we exist on this planet and provide a temple for our spirits, they are but one level of a larger energy or "auric" field. This field is comprised of a multi-dimensional and overlapping system that includes our other bodies, which are more subtle in nature and which comprise our emotional (vital), mental, astral (heart), etheric (the fifth or throat level where sound creates matter), and celestial (third eye, ecstatic level), spiritual or crown (ketheric, supramental or intuitive), bodies. Care of and attention to these bodies—as well as the earthstar chakra below our feet by which we connect to the elemental realms and the galactic center above our head through which we can extend our consciousness to the wider Cosmos—is central to making them worthy vessels of the deep processes and refined vibrations of transformation and transmutation. Connection with the deep psyche always affects these bodies, hence physical activity and exercise, yoga, chakra medicine, massage, other kinds of body work (such as cranio-sacral therapy), creative expression, art work, movement and dance, and dietary considerations must all be included in a holistic healing approach that goes beyond the "talking cure" employed in traditional modern psychotherapy. Today, alternative approaches to healing, such as homeopathy, Chinese medicine, ayurveda, acupuncture, yoga and meditation, are increasingly being used to augment allopathic approaches, as they include an appreciation for the quantum level of the body—the power of the non-local or morphic field, the implicate order or psychoid realm beyond time and space—and its subtle creative potential to create health, wellness, and emotional and spiritual well being. Unlike the "one size fits all" approach of allopathic medicine, these healing modalities can be tailored to the individual's needs.[8] Although it is beyond the bounds of this book to go more

---

8 I am aware of the limitation here of not going more fully into these alternate approaches, but would refer the reader to other sources, for example, Amit Goswami, *The Quantum Doctor* (Charlottesville, VA: Hampton Roads, 2004); Arnold Mindell, *Quantum Mind and Healing* (Charlottesville, VA: Hampton Roads, 2004); Larry Dossey, *Healing Beyond the Body* (Boston: Shambhala, 2003); Rosalyn Bruyere, *Wheels of Light, Fireside* (New York: Simon & Schuster, 1994); Barbara Brennan, *Hands of Light* (New York: Pleiades Books, 1987); Edgar Cayce, *Auras* (Virginia Beach, VA: A.R.E. Press, 1973); F. Capra, *The Tao of Physics* (Boston: Shambhala, 2010), Richard Wilhelm, *The Secret of the Golden Flower* (New York: Harcourt Brace, 1973).

thoroughly into this all-inclusive approach to the body, I have included a "further reading list" at the end of this book.

Moreover, the ancient healing sanctuaries of the Mediterranean world are a rich source of knowledge that have much to teach us about an approach to subtle realities and the deeply felt experiences that belong to them. Those who used them seem to have understood the seamless connection between psyche and matter, and to have emphasized body work and creativity as much as dream incubation and meditation as supportive endeavors when the initiate was preparing to access the timeless wisdom of the Other world while remaining grounded in this one.

I have already suggested there is a relationship between star systems, mystical cities, and their alignment and connection with sacred sites distributed throughout our Earth. Here I would add that the celestial cities, perhaps, can be imagined as finding earthly form in association with the Mystery Schools, Sacred Colleges, and Healing Temple Sanctuaries familiar from ancient Egypt, Greece, India, England, other parts of Europe, and Mexico, as well as other sacred places on the planet, such as oracular shrines like Delphi. I would propose that these Sanctuaries, Schools, and Shrines, were located at domains where the veil between the human, etheric, astral, and cosmic planes were, and in some cases still are, particularly permeable. I believe that contact with the mystical cities was even cultivated by these Schools, as part of a training to remain in contact with the guidance and wisdom of our stellar psychopomps during the search for the elixir of life and the establishment of the immortality of the soul, not only in preparation for the after-life, but also the establishment of the immortality of the soul in the creation of the "resurrection body," "Celestial I," or bardo body before death.

Ritual practices associated with initiation to the mysteries, and sacred places associated with healing, were designed specifically to keep alive the soul's connection to the stars, to the soul's source and final destination.[9] We know from our own lives how easy it is to forget who and what we truly are, where we come from, and what vision of vocation life holds for us. The profound separation from this knowledge has endangered our planet to the point of threatening extinction, whether environmentally through lack of

---

9   See, Joseph Campbell, Ed., *The Mysteries: Papers from the Eranos Yearbooks* (Princeton, NJ, Princeton University Press, 1955).

care for the ecological balance of life systems that we depend upon and of which we are a part, or through the madness of continuing violence toward our brothers and sisters designated erroneously as "enemy," both at home and in other places in the world.

I feel that our violence is the face of a desperate, frantic, consuming and unacknowledged grief resulting from amnesia about our inherent radiance and divinity. However, there is hope for us. Once truly glimpsed, this radiant "self" can no longer act as if it exists alone, but only and always in attunement to the earthly and galactic community of which we are each a tiny and marvelous cell. A dream I had several years ago draws attention to this dawning realization.

THE TERROR OF HUMAN DIVINITY

I am in a bucolic landscape, very green and lush. There are several people, men and women, who seem to have gathered for a picnic, perhaps a celebration of some kind. I am in a boat with others going backwards into a still pool of water with lots of tall reeds in it. We are having fun in a relaxed kind of way. I feel almost as if I am in the landscape of Shakespeare's A Midsummer Night's Dream, *that is, in a subtle imaginal landscape.*

Then it becomes apparent that one of our companions, a woman, has had an unusual encounter with a small yet powerful being from another realm, who has disclosed some secrets to her concerning our current situation on Earth. Now she is going to share this message with us. This being, whose form is a bluish glowing light, revealed to her that humans are really gods, but this knowledge has been too frightening for us to handle thus far, and our terror about this awesome realization has made us run away in fear. Our fear has been so profound that the only means of expressing our terror, with the power currently at our disposal, has been to create attitudes, technologies, and weapons of destruction that have almost succeeded in annihilating the Earth. (In other words, we have acted out the shadow of our divinity, its demonic side.)

The extent of the devaluing of life on Earth has become so extreme in recent years that there have been interventions made from other realms to help humans take on the responsibility of our divine natures. They have tried to help us accept our awesome power in the service of the sacred, in harmony with the whole of creation, both invisible and manifest, in the service of creative effort, not destruction, and in loving regard for all beings, instead of fear, which only results in expressions of hatred and violence. This dread-become-fear needs to be transmuted into the awe reserved for an appropriate response to the wondrous beauty of creation.

The chaos of our impoverished times, in which the tension of the separation between humans and the divine has reached critical proportions, has constellated the need for a profound transformation in the hearts of all of us. On many different levels, and in a diverse variety of ways—through stones and sea creatures, visionaries and children, the silent and invisible ones and the active and outspoken—Earth is receiving tremendous aid in shifting its paradigm of reality from an overly constricted view based in fear, to one that calls us back to our angelic resonance.

As I was awakening from the dream, I heard these words: *Morning of May 1: "May Day, May Day," alarm or celebration? Our destiny is held in a delicate balance.*[10]

<hr/>

Recovering this divine self—a self that not only has an origin in historical time and space, but also has a transpersonal Source from the stars and in the luminous cities of the soul—is the work of incarnating the songlines of our souls. This work engages the different layers of our various bodies in the energies of transformation. We must "wake up" to ourselves, and reclaim the sacred knowledge which is our birthright, and which will help restore a much needed commitment to the ongoing creation of our Earth home and its place in the galaxy. Reclaiming and remembering this wider gnosis and deep wisdom kept alive in the mystical cities was the aim and function of mystery schools and healing sanctuaries. For example, it is now well known that the Egyptian Giza pyramids were most likely not the tombs of Kings and Queens—in fact there is no evidence of tombs in these pyramids—but also sonic structures designed on sacred geometrical principles linking earth and heaven, aligned precisely with the three major stars of Orion's belt, and associated with Schools of Initiation. The empty sarcophagus found in the King's chamber in the Great Pyramid was probably a sounding chamber of incubation in which the initiate, after many years of preparation and training, would "die" and be "reborn" to an identity that included a gnosis of his or her divine, stellar, as well as human, nature.[11]

In a similar fashion, Mayan temples with their vast astronomical and esoteric knowledge coded on their walls, were ceremonial centers honoring

<hr/>

10 Author's dream journal, May 1, 2001.
11 John Anthony West, *Serpent in the Sky, The High Wisdom of Ancient Egypt* (Wheaton, IL: Quest Books, The Theosophical Publishing House, 1993).

their sacred connection to the cosmos and to the vast cycles of time, and they enjoyed a connection with the Pleiades star system.[12] And, of course, there were many such Temple sites and other oracle centers, such as Delphi, distributed throughout our planet, places such as the stone circles of Avebury, Stonehenge, Callanesh, Newgrange, and Carnac, and most likely the ritual and meditation portals associated with the Nazca lines in Peru. Gothic cathedrals, arising seemingly out of nowhere around the eleventh century A.D., are Western Europe's pyramids, astounding embodiments of spirit in stone built on sacred geometric principles that also use sound to enhance consciousness, and are associated with esoteric Wisdom schools.[13]

How can we explain these architectural connections between Earth, other celestial bodies, and various star constellations in our galaxy if the ancients were not seeking to maintain an ongoing relationship with these energies through ritual, incubation techniques, music and ingestion of sacred plants? These things were done for the purposes of re-membering, keeping the sacred lineage open, up and running, as it were.[14] We say somewhat dismissively that these cultures had a special relationship with the stars, with the sun or with the moon, but we do not pause to think precisely what this relationship might have actually entailed. The suggestion that the star connection had to do with life after death seems to be a "Christian" imposition onto facts that may hide other mysteries that orthodox Christianity has concealed, if not outright suppressed. I say this because here we are hundreds and even thousands of years later being addressed by all sorts of anomalous experiences—not to mention the practices of the planet's indigenous and native cultures to this day—that are initiating individuals into reclaiming and continuing to honor this ancient heritage with the Earth and the stars.

---

12 See Parker, Schele, Freidel, *A Forest of Kings: The Untold Story of the Ancient Maya and Maya Cosmos: Three Thousand Years on the Shaman's Path*. Ibid

13 M. Louis Charpentier, *The Mysteries of Chartres Cathedral* (Paris: Robert Laffont, 1975). See also, Norman D. Livergood, "Tansformative Sanctuaries," www.hermes-press.com

14 *Shikasta*, book one of five in Canopus in Argos Archives by Doris Lessing, is written on this theme, losing our connection with a cosmic community and trying to find ways to reestablish it.

Newgrange: A Story of Healing

In a lecture on the Asklepeia, the healing sanctuaries of ancient Greece, Michael Kearny, a physician who includes work with dreams and images in his medical practice, tells of the numinous dream-vision of a dying patient in Dublin, Ireland. The patient related how in the middle of the night he felt someone touch his arm. He awoke to see a certain professor standing next to him. The professor tells the patient that he (the professor) is going to die and they need to visit Newgrange just north of Dublin, a place the patient had never been. When they get there, the professor asks the man to start digging. He is told that, "under Newgrange is another city." The patient was so impressed by the dream that he felt the urge to gather his family around him and to tell them the dream. Kearny recounts that, although at the time, the patient did not have conscious knowledge of his terminal illness, he knew from the dream-vision that it was not the professor who was going to die, but he himself. The patient died peacefully two weeks later. Dr. Kearny adds that although in this case there was no physical cure, the man died healed, that is, made whole by his dream. It is Kearny's feeling that in order to bring the values of the ancient Asklepeia back into contemporary medical practice, patients need to be treated in a whole way, that is, they not only need to be treated symptomatically and cured of disease, they need for their doctors to address the needs of the soul through the inclusion of such mysterious and powerful dreams and visions.[15]

Newgrange, an ancient temple burial mound built over five thousand years ago —about 3200 BC—situates the inhabitants' response in relation to the majestic forces of the cyclical processes of the moon, sun, and stars. It is aligned in such a way that for a few days on either side of the winter solstice—and for that time only—the light from the rising sun infiltrates the narrow entrance to the chamber and reaches to the furthest recesses, illuminating cut circles on a great stone slab. For the rest of the year, the interior is in darkness. Newgrange is considered a sacred site that was most likely an initiation or ritual center that both celebrated the forces of regeneration on the earth at the winter solstice with the rebirth of the light during

---

15 Micheal Kearny, Imagination and Medicine Conference, Pacifica Graduate Institute, April 27–29, 2007.

the darkest day, and also the renewal of the dead, as described above in the patient's dream, in the cities beyond time.

It is quite possible also, that in the underground chamber, rituals of dream incubation, shamanic journeying, and sacred song were practiced, honoring the death of single vision and the second birth that arises out of awakening to knowledge of other dimensions of consciousness. In Neolithic imagery, death is always viewed as inseparable from new life. At the front of the doorway to the temple, there is a huge oblong horizontal rock decorated with spirals and wavy lines, seen elsewhere throughout Old Europe. These signatures suggest the cyclical processes of the rising and falling of the moon—life, death, and rebirth—the serpentine subtle energies of transformation and healing, and the water imagery that is almost always a feature of sacred healing centers. These are all symbols of the ancient Goddess religions that indicate the deep union of psyche and matter, the wisdom of initiatory processes that keep us linked with the ancestors in the land of the dead, and the urgency in our time for the recovery of deep feeling and the healing power of compassion. The megalithic stone itself suggests not only the endurance of the soul beyond death, and the hope for protection from the ancestral spirits, but also the strong and resonant forces of a spiritual life deeply anchored in the body during life.

It seems to me that we must do everything we can to foster a recovery of this ancient knowledge, to work through the loss, grief, and anxiety that lead us to raging and unspeakable acts. As Jungian analyst Arnold Mindell says, we need to fall over "The Edge to the Universe," until it and everything in it becomes more familiar once again. A willingness to participate in this "great awakening" will revivify our devotion and natural humility to a purpose not only on behalf of ourselves but also in service to humanity and the world at large. We will recover our vocation and the destiny with which we have been entrusted and for which we have come to this jewel of a planet. Jung speaks of individuation as leading to this broader commitment, gathering the world to oneself. Beyond working on our individual complexes, he suggests, we are each responsible for offering something back to our culture.

Let us look a little more closely now at the ancient healing sanctuaries with a view to appreciating how the comprehensive approaches to healing found in them can fruitfully be used to augment modern healing methods, particularly with the intention of incarnating the songlines of the soul and the subtle body of the world. Our task today, indeed our ethical obligation, is to continue this work of incarnation.

The Ancient Greek Healing Sanctuaries

The Asklepeia, Healing Temples, whose main sanctuary was located at Epidaurus, but which were to be found in other venues such as Corinth, Kos, Crete, and Pergamum in Turkey, flourished in ancient Greece for almost one thousand years, from the sixth century B.C.E. to the third century C.E. (and in some places to the fifth century C.E.). These cult centers were dedicated to the Divine Physician, the god Asklepius, and were a response to the soul in the case of physiological or psychological sickness. Asklepius was the son of Apollo, god of oracles and incubation, arts and music, and a mortal woman called Koronis (the "crow maiden" or "dark beauty") whom Apollo killed out of a jealous rage when a raven reported seeing her lying with another man. Asklepius was rescued by Apollo from the womb of Koronis as she lay on the funeral pyre and was put into the wise care of Chiron from whom he learned the healing arts of divination, astrology and shamanism. Chiron, mythologically, was the priest-king of the Centaurs who were half men/half horse. He initiated healers, warriors, and magicians. From Asklepius' origins we can already see the theme of healing as arising from a birth out of death, "the death before you die." Chiron too is associated with this theme of "life in death" for his own wound from a poisoned arrow awakened his instinctual knowledge of healing rituals and medicinal salves, and he is known as the "wounded healer."

In contrast to our modern preoccupation in medicine with treating illness with biological observation and scientific technologies, in antiquity everything that had to do with the psyche and the body was embedded in "religion." This "linking back" of the emotional/physical symptom to its correspondence in the soul was based on the perception of the inseparable unity between bodily sickness and psychological deficit. Or we might say, "illness" was an invitation to heal the rupture or separation from the divine, from the integrity of our wholeness. Thus, in the case of physical or psychological ailments, conditions were sought that would constellate the healing power of the numinous—including the erotic abandon and access to wild nature associated with Dionysus, in place of a doctor to prescribe medicine or a dream interpreter, as these were deemed unnecessary. Those who attended the ones who were suffering in the sanctuaries were the priests or *therapeutae* of the god.[16]

These Healing Temples were created in alignment with the Mystical Cities of the Soul, and were the earthly physical manifestation, the closest possible mirror, of these luminous places of spiritual advancement and wholeness. The conditions for healing in the temple sanctuaries reflect a profound regard for the richness, complexity, and multidimensional layering of human nature. This is a process that we hardly begin to approach today, or perhaps are just beginning to remember and recover as we link modern medicine with ancient energy healing systems, reconnecting science and spirituality once again. Synchronistically, the planetoid Chiron (whose orbit lies between Saturn and Uranus) was "discovered" in 1977 and therefore signals the possibility of recovering ancient esoteric techniques for the transformation of body and soul.

The aesthetic quality of beauty and its link to deep remembering, the nature of the environment, access to direct knowledge of all things and the importance of how our thoughts or the state of our consciousness help co-create reality, were also features characteristic of the ancient healing sanctuaries. Perhaps the most important feature of such places was the presence of the compassionate love of the "luminous ones," who are our guides in the mystical lands beyond ordinary time and space, and who were present during the healing process. Furthermore, Richard Leviton's book, *The Galaxy on Earth*, which discusses the subtle levels of visionary geography relating to sacred sites, confirms the direct access we have, here and now, to these higher frequency landscapes. They can be accessed for assistance in our healing, spiritual evolution, and continuing creation.

The location of each sanctuary was of utmost importance. Lissos on Crete, which I mentioned in connection with crop circles earlier in this book, is accessible only by either boat or a long hike through a rocky gorge, up a

---

16 See, for example, C. A. Meier, *Healing Dream and Ritual* (Einsiedeln, Switzerland: Daimon Verlag, 1989); and Michael Kearney, *A Place of Healing: Working with Nature and Soul at the End of Life* (New Orleans: Spring Journal Books., 2009) for a discussion of the Asklepian Healing Rites.

steep hill, across a plateau, and down a precipitous stony path into the beautiful hidden valley below. The ancient temple with its mosaic remains, some of whose patterns are amazingly reflected today in the crop circle designs and which offer portals for deep meditation, nestles up against the foot of the mountain. The original spring still flows with clear drinking water providing a welcoming quenching of thirst after the long climb, and buzzing bees hover around its fount reminiscent of the "melissae" or bee priestesses of the Goddess. Stone dream incubation mounds with their vaulted ceilings are still visible on the side of the hill, and a small beach allows relaxation, healing and cleansing in its welcoming salty waters. The hike into the valley can be undertaken as a pilgrimage and the effort extended in getting there already stimulates the whole psycho-somatic system, facilitating an enlivened—if fatigued—body open to the contemplative and transformative possibilities once you arrive there.

Epidaurus, too, is situated in a venue of great natural beauty, out in the country, away from the mundane world of the city. In a valley surrounded by forested mountains, the sacred grove was chosen as a place where earth opens to a vortex of healing energy that immediately opens the heart, and the soul of the land begins speaking to the souls of the supplicants. Its clean air, proximity to the ocean, and springs of healing waters that were pumped into the sanctuary invited the sick into a deep communion with the depths of the earth, the subtle body vibrations of its imaginal geography, and the Other world experience that would bring about cure.

At Epidaurus, statues of the god Asklepius and his female companions, Hygeia (sometimes wife, sometimes daughter), Panacea, Epione, Iaso, and others, and of his sons, Machaon and Podalirius, were distributed throughout the sanctuary. The chthonic representation of the god in the form of serpents was also everywhere to be seen and this union of god and serpent draws our attention to the divine in matter, and the seamless connection between psyche and matter. Moreover, the snakes, associated with Asklepius because of their keen sight, instinctual wisdom, and powers of self-rejuvenation by casting off their skins, are one of the earliest cross-cultural symbols of healing. This snake is also a symbol of initiation, of the death and rebirth that inevitably accompanies the passage from sickness to health.

Snakes also provide an image for us of the body's kundalini energy system that links the chakra system from the root at the base of the spine (or bottom of the feet) to the transpersonal point above the head. This chakra system speaks of the necessary alignment of subtle energy, with its link outward to the universal energy field, and inward to the organs of the physical body, that is required for optimum vitality and health. Meditation practice and yoga facilitate the proper functioning of this subtle energy system, enabling a return to balance with a grounded connection to the earth as well as a healthy functioning of our connection to altered states of consciousness. These states re-link us to the immortal guides and those domains that remind us that all of creation is a pulsating field of consciousness guided by a loving and creative intelligence.

Peter Kingsley points out how the hissing of snakes is also a sound related to entering another world, a vibration that signals an altered state of consciousness. He further comments that in India this hissing sound is a prelude to samadhi, or the arousing of the kundalini serpent energy and power. Hissing is also related to breathing exercises that facilitate entrance to Other worlds and, paradoxically, to the sound of silence, the sound of creation, and the harmony of the planets and stars.[17] Interestingly, a "trilling sound" has also been heard and tape recorded in relation to crop circle formation. Crop circle researcher, Freddy Silva, notes that the Australian Aborigines have a sound similar to this unusual trill. "During their ceremonies to contact their "sky spirits," he writes, "a bora (a specially shaped piece of wood) is attached to the end of a long string and whirled, creating a noise practically identical to the crop circle hum."[18]

The culminating ritual in these healing sanctuaries was incubation in the sacred precinct to induce the healing dream or vision of the god or one of his representatives. Dream incubation was preceded by elaborate rites of purification and ablutions that prepared the body, cleared the mind, and purified the soul from the contaminations of disease or despair. Suppliants would don special robes to remind themselves of the great mystery of their being that had been temporarily eclipsed. Different kinds of music would

17 Kingsley, *In the Dark Places of Wisdom* (Inverness, CA: The Golden Sufi Center, 1999), p. 128.
18 Freddy Silva, *Secrets in the Fields: The Science & Mysticism of Crop Circles* (Charlottesville, VA: Hampton Roads, 2002), p. 209–210.

be played to stimulate emotional release, facilitate connection to Dionysian instincts, and realign the energies in the body. Garlands of flowers would be hung from the stone pillars and fragrant petals would be strewn everywhere on the temple floors. Candelabras would be carefully placed to create soft lighting and an attitude of receptivity to the unknown and to the mysteries. Scented oils would fill the air with their stimulating and healing aromas. Suppliants would participate in processions to honor the gods and goddesses and open themselves to galactic influences. There was massage, meditation, and gymnastics to strengthen the physical form and facilitate the flow of stuck energy. Participation at theatrical performances of the Greek dramas—(Dionysus was also the god of masks and carnivals and the patron of actors)—in the acoustically perfect amphitheatre would arouse the patients' emotions and bring about emotional catharsis, as the great universal themes and stories of the human soul were enacted upon the stage in an atmosphere of powerful collective healing energy.

Too, there was room for outrageously lewd sexual humor, allowing for full participation in a sensual belly laugh in honor of that irreverent, "between-the-legs" sorceress of a goddess, Baubo! The recognition prevailed that a few basic obscenities could help lift depression, restore a healthy connection to the instincts, and set the life energies flowing again.[19] Today, the place of humor in healing is once again being reclaimed in books such as *Humor and Healing* by Bernie Siegal (well known author of *Love, Medicine, and Miracles*), and *The Healing Power of Humor* by Allen Klein. This approach to illness was perhaps first explored in Norman Cousin's classic, *Anatomy of an Illness*.[20] Laughter therapy is also used in cancer treatments, and there is now even "laughter yoga." We can perhaps all relate to a feeling of well being when we think of a really good joke or one of our favorite funny movies, be it a Charlie Chaplain or Woody Allen film, or *The Princess Bride* (1987), *A Fish Called Wanda* (1988), *Office Space* (1999), *Keeping the Faith* (2000), and the recent *Walk Hard* (2007)—to name five of my own preferences!

After the preliminary sacrifices were made, the sick slept in the *abaton*, the

19 Clarissa Pinkola Estes, *Women Who Run With the Wolves* (New York: Random House,1992), chapter 11.
20 Bernie Siegal, *Humor and Healing* (Boulder, CO: Sounds True, 1990); Allen Klein, *The Healing Power of Humor* (New York: Jeremy P. Tarcher/Putnam Penguin, 1989); Norman Cousins, *Anatomy of An Illness* (New York: W.W. Norton, 2005).

"inmost sanctuary." This may have been preceded by attendance at the *tholos*, "place of the altar or of sacrifice," although it is not known for sure (as with many of the buildings), what the purpose of this sacred space was. Because of its circular structure with labyrinthine basement and patterning, I would suggest it was most likely a dromenon, like the ancient labyrinth still to be seen on the floor of Chartres cathedral, and predating it. A dromenon or labyrinth was designed for walking meditation, where movement through each of the four quadrants or elements making up the circle recovered the shaman's path. This symbolic journey, the mystic's path, involved seven turning points that were imagined as the seven chakras of the body. The reenacted spiral movement, by turning in and out of power—the clockwise direction—and walking the life and death path—signaled by the counter-clockwise direction—helped the meditator to imaginally weave the world together, and purify and prepare herself or himself to go to "the edge of within," the *nemeton* or sacred grove, perhaps in this case symbolized by the abaton.[21] Too, the circular structure recreated the *mandala* or magic circle with its protective and balancing properties, and was reminiscent of the full moon and the healing powers that were once the province of the ancient Great Goddess.

The *abaton* or *adyton* was also the "place not to be entered unbidden." This suggests some oracular (or other) means of calling the sick into the temple for the culminating experience, perhaps only when they were adequately prepared. This recalls the importance of *kairos*, right timing, divine timing, a feature of synchronicity. It was important to have the right dream while sleeping, so readiness was a significant consideration in constellating the healing aspect of the god. Statues of the gods of sleep, Hypnos and Epidotes, and the god of dreams, Oneiros, were sometimes present, as were images of Hygieia. An immoveable sick person could have a representative do the dreaming for him or her—a phenomenon not unfamiliar in analysis where occasionally a spouse or partner, or even the analyst, has the dream for the client, or indeed the client has a helpful dream for the therapist—and perhaps this points also to faculties of remote or long distance energy healing, supported by modern prayer research. The sick often lay on a "kline" or couch, a vulnerable position that induces receptivity to the unconscious or

---

21 David Patten, February 1989, *Nine Gates Mystery School*, unpublished lecture. Go to www.ninegates. com for more information.

other healing dimensions or non-ordinary states, a practice picked up two thousand years later by Freud and his followers. The practice of Breathwork techniques designed by Stan Grof and his colleagues also uses a prone position to facilitate access to alternate realities. Perhaps supplicants engaged in exercises to open them to deep levels of consciousness beyond the local self (such as Grof and Bache describe), to the non-local, quantum healing domains of cosmic knowledge and remembering.

The dialectical method of Jung's treatment usually involves doctor and patient sitting face to face, yet C. A. Meier gives an example of the "kline" (couch) appearing symbolically in a contemporary dream, evoking the epiphany of the gods. Meier points out that, "Probably being bidden by the god was the original significance of incubation,"[22] such as in modern times suffering, or a large dream, can be the call of a god into a relationship with one's depths, dreams, healing, and vocation.

The god Asklepius might appear in dream or vision, as himself in statue image, or in his theriomorphic form as serpent or dog, or one of his female goddess companions might be the instrument of the suppliant's healing. Hygeia in particular seems to have had a particularly good relationship with the snake, as if Asclepius healed through the agency of his wisdom imaged by the feminine soul. According to accounts, the god or his chthonic form, touched the affected part, and then vanished. It could be that the sick one would stay several nights in the *abaton*, until the healing experience was constellated. Sometimes this might never occur.

Everyone was obliged to record his or her dream, or have it recorded (an invitation made of patients today), and this constituted a "thank offering." I wonder how many of us today greet our dreams with an attitude of gratitude? Practices that engage the use of loving feelings combined with gratitude are a part of Buddhist practice. They also have a healing effect, as can be seen in Masaru Emoto's beautiful photographs of water crystals in his book, *The Hidden Messages in Water*.[23] These photos demonstrate visibly the reciprocal effects of consciousness on matter. Sometimes there was a sacrifice of some personal object, or the bandages of sickness were dedicated to the temple, or transferred to one of the sacred trees in the grove, in

---

22 C. A. Meier, *Healing Dream and Ritual*, pp. 51–52.
23 Emoto, *The Hidden Messages in Water* (Hillsboro, OR: Beyond Words Publishing, 2004).

order for nature to absorb and transmute the energy of illness and heal it. Meier sees the archetypal background to the idea of transference in this act, whereby the doctor absorbs, digests, transmutes, projections and complexes into digestible elements of consciousness for the patient to take back.[24]

There was also the payment of a fee involved. Asklepius preferred a cock, an animal associated with Hermes, the figure associated with transformation on the borderland crossings between the material and spiritual worlds. Furthermore, Asklepius was regarded as helpful to the dying at the moment of crossing over into another dimension of consciousness, and Socrates remembered him at the point of his death. The cock was sacrificed at the altar outside the doorway facing east and the rising sun, at dawn after the night spent sleeping and dreaming in the temple.[25] No doubt there were other concluding ceremonies and rituals. Much is left to our imagination and speculation.

The Asklepeia emphasize the importance of sleep and the healing potential of dreams, as well as the healing possibilities to be found in altered or nonordinary states of consciousness. In sleep, the patient submits to a process going on "within" him, outside the ordinary realm of other people and life. In antiquity, dreams were held in highest esteem as messages from the gods, so conditions such as the incubation rites were created to cause significant dreams and exert great influence. By understanding how to constellate powerful archetypal energy within the safe container of ritual, and a right attitude toward these holy mysteries, namely that the numinous belonged to the realm of gods and goddesses and not humans, the ancient Greeks knew how to facilitate healing and cure. So too, soul does not depend on personal life but on a relation to archetypal powers, or the gods and goddesses. This knowledge was prepared for by sacrifice, initiation, and dream. The world was the place of divine enactment and the gods— recovered by quantum physics in modern times as hyperspace and the wave form of everything—were everywhere.

Today, because we have forgotten the mysteries of death and renewal, grief and rebirth, in our secularized world, we tend to overburden our egos with the weight of transpersonal energies. Incubation is one way in which the individual, via a belief in the "divine" nature of sickness, finds her or his way back to a relation with the god or goddess, to the Other world. When

24 Meier, *Healing Dream and Ritual*, p. 69.
25 Kerenyi, 1959, p. 59

the soul has lost this relationship, it is cut off and sick. The psyche herself, which is beyond the control of the personal self, if properly related to, will autonomously constellate the healing energy of the quantum Self, one of whose images is the divine physician Asklepius. This produces a new element in the psyche, the divine child, signifying a rebirth of the personality. Like the celebration of the other Greek initiation mysteries, the individual, by his or her participation and journey to the underworld and dreamtime, and the disclosure of unspeakable revelations, is reconnected to the eternal. In this way the patient can re-member the god, goddess, or immortal guide of the soul, who wants to be known and who wants to receive sacrifices.

The healing image of Asklepius points to the timeless laws of the psyche, despite differences in approach throughout history. The significance of the healer god, psychologically speaking, is the recognition that in every cure or transformation, something transpersonal, something beyond the psyche of therapist and patient, something "divine" is involved. It helps us to recognize that healing is a mystery, a gift of grace, from the wisdom of those imaginal worlds and other dimensions of consciousness beyond time and space.

The following dream illustrates how the union of psyche and matter gives way to a potent subtle embodiment of the divine experienced, as it were, from below. The dream draws attention to how such subtle experiences of the divine in matter—the psychoid realm—rather than a dissociated spiritual experience, relate specifically to the "reemergence of Hagia Sophia, the feminine wisdom hidden in nature and in us" and the recovery of eros awareness.

INITIATION TO SNAKE:
TRANSCENDENCE AND THE DEEP FEMININE

I am going to a house to meet with some Pacifica Graduate Institute colleagues of mine who are teaching in a new program in Depth Psychotherapy, to discuss that program. (In reality, on this Sunday I was teaching Session Two in that program, and these colleagues were coming to my house for a dinner meeting that evening. My class was on synchronicity, UFOs, and the psychoid archetype.) I am at the house (which is unknown to me in the dream) and I come out of a room (bathroom?) into a corridor (on my way to meet the group), and see two huge snakes at each end of the corridor. I think to myself, "there is NO WAY I can escape this."

Next: I am in a circular room adjoined to this corridor, with a stone floor and a central pool of water in the middle. This is the "Initiation Room." The two massive snakes are entwining themselves around me. At one point, I remember feeling the weight of one of the snakes on my back. It is warm, soothing, and healing. I am thinking that I must not let the snakes see how fearful I am as they could bite or poison me perhaps. It is essential that I keep the right attitude and let them do their thing. There is an awesome, terrifying feeling to this whole event, yet being enfolded by the snakes is absolutely necessary for the initiation process. The event is far from ordinary consciousness and reality, yet there is an ancient feeling about what is happening. It is difficult to convey the strangeness of the whole procedure.

There is a woman present. She is the helper, one of the "therapeutae" (known to assist in the ancient Asklepieian healing sanctuaries described above). The whole process is completely natural to her. I must have gone unconscious because in the next part she's somehow extricating me from the ritual of the snakes. I sense that the snakes must have entered my body and gone down my throat into every area of my insides (intestines). I know this penetration has occurred as there is something left that is now coming out of my mouth, like an endless string of gauze—or is it the snake skin left behind by their being in my body?—and I am pulling it out.

The feelings are intense and numinous in an awe-filled way. My body cells are alive with the snake energy. I am vibrating all over with the instinctual energy of the powerful serpent god/goddess. These beasts are so far beyond/below the human dimension of reality. I cannot describe adequately the feelings associated with this experience. It is as if my whole body is alive with a cosmic orgasm.

At one point I notice all the others are in another room, but I never make it there. I have to leave to try to get home. I am concerned that it's getting late and Robert might wonder where I am and be worried. My body/psyche is changed irrevocably. I am far from human consciousness in this state. Although I leave, I am drawn back again to the house. The woman (therapeuta) says to me, "The snakes are not done with you yet."

Then I leave the house a second time. It is very dark, night-time. Now I have the snakes with me, one on either side, they are like my guardians or allies that accompany me now. I need to descend a hill to reach my car. I am hoping the darkness will hide the snakes from view so people won't be wondering what I'm doing with two snakes!!

A voice says, "You need to truly know about what is meant by the UNKNOWN"—the implication being that all my not knowing or deciding about my life—what to focus on, how to proceed—on a deeper level, is about this initiation into the truly unknown, a coming to terms and wrestling with the objective psyche. The voice continues, "Look at the images of Aion (Mithras

sculpture from the Vatican museum), of the Cretan Snake Goddess, the alchemy picture of the
adept entwined by the serpent, the snakes associated with Asklepius, and the Kundalini serpent.
You must know about the snake—these are images of the depths of instinct, initiation, embodi-
ment, transformation. The depths of instinct also connect back to the goal, the lapis, the immortal
body, healing, and gnosis—gnosis that reaches from the spiritual realms, to the body, incarnation,
individuation (discrimination of opposites), down to the elements, nature, stones, earth, shadow,
shadow as enlightenment. The Snake is the most powerful symbol, cross culturally. All knowledge,
wisdom, shadow, is associated with it. Only those who do not know, know. A Jung Institute,
or a Pacifica, will never hold you. You must find your own way, even if you are a part of these
organizations. Only by not knowing will you truly know."

Again, the voice emphasizes, "This is the time for the INITIATION TO SNAKE."[26]

Ever since this dream, I have felt compelled to remain with the unknown, to keep open to where the journey is taking me, not to allow myself to decide prematurely on certain things in a concrete way, but to remain present with/flow with the deeply mysterious process and to trust it, even if I do not know with full certainty where it is going. Partially, what has arisen out of remaining in this unknown place is the emergence of the idea of supplementing psychotherapy and Asklepieian healing traditions—subtle body medicine, meditation and visioning, music, mantic methods and astrology, and physical exercise, humor and theatre—with hydrotherapy practices, water immersions or mineral spring baths, as a way of recovering the ancient healing sanctuaries in contemporary times. Staying close to Snake in my imagination, I instinctively feel that water therapies offer a benign and "feminine" treatment option for the support of the subtle body, for connecting with the invisible guides of the soul, and for contacting our creative self *that is born from direct encounters* with the non-local, quantum mind. There is even a pool of water in my dream above. And after all, the Great Bath, or Sacred Bath, was part of the ritual to Aphrodite mentioned in relation to Crop Circles earlier in this book, and water was mentioned as a central symbol of the death and regeneration processes in Candy Kleven's visionary dream in chapter 10. I explore this connection of snakes, water, and the subtle body in the next chapter.

---

26 Author's dream journal, Sunday, March 12, 2006.

Chapter Thirteen

Eros Consciousness, Water, and the Moon: Songlines and the Return of the Cosmic Soul

The human being holds a universe within, filled with overlapping frequencies,
and the result is a symphony of cosmic proportions.[1]

"When enough unexplainable new phenomena pile up, there is sometimes a shift in
consciousness that moves us quickly and suddenly to recognize a new pattern that explains
all of these things that have been mysterious in the context of the old way of thinking.
That's what we're on the cusp of right now."—Al Gore

I have noted throughout this book that we are on the cusp of a shift in consciousness that emphasizes our encounters with the imaginal world, the interdependent nature of reality, and a connection with the cosmos through eros awareness. Eros awareness emphasizes intuitive knowledge, deep emotion, and the recovery of dark wisdom through direct experiences of the soul that deepens our capacity for compassion and ethical care of self and others, including our planet. This chapter proposes that eros awareness is related to the Moon. Because astrologically and in alchemical and mythological traditions the Moon is particularly connected with water, I want to suggest that we can be supported in our incarnation of the "new pattern" through immersion in water. Perhaps we should note that the New Age of Aquarius has the Water Bearer as its symbol, or alternatively a figure who

---

1   Masaru Emoto, *The Hidden Messages in Water* (Hillsboro, OR: Beyond Words Publishing, 2004), p. 47.

pours water out of a vase! Water treatments can assist us in deepening our awareness of the songlines of our souls.

Water has always been important in healing, purification and ablutions. It has always accompanied the initiation mysteries and, as I noted in the previous chapter, healing sanctuaries and oracle sites are inevitably situated near the sea or a sacred spring associated with a divinity. The spring water at Lourdes, for example, one of the many Marian vision sites, is considered to have healing properties. Masaru Emoto comments on the photograph of a crystal from this spring, observing that its shape is similar to the crystal formed from water that has been shown the word "angel."[2] Freddy Silva, dowser and student of Earth Mysteries, points out that both crop circles, stone circles, Egyptian pyramids and European cathedrals, which are built on older Druidic and Celtic sites, are all situated on pivotal locations along the energy grid of the Earth. This grid, he says, is related to subtle energies amplified by underlying water courses that enable heightened states of awareness and healing.

Symbolically, water is specifically linked with the divine feminine. As I was completing this manuscript, the Lady Melissa from the City of Ladies (mentioned in chapter 9), appeared once again, this time in a dream, revealing herself as the "Moon Lady." Relevant sections of the dream follow:

DREAM: MOON LADY

There is a ritual being celebrated in a beautiful sand-colored cathedral, filled with a beautiful light. Many are involved. The ritual is a mystical celebration of an archetypal event: two streams are coming together, one from the East and one from the West. They are giving birth to a new order that joins and transcends both. The "new order" is symbolized by the presence, not of a Jesus or Buddha-type figure, but by a young woman. In the dream the young woman has a Persian/Sufi-type mystical name (that I cannot produce or remember, but it would be "foreign" and unfamiliar anyway). However, I am told that the translation of the woman's name is "Moon." She has a beautiful dark complexion and is dressed in a beautiful garment with richly colored brocade, and gold and silver threads. She carries the opposites of dark and light in her form, and has knowledge of all things.

---

2   Emoto, *The Hidden Messages in Water*, p. 128.

I am participating in the ritual. I have gathered together the history of this archetypal event, and am going to say something at the ritual. I have books and papers in my possession, relating to all of this. I am preparing.[3]

An exploration of the dream guided me to the creative possibility of water initiations in the "new order" and their assistance in realizing the songlines of the soul.

The Moon and Water

In the dream, I am witness to a new possibility represented by the union and transformation of opposites—"East and West"—in a third realm, symbolized by a woman whose name translates as "Moon." The moon lady embodies light and dark, silver and gold, and owing to her exposure to the complexity of the knowledge of how things really are, she embodies the opposites and a range of possibilities in between. Moon suggests a consciousness that waxes and wanes, is born, lives to the full and dies, going into the dark and toward death, yet arising again. Hence the moon suggests the possibility of transformation, of death, regeneration and renewal. As an expression of the Goddess, of the archetype of the divine feminine, she is related to feeling and relationship values, to intimacy and eros, to emotion and emotional development; to deep intuition and visionary gnosis occluded in the bright sun's rays; to the cyclical and organic processes of life, to time and cycles, growth and decay, and eventual rebirth. Perhaps she embodies energies of the Black Madonna and the many faces of Tara who is also called "Wisdom Moon."[4] As a light that shines in darkness, a light that reflects, she represents the wisdom of the imagination. She is a figure devoted to being, becoming, eternity, and Presence, and to the knowledge of the heart. This mandala feminine symbol suggests psychic sensitivity and the ability for compassionate service. All these qualities belong to a consciousness steeped in eros awareness.

---

3 Author's dream journal, August 24, 2006.
4 China Gallant, *Longing for Darkness: Tara and the Black Madonna* (New York & London: Penguin Books, 2007), p. 332

Most notably, however, the Moon in all mythology and folklore cross-culturally, is connected with water, and thus to one of the major alchemical operations. This operation is known as *solutio*, "dissolving," and is sometimes called "the root of alchemy"[5] since images of water—be they individual tears or floods that affect large groups—often lead us to experiences of breakdown and breakthrough. Water takes us to dissolution, containment, gentleness, and rebirth. Jungian analyst, David Rosen, gives an affecting example of the healing power of tears. He writes about a time when he was suffering from severe melancholy due to a marriage that was breaking down, and feeling as if he were dying. But then he had a moment of reprieve when "tears started flowing while I walked on a wooded path by a stream." He adds, "All forms of water, whether rivers or tides, are healing."[6]

There are moon gods as well as moon goddesses, and ancient lunar myths often relate to dismemberment processes and renewal through tears and deep feeling which educates us through deep subjectivity, heartfelt values, and initiation. The Isis/Osiris myth is one example.

The Moon and the Waters of Life

I have always loved the water, the experience of and pleasure with mineral springs and saltwater pools. I live by the ocean, walk often on the beach, swim regularly, and (perhaps owing to my English upbringing) have always preferred baths over showers. In the last twenty years or so, I have frequently used aromatherapy treatments in my baths, keeping supplies of lavender, eucalyptus, bergamot, basil, rosemary, geranium, rose, and ylang ylang essential oils on hand for their relaxing or healing properties. Moreover, I have explored some of the spas of Western Europe where hydrotherapy is a more integral part of medical treatment than it has been in the United States, though this is now changing with an increased interest in the U.S. in prevention and well-being that spa culture helps provide. Hot springs arising directly out of the earth, though they often

---

5 E. Edinger, *Anatomy of the Psyche: Alchemical Symbolism in Psychotherapy* (La Salle, IL: Open Court, 1988), p. 47.

6 David Rosen and Joel Weishaus, *The Healing Spirit of Haiku* (Berkeley, CA: North Atlantic Books, 2004), p. 12.

provide the venue for spa hotels offering massage and other body treatment options, invariably have pools of mineral waters that are available to the general public at minimum or no cost. For example, in the mediaeval village of Pari south of Siena, there is a small medical facility connected to very hot sulphur springs that pour into the local river at the bottom of a deep valley. Though the medical clinic provides massage and other hydro-treatments, the hot springs are available to all and are frequented by locals and visitors alike. These springs and the beautiful warm mineral waters at the small Roman spa town of Bagno Vignoli in Tuscany were the venue for many of the insights generated for this book.

In the United States there is a healing sanctuary called Ojo Caliente in the high desert of northern New Mexico. This ground is sacred to Native American peoples and is famous for its several healing mineral springs—lithia for depression and digestion, iron for the blood, soda for relaxation and digestion, and arsenic for various skin conditions, arthritis, and stomach problems. These waters have been coursing up from a volcanic aquifer deep within the Earth for thousands of years. Various body treatments are available at this spa, including a meditation room you can use following the arsenic mineral water baths. In this room you are wrapped in cotton muslin and heavy wool blankets that make you sweat out toxins. In my experience, this modern "incubation room" can aid in travel to other dimensions of consciousness, and it was in that setting that I had the experience with my shaman teacher Ash*tiana Sundeer (noted in my account of missing time in chapter 11) of accessing several past lives and their relevance for this present incarnation.

Nothing can live without water. We not only bathe in it, we cook with it and drink it. Water is the origin, the mother of life. It represents the energy of life. Shrines were often built where water coursed up out of the earth because of this sacred connection. Water figures in creation as well as in deluge or flood myths, which are always followed by the birth of a new humanity or creation. We ourselves slowly emerged out of the ocean onto the land, and we replicate this evolution *in utero*. Our bodies—like the Earth herself—are composed of 70 to 80 percent water.

The moon—owing to her own rhythmic nature, swelling slowly into fullness and then diminishing toward decline, and disappearing into blackness only to be reborn—governs all things with a periodic or cyclical nature: the tides, rains, plant life, fertility, and menstrual cycles.[7] Moon divinities are invariably related to water, to moisture, to rain and to dew. The Sumerian Inanna holds the vessel of the water of life as a gift, the Mycenaean goddess has wavy patterns on her body suggesting the fertilizing power of water and rain, the Greek Artemis of Ephesus has milk flowing as nourishing rain from her breasts, the Iranian moon goddess Anahita is also goddess of the waters. The Babylonian god Sin stands on his crescent moon boat and sails across the heavenly sea in the sky, filling the Euphrates river; the Egyptian moon god, Khons or Khensu, the "traveller," is the one who is likened to a bull and who controls the waters of the Nile. Osiris, as moon, water, and vegetation, is the pre-eminent figure related to the waxing and waning of the moon and the rising and falling of the Nile, while his sister-bride, Isis, carries the circle of the full moon within the crescent upon her head, and cries the tears that bring back the river after darkness and drought, reproducing new plant life from the watery semen of Osiris's inundation.

In India, the Hindu moon god Soma was "Lord of the Waters," and he stored the rain in his luminous orb, while Shiva, among his many names, is moon god of the mountains and carries the crescent moon in his hair. Furthermore, there are goddesses of the dew, also known as "moonwater." These were involved in rites to secure the beneficent effects of dewy moisture and to fertilize the green fields. Athene, "the All Dewy One," had pre-Zeus origins in Crete, and sometimes carried the full moon instead of the Gorgon's head upon her shield. She also had a moon sliver on her coins in addition to an owl and olive branch.

The Greeks, Celts, North American Indians, Mexicans, New Zealand Maoris, Eskimos, the Chinese and the Japanese, all linked the moon with water or oceans in one way or another, and these examples, together with the mythic stories to be found in their traditions, demonstrate how universal and long lasting is the archetypal pattern between the lunar orb and her

---

7   For books on moon symbolism, I used especially Jules Cashford, *The Moon: Myth and Image* (London: Cassell Illustrated, 2003), Anne Baring & Jules Cashford, *The Myth of the Goddess: Evolution of an Image* (London, Arkana Penguin, 1991), Mircea Eliade, "The Moon & Its Mystique," in *Patterns in Comparative Religion* (Cleveland & New York: Meridian Books, The World Publishing Company, 1963), and Erich Neumann, "The Moon and Matriarchal Consciousness," in *The Fear of the Feminine & Other Essays on Feminine Psychology* (Princeton, NJ: Princeton University Press, 1994).

fertile properties. Dionysus, for example, is both moon god and god of vegetation, and becomes a symbol, therefore, of inexhaustible life.

However, the moon also wanes, and in her decline brings the waters of death and decay. Do we not feel at times in some deep place within ourselves, in a memory that rises like some ancient tide, a sense of loss and mourning as the moon withdraws into darkness, followed by a longing for the return of her light and promise with the delicate new crescent? In ancient times the planting of seeds would take place in the waxing phase, while the cutting or harvesting of plants would take place in the waning phase, to harmonize with the rhythms of nature. This harmonious activity is still replicated in parts of the world today. We too might feel the rising tide of creative energy as the moon waxes toward her full abundance and a diminishment as she wanes toward extinction, a pattern that like the seasons continues in endless rhythm.

The Moon and Snakes

At the end of the last chapter, I related how the *Initiation to Snake* dream showed the way toward incorporating hydrotherapy as a pathway to inner guidance and the support of the subtle body. Water assists in deep reflection and in helping us travel to the mystical cities of the soul, revealing to us our psychic abilities and deepest intuitions. Furthermore, this kind of flow connects us with the wisdom of deep eros, an awareness that links us to the moon.

In mythology, certain animals, because their behavior was akin to the rhythms of the moon—for example, the bear that hibernates in winter and returns in the spring—were seen to be symbolic, or even an embodiment, of the moon. This is nowhere more prevalent than with the snakes that from time immemorial were associated with the early representations of the Goddess as Moon. Like the prehistoric lunar etchings on bone that marked time as a serpentine path toward fullness and then decline, the snake too lives, sloughs its skin, remains alive, and is reborn to new life. The wavy motifs on ancient artifacts also ally the serpent, water, and the tidal moon movements, as do the associated motifs of the spiral, labyrinth, and wavy meander found on stone, rock, and in caves going back thousands of years. These spiraling, serpentine patterns are found also in seashells, conches, and snails, opening into larger circles and flowing back to a central point, evoking the rhythmic movements of expansion and withdrawal of the moon as well as a woman's way of being. The snake because it disappears and reappears, sloughs and renews its skin, is a symbol of rebirth, even immortality. As a "moon force," it can mediate a vision directly from the collective unconscious, bestowing fecundity, knowledge as prophecy whose shadow is expressed as lun-acy, madness, and knowledge as intuitive gnosis. Coleridge's water snakes that leave traces of golden fire in the shadow of the ship on a moonlit night, in his poem, *The Ancient Mariner*, hint at this way of knowing.

The great goddesses (Inanna-Ishtar, Isis, Hera, Demeter, Artemis, Athene, and Hecate, to name a few) were often imaged entwined with serpents, or holding serpents like the now well-known Cretan snake goddess, or as having snakes for hair (the Gorgon). Snakes were also represented by the uraeus on the headdress of Egyptian gods and goddesses. The goddess Mucalinda supports the Buddha and protects him from the destructive powers of the universe, suggesting her connection with the spiraling energies of life and death, time and eternity. She holds these opposites together, even expressing the subtle background unity of existence from which opposites arise.[8]

In their association with fecundity, snakes are particularly associated with women and their menstrual cycle, and even to this day in some cultures, the moon as serpent is thought to copulate with women, and then disappear. Snakes are also thought of as a woman's "first mate," and are used in the form of stone statues to arouse fertility in young women. There is even a story in parts of Europe that women were afraid that a snake would slip into their mouths while they were sleeping and make them pregnant, reminiscent of my dream in the previous chapter.[9] This belief rests on an earlier tradition and can be seen in a sculpture from the Pyrenees in France, going back to Gallo-Roman times (or earlier), in which the goddess is giving birth to a snake and suckling it. Perhaps the goddess' serpent power is connected with her instinctual nature, and the vital power of her sexuality and fertility.

Furthermore, witchcraft and magic are thought to be bestowed by the moon either directly or indirectly via snakes. Because snakes are lunar and

8   See especially, Baring & Cashford, *The Myth of the Goddess*, pp. 64–67, 109–111, 499ff.
9   Eliade, "The Moon & Its Mystique," pp. 165–166.

live underground, embodying the souls of the dead, they also have access to the source of all wisdom in the Other world and can foretell the future. The widely believed notion that anyone who "eats a snake" has access to Other worlds and the secrets of transcendent reality goes back to antiquity. Moreover, the serpentine companions of the great goddesses in touch with the sacred and cyclical nature of moon and earth, who express the possibility of "change" and immortality, are related to ceremonies of initiation. Many traditions also make a link between snakes and water or the type of rain supplied by the moon. Often snakes or dragons are guardians of springs, dwell in pools, govern clouds, and keep the world supplied with water. In India, for example, a ceremony honoring the snake begins on the day of the full moon at the beginning of the rainy season.[10]

The Nectar of the Moon: Waters of Immortality

In the early seventeenth century, Galileo saw "seas of rain" on the moon through his telescope. The watery moon with its serpentine path through the dark night sky rises to its fullness and slowly disappears and "dies." But her rebirth every month out of her dark phase also linked the moon with an immortal liquid called soma or mead. In India, soma is called *amrita* and was one of the names for the moon god as well as for rain—a dew, a sap, milk from the sacred cow, and blood—all of which represent differing states of the drink of immortality poured out by the moon, offering healing medicine, sexual potency, and poetic inspiration, and available also after death as a nourishing potion. "The Churning of the Ocean of Milk" is the story that tells how the liquid soma was created out of friction and conflict using the King of Serpents, Vasuki, as a rope that was pulled back and forth. The production of the elixir points to the achievement of a consciousness that can sustain and transcend opposites, finding a liberating vision at the still point of the turning world.

In Norse mythology this soma is called mead, a fermented honey potion drunk by the dead warriors in the afterlife restoring them to life and joy. The root of the word "mead" goes back, in fact, to Indo-European origins and suggests a drink of celestial potency that gave rise to a feeling of oneness

10 *Ibid.*, pp. 170–171.

with the gods. Interestingly, at the stone circle of Callanish in the Hebrides, aligned to the rising and setting moon, and possibly also to the Pleaides, a mead-like beer was discovered together with cups, and so perhaps was used to induce an altered state of consciousness that would assist in these celestial and cosmic rituals.

The Lunar Waters of Initiation

The moon in its dark phase symbolizes the realm of death. Many highly developed cultures imagine this realm of death as an afterlife abode. The dark of the moon gives birth to new life, and hence there is a relationship between the moon, symbolic death, and journeys of initiation. Because of the connection of moon and water, I am proposing that we allow immersion in water—today—to assist us in these lunar rituals of death and rebirth and to travel to other dimensions to seek wisdom and guidance.

In her beautiful book on Sophia, Susanne Schaup includes a meditation at the end of Chapter Five that invites contemplation of water's gentle, supple power that "overcomes resistance by constant movement," and how its flowing movement suspends time, "as it is always at the beginning and always at the end." She describes how water connects us with everything as it flows through the blood in our bodies and along the rivers as the veins of the Earth. She reflects on water and its still, bubbling, or rushing sounds as the goddess alive in creation, sending her roots into densest matter and transmuting obstacles into vision. She evokes the goddess enthroned on the lotus above the nourishing waters, her roots deep in the dark mud below. This idea is common in our culture—we speak of creative states as the experience of being "in the flow," as "being carried by a force larger than ourselves" like a "leaf in a stream." As Schaup writes, water is "matter in motion *and* creative spirit: the one merging with the other."[11]

Immersion in water, hot springs, or mineral baths can help us access these subtle states of a psychophysical reality beyond ordinary time and space, curiously felt in the body, in the heart, and in what is most real. Water dissolves us, slows us down, works to undo our fixed and limited ideas, destroys what came before, and puts us in harmony with our deeper self,

---

11 Susanne Schaup, *Sophia* (Lake Worth, FL: Nicolas-Hays, 1997), pp. 194–5.

re-establishing our eternal or cosmic rhythm that was One before it fractured into parts in ordinary time.

The following story comes from Judith Orodenker, one of my dissertation students at Pacifica Graduate Institute. She was writing on the reemergence of the archetypal divine Feminine in her own life and in the artwork of her therapy patients. In this account, Judith describes what happened to her consciousness as she was receiving a water massage treatment called Watsu, a form of aquatic bodywork. The work takes place in a saltwater pool heated to body temperature. Judith explains that the therapist cradles your body and gently pushes and pulls your body through the water, sometimes submerging you in the water. It is a continuous series of gentle movements and stretches, with each movement flowing into the next. The following is what she recorded in her journal after receiving her Watsu treatment:

"Floating in the Greater Rhythms of the Cosmos"

My body was fluid. I felt completely supported and completely released at the same time. As my body stretched and swirled in the water I could feel my muscles become deeply relaxed and pliable. I felt places open and release in my body. I felt myself go so deep into my body, so deep into my unconscious, that I came to a place where I began to experience a feeling of oneness with all things. I experienced the memory of being a flower, of being a snake, of being the sky. At one point Lilia (the massage therapist) held my ear against her heart as she cradled me in the warm water. All I could hear was the sound of her heart beating. It was deafening. My heartbeat connected with hers and at once I was connected with the pulse of the earth and then the pulse of the universe. At first I felt an experience that I think was one of being in the womb, of being safe, warm, nurtured, totally embraced, feeling my heartbeat as one with another's heartbeat. From this inward place I then moved to a feeling of expansiveness and to a place where I experienced myself far above the earth, making my way down toward the earth. I was floating and flying. I felt a yearning and love for the earth as I grew closer to it. I must remember this expandedness so that I can return to it."

Commenting on her water massage, Judith says:

"Through the non-ordinary state of consciousness I experienced during the Watsu massage, my perception expanded to include the greater rhythms of the cosmos. Through this expanded perception,

I knew myself as part of the cosmos. I experienced my unity with all things. Because I was connecting with my body on a very deep level, I was able to access my personal unconscious and then move to an even deeper level to access the collective unconscious, the archetypal psyche, the transpersonal dimension of consciousness. Being in this expanded state gave me so much pleasure that I wanted to bring it back with me into my ordinary state of consciousness. I wanted to remember and embody my connectedness with all things. In my expanded state I felt love, peace, and joy. This transformative experience was an experience with the unseen dimension of life, a dimension of life that is both subtle and powerful at the same time. It is a dimension of life that can be accessed through non-ordinary states of consciousness, the same states of consciousness beheld in visionary experience."[12]

In some respects, this experience of Judith's, though it took place in water, reminds us of Jung's feeling and description of "floating in the womb of the universe" in his near-death experience. However, unlike Jung, Judith felt connected and was happy to return to the earth. Nevertheless, both accounts witness the same feelings of inexpressible joy, inspiration, and guidance, and constitute a confirmation of another, autonomous world more real in some respects than this one.

Micea Eliade gives eloquent expression to the moon and its mode of being, which creates "harmonies, symmetries, analogies and participations which make up an endless "fabric," a "net" of invisible threads, which "binds" together at once humankind, rain, vegetation, fertility, health, animals, death, regeneration, after-life, and more."[13] He suggests that this binding quality helps us see why the moon in so many traditions is personified by a deity, or lunar animal, that "weaves" a cosmic veil or net. In many of the images of the goddess she is wearing a garment with either spiral designs, crescent or laby-

---

12 Judith Orodenker, *The Voice of the Goddess: The Reemergence of the Archetypal Divine Feminine*, Pacifica Graduate Institute, 2007, Unpublished Dissertation, pp. 81–84.
13 Eliade, "The Moon & Its Mystique," p. 180.

rinthine motifs, or net-like patterns. These rich associations reveal the moon as a beautiful symbol for initiation into the subtle body and subtle worlds.

The Minoan bee goddess or priestesses, *melissae*, famous as seers and diviners, are also united with moon and bull in a symbolism of death and renewal. Honey was important in both embalming and the making of mead, the drink of immortality. Honeycombs likewise are created in a net design, and Anne Baring and Jules Cashford point to the fascinating etymological link in Greek that unites the "ideas of the honeycomb, goddess, death, fate, and the human heart, a nexus of meanings that is illuminated if we know that the goddess was once imagined as a bee."[14] Too, the moon is the weaver of destinies, represented by a spider in many mythologies, suggesting not only fate, but the necessity to create, to make something of one's essence and the "hand dealt" to one, as a spider does when spinning its web.

This "living whole" or integral vision of reality comes back to us today, whether it be in images of the cosmic web (or worldwide web) and the interrelationship of all being, pictures of the earth from the moon, or the mandala symbols found in many of the crop circles. It is found in the suggestion of an implicate order (the new physics) or the psychophysical whole behind manifest reality in which that wholeness is expressed in every part— the Akashic field or non-local quantum holographic phenomenon residing in the zero-point field[15]—or in the urge toward a lived expression of the *unus mundus* world in a subtle and richly textured layering of felt reality. Likewise, just as water, the source and mother of all life, holds the potentiality of all forms in unbroken wholeness, so immersion in water symbolizes a return to that pre-formed potential, and to the possibility of renewal and rebirth. Emerging from the water is a repetition of the act of creation. In initiation rituals, water confers a "new birth" and hence is a symbol of life, the "water of life." "Living water" heals. It gives life, endows strength, restores youth, and assures eternity.

Immersion in water was done before all major religious acts as a preparation for entering the temple of the sacred. Ablutions were performed before entering temples and before sacrifices. Eliade writes, "The ceremony

---

14 Baring & Cashford, *The Myth of the Goddess*, p. 120.
15 Ervin Laszlo, *Science and the Re-enchantment of the Cosmos: The Rise of the Integral Vision of Reality* (Rochester, VT: Inner Traditions, 2006), p. 128.

of the sacred bath was generally performed in the cult of the great goddesses of fertility and agriculture."[16] Statues of the goddess were immersed as well to ensure rain and fertility. Water immersion prevails in modern Christianity in the form of baptism, a symbol of spiritual regeneration and second birth.

Cults and rites associated with springs and rivers and their sacred and healing qualities have persisted throughout history. For example, in England, springs near some of the stone monument circles or ancient Celtic wells are believed to have restorative powers and prophetic power was associated with the ocean, "the home of wisdom," particularly in the mythical figure of the Babylonian Oannes, half man, half fish, who rose from the depths and revealed to humankind culture, writing, and astrology.[17] In Greece, animals were sacrificed to powerful Poseidon and the divinities of the sea and rivers, especially Achelous who was considered a great water god throughout Greece. Numerous nymphs, too, resided in springs and fountains, magically created by the babbling water or mists arising from it, or found in caves near water. Oracular, prophetic, or healing qualities of water initiations are present in these beliefs. One should not forget, however, that these beings were not only benign but also were to be feared as they could induce fascination or derangement, as in the case of Actaeon who chanced upon Artemis bathing with her nymphs.

Though people can, of course, drown in water, and there are many cross cultural flood myths that signify endings and beginnings, immersion in this "matter in motion" dissolves and transforms, promising germination, re-creation, and re-vitalization. Even in modern times, creatures of the depths such as dolphins are used in healing rituals, known to be effective especially with children, as indicated for example, the dolphin work done with children with autism. The dolphin's ancient wisdom is thought to be accessible telepathically via immersion in water, either actually or via the imagination using meditation techniques. Rituals involving water bring into the present that Other world, the *mundus imaginalis* that assists in the birth of the new woman or man. As Eliade summarizes: "Any use of water with a religious intention brings together the two basic points in the rhythm of the universe: reintegration in water—and creation."[18]

---

16 Eliade, "The Moon & Its Mystique," p. 195.
17 *Ibid.*, p. 202.
18 *Ibid.*, p. 212.

My dream of the Moon Lady cited earlier and its associations speak to the possibility of a new dispensation involving eros awareness, the return of Sophia and the reclamation of the divine feminine. The dream also speaks of a union of East and West, pointing once again to the close spiritual proximity of Buddhism and Christianity. Closely related to this possibility is a dream of Marie-Louise von Franz shortly before her death, recorded by Remo Roth, a Zurich analytical psychologist who worked closely with her for over 25 years. He writes:

> In the summer of 1994 [Marie Louise von Franz] was visited by a woman, a medium, who wanted to convince her to collaborate with her; she was certain that the Christian and the Buddhist spirit were presently uniting on the other side in order to save the world. Marie-Louise promised nothing—she wanted first to see what she might dream. The following night she had this dream: "She is working in the laundry at the cloister in Einsiedeln [where there is a shrine to the Black Madonna]. She is given to understand that Jung would come down from heaven to the wedding of the Black Madonna. Marie-Louise is among the one hundred elect who are permitted to take part in the wedding."
>
> She then said that the unconscious was indeed preparing a remedy for the world and a union, to be sure not one "above in the spiritual realm," but a union of above and below, a union of spirit and matter. Very early on the Virgin Mary was thought to be "the earth;" the Black Madonna was a nature goddess. And yet the union comes about in a Christian framework, which she (Marie-Louise) never could accept. But still the dream filled her with the highest happiness.[19]

Roth continues that this dream was shared at Marie-Louise's funeral, giving the world, and particularly the Jungian community, a parting symbolic message about the constellated future developments described in this archetypal dream: the incarnation of the divine feminine in the body of men and women, and the sacred marriage union of psyche and matter that gives

---

19 See Dr. Remo Roth's website: www.psychovision.ch/rfr/roth_e.htm

rise to the subtle body. Although the union of East and West is not specifically mentioned in von Franz's dream, it is present in the context of the woman who visited her and spoke of a Christian-Buddhist connection. We might take her dream, therefore, as a suggestion that the union of East and West could also refer to how Buddhist meditative practice can supplement Jungian analytic work in its focus on happiness, liberation, and the interrelated wholeness of humanity with nature and the cosmos. Perhaps that is why when von Franz awoke she was filled with the highest happiness. My own feeling is that the direct experiences of the imaginal realm recounted in this book can be viewed as different ways of accessing the wisdom of the Buddhist tradition.

In the Jewish mystical traditions there is a beautiful passage that situates this image of union within another context: "When the moon shall shine as bright as the sun, the messiah will come." In other words, when the Sophianic/Eros awareness of lunar consciousness is brought into being as a subtle intermediate world from deep within the resources of the psychoid psyche, and this lunar awareness of creative imagination and love is recognized as being just as central to life as our solar achievements in logos consciousness, then the ancient spirit and natural resource of wisdom will become available to our planet. I suggest that this evolution in consciousness is already constellating, and this book *Songlines of the Soul: Pathways to a New Vision for a New Century*, bears witness to its epiphany. Water treatments and ancient Greek dream incubation practices may assist us in embodying this energy.

In this regard, it is important to mention, once again, Masaru Emoto's book on the mysteries of water. His research shows, through the photographs of water crystals, not only how consciousness affects the beauty or distortion of the designs, but how this points to the non-local union of psyche and matter. He writes not just of the effect of words themselves on water, whether they are loving or harsh (or of the effects of music and landscapes), but of the spirit contained within the words (music and landscapes), as different languages produce similar results on the water crystals. In turn, water crystals—like crop circles—and their extraordinary beauty, have the power to affect people, inducing deep feelings of love, beauty, and healing, changing the consciousness of those looking at the designs. He comments that this reciprocal motion is possible because, as we know from quantum physics, everything vibrates and produces sound, whether you can hear it or not. Emoto emphasizes that sound, at various frequencies, means that relationships take place in a resonant field of experience (both positively and negatively) *non-locally*, beyond the confines of time and space. Water is the "master listener," he writes, mirroring back to us the state of our souls. Emoto even says that water comes from elsewhere in the galaxy, and is the carrier of cosmic memory.

Emoto inspires us to have deep respect for water and its wisdom properties, to be aware of how words, or a gaze, carry energy, and to be responsible moment to moment for holding an attitude full of gratitude and love, as opposed to hatred, indifference, or control. His research confirms my interest in using water in healing and the search for creativity and wisdom. His book, *The Hidden Messages in Water*, might change your life. Water is a medium for non-local consciousness and carries the songlines of our souls. Emoto writes: "there is another world in addition to the one that we live in. When looking at our world from that world, we can see things that we cannot now see."[20] These chapters have been a witness to that Other world.

Water, Music, and the Songlines of the Soul

Amplifying Emoto's remarks about water and sound, there is a strong relationship among sound, water, and sacred sites that activates the reconnection of human and cosmic consciousness. Crop circle researcher, Freddy Silva, writes of how subtle earth energies interact with the energies of the human body, amplified by both underlying water courses and, in the case of stone circles, temples and cathedrals, the actual quality of stone used in the buildings. Together with the coded patterns of sacred geometry found in alchemy, ancient philosophical schools of learning, as well as in the crop circles today, the vibration of sound based on the music scale that is governed by the same mathematical ratios as geometry, is known to assist in the transformation of the seeker or initiate. Silva writes:

> By 4000 B.C., geometry and sound were inextricably linked, at which time it was already established that the laws of geometry governed the mathematical intervals that made up the musical scale.

---

20 Emoto, *The Hidden Messages in Water*, p. 91.

This inseparable bond was certainly taught at the Egyptian Mystery Schools, since many of the temples associated with knowledge and transformation structurally encode the same harmonic ratios found in music (Schwaller de Lubicz 1977; West 1993). In fact, the relationship of form and substance to tone was understood to such a degree that structures such as the colossal statues of Memnon used to emit an audible tone when struck by the rays of the rising Sun.[21]

Pyramids, like Gothic cathedrals, were and are vast sonic temples. Again, we can remind ourselves that in both Eastern and Western religious traditions, sound, vibration, word or tone is present "before" creation and is the force behind the visible manifest world. Think of the "OM," or as some describe it the "AUM," also reflected in the Egyptian "amun" and later Christian "amen." The frequency of this sounding mantra arises from the solar plexus chakra and is used to center and ground the praying individual or group. Sound was so fundamental to an understanding of the universe that many of the teachers in the ancient mystery schools were musicians as well as initiated philosophers. Sound is thought to be involved in moving the massively huge stones vast distances to create the ancient stone circles and temples. Spiritual psychologist Robert Sardello in his article on angels gives the example of Tibetan monks who use the sound vibrations of their musical instruments in combination with the singing of mantras to help move otherwise immoveable blocks of stone up a steep cliff.[22] And in physics today the ancient music of the spheres returns in string theory that now envisions invisible frequencies behind the constitution of so-called matter. The cosmos is a vast musical score.

Since ancient times, music has been used in healing, from Aboriginal didjeridus, to Gregorian chant, to Indian classical raga music, and modern day ultrasound. Music alters awareness and can assist in making us feel deeply and spiritually. I remember a moment during my painful divorce in the early 1990s when, falling exhausted one night on the sofa in my living room, I heard Beethoven's Fifth Piano Concerto on the radio, and suddenly

---

21 Freddy Silva, *Secrets in the Fields: The Science & Mysticism of Crop Circles* (Charlottesville, VA: Hampton Roads, 2002), p. 205.
22 Robert Sardello, Ed., *The Angels* (Dallas: Dallas Institute Publications, 1994), p. 60.

I could feel every chakra in my body from my feet to the top of my head, realigning my energy to create balance and harmony, awakening me out of the depths of despair toward life once again. I also think of how important music is for teenagers who, having almost no help from their elders to transition from childhood to young adulthood, often instinctively seem to feel the transformational power of music to assist them. And it goes without saying how central music is to love and lovers bypassing thought and giving direct expression to joyous or tormenting passion. Moreover, just think of songs and particular pieces of music that were important to you at various stages of your life. Recalling these will bring back those times of change as if they are still present now.

Silva also describes the crop circles as contemporary (and temporary as they are mowed down every autumn during the harvest season!) initiation temples that are known to alter people's states of awareness, and even to heal illness. The "trilling sounds" that have been heard in or near crop circles around the time they appear, are comparable perhaps to the effects of Aboriginal didjeridus used by shamans to open pathways to different levels of existence. Likewise, Tibetan overtone chanting, which is thought to unite the feminine and masculine elements of the creative spirit, and sacred music that activates the spirit and opens the soul to cosmic consciousness, are also examples of the transformational effects of sound.

As another contemporary example of the ancient healing sanctuaries, the salt mineral springs spa in the medieval village of Bad Sulza near Weimar in Germany has a "Liquid Sound Temple" as well as light treatments focusing on the different chakras in their famous baths. Water, sound and light are combined in the ancient ritual of The Great Bath (already noted by Eliade), to enhance transformation, healing, and renewal. After one such soak in the Liquid Sound Temple and feeling that the waters were "melting" my heart open, I wrote: "Boundaries dissolving, feeling at one with the water, liquid gold, I too have been dolphin, plant and star. I am at one with the universe, a note in a musical score."[23]

---

23 www.hotel-an-der-therme.de. See also Professor Jonathan Paul de Vierville's website: www.spacultures.com, and an article titled "Into a Dream" in Spa Magazine, April 2009, by Margaret Pierpont, on de Vierville's annual 5 day workshop: "Spa Cultures, Dreams and Healing Waters," that my husband and I attended in 2008.

Moreover, The Lady Melissa who has been so important in my dreams connecting me to the moon, and who gives expression to the deep feminine mysteries of Sophia, Isis and Aphrodite, is connected to the throat chakra. The throat chakra is related to the power of right speech and creative expression and is thus also intimately related to sound, vibration, and music. It is an elegant fact for me that the music I loved as a child, when I insisted on playing the piano at age 5 and continued through High School, only to put it aside at college to pursue my interests in spiritual traditions and the mysteries, returns transformed now much later in life as an intimate expression—both literally and symbolically—of those mysteries.

Songlines and the Return of the Cosmic Soul

I come now to the end of my journey. Through a tapestry of reflections and accounts of experiences from my own life and the lives of others, I have suggested and alluded to the fact that in the breakdown of ordinary reality as we know it, a different kind of gnosis is occurring all around us. At the turn of the Aeon, it brings us a new kind of knowledge—revealed rather than rational knowledge—that wishes to make itself felt.

This disclosure hints at the union of soul and life in a revelation of love: our human love, and the love of the cosmos for us. Held within this larger perspective we come to know what not only the Ancients, the Mystics, the Gnostics, and the Alchemists once knew, but also what we know today through our dreams, visions, and anomalous experiences, which perhaps we have kept secret for too long, but which now cry out for each of us to add to the chorus that is singing the songlines of the soul. Lift up your voices, let them resonate as far as the stars, let them echo throughout all creation that we are the microcosm of the macrocosm, that our bodies hold the secrets of creation, and that the Self and the Cosmos are One.

Appendix

MEDITATIONS

In order to facilitate a living experience of the issues discussed in this book, I offer a series of meditative exercises that the reader can practice. The intention here is to open the imagination to these realities, which, as I have been saying throughout this book, cannot be fully appreciated by reason alone. This chapter will present several meditations to help us become more attuned to the songlines of our souls.

In addition, these exercises might support epiphanies of this Other world that readers have already had.

I. AN EXPERIENCE IN SOCIAL DREAM INCUBATION[1]

I have used this exercise in classes with students at Pacifica Graduate Institute. This "group dreaming" has also been used as part of consulting efforts in a variety of organizational settings and groups, and at meetings of Jungian analysts and therapists all over the world. It is a way of hosting a sharing of images from our depths and is a powerful way of creating the subtle body field of the mundus imaginalis and an opening to the mystical cities of the soul.

How is it done? You can lie on the floor or remain seated in chairs. First, ask for a volunteer who is willing to record the images that arise in the group as these will be read out at the end of the exercise. Then, select someone willing to lead an opening meditation in which there is an effort

1   In this description of social dreaming, I have adapted a write-up of it by my colleague Dr. Patricia Katsky in a seminar for students that we co-taught in the Depth Psychotherapy Program at Pacifica Graduate Institute, Fall 2007 and 2008. For further references on social dreaming, see W. G. Lawrence, (Ed), *Experiences in Social Dreaming* (London: Karnac, 2000).

to quiet the ego mind. I usually instruct participants to try to let go of who they were when they entered the room and, following the natural rhythm of their breath, to allow themselves to go to the deepest place that they know, sinking deeper and deeper with each breath. To assist this process you can imagine both the crown of the head and the ground underneath the feet opening up to allow universal energy and earth energy respectively to spiral down and up into the body through all the major chakra centers. The idea is to focus on getting in touch with what is most important in this moment, allowing one to be addressed by the wisdom of the soul, freeing oneself from distractions and passing concerns.

After the meditation, to start the process, I begin with a dream or dream image. Naturally, someone else can start this process as well. What happens next is up to our deeper selves. Participants are invited to choose to answer with an image of their own—one coming from a dream or dream image, from an active imagination, or one occurring right now—something elicited from the energy of the moment. You may also feel free to change the direction of the moment by contributing an image or dream that is not related to what has gone before in a direct way, but one that you feel moved to contribute at this point in the process. The goal of this experiment is not to look at these images in terms of the person presenting them, but rather to host these images as guests who have come to share themselves with us, bringing their own unique mix of light and dark, of past and future, of intimacy and expansiveness. The process of sharing these dreams and images continues for as long as it feels intuitively right. I have found that it usually takes about half an hour, but it depends somewhat on the size of the group. Often, especially at the beginning, there are pauses and silences between sharing, as participants "fall" into the space of co-creating the imaginal world. If you notice, these silences are often "full" and pregnant with energy and meaning and are part of the field being created.

When it feels as if it is time to conclude this part of the sharing process, I suggest to the group that they imagine now that all the images are being woven into a beautiful tapestry or blanket and that we are each holding on to the edge of it. Then, we let the blanket go out into the cosmos, out to the other galaxies, stars, and dimensions, and then let it fall back into our midst. After we are finished, our recorder will read back a composition of what has been shared.

We recognize that the attempt to record these images will be necessarily partial and selective, since it is not possible to remember each and every image that will come forth. One of us has graciously agreed to be our recorder, writing down what has been shared as best as possible, while recognizing that the recording process is like the sharing itself. Some things will inevitably be remembered, some lost. We all need to remain humble in our efforts to contact the soul and retrieve its gifts as best we can.

After a break in which we remain quiet and hold the energy created by the experience in a respectful manner, we return to share some of our feelings and responses.

The goal of this experience is that each of us will be enriched and seeded in our being with images that may speak to us and move us. Images are like seeds—when seeds are sown, it is not always possible to predict the growth that will come. In a similar way, learning at the level of the deep unconscious is like planting and sowing. The results may take many moons to bear fruit. Each of our souls may be nourished in unique and synchronistic ways by the images that others may share with us. And perhaps we will have dreams following this experiment that speaks to what we have heard.

2. INCUBATION

You can repeat the spirit of the above exercise by doing it yourself. Create a quiet space where you will not be interrupted. Follow the guidelines above (or do your own) for a meditation to quiet the mind. Allow yourself to be open to whatever wishes to address you from the depths of your being at this moment. Give yourself about twenty minutes for this meditation. Spend some time writing down what happened. Who or what addressed you? What needs to die or be reborn in your soul? How can you become even more fully who you are?

3. GRAIL CASTLE AND DEEP COSMIC REMEMBERING

What West African "Keeper of Rituals" Sobonfu Some calls the "web of light" is the subtle energy field of the earth where we find, among other things, the mystical cities of the soul. Though these cities are related to sacred sites on the planet that we can also visit, through meditation, we can practice accessing the wisdom to be found in these imaginal geomythic landscapes. The following is based on Richard Leviton's book, *The Galaxy on Earth.*[2]

The Grail Castle—also known as Yima's Var—is associated with one of the eight celestial cities surrounding Mount Meru, home to the three chief Hindu gods according to the Sanskrit Puranas. The city is called Sankara, Yasovati or Lankara, and is associated with the North cardinal direction. It is the realm of Kubera, lord of wealth and endless riches. The Grail Castle's gift to us is deep cosmic memory. It is located at the sacred sites of Delphi, Glastonbury, and Montsegur, and among other places such as the Acropolis and the Dome of the Rock.

First, contact the angelic "star" guidance near your belly button.[3]

This star is an angelic order called the Ofanim, which comes from the Hebrew meaning "wheels" or "thrones;" they provide guidance and help us to remember who we truly are:

- Sit in a comfortable chair in a room free of distractions. Relax and place both feet, uncrossed, on the floor. Close your eyes and take a few deep breaths. Do this without effort or strain. Spend a few moments observing your breathing, noting that the inhales and exhales come and go without effort on your part.

- As you relax into the natural rhythm of your breathing, allow your lips to form a little smile with each out-breath, as if you are amused, or feeling affectionate.

- Now focus your attention on a point two finger's width above your belly button and the same distance inside. Imagine a pinprick of light at that spot, a tiny blazing star of brilliant light. It is very tiny but brighter than seems possible. As you exhale, breathe to this little bright star with a smile. Let every exhale work as a bellows, making the star just a little brighter.

- As you exhale, send your smile to that little pinprick of brilliant light, to that little blazing star at the center of your body. Breathe to it with

---

2   Richard Leviton, *The Galaxy on Earth* (Charlottesville, VA: Hampton Roads, 2002), p. 57.

3   See Leviton, *The Galaxy on Earth*, pp. 3–4, and www.blueroomconsortium.com/About the Ofanim.

some fondness, as if somehow it is an old almost forgotten friend suddenly returned to you after a long absence. Breathe to this star with a sense of fondness, affection, and with a smile of recognition. It may surprise you to notice from time to time that it seems the star is twinkling at you, even winking, if this were possible. No effort is required; just a smile and your natural breathing.

- You may notice that this point of light begins to grow a bit larger. It may be the size of a marble now. Soon it becomes the size of a golf ball. Now a peach. Now a softball. Now a basketball. It keeps growing. Continue to breathe with the sense of quiet fondness to this growing point of light until it is as big as a house in front of you, a round house of brilliant light. If you wish, walk right into this brilliant sphere or allow it to roll over and through you. No effort is required.

- You are now inside your own blazing star and within the energy field of the Ofanim. Keep breathing with that smile, and enjoy the angelic presence.

- If you wish, you may now picture the planet Earth as seen from space. Place this image of the blue-and-white planet Earth inside your blazing star at the center of your body. Simply put the Earth inside the star, and continue to breathe to it with fondness and regard. You can now amplify that fondness to something called Love from Above. This is the way the spiritual world regards humans and our planet. Keep breathing Love from Above to planet Earth inside the blazing star at the center of your being.

- Allow yourself to feel like a cosmic parent to the Earth, that you are nurturing it inside this blazing star at the center of your being. Continue to breathe as Love from Above to the Earth inside your star for a few moments.

Now to the Grail Castle:

- Next, move your attention to the top of your head, to the crown chakra. Let that area soften and open like a lotus flower while you keep breathing in an effortless manner. Now imagine that the lotus flower opens up to the Grail castle. You are now in a temple that houses the Grail. Look around, what do you see? There is a round table with people gathered. Who is there? Take a moment. In the middle of the table is the grail. The grail is both an object—sometimes a stone, sometimes a cup or chalice, sometimes a platter—but it is also a process. That process is the regeneration of the human through retrieving cosmic memory. The potential reclaimable riches of cosmic memory are almost inconceivable, which is why Kubera is said to be the Lord of wealth.

- The world is a wasteland and the Rich Fisher King has become the Wounded Fisher King because he and we have forgotten our vast past. The Grail is the process of regaining that memory and healing the wound in consciousness. Deep cosmic memory is pre-incarnational memory, pre-Fall memory, full cosmic knowledge of all the past cycles of time.

- The Grail King is the Lord of the Sea, King of the Waters, the watery abyss of primordial chaos. But it is only chaos because it is so much consciousness that it potentially overwhelms our self-identity and structure of consciousness based on our comparatively parochial sense of spacetime.

- The Grail Castle is Noah's Ark and the Boat of the Vedas floating on the waves upon the cosmic sea during the time of Deluge. This refers both to the location of the Grail Castle in the highest level of the etheric realm (on top of the Sea or above your crown chakra) and to its function to preserve knowledge from one Day of Brahma, and Year of Brahma, to the next, the interregnum being marked by a Flood, or inundation of matter-based spacetime by a surfeit of galactic consciousness. These are vast cycles of time, calculated in the billions of years.

- Now, allow yourself in this moment to ask a question. It could be what spontaneously occurs to you, or it could be the grail question: What ails thee? Or, Whom does the Grail serve? Await an answer.

- When you are ready, bring your awareness to your body, wriggle your fingers and toes, and slowly open your eyes. Write in a journal what happened in your meditation.

4. OPENING TO THE HEART

Reflect on experiences that have helped open your heart. Write them down and meditate on them. Can you design a meditation or exercise to keep heart consciousness in awareness? This will enable you to stabilize eros awareness, particularly in the face of the pull to old or unconscious patterns of relating to self or other.

Read books by His Holiness the Dalai Lama, Thich Nhat Hanh, or Robert Thurman on Buddhism that aim to help you open the heart of compassion toward yourself, your fellow human beings, and to the planet. Learn from Indigenous Traditions. Read also Drunvalo Melchizedek's book, *Living in the Heart: How to Enter into the Sacred Space within the Heart*. See the articles at goldensufi.org and workingwithoneness.org.

5. USING MUSIC TO HELP OPEN THE HEART

The following pieces of music are also aimed to facilitate contact with feelings and an opening of the heart. They come from The Bonny Institute website.[4] Helen Bonny designed The Bonny Method of Guided Imagery and Music which is a process focusing on the conscious use of imagery arising in response to a formalized program of relaxation and classical music. She writes: "Music, as a structured envelope of sound, is probably the most effective and safe opener to the doors of the psyche. It reaches beyond personal defenses to the realities and beauties of the person. Music gives access to the discovery of inner strength, uncovers the potential for creativity, and manifests ways in which life can be lived from a center of inner security." Music also reconnects us with the sacred and with the wider cosmos of which we are a part.

During a session, guided by a trained facilitator, imagery is evoked in the form of symbols, memories or feelings. Carefully selected music serves

---

4   www.bonnieinstitute.org. My thanks to Lindsay Beaven for this suggestion.

as a catalyst to encourage spontaneous verbalizations, movements, and insights to create an opening for healing and change to occur. The totality of the experience enhances self-understanding, therapeutic goals and spiritual transformation. Here are the sample suggestions to practice on your own: (The majority of these music suggestions come from the Western classical repertoire, but you can add your own selections as I have done)

Suggested music for imaging experiences:

Ravel, *Daphnis and Chloe*; Introduction and Allegro
Vaughan Williams, *Variations on the theme of Greensleeves*; *Rhosymedre*
Debussy, *Afternoon of a Faun*; *Dances Sacred and Profane*
Pierne, *Concertpiece for Harp and Orchestra*
Holst, *The Planets*: Venus, Neptune, Jupiter
Copland, *Appalachian Spring*
Respighi, *The Pines of Rome*
Warlock, *Pieds-en-l'air*

Suggested music for release of feelings:

Anger, frustration:

Holst, *The Planets*: Mars
Bach, *Passacaglia and Fugue in C*, orchestra transcription
Mussorgsky, *Pictures at an Exhibition*: Baba Yaga and the Great Gates of Kiev

Sadness, grief:

Marcello, *Oboe Concerto in C minor*
Rodrigo, *Concerto de Aranjuez*, Adagio
Paul Schwartz, *State of Grace*
Michael Hoppe, *Solace*
Hoppe, Tillman, and Wheater, *Afterglow*

Longing, reminiscing:

Grainger, *Danny Boy*
Satie, *Gymnopedie #3*
Massanet, *Meditation from Thais*

Nurturing, comforting:

Villa-lobos, *Bachianas Brasilieras, No. 5*
Canteloube, *Songs of the Auvergne:* Brezairola
Haydn, *Cello Concerto in C,* Adagio

Suggested music for spiritual upliftment:

Vaughan Williams, *Variations on a Theme of Tallis; Lark Ascending*
Brahms, *German Requiem*
Bach, *B minor Mass*
Beethoven, *Symphony #9; Piano Concerto #5*
Brahms, *Piano Concerto #2*
Elgar, *Enigma Variations #s* 8 and 9
Faure, *Requiem*
Durufle, *Requiem*
Olga Kharatidi & Jim Wilson, *Entering the Circle*

Suggested music for relaxation:

Kelly, *Seapeace; Perennials*
Deuter, *Ecstasy; Land of Enchantment*
Jones, M., *After the Rain*
Lind Institute collection: *Relax with the Classics*

If these musical experiences strike a chord with you, you might also enjoy reading *The Mysticism of Sound and Music: The Sufi Teaching of Hazrat Inayat Khan.*[5]

---

5   Boston & London: Shambhala, 1996.

6. MEDITATION FOR OUR CONNECTION TO THE COSMOS:

Steven Greer's Group Meditation for Contacting ET Beings and a Prayer for the Earth.[6] *Use accompanying music of your choice.*

Sit in silence and center yourselves, taking deep cleansing breaths, and feeling your consciousness expanding. Breathe in light and life; breathe out all negativity, tension, and fears, and feel yourself settling into a deep peace. See that you are centered in a vast ocean of silent consciousness.

Gently, without straining, allow yourselves to see the awake-ness that is watching the breath. Observe that you are awake, and that this awake-ness is silent. Now, see that this awake mind, which is still and steady, is observing all the sounds, the thoughts, the feelings, all perceptions, and yet the mind itself is quiet.

Dive deeply into this vast ocean of quiet awareness. Going more deeply now, see that all the perceptions are receding, becoming more distant, and quiet, and you are being established more deeply, in this ocean of awake-ness within.

Now, settle more deeply into this ocean of quiet awareness, where all perceptions are like distant ripples on the surface of the ocean. And you perceive that this vast awake mind extends infinitely in all directions. And you see that this awake-ness is omnipresent. It is not bound by space or time. And so it is infinite, and it is eternal. This is the true nature of the awake-ness whereby we perceive our own breath, our own self, sight, sounds, and thoughts. We feel the joy and peace of knowing that this awake Being, this Mind is ever present with us.

Now, release yourselves from all attachment to perception or even self, and see the unbounded quality of this awake-ness is universal. Though you are awake and a unique individual, the light of awareness is a singularity, and that awake-ness is one, and we are one being in many bodies, one light illuminating every soul and conscious mind.

We see this same vast awake-ness permeating the earth beneath us and expanding into the sky above us. And soaring on the wings of this vast and limitless awareness, we expand upward into the sky, and we see that the

---

6 Steven Greer, *Hidden Truth Forbidden Knowledge* (Crozet, VA: Crossing Point, 2006), chapter 46, pp. 321–325 (with some minor changes). You can also do this meditation alone.

entire earth is shining in the light of this awake-ness, and beyond us, space, and the planets of our solar system, all spinning, swimming, in an ocean of awake mind.

This simple awake mind within us is the same awake mind that permeates all things, which is omnipresent, omniscient, and eternal.

As we expand further into the vastness of space, we see the entire solar system, with the beautiful blue earth now an orb before us, and we see that she is conscious, and is her own individual being, and she is awake, with the same light of awareness whereby we are conscious, whereby we have awareness.

The sun, and all the planets, each have their own conscious identification and are all unique beings. And yet the awake-ness within them, within every atom, within every photon, permeating the space of our solar system is the same awake mind that is within us.

As we expand further, we go beyond our solar system, and we soar through the entire Milky Way galaxy, and expand through the vastness of 100,000 light years of space and beyond the outer edge of the Milky Way into inter-galactic space, and we behold the beautiful spiral galaxy of our Milky Way, and we see that it is awake, pure consciousness shining, phasing as stars and planets and an infinite number of awake beings.

Gazing then beyond the space of our Milky Way galaxy, we behold inter-galactic space, and we see stretching in all directions an infinite and endless cosmos with billions of galaxies, each with billions of star systems, and planets teeming with intelligent life.

Now effortlessly, we dive into this vast cosmic awareness, and find the infinite peace, an infinite, endless awareness permeating the entire creation, and we behold that this cosmic mind, this omnipresent awareness, is always indivisible and is the same awake-ness whereby we are conscious here and now and always.

Being thus awake, we now perceive that the universe, which is itself endless, has advanced extraterrestrial life forms, and all are awake even as we are conscious. And through this connection, we are one. We know that there is one conscious Being, shining, standing, within all life. And through that, we connect to them. As we gaze across the cosmos, through the galaxies, within the Milky Way, within our solar system, around the earth, we allow ourselves to see any extraterrestrial people with their beautiful celestial spacecraft.

As we see them, we ask permission to gaze within, and as we see these beings, we invite them to join us here on earth as we join together as people celebrating the time of universal peace and the establishment of an enlightened civilization on earth.

As we see each of these beings, we see that they are connected to an inter-planetary council—highly evolved spiritual and ambassadorial in nature. We invite them to join us here as we show them our galaxy. And as we zoom in ever more closely to our solar system, we show them this beautiful planet Earth, the third planet from our star, the sun.

As we connect to their minds and to their guidance system, we show them our exact location. As we come zooming in more closely, we show them this place and we invite them here, in a spirit of universal peace, acknowledging our oneness with them through the universal awake Being within us, this cosmic Mind, shared by all beings.

Now, as we see these beings, aware of us, and in our mind's eye, we see them, we ask that they join us at this time in a meditation and a prayer for Earth and for its transition to the time of its destiny as a place of peace and enlightenment. As we make this invitation we see that there are extraterrestrial beings, celestial beings, the great Prophets, and the enlightened ones, all joining with us. If in a group, send from person to person, around this circle, counterclockwise, a golden light in our conscious awareness, a beautiful astral light empowered with oneness, peace and love. And as this light goes from left to right, making a beautiful circle, it becomes a ring of light. If alone, imagine a ring of light.

In our minds, we empower this ring of light with tremendous energy, and we send it upward as a column of light rising from this spot, going into space as a beacon, carrying with it the love of Earth, the oneness we share, and the time of peace that we are establishing.

This beacon is calling to all beings, joining with us in peace. And we see it connecting to every world, every star, every heart, and every life. It spreads out and diffuses throughout the cosmos, this beautiful golden light. As it spreads we see every heart is illumined, and every mind awakened and every dark place is filled with light.

In this state of illumination, we ask the great Being to give peace to the Earth, to turn every selfish heart into an open fountain of love and generosity. And wherever there is hatred and enmity, we see peace being established. And wherever there is greed, we see altruism and generosity. And wherever we see separation and sadness, we see the joy of oneness and love.

As we do this, we see the cosmos and all enlightened beings, material, celestial and divine joining with us, pouring forth this vision, and the Earth coming to its time of peace, and the chaos ending.

Now stretching before us, we see thousands of generations of humans living together in peace on the earth with wondrous new technologies and sciences that enable us to be in harmony with the Earth. And with abundance we banish all disease and poverty, and all injustice and all want.

On the foundations of this peace and prosperity, we see the hearts of all humanity turning to the pursuit of enlightenment. And in this state we are welcomed into the vast regions of the stars, and we become an inter-stellar species, and are welcomed into the family of planetary societies.

As we gaze down through the ages, we ask the great Being at this moment to set us forth in the direction of enlightenment. And in that instant, we see the time where every man, woman, and child abiding on earth, is in a state of cosmic awareness, of God consciousness. The divine sciences and enlightenment prevail. We ask the great Spirit that we may be channels, vehicles, tools, for the establishment of this peace and the entry of humanity into enlightenment. We see that we are joined by beings celestial, extraterrestrial and divine, and that we are not alone and we have never been alone. And we ask that this Great Being enable us to all work together in the establishment of universal peace and a universal civilization.

This we leave as our cherished gift to our children, and our children's children. And we are certain that this beautiful vision is already manifest, that the Creator has already given to us the knowledge, the sciences, and the wisdom to create this world and to manifest this reality. And we consecrate our lives to the establishment of this divine civilization.

Namaste.

Coda

SINGING YOUR SONG

Small and invisible as the contribution may be, it is yet an opus magnum....
The ultimate questions of psychotherapy are not a private matter—
they represent a supreme responsibility.[1]

The more the critical reason dominates, the more impoverished life becomes;
but the more of the unconscious, and the more of myth we are capable of making conscious,
the more of life we integrate.... Consider synchronistic phenomena, premonitions,
and dreams that come true.[2]

In speaking of therapy, Jung comments on the fact that it is not only a personal matter, but important also for society, and "indeed for the moral and spiritual progress of mankind." This seems counterintuitive. Surely when we sit in our therapy offices, in either the patient's or therapist's chair, we are just working on ourselves. But as Jung went to great pains to point out throughout his work, our individual symptoms unite us with the universal archetypal dimensions of consciousness that not only bring individual healing, but reconnect us with an "always and everywhere" realm of being that is vertical, non-local, eternal, and immediate. I have gone further and made the claim that this landscape, a *mundus imaginalis* inhabited by subtle imaginal beings, is a psycho-cosmic geography that is more spiritual than material, yet more earthy than spirit, to which many of Jung's own experiences attest. From these direct experiences of our relationship to something beyond ourselves, we are encouraged to speak on behalf of a broader vision. This is what I have attempted to do in this book.

---

1   C. G. Jung, *The Practice of Psychotherapy*, CW 16, par. 449
2   C. G. Jung, *Memories, Dreams, Reflections*, p. 302

Jung's later work on the psychoid archetype emphasizes the unifying psychophysical background behind the world, and the co-creative possibilities of our direct intersection with it, especially through active imagination processes and the employment of the true or visionary imagination of alchemy. At the time, quantum physics was arriving at comparable insights concerning the participatory nature of the universe and the centrality of the observer effect. In this way, our individual effort lends itself not only to enriching the collective consciousness of our social group, but also to the larger work—invisible as this may be to ego consciousness—of active participation in the long, aeonic, spiritual development of humanity. Because of the psychic aspects of matter and the material aspects of psyche, we can now envision the subtle body world as a third realm that unifies soul and body, psyche and cosmos. This celestial earth is always potentially present to us. It has the ability to emerge and develop as our attunement to it grows stronger. In Avalon, Shambhala, or Hurqalya, we resume our spiritual progress as cosmic citizens who know that we are both particle and wave, and come into awareness of our differentiated unity. There we exist in devotion to a destiny that we can assume with ethical care and commitment on behalf of a larger vision for the highest good of all earth creatures and beyond to our galactic neighbors.

Yet, it is so easy to forget who we are. A millennial separation, an enormous *disiunctio* has occurred, in service to one type of evolution, that of the individual ego. But this has come at a great price to the soul of humanity as a whole and to the health—and even survival—of our planet. Only a return to a process akin to the dismemberment and recollection mysteries will suffice to transform consciousness from ego, convention, and forgetfulness toward remembering and recovering the songlines of the soul. Traditional therapy has increasingly numbed itself against this great undoing and rebirth, blindly continuing to pursue time-limited, goal-oriented strategies that are inherently unsatisfying to the soul. Individuals are now seeking deeper personal changes outside the usual norms. Often these changes are fostered upon them from without in ways that need to be taken notice of so that modern therapists can adapt the strategies to meet the psychological needs of the times.

Initiations were always known to court danger, because in seeking a restoration of the whole, the initiate must break down the barriers that normally veil and protect one in the ordinary world, and travel (by being quiet and still and adopting a "religious" attitude) to those realms of neither dreaming, waking nor sleeping where one can hear the voice of the guides of the soul. Unless we are willing to go to those places that grant us a gnosis of the whole, we will not be deflected from the dangerous destructive course currently being pursued by nations and groups all over the world. Only such a vision of wholeness will give us the courage to move forward from our reckless path to the kind of spiritual progress Jung suggests is sorely needed in our times.

Synchronicities, UFO/ET contact, crop circle mysteries, travel to the mystical cities, and NDE phenomena have arisen as emblems of an increasingly broader interest in the anomalous and paranormal in general. But beyond this interest, *experiences* of these phenomena lead to the search on the part of many for alternate ways of ethical living and being in the world that honor the interconnectedness of us all—animal, human, flower, tree, river, stone and star. The soul is once again being *awakened* on a global scale to the memory of its love, beauty, sorrow, and wisdom so that it can once again sing its song of creation. Like the shamans whose song *is* the initiation experience, because it captures the depth of its symbolic complexity and embodies the healing note, individuals are now gathering either alone, in small groups, or in larger collectives to attend to a new awakening on our Earth of the Mysteries that include, once again, the Invisible Ones.

Towards the end of *Memories, Dreams, Reflections,* in the chapter "On Life After Death," Jung records some of his own UFO dreams. After relating his dream that hints that his earthly life is really the projection of a meditating yogi, Jung suggests that UFO dreams too are a kind of reversal of our usual understanding of things, that perhaps it is not us "projecting UFOs" but them projecting us. In Jung's UFO dream, a magic lantern is attached to the UFO. This lantern "projects" the visible personality, like the yogi whose meditative pose is dreaming Jung who is using his life experiences in the three-dimensional world to further his own path toward realization. Jung makes an astonishing comment here: it appears that in the opinion of the "other side," our pre-natal existence is the real one and that our life here in the world is "a kind of illusion, an apparent reality constructed for a specific purpose," an observation similar to the oriental idea of Maya.[3] Furthermore, just as the ego is required to participate in the fulfillment of its destiny by helping to make the Self conscious, the analogies of "other side," UFO, and yogi as spiritual guide, suggest also the possibility for our interaction with them.

My own experience, together with the reports of many other witnesses confirms this possibility and supports the claim that the UFO phenomena are not just "unconscious projections." Like Jung, who wondered if they are, in fact, real, we feel that we are indeed being contacted from other realms, dimensions of consciousness, extraterrestrial or interstellar intelligences, or parallel worlds. The Invisible Ones, like Jung's yogi, or Christine de Pizan's Celestial Ladies, are making their presence felt for the purposes of guidance, healing, and the spiritual progress of humankind. This healing, dynamic, and creative urgency is represented by individuation as a path to self-realization and the establishment of the subtle body, culminating in an erotic-spiritual union, an embodied *coniunctio* that finds the figure of Eros/ Sophia at its center. This union of psyche and matter as a never-before- produced-creation is the new archetypal constellation erupting as we move from Pisces to Aquarius. Crop Circles are a signature of this union and, perhaps, ETs in UFOs are here to watch us transform and birth a new con- sciousness on Earth.

As many contemporary authors such as Anne Baring, Christopher Bache, and Betty Kovacs[4] confirm from their own dreams and visions, along with many NDEers and Close Encounter Experiencers, Love is at the center of creation. Love is the songline of the soul, the engine of creation coming to know itself. In both Christian mysticism and Eastern meditative prac- tices, self-knowledge is the road to knowledge of the divine, and this effort produces the "golden germ, or yellow castle"—(as I write this, a golden yel- low bird with blackish wings has just landed on a branch outside my window and is singing away)—which are images of the immortal body. We need now for our wisdom and our love to make the leaps and bounds beyond what

---

3   *Memories, Dreams, Reflections*, p. 324.

4   Anne Baring, *The Dream of the Cosmos* (Forthcoming, see excerpts at www.annebaring.com), Christo- pher Bache, *Dark Night Early Dawn* (Albany, NY: SUNY Press, 2000), and Betty Kovacs, *The Miracle of Death* (Claremont, CA: The Kamlak Center, 2003).

our technological ability has heretofore achieved. Our friends in the larger universe are helping us with this through UFO initiations, Near-Death events, shamanic journeys, and crop circle mysteries. We are being directly addressed by this breaking down of the usual distinctions and coordinates of reality. It is now up to us to choose to participate in a co-creative manner in this difficult yet wondrous epiphany.

Moreover, these experiences should also help remove our fear of death as an end, and assist us in embracing death as a part of life. This realization can act as a wake-up call for us to fulfill our wildest dreams here on Earth. This is possible if we truly know that when our time here comes to an end, that "ending" is more accurately a process and transition to another dimension of consciousness. Certainly NDErs, with their repeated descriptions of a feeling of calm; a restoring of health; fast travel through a tunnel toward light, radiance, and unconditional love; and their meeting with a being of light, followed by a life review and a change of heart, seem to confirm this view. Of his many reflections on death and life after death, Jung writes empathetically in a letter on July 11, 1944 (shortly after his own NDE) to an anonymous correspondent who had lost a child:

> What happens after death is so unspeakably glorious that our imagination and our feelings do not suffice to form even an approximate conception of it …. The dissolution of our time-bound form in eternity brings no loss of meaning. Rather does the little finger know itself a member of the hand.[5]

In this book, I have tried to demonstrate, beginning with imaginal events and synchronicities and continuing with accounts of UFOs, Crop Circles, Mystical Cities and comparable experiences, that a new worldview is arising in our midst. We are crossing a threshold to a new and expanded spiritual awareness, one that includes the other dimension of the subtle world, a dimension that takes us beyond the ordinary three dimensions of space and the fourth dimension of time. This new story balances rational achievement and understanding with intuition, compassion, and a whole new order of being. This new way of being includes the powerful insight that our imaginative capacity

---

5   C. G. Jung, *Letters 1*, 1973, p. 343.

contributes to new creations in spontaneous and ongoing ways. This shows us that we experience life not only in a historical time-bound manner, but that we also have access to the timeless wisdom of the invisible realms that move us beyond history to a relationship with the mystical cities of the soul and their guides. This vaster vision of reality means that we are grounded on earth and living in our bodies, yet simultaneously open to the stars. We can now view life in the subtle dimension as collapsing past present and future into a continual present moment with which we can intersect *at any moment* in creative or destructive ways. How we choose effects not only our personal future, but also the future of all humankind and beyond.

As the Kabbalah indicates, creative imagination is a higher form of consciousness than merely thinking. *Imaginatio vera* honors the depths of the soul's reality, its dreams, its waking visions, its connections with the immortal guides, and the bringing back of wisdom to our troubled world. Thinking of necessity divides and discriminates; imagination reunites and heals, makes whole. We are being called to move beyond the current limitations of consciousness toward remembrance, toward each becoming the shaman, mystic, or Orphic presence so that we can recover the songlines of our souls. In so doing, we can hear the songs of the cosmos ring out once more. Taking on this daring task with increasing awareness will ensure not just *that* the new era will come, but more precisely *how* it will be incarnated in a continuing creation sourced by wisdom and love.

Final Note

As I was nearing the completion of a first draft of this book, I found myself being drawn to join a local singing group.[6] The aim of the group was less "to become a singer" in the conventional sense than to allow members to develop their authentic voice. Each member of our group went through a painful process of facing all the old woundings and "complexes" that prevent this authenticity from emerging in an effortless fashion. Each individual began to find his or her authentic sound by doing exercises involving breathing deeply into the diaphragm. Within two months almost everyone

---

6   Breakthrough Performance Workshop at: www.bigembrace.com, and info@bigembrace.com.

had an experience of this unique sound or vibration coming through their bodies on the breath. Getting in touch with this sound was also linked to movements that we did to help awaken the vital and subtle energies concealed and hidden in the body.

Early on in the process I had a dream in which one of our facilitators guessed or somehow knew my secret name, a name I have had for many years and that is known to no-one except my husband. Astonished, I asked her how she could possibly know this name. Her response was equally amazing. She said, "Let's just say that your secret name connects you to the angelic realm." About two weeks later, a colleague who had just returned from a visit to India, commented that according to some Hindu beliefs, each person's essence is linked to the invisible guides or angelic realm through the power of sound, and that each one of us has a "note," a vibratory resonance that is ours.

The activity of singing drew me nearer in an embodied way to the mysterious songline of my own soul. In addition, I had the privilege of seeing this happen to others. This was a tremendously exciting and transforming process for all, especially as the emergence of greater authenticity of voice through sound and song also led to profound changes in other areas of people's lives. For example, some of us found ourselves speaking up with greater clarity, ease, and confidence in our work situations, to be fully present in a relaxed kind of way. I also became more attuned to the effect of voice in teaching in general, and how sound as well as silence carries a wealth of emotion, image, nuance, and evocation, as well as idea.

As I continued with the singing group, we were encouraged to write a song or two out of the dreamtime. As a way of completing my manuscript, and as an offer of gratitude to all those beloved ones and friends, and invisible guides of the soul who have accompanied me on this long and arduous journey of writing, I offer you the following song with the hope that, from deep within, we all discover the songlines of our own souls, and all achieve the evolution of consciousness toward a new union of psyche and matter, toward the establishment of the subtle body, and toward the establishment of wisdom, love, and heart knowledge on our beautiful planet earth.

Secret Name

There's a secret name inside you
That belongs to the stars
There's a secret name inside you
That is truly yours

There's a secret name inside you
That belongs to the wind
There's a secret name inside you
That is yours to find

There's a secret name inside you
That belongs to the trees
There's a secret name inside you
That you'll hear in the breeze

There's a secret name inside you
That belongs to the waves
There's a secret name inside you
This the Wise One says

There's a secret name inside you
That is deep in your soul
There's a secret name inside you
Which is the angel's goal

There's a secret name inside you
That belongs to the stars
Wind, trees, waves, soul
Take what is yours.

And live it!

FURTHER READING

Alexander, S. & K. (2008). *Crop Circles: Signs, Wonders, and Mysteries.* Edison, NJ: Chartwell Books.

Baring, A. & Cashford, J. (1993). *The Myth of the Goddess: Evolution of an Image.* London: Arkana Penguin.

Clow, B. H. (2004). *Alchemy of Nine Dimensions: Decoding the Vertical Axis, Crop Circles, and the Mayan Calendar.* Charlottesville, VA: Hampton Roads.

Corbin, H. (1977). *Spiritual Body and Celestial Earth.* Princeton: Princeton University Press.

Gieser, S. (2005). *The Innermost Kernel: Depth Psychology and Quantum Physics. Wolfgang Pauli's Dialogue with C. G. Jung.* Berlin-Heidelberg-New York: Springer-Verlag.

Glickman, M. (2009). *Crop Circles: The Bones of God.* Berkeley, CA: Frog Books.

Goodchild, V. (2001). *Eros and Chaos: The Sacred Mysteries and Dark Shadows of Love.* York Beach, ME: Nicolas-Hays, Inc.

Goodrick-Clarke, N. (2008). *The Western Esoteric Traditions: A Historical Introduction.* Oxford: Oxford University Press.

Goswami, A. (2001). *Physics of the Soul.* Charlottesville, VA: Hampton Roads.

Goswami, A. (2004). *The Quantum Doctor.* Charlottesville, VA: Hampton Roads.

Greer, S. (nd). *Hidden Truth Forbidden Knowledge.* Crozet, VA: Crossing Point, Inc.

Jung, C. G. (1989). *Memories, Dreams, Reflections.* New York: Vintage Books.

Jung, C. G. (2009). *The Red Book.* London: W.W. Norton & Co.

Kingsley, P. (1999). *In the Dark Places of Wisdom.* Inverness, CA: The Golden Sufi Center.

Kingsley, P. (2010). *A Story Waiting to Pierce You.* Point Reyes, CA: The Golden Sufi Center.

Kundalini Rising. (2009). Boulder, CO: Sounds True.

Laszlo, E. (2007). *Science and the Akashic Field: An Integral Theory of Everything.* Rochester, VT: Inner Traditions.

Laszlo, E. & Currivan, J. (2008). *CosMos: A Co-Creator's Guide to the Whole-World.* Carlsbad, CA. & New York City: Hay House, Inc.

Leviton, R. (2005). *Signs on the Earth: Deciphering the Message of Virgin Mary Apparitions, UFO Encounters, and Crop Circles.* Charlottesville, VA: Hampton Roads.

Lindorff, D. (2004). *Pauli and Jung: The Meeting of Two Great Minds.* Wheaton, IL: Quest Books.

Mack, J. (1999). *Passport to the Cosmos.* New York: Crown Publishers.

Mayer, E. (2008). *Extraordinary Knowing*. New York: Bantam Dell.

McTaggart, L. (2008). *The Field: The Quest for the Secret Force of the Universe*. New York & London: Harper.

Melchizedek, D. (2007). *Serpent of Light Beyond 2012: The Movement of the Earth's Kundalini and the Rise of the Female Light, 1949-2013*. San Francisco, CA/Newburyport, MA: Weiser Books.

Michell, J. (1983). *The New View Over Atlantis*. London: Thames & Hudson.

Mindell, A. (2004). *The Quantum Mind and Healing*. Charlottesville, VA: Hampton Roads.

Mitchell, E. (1996). *The Way of the Explorer: An Apollo Astronaut's Journey Through the Material and Mystical Worlds*. London: G. P. Putnam.

Moody, R. (2001). *Life After Life*. San Francisco: HarperSanFrancisco.

Moorjani, A. (2012). *Dying To Be Me: My Journey from Cancer, to Near Death, to True Healing*. Carlsbad, CA: Hay House, Inc.

Prechtel, M. (1999). *Secrets of the Talking Jaguar*. New York: Jeremy P. Tarcher/Putnam.

Roth, R. (2011). *Return of the World Soul: Wolfgang Pauli, C. G. Jung and the Challenge of Psychophysical Reality*. Pari, Italy: Pari Publishing.

Silva, F. (2002). *Secrets in the Fields: The Science & Mysticism of Crop Circles*. Charlottesville, VA: Hampton Roads.

Tarnas, R. (2006). *Psyche and Cosmos*. New York: Viking Press.

Van Lommel, P. (2010). *Consciousness Beyond Life: The Science of the Near-Death Experience*. New York: HarperCollins.

DVD and Websites

www.temporarytemples.co.uk. Steve Alexander has been photographing the crop circles for twenty years. During that time he and Karen Alexander have provided an important service to the crop circle world by supplying professional quality photographic imagery of the circles to researchers, the media and the general public. Since 1999 they have produced an annual Year Book showcasing the very best formations of each year along with a written commentary researched by Karen Alexander. *The Crop Circle Year Book* books are beautifully produced and considered to be the most important crop circle documents available. To keep up with the latest circles as they happen you can subscribe to their free newsletter available at their website.

www.annebaring.com. See especially *The Dream of the Cosmos*.

Suzanne Taylor, [Producer]. (2009). *What on Earth? Inside the Crop Circle Mystery*. CA: Mighty Companions, Inc.

ABOUT THE AUTHOR

Veronica Goodchild, PhD, is a professor of Jungian Psychotherapy and Imaginal Psychology at Pacifica Graduate Institute. She received her PhD from Pacifica (1998) and has a Masters in Clinical Social Work from Columbia University, NYC (1980). She has practiced as a Jungian psychotherapist for almost 30 years, and is the author of numerous articles as well as *Eros and Chaos: The Sacred Mysteries and Dark Shadows of Love* (Nicolas-Hays, 2001). Veronica was elected as an Affiliate Member to the Inter-Regional Society of Jungian Analysts (IRSJA) in Spring 2012. She lives in Summerland, CA, with her husband Robert Romanyshyn.